A TEXT BOOK OF

NUMERICAL ANALYSIS AND COMPUTATIONAL METHODS

For

SEMESTER – VI
THIRD YEAR DEGREE COURSE
IN MECHANICAL ENGINEERING

AS PER NEW REVISED SYLLABUS OF
NORTH MAHARASHTRA UNIVERSITY, JALGAON

MV RAWLANI
M.E. (Mechanical)
Associate Prof., Department of Mechanical Engg.
SSBT's College of Engineering
Jalgaon

VN CHOUGULE
M.E. (Mfg. Engg. & Automation)
Associate Professor & HOD
Mechanical Engg. Deptt.
M.E.S. College of Engineering,
Pune.

MT PURANIK
M.E. (Design)
Deputy Manager (Training & Apps.)
SMC Pneumatics (India) Pvt. Ltd.,
Formerly, Mech. Engg. Deptt. VIT
Pune.

N 3347

NUMERICAL ANALYSIS & COMP. METHODS (TE MECH. SEM - VI NMU)   ISBN 978-93-5164-400-2

First Edition : February 2015

© : Author

The text of this publication, or any part thereof, should not be reproduced or transmitted in any form or stored in any computer storage system or device for distribution including photocopy, recording, taping or information retrieval system or reproduced on any disc, tape, perforated media or other information storage device etc., without the written permission of Authors with whom the rights are reserved. Breach of this condition is liable for legal action.

Every effort has been made to avoid errors or omissions in this publication. In spite of this, errors may have crept in. Any mistake, error or discrepancy so noted and shall be brought to our notice shall be taken care of in the next edition. It is notified that neither the publisher nor the authors or seller shall be responsible for any damage or loss of action to any one, of any kind, in any manner, therefrom.

Published By :
NIRALI PRAKASHAN
Abhyudaya Pragati, 1312, Shivaji Nagar,
Off J.M. Road, PUNE – 411005
Tel - (020) 25512336/37/39, Fax - (020) 25511379
Email : niralipune@pragationline.com

Printed By :
REPRO INDIA LTD,
Mumbai.

DISTRIBUTION CENTRES
PUNE

Nirali Prakashan
119, Budhwar Peth, Jogeshwari Mandir Lane
Pune 411002, Maharashtra
Tel : (020) 2445 2044, 66022708, Fax : (020) 2445 1538
Email : bookorder@pragationline.com

Nirali Prakashan
S. No. 28/27, Dhyari,
Near Pari Company, Pune 411041
Tel : (020) 24690204 Fax : (020) 24690316
Email : dhyari@pragationline.com
bookorder@pragationline.com

MUMBAI
Nirali Prakashan
385, S.V.P. Road, Rasdhara Co-op. Hsg. Society Ltd.,
Girgaum, Mumbai 400004, Maharashtra
Tel : (022) 2385 6339 / 2386 9976, Fax : (022) 2386 9976
Email : niralimumbai@pragationline.com

DISTRIBUTION BRANCHES

NAGPUR
Pratibha Book Distributors
Above Maratha Mandir, Shop No. 3, First Floor,
Rani Jhanshi Square, Sitabuldi, Nagpur 440012,
Maharashtra, Tel : (0712) 254 7129

BENGALURU
Pragati Book House
House No. 1, Sanjeevappa Lane, Avenue Road Cross,
Opp. Rice Church, Bengaluru – 560002.
Tel : (080) 64513344, 64513355,
Mob : 9880582331, 9845021552
Email:bharatsavla@yahoo.com

JALGAON
Nirali Prakashan
34, V. V. Golani Market, Navi Peth, Jalgaon 425001,
Maharashtra, Tel : (0257) 222 0395
Mob : 94234 91860

KOLHAPUR
Nirali Prakashan
New Mahadvar Road,
Kedar Plaza, 1st Floor Opp. IDBI Bank
Kolhapur 416 012, Maharashtra. Mob : 9855046155

CHENNAI
Pragati Books
9/1, Montieth Road, Behind Taas Mahal, Egmore,
Chennai 600008 Tamil Nadu, Tel : (044) 6518 3535,
Mob : 94440 01782 / 98450 21552 / 98805 82331, Email : bharatsavla@yahoo.com

RETAIL OUTLETS
PUNE

Pragati Book Centre
157, Budhwar Peth, Opp. Ratan Talkies,
Pune 411002, Maharashtra
Tel : (020) 2445 8887 / 6602 2707, Fax : (020) 2445 8887
Pragati Book Centre
Amber Chamber, 28/A, Budhwar Peth,
Appa Balwant Chowk, Pune : 411002, Maharashtra,
Tel : (020) 20240335 / 66281669
Email : pbcpune@pragationline.com

Pragati Book Centre
676/B, Budhwar Peth, Opp. Jogeshwari Mandir,
Pune 411002, Maharashtra
Tel : (020) 6601 7784 / 6602 0855
PBC Book Sellers & Stationers
152, Budhwar Peth, Pune 411002, Maharashtra
Tel : (020) 2445 2254 / 6609 2463

MUMBAI
Pragati Book Corner
Indira Niwas, 111 - A, Bhavani Shankar Road, Dadar (W), Mumbai 400028, Maharashtra
Tel : (022) 2422 3526 / 6662 5254, Email : pbcmumbai@pragationline.com

www.pragationline.com   info@pragationline.com

Dedicated to...

Our Beloved Parents

Authors

PREFACE

We take an opportunity to present this book entitled **'Numerical Analysis and Computational Methods'** for the students of Third Year Degree Course in Mechanical Engineering. It is strictly written as per the New Revised Syllabus of North Maharashtra University, Jalgon.

The object of this book is to present the subject matter in a most concise and simple manner.

The Book Contains Five Constructive Units :

- **Unit I :** It include Software Development in that Algorithm, Flowchart etc. and Solution of Transcendental Equation in that different methods such as Bisection, Hornerls etc.
- **Unit II :** It include Numerical Integration and Solution of Ordinary Differential Equation.
- **Unit III :** It include Interpolation in that Different types of Interpolation and Curve Fitting.
- **Unit IV :** It include Solution of Linear Algebraic Equation and Iterative Method.
- **Unit V :** It include Finite Element Analysis (FEA). Solution of various Equations and Introduction to Finite Difference Method.

We take this opportunity to express our thanks to Shri Dineshbhai Furia, Shri Jighnesh Furia and Shri. M.P. Munde for publishing this book in time.

We also take this opportunity to express our thank all the staff members of Nirali Prakashan namely, Mrs. Deepali Lachake (Co-ordinator), Mrs. Neeta Kulkarni and Miss. Mandakini Jadhvar, for their tremendous dedication and hard work in bringing out this book in an excellent form.

We are also thankful to **Mr. Pruthviraj M. More,** Branch Manager, Jalgaon office for his valuable help and efforts for promotion of our book.

Any undectected and unintentional errors, omissions, suggestions etc. from students and for improvement brought to our notice in good sprint are most welcome.

February 2015
Pune   **Authors**

SYLLABUS

Unit I : Software Development and Solution of Transcendental Equation   Marks 16
(a) Software Development : Principles, Mathematical Modeling Problem Solving, Algorithm, Flowchart, Errors, Graphical method.
(b) Solution of Transcendental Equation : Bisection method, False position method, successive approximation method, Newton-Raphson method, Horner's method, rate of convergence.

Unit II : Numerical Integration and Solution of Ordinary Differential Equation Marks 16
(a) Numerical Integration : Trapezoidal Rule, Simpson's 1/3rd , Simpson's 3/8th Rule, Gauss Quadrature method : 2 point.
(b) Solution of Ordinary Differential Equation : Taylors series method, Euler's method, Improved and modified Euler's method, Fourth order Runge-Kutta method.

Unit III : Interpolation and Curve Fitting   Marks 16
(a) Interpolation : Linear and quadratic interpolation, Lagrange's interpolation, Newton's forward interpolation, Newton's backward interpolation, Newton's divided difference interpolation, Stirling interpolation.
(b) Curve Fitting : Linear and quadratic regression, Logarithmic curve fitting, Exponential curve fitting.

Unit IV : Solution of Linear Algebraic Equation and Iterative Method   Marks 16
(a) Solution of Linear Algebraic Equation : Gauss elimination method, Gauss Jordan method LU, decomposition method.
(b) Iterative Method : Jacobi iteration method, gauss seidal interactive method, cholesky method.

Unit V : Finite Element Analysis and FDM   Marks : 16
(a) Finite Element Method : Introduction, steps used in finite element analysis, general approach, interpolation function and finite element application on one dimension, solution of elliptical equations, for various boundary conditions, solution of parabolic equation by explicit implicit.
(b) Introduction to Finite Difference Method : Comparison with Finite Element Analysis, Crank-Nicholson method.

CONTENTS

Unit - I

Chapter 1 : Software Development   1.1-1.38

Chapter 2 : Solution of Transcendental Equation   2.1-2.48

Unit - II

Chapter 3 : Numerical Integration   3.1-3.42

Chapter 4 : Solutions of Ordinary Differential Equations (ODE)   4.1-4.54

Unit - III

Chapter 5 : Interpolation   5.1-5.46

Chapter 6 : Curve Fitting   6.1-6.54

Unit - IV

Chapter 7 : Solution of Linear Algebraic Equation and Iterative Method   7.1-7.52

Unit - V

Chapter 8 : Finite Element Analysis   8.1-8.10

Chapter 9 : Finite Difference Methods   9.1-9.48

◈ ◈ ◈

Unit - I

Chapter 1
SOFTWARE DEVELOPMENT

1.1 INTRODUCTION

In this subject, we are going to study various numerical methods to solve variety of engineering mathematical problems. The objectives of learning of this subject can be assumed as below :
1. To understand the engineering problem situation.
2. To convert it into mathematical form, i.e. prepare a mathematical model.
3. To solve the mathematical expressions to reach conclusive solutions.
4. Predict and understand existence of inaccuracies in the final solutions.
5. Simplification and reduction in laborious repetitive calculation work so that the solutions will be obtained efficiently and without much loss of time.

To understand these objectives, let us take a simple example as below.

Example

A person is owning and running a mass production unit to make candles. He is in a financial crunch due to a huge rejection of candles produced per day. One day, he observed that 1250 candles are rejected. Then he decided to cut down the rejection to half every next day.

As numerical solution provider to engineering problems, he needs your assistance to determine number of days to practically reach zero rejection in candles production. Also he needs number of candles rejected from this day onwards till reaching the day of zero rejection.

Mathematical Thought Process

The situation of the problem demands division of 1250 by 2 and iteratively the answer divided by 2 till we reach zero.

So mathematical equation is

$$a_{i+1} = \frac{a_i}{2}$$

where, a_i = 1250 when i = 1.

Thus, a_i is number of candles rejected on the day number 'i'.

So number of days to reach zero rejection is value of 'i' when a_i = 0.

And number of candles rejected till that day is $\Sigma\, a_i$.

Now, practical problem in the process of getting the solution will surface out when we start the calculation.

The day number i →	1	2	3
Candles rejected →	1250	625	312.5

Here, we understand that a half candle cannot be rejected, so rejected candles must be either 312 or 313. The basic rounding rule forces us to select upper value. So the observation table may be prepared as :

Table 1.1

Day No. i	Candles Rejected a_i	Rounding Done (Yes / No)
1	1250	No
2	625	No
3	312.5 ≐ 313	Yes
4	156.5 ≐ 157	Yes
5	78.5 ≐ 79	Yes
6	39.5 ≐ 40	Yes
7	20	No
8	10	No
9	5	No
10	2.5 ≐ 3	Yes
11	1.5 ≐ 2	Yes
12	1	No
13	0.5 ≐ 1	Yes
14	0.5 ≐ 1	Yes
15	0.5 ≐ 1	Yes
.	.	.
.	.	.
.	.	.

Table 1.1 indicates that we cannot reach zero rejection even after infinite number of days.

Practical Considerations

To reach the practical solution, we will modify the basic rounding rule to select lower value. So the table will become as below :

Table 1.2

Day No. i	Candles Rejected a_i	Rounding Done (Yes / No)
1	1250	No
2	625	No
3	312.5 ≐ 312	Yes
4	156	No
5	78	No
6	39	No
7	19.5 ≐ 19	Yes
8	9.5 ≐ 9	Yes
9	4.5 ≐ 4	Yes
10	2	No
11	1	No
12	0.5 ≐ 0	Yes

Here, we get a solution as "on 12th day, there will not be any rejection". Simultaneously, we know, we have done some wrong assumption to reach the solution. So for practical solution, we may use basic rounding rule without modification till we reach rejection = 1 and then take decision to modify the rule.

Thus, the answer is that the plant will observe zero rejection on the 13th day (Refer Table 1.1) and the number of candles rejected is summation of the second column as :

1250 + 625 + 313 + 157 + 79 + 40 + 20 + 10 + 5 + 3 + 2 + 1 = 2505.

Inaccuracies

Now, the error or inaccuracy in the solution is difference between the theoretical and practical answers. In this case, practical answer is 2505 candles and the theoretical answers is Σa_i without rounding. Thus, theoretical answer is :

$$\sum_{i=1}^{\infty} a_i = 1250 + 625 + 312.5 + 156.25 + 78.125 + 39.0625$$

$$+ 19.53125 + 9.76525 + 4.8828125$$
$$+ 2.44140625 + 1.220703125 + 0.610351562$$
$$+ 0.30517781 + 0.15258789 + 0.076293945 + ...$$
$$= 2499.37439$$

For more precise answer, we may add a few more a_i terms and we will get the theoretical answer as 2500 which is twice of 1250, the first day rejection.

Thus, in numerical solutions due to reasons like rounding and other assumptions, the final solution may vary from theoretical answer. An engineer, while presenting the final solution, must be aware of this existence of inaccuracy and predict its magnitude.

Computer's Assistance

Referring back the objectives of learning, we have discussed first four objectives. Now the last objective tells us to use computer softwares either as solver or programming language. In this book, we will learn use of C programming for various numerical methods. In addition, we will learn use of solvers like MS-Excel and MATLAB.

As an engineer or a numerical solution provider, we must know that the mathematical expression cannot be directly fed into the computer. Hence, it must be properly arranged and iteratively or directly solved in step by step manner. Developing this step by step process of approaching, the solution can be achieved using some techniques as Pseudo Codes or flow charts etc. Coming back to the problem of candles, to reduce repetitive work of division of answer by 2 and summation of all answers to get final solution, we may develop a computer program which will include the practical assumptions and will provide us the desired solutions.

Algorithm or Pseudo Code

The steps for development of the program will be :
1. Get the first day's number of candles rejected i.e. 'a' and set i = 1 for day no. 1 and sum = 0.
2. Check whether a is even or odd, if odd a = a + 1.

3. Perform summation as sum = sum + a and division as a = $\frac{a}{2}$.
4. If a = 1, we have reached the solution, so go to step 5 else for further calculations of next day rejections, increment day number as i = i + 1 and go to step 2.
5. Print the answers for number of days as (i + 1) and number of candles rejected as (sum + 1).
6. End.

The step by step process of approaching the solution presented above is called Pseudo Code technique because it uses mathematical expressions those can be directly used in computer program but rest part of the sentences cannot be "as it is" typed in the program.

The graphical presentation of this pseudo code is known as flow chart. Naturally, presentation of flow chart needs some standard symbols listed below :

Name	Purpose	Symbol
Terminal box	Start or Stop of flowchart	⬭
Process box	Mathematical expressions	▭
User interface	Input from user or output to user	▱
Diamond box	Decision-making	◇
Hexagonal box	Loop structure	⬡
Circle	Connector	○
Pentagon	Off page connector	⬠
Arrows	Flow lines	↑↓ ⇄
Bracket	Annotation	----[

Using these symbols, above pseudo code may be converted into flow chart as below :

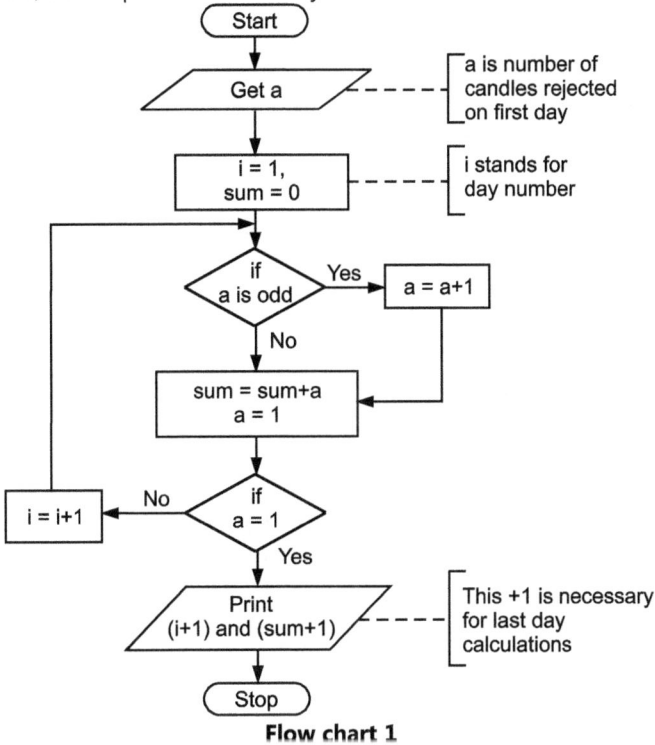

Flow chart 1

1.2 C Programming

As engineering students, you have already learned C programming. In this section, we will revise various functions required in C program.

The outline of C program is always as below :

```
#include<-------->
#include<-------->
main()
{
    int a;
    float b;
    clrscr();
    printf(--------);
    scanf(---------);
    a = --------;
    b = --------;
    printf(--------);
    getch();
}
```

Standard Terms in C Programming

Here, #include statements are required to include predefined codes. These statements are known as pre-processor statements and normally they instruct the compiler to include header files like "stdio.h", "conio.h", "math.h" where various functions like printf(), scanf(), clrscr(), getch(), sqrt() etc are predefined. Next statement is main() which indicates that the program is executed in this MAIN function. We must remember or we must know that there can be other user defined functions which can be called by main(). Further, it is quite compulsory to write complete program inside the pair of curly bracket. The program inside the curly bracket starts with declaration statements. These statements declare names and data types of the variables those will be used in the program.

Then comes clrscr(), which is a statement that clears the program execution screen. The program uses printf() function to instruct user or to display answers. And uses scanf() function to receive data from user.

There can be multiple mathematical expressions or decision making statements or loop structures in a program.

At the end, we observe getch() function which is used to hold the execution screen till user presses any key on the keyboard. Without this statement, program control (compiler) may automatically close the execution screen.

Here, we will develop C program for the problem of candles and then will go in details of datatypes, functions, arithmetic operators, loop structures etc.

Program for the example of rejection of candles :

```
CANDLES.C
#include <stdio.h>
#include <conio.h>
#include <math.h>
main()
{
int a,i=0,sum=0;
clrscr();
flushall();
printf("****************************************************");
printf("\n\tTE (Mechanical) CONM Book by");
printf("\n\tM. T. Puranik & V. N. Chougule");
printf("\n\t\tNirali Prakashan");
printf("\n****************************************************");
printf("\nProgram to find no. of days for ZERO rejections of candles");
printf("\n****************************************************\n\n");
printf("Enter first day's rejection: ");
scanf("%d",&a);
repeat:
i++;
```

```
sum=sum+a;
if(a%2==0) a=a/2;
else a=a/2+1;
if(a>1) goto repeat;
printf("No. of days to reach ZERO rejection = %d",i+1);
printf("\nNo. of candles rejected in these days = %d",sum+1);
getch();
}
```

Structured Programming

The program demonstrated above uses "goto" statement. This statement helps beginners but a matured programmer will always try to avoid use of "goto" statement. As this statement makes program control to jump abruptly from one step to any other step, it becomes difficult to trace the program control location. One may not understand this difficulty while developing the program. But will realize it while debugging or while modifying the program.

The program with "goto" statement is hence called as unstructured program. Compiler of C program has loop structures like "for" construct, "while" construct etc. to eliminate use of "goto" statement and make the program as a "structured program".

Let us now get introduced to various terminologies for C programming.

Data Types

Not only C program but computer in general handles data of different types such as numeric and alphanumeric. In numeric, the data may be integer numbers or fractions. Hence, before developing program, it is necessary to know the types of data variables.

The commonly required data types those are supported by C compiler are :

- **int** : Integer that can store positive or negative numbers including zero.
- **float** : Floating point numbers that can store real numbers such as – 23.91, 0, 37.5 etc.
- **char** : Character that can store one character at a time like : a, b, c, A, B or 0, 1, +, –, #, $.

In general, char stores a character that can be displayed on screen using keyboard.

Here, it is important to note that, if a variable is declared as "int" but the value assigned to it is real, the variable will store only integer part of the number. For example, if a is declared as "int" and a = 4.3 then a will store only 4. If a = 7.99 then also a will store only 7. Thus, there will not be any rounding assumed by compiler.

Similarly, if a variable is declared as "float" and an integer value is assigned to it, the value will be added with a decimal point. For example, if variable x is declared as "float" and x = 15 then compiler will store 15.0000 in memory.

If a variable is declared as "char" and we try to assign a numeric value to it then it will be taken as symbol and not numeric value. The symbol will be the ASCII symbol. ASCII stands for American Standard Code for Information Interchange. The C compiler supports total 256 ASCII symbols, shown in Table 1.3.

Table 1.3

Int	ASCII	Int	ASCII	Int	ASCII	Int	ASCII	Int	ASCII	Int	ASCII	Int	ASCII	Int	ASCII
0		32		64	@	96	`	128	Ç	160	á	192	└	224	α
1	☺	33	!	65	A	97	a	129	ü	161	í	193	┴	225	ß
2	☻	34	"	66	B	98	b	130	é	162	ó	194	┬	226	Γ
3	♥	35	#	67	C	99	c	131	â	163	ú	195	├	227	π
4	♦	36	$	68	D	100	d	132	ä	164	ñ	196	─	228	Σ
5	♣	37	%	69	E	101	e	133	à	165	Ñ	197	┼	229	σ
6	♠	38	&	70	F	102	f	134	å	166	ª	198	╞	230	μ
7		39	'	71	G	103	g	135	ç	167	º	199	╟	231	τ
8		40	(	72	H	104	h	136	ê	168	¿	200	╚	232	Φ
9		41	)	73	I	105	i	137	ë	169	⌐	201	╔	233	Θ
10		42	*	74	J	106	j	138	è	170	¬	202	╩	234	Ω
11		43	+	75	K	107	k	139	ï	171	½	203	╦	235	δ
12		44	,	76	L	108	l	140	î	172	¼	204	╠	236	∞
13		45	-	77	M	109	m	141	ì	173	¡	205	═	237	φ
14	♫	46	.	78	N	110	n	142	Ä	174	«	206	╬	238	ε
15	☼	47	/	79	O	111	o	143	Å	175	»	207	╧	239	∩
16	►	48	0	80	P	112	p	144	É	176	░	208	╨	240	≡
17	◄	49	1	81	Q	113	q	145	æ	177	▒	209	╤	241	±
18	↕	50	2	82	R	114	r	146	Æ	178	▓	210	╥	242	≥
19	‼	51	3	83	S	115	s	147	ô	179	│	211	╙	243	≤
20	¶	52	4	84	T	116	t	148	ö	180	┤	212	╘	244	⌠
21	§	53	5	85	U	117	u	149	ò	181	╡	213	╒	245	⌡
22	▬	54	6	86	V	118	v	150	û	182	╢	214	╓	246	÷
23	↨	55	7	87	W	119	w	151	ù	183	╖	215	╫	247	≈
24	↑	56	8	88	X	120	x	152	ÿ	184	╕	216	╪	248	°
25	↓	57	9	89	Y	121	y	153	Ö	185	╣	217	╜	249	·
26		58	:	90	Z	122	z	154	Ü	186	║	218	╓	250	·
27	←	59	;	91	[	123	{	155	¢	187	╗	219	█	251	√
28	∟	60	<	92	\	124	|	156	£	188	╝	220	▄	252	ⁿ
29	↔	61	=	93	]	125	}	157	¥	189	╜	221	▌	253	²
30	▲	62	>	94	^	126	~	158	₧	190	╛	222	▐	254	■
31	▼	63	?	95	_	127	⌂	159	ƒ	191	┐	223	▀	255	

These may be seen on screen by following program :

```
#include<stdio.h>
#include<conio.h>
#include<math.h>
main()
{
    int a = 0;
    repeat :
    printf("%c \t", a);
    a = a + 1;
    if (a < 256)
        goto repeat;
    getch();
}
```

So, if a variable is declared as "char", it should be assigned value as 'a', 'm', '1', '+', '$' etc., always in single quotation marks.

The data types are declared as "int", "float", "char" etc. and they are accessed in the program in printf() or scanf() functions by respective format specifiers. The format specifiers for the three data types are listed below :

Data Type	Format Specifier
int	%d
float	%f
char	%c

Arithmetic Operators

The compiler of C supports +, −, * and / as basic arithmetic operators for addition, subtraction, multiplication and division respectively. Further, it also supports % to determine remainder of integer division.

For example,

16%2 is equal to	0
31%2 is equal to	1
16% 7 is equal to	2
2137% 100 is equal to	37

Assignment Operator : The equal sign "=" is used as assignment operator.

Logical Operators : These operators are used for comparison of variables or comparison of variables and a value.

Operator	Meaning
= =	Equality*
<	Less than
>	Greater than
< =	Less than or equal to
> =	Greater than or equal to
!	Not
! =	Not equal to
&&	And
||	Or

You must be already aware of use of these operators. If not, it will be clear through some exercises at the end of this topic.

Loop Structures

These structures help us to make our programs structured. Due to use of these constructs, programmer puts all those statements which are to be repeated in a separate pair of curly bracket. Thus, one can understand, which statements are repeated and how many times.

There are various loop structures as "for loop", "while loop", "Do ... while loop". These are illustrated by a common example as below :

Example 1.1 : *Develop a C program to display integers from 1 to 10 on separate lines using :*
  (a) "If ... goto" statements
  (b) "while" loop structure
  (c) "Do ... while" loop structure
  (d) "For" loop structure

Solution :

(a) Using "If ... goto" statement :

```
#include<stdio.h>
#include<conio.h>
#include<math.h>
main()
{
    int a = 1;
    clrscr();
    repeat :
    printf("%d \n", a);
    a = a + 1;
    if (a < = 10)
        goto repeat;
```

---

* Single equal symbol is assignment operator whereas double equal symbol is comparison for equality.

```
        getch();
}
```

(b) Using "while" loop structure :
```
#include<stdio.h>
#include<conio.h>
#include<math.h>
main()
{
    int a = 1;
    while (a <= 10)
    {
        printf("%d \n", a);
        a = a + 1;
    }
    getch();
}
```

(c) Using "Do ... while" loop structure :
```
#include<stdio.h>
#include<conio.h>
#include<math.h>
main()
{
    int a = 1;
    do
    {
        printf("%d \n", a);
        a = a + 1;
    } while (a <= 10);
    getch();
}
```

(d) Using "For" loop structure :
```
#include<stdio.h>
#include<conio.h>
#include<math.h>
main()
{
    int a;
    for (a = 1; a<=10; a = a + 1)
        printf("%d \n", a);
    getch();
}
```

Additional Mathematical Operators :

These operators may be used to reduce length of mathematical expressions. They are listed below :

Mathematical Expression	Reduced Expression
a = a + 1	a++
a = a – 1	a– –
a = a + 3	a+ = 3
a = a – 7	a– = 7
a = a * 3	a* = 3
a = a/5	a/ = 5

Escape Sequences

The C compiler has some special print characters which are also known as printf() escape sequences.* The sequences we will commonly use are as listed below :

Escape Sequence	Meaning	Application
\b	Backscape	Developing password programs
\n	New line	Pass print control (cursor) to next line
\t	Tab	Pass print control (cursor) horizontally rightwards by pre-decided spaces

Library Functions

C compiler commands are known as functions. These functions are predefined in header files. For example, printf(), scanf(), sqrt(), clrscr(), getch(), etc.

Some mathematical library functions which we will require in this subject are as listed here :

Math function	Description	Example
abs()	Returns absolute value of given integer	abs (–20) = 20
fabs()	Returns absolute value of given real number	fabs (–5.3) = 5.3
sqrt()	Returns square root in real number form	sqrt (25) = 5.0000
pow()	This is power function, returns x^y	pow (4, 3) = 64.0000 pow (27, 1/3) = 3.0000
exp()	Returns exponential value	exp (2.5) = $e^{2.5}$ = 12.1825
log()	Natural logarithm is determined	log(12.1825) = 2.5000

contd. ...

---

* We have already used \t in ASCII characters printing program and \n in rest of the programs.

log10()	Common logarithm or logarithm to the base 10 is determined	log10(1000) = 3.0000
sin()	Sine ratio of angle given in radians	sin(1.047198) = 0.8660
asin()	Arc sine or sine inverse of the real number	asin(0.866) = 1.047198
cos()	cosine ratio of angle given in radians	cos(0.523599) = 0.8666
acos()	Arc cosine or cos inverse of the real number	acos(0.8666) = 0.523599
tan()	Tangent ratio of angle given in radians	tan(0.7854) = 1.0000
atan()	Arc tangent or tan inverse of the real number	atan(1) = 0.7854
ceil()	Rounding to upper integer number, but return type is float	ceil(23.7) = 24.0000 ceil(23.2) = 24.0000 ceil(–23.2) = –23.0000
floor()	Rounding to lower integer number, but return type is float	floor(23.7) = 23.0000 floor(23.2) = 23.0000 floor(–23.2) = –24.0000

User Defined Functions : The user i.e. programmer can write his/her own functions. For example, it is required to calculate factorial of many numbers in one mathematical expression. But the C compiler does not have library function for factorial. Hence, programmer can write a function and call it whenever required in main() function. To understand this, let us develop a program for permutations and combinations as below :

Example 1.2 : *Determine permutations and combinations if 3 students out of a batch of 7 are called in a group for photo session.*

Mathematical solution :

$$\text{Permutations} = {}^nP_r = \frac{n!}{(n-r)!}$$

$$= \frac{7!}{(7-3)!}$$

$$= 210$$

and

$$\text{Combinations} = {}^nC_r = \frac{n!}{r!(n-r)!}$$

$$= \frac{7!}{3!(7-3)!}$$

$$= 35$$

Now let us develop C program for the same.

Permutations and Combinations :

```c
#include <stdio.h>
#include <conio.h>
#include <math.h>
main()
{
int n,r,npr,ncr;
int facto(int);
clrscr();
printf("****************************************************");
printf("\n\tTE (Mechanical) CONM Book by");
printf("\n\tM. T. Puranik & V. N. Chougule");
printf("\n\t\tNirali Prakashan");
printf("\n****************************************************");
printf("\nProgram to find permutations and combinations");
printf("\n****************************************************\n\n");
printf("Enter no. of students in a batch: ");
scanf("%d",&n);
printf("Enter no. of students called for photo: ");
scanf("%d",&r);
npr=facto(n)/facto(n-r);
ncr=facto(n)/(facto(r)*facto(n-r));
printf("Permutations = %d\nCombinations = %d",npr,ncr);
getch();
}
int facto (int a)
{
int p=1,i;
for(i=1;i<=a;i++)
p*=i;
return(p);
}
```

Subscripted Variables

These are also called as ARRAYS. Arrays can be usually one dimensional or two dimensional. For example, a[10] is a one-dimensional array that can store 10 data values. Variable "a" is called subscripted variable because a_0, a_1, a_2, ... a_9 such ten values can be handled with single variable name. Similarly, b[5] [4] is two-dimensional array which can handle 20 different data values. In mathematical terms, these variables are matrics. Following program, which accepts number of rows and number of columns from user, further accepts all values, then displays them in matrix form (i.e. row and column form) and also displays transpose will clear all the doubts like "how to declare array", "how to input the matrix elements", "how to access them" etc.

Program :

```c
#include<stdio.h>
#include<conio.h>
#include<math.h>
main()
{
int a[10][10], i, j, m, n;
clrscr();
printf("****************************************************");
printf("\n\tTE (Mechanical) CONM Book by");
printf("\n\tM. T. Puranik & V. N. Chougule");
printf("\n\t\tNirali Prakashan");
printf("\n****************************************************");
printf("\nProgram to find transpose of matrix");
printf("\n****************************************************\n\n");
printf("Enter no. of rows: ");
scanf ("%d",&m);
printf("Enter no. of columns: ");
scanf ("%d",&n);
for(i=0;i<m;i++)
 for(j=0;j<n;j++)
  {
   printf("Element(%d,%d)= ",i,j);
   scanf ("%d",&a[i][j]);
  }
printf("Press any key to see the matrix ...");
getch();
clrscr();
for(i=0;i<m;i++)
{
```

```
 for(j=0;j<n;j++)
  printf("%d\t",a[i][j]);
  printf("\n");
 }
 printf("Press any key to see transpose ...");
 getch();
 clrscr();
 for(j=0;j<n;j++)
 {
  for(i=0;i<m;i++)
   printf("%d\t",a[i][j]);
   printf("\n");
 }
 getch();
}
```

1.3 SOLVERS

Solver is a generalised which can handle the data and can produce mathematical results as desired. Microsoft Excel is one such solver. Other solver which is dedicated to mathematical calculations is MATLAB.

1.3.1 MS-Excel

Let us see how we can use MS-Excel to solve the problem of candles rejection.

- After opening MS-Excel worksheet, type and enter first day's rejection i.e. the number 1250 in cell A1, as shown in Image 1.1.
- Then type formula "=ceiling(A1/2, 1)" in cell A2.
- Here we are using "ceiling" function for rounding the division to upper integer. The number 1 after comma indicates the range for rounding. For example, if we type formula "=ceiling (A1/2, 2)" we get answer as 626 because 625 is not multiple of 2 and 626 is upper nearest multiple of 2.
- Similarly, if we type "=ceiling (A1/2, 7)" then we will get 630 because 625 is not multiple of 7. And 623 is multiple of 7 but lower than 625. So 630 which is multiple of 7 and upper nearest number to 625, is returned as the answer.
- The typed formula is shown in Image 1.2.
- Then copy A2 down from A3 to a sufficient number of cells, say A3 to A15, as shown in Image 1.3.

- We know, once we reach division equal to 1, we will change the rounding rule, hence A12 is the last cell required for our solution. So cells from A13 to A15 are redundant and therefore removed as shown in Image 1.4.
- Thus, the excel sheet tells us the number of candles rejected everyday. The row numbers indicate the day number.
- Now, type formula "=sum(A1:A12)" in cell A13 as shown in Image 1.5.
- Now the MS-Excel solver is ready with both the answers we need. Refer Image 1.6. It indicates that in 12 days after total rejection of 2505 candles the plant will reach the zero rejection status.

MS-Excel is a powerful solver which can handle matrices of a large number of rows and a large number of columns. It is very easy to find determinant, inverse, transpose of these matrices and even it is not difficult to multiply the matrices.

Refer Image 1.7 to understand how determinant of a matrix can be found.

Refer Image 1.8 and Image 1.9 to understand how to find inverse of matrix. Remember for getting inverse of matrix you must select range of columns and rows equal to the given matrix, then type the formula as "=minverse(----- : -----)" and DO NOT press simply enter key; press CTRL+SHIFT+ENTER.

To find transpose of a matrix, select all the cells representing matrix elements. Copy all the cells by ctrl-C as shown in Image 1.10. Then go to a cell where you want first element of transpose to appear. Then move cursor (mouse pointer) to an arrow on right side of Paste icon in toolbar and click it to get a pop-up menu as shown in Image 1.11. Click the "Transpose" option to get the transpose of the matrix as shown in Image 1.12.

Matrix multiplication can also be easily performed using MS-Excel. Refer Image 1.13 where two matrices are defined. Then locate a cell where you wish to have first element of multiplication of matrices. Then select rows and columns equal to the expected matrix dimensions and type formula as "=mmult(----:----)" as shown in Image 1.14. Again remember – DO NOT press simply enter key. Press CTRL + SHIFT + ENTER together to get result of multiplication as shown in Image 1.15.

1.3.2 MatLab

MATLAB is a software developed by the MathWorks Inc. MatLab stands for MATrix LABoratory which provides a numerical computing environment and programming language that is used to perform engineering and scientific calculations.

Running MatLab creates one or more windows on your computer screen. One of these windows, named MATLAB is commonly known as MatLab desktop. Within this window you will find command window which is primarily used to interact with MatLab. The prompt >> is displayed in the command window. Refer Image 1.16 for knowing these windows. Except command window you may close all other windows.

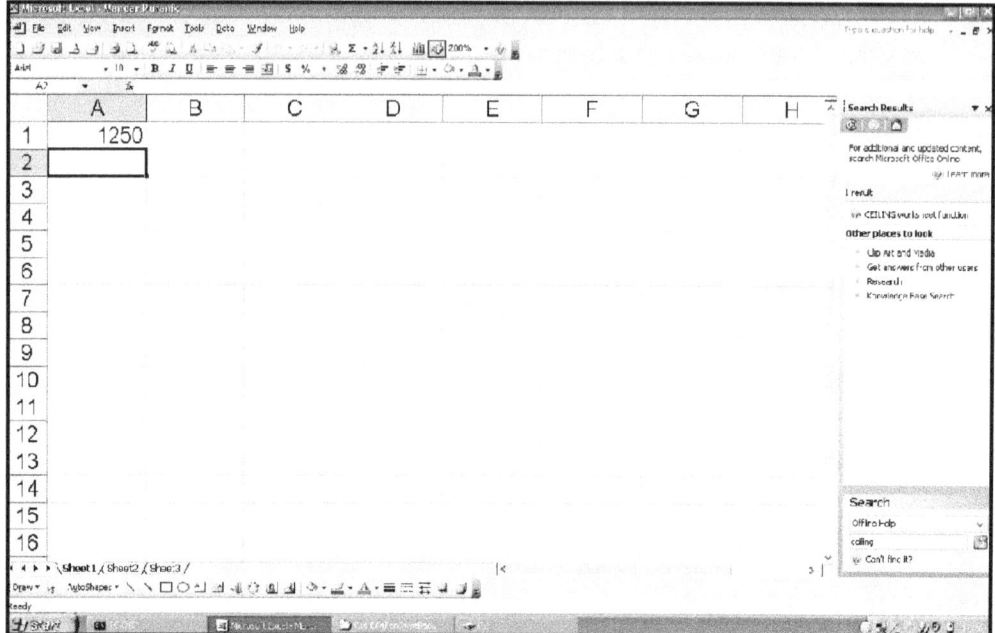

Image 1.1

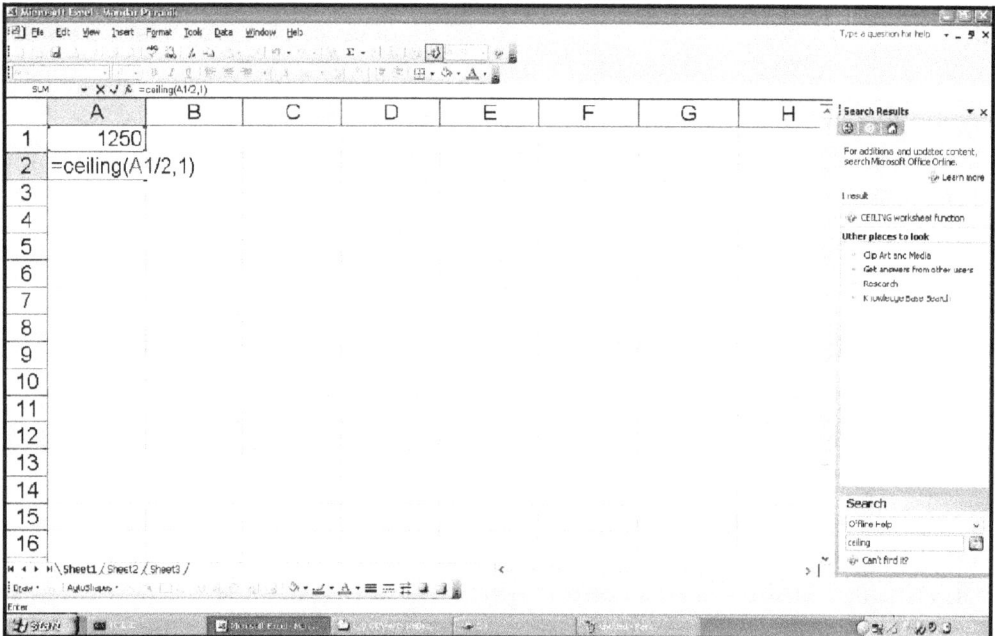

Image 1.2

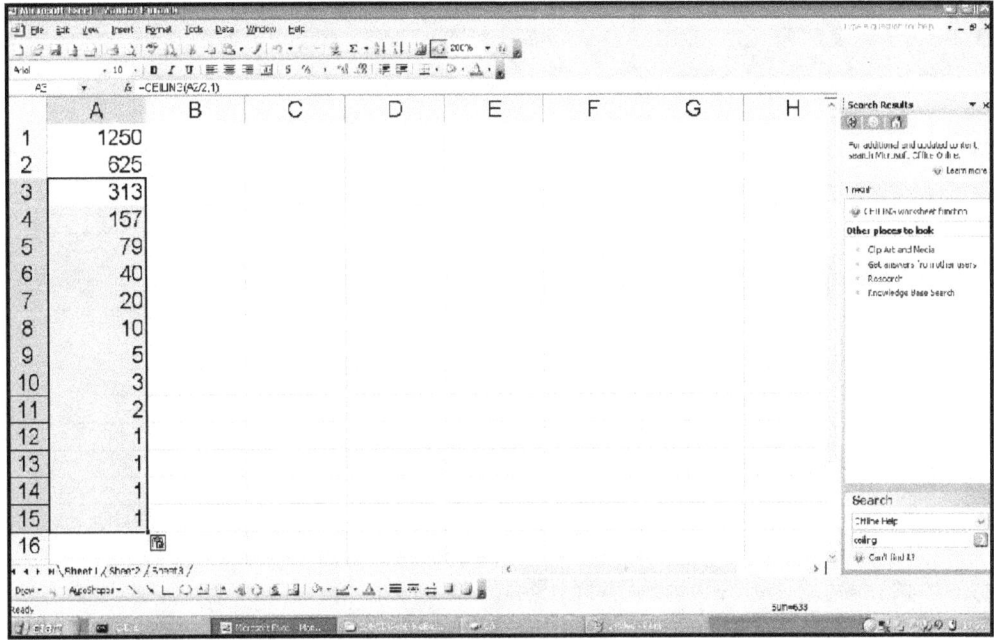

Image 1.3

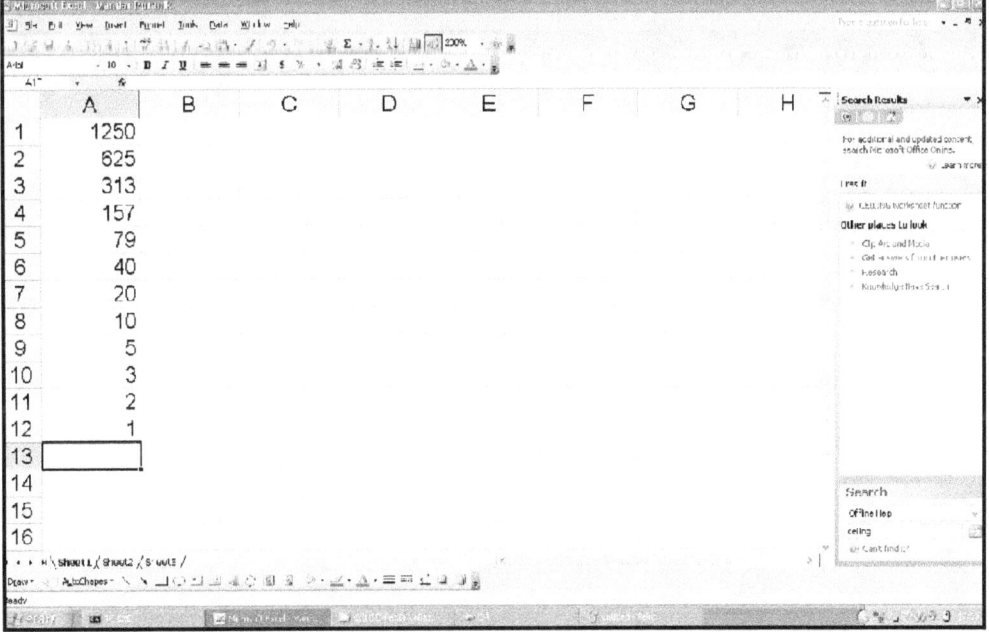

Image 1.4

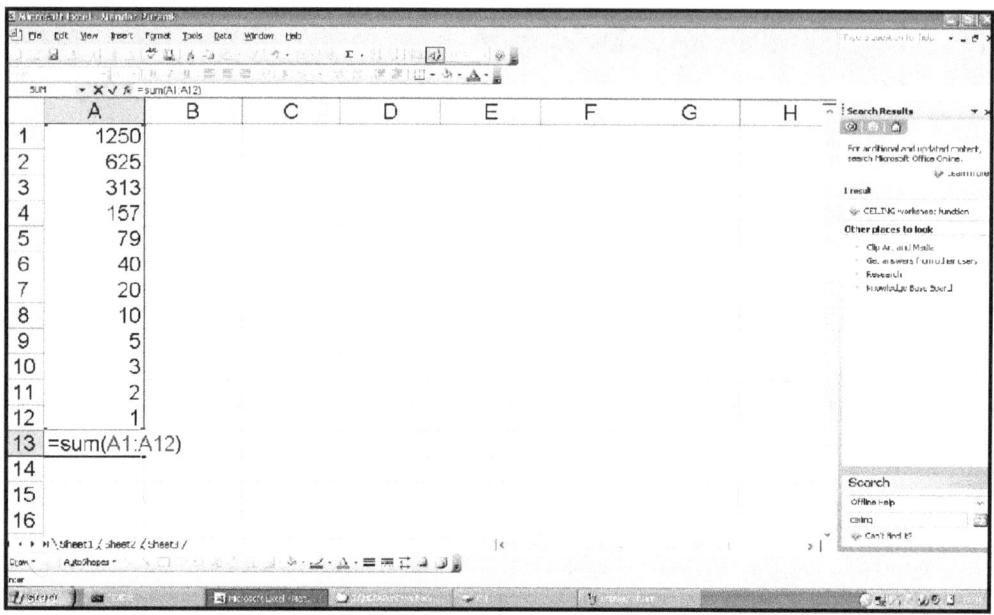

Image 1.5

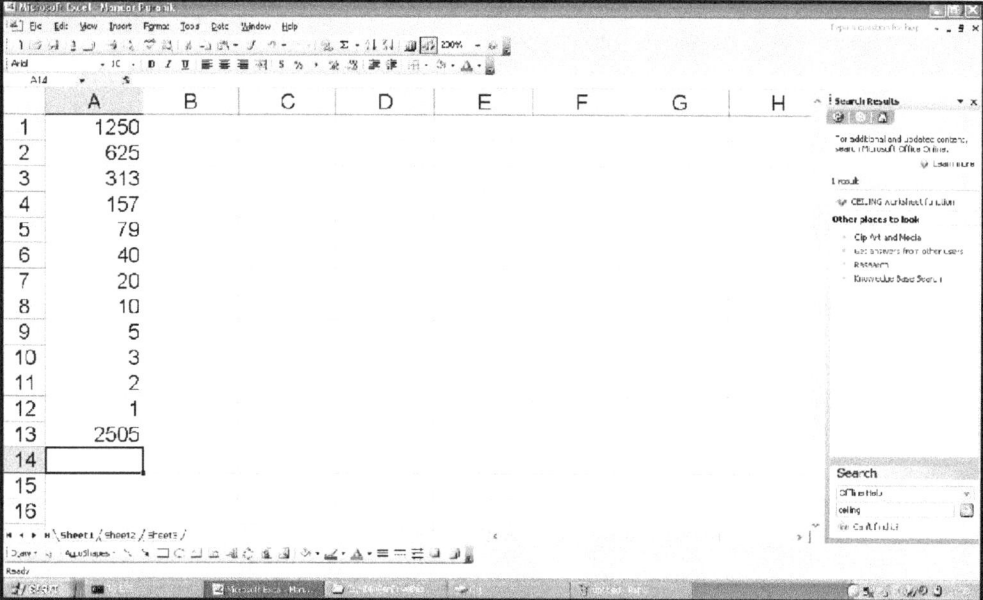

Image 1.6

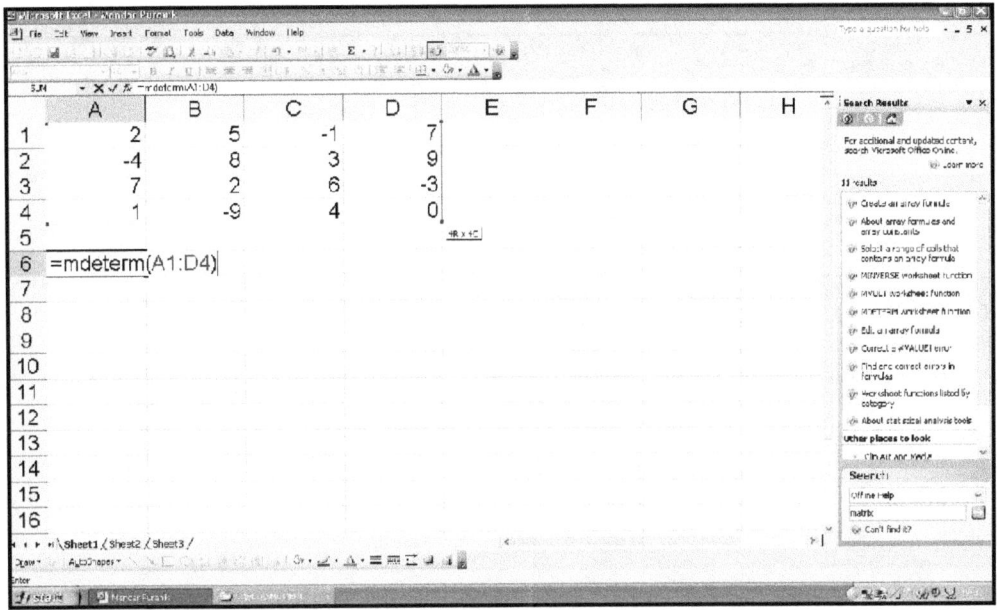

Image 1.7

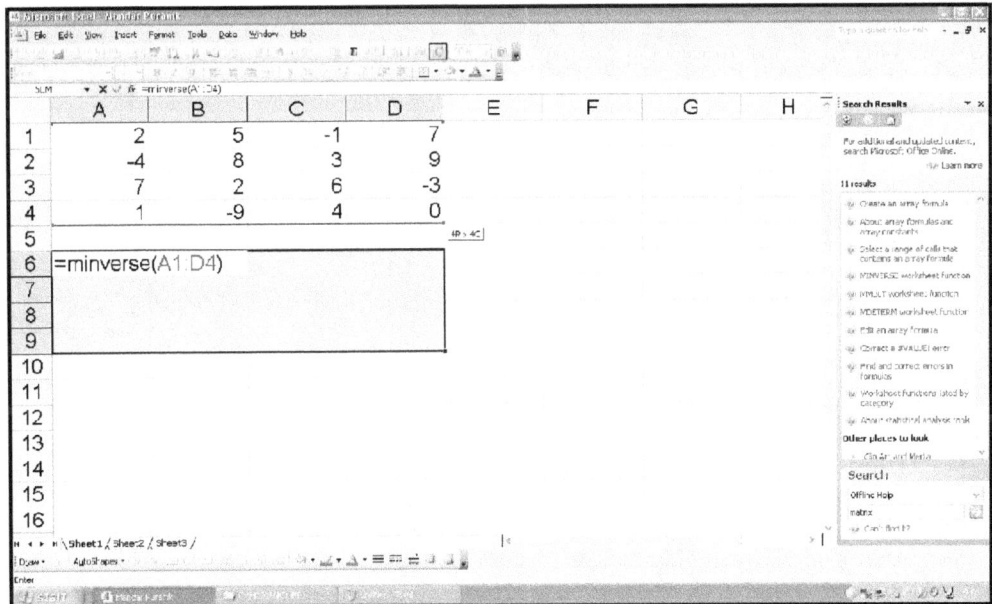

Image 1.8

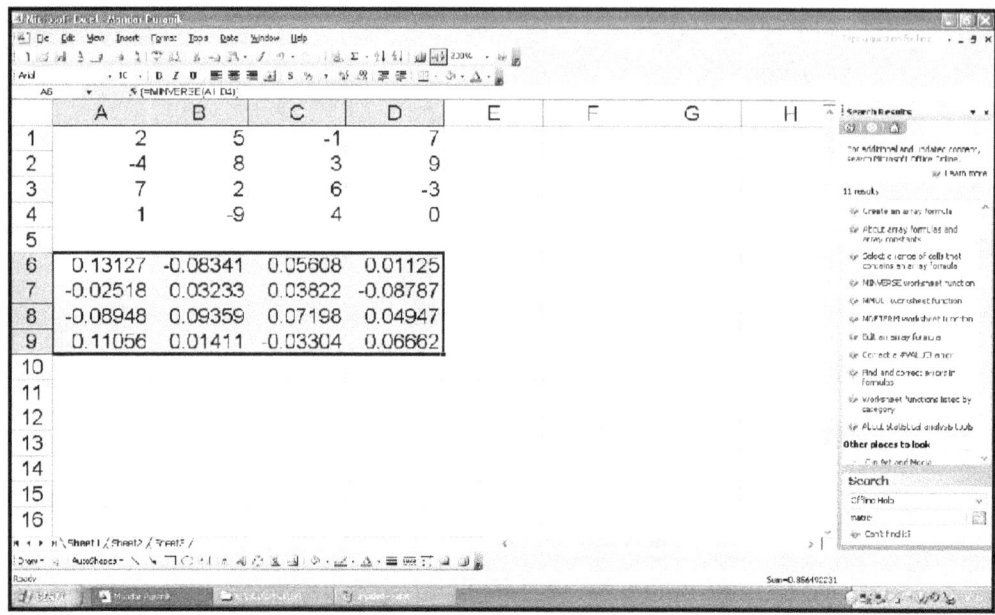

Image 1.9

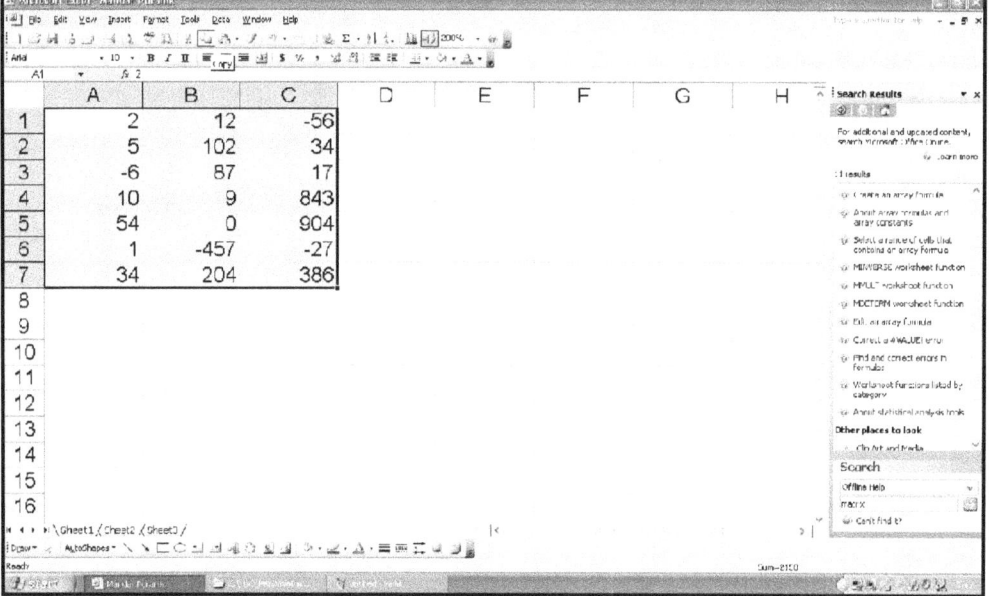

Image 1.10

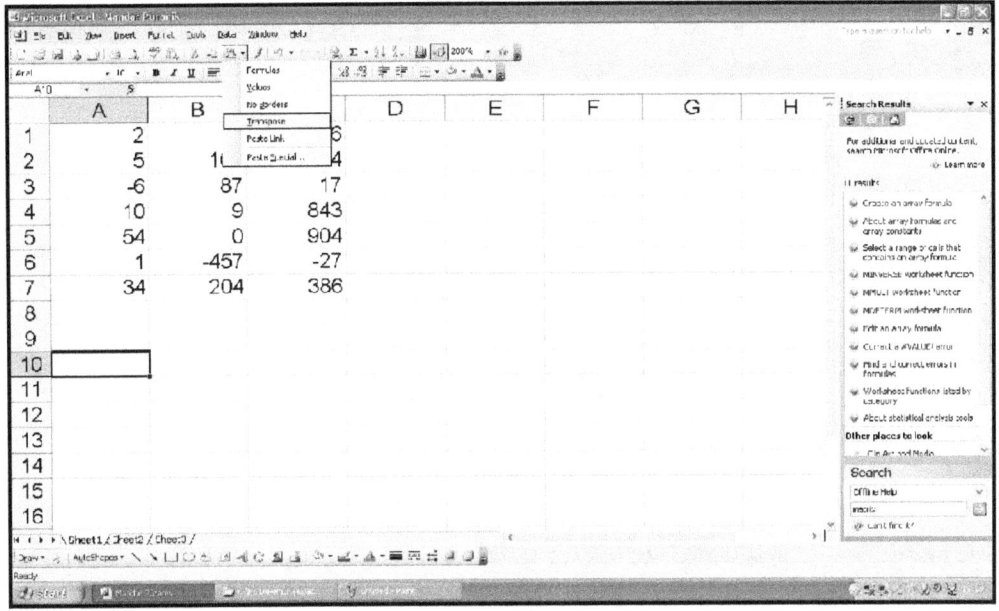

Image 1.11

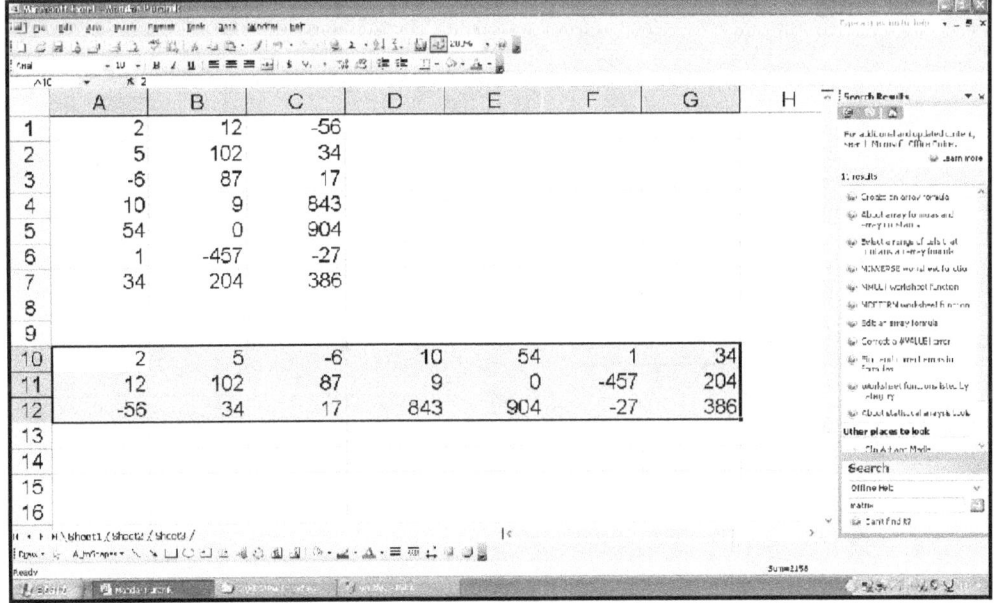

Image 1.12

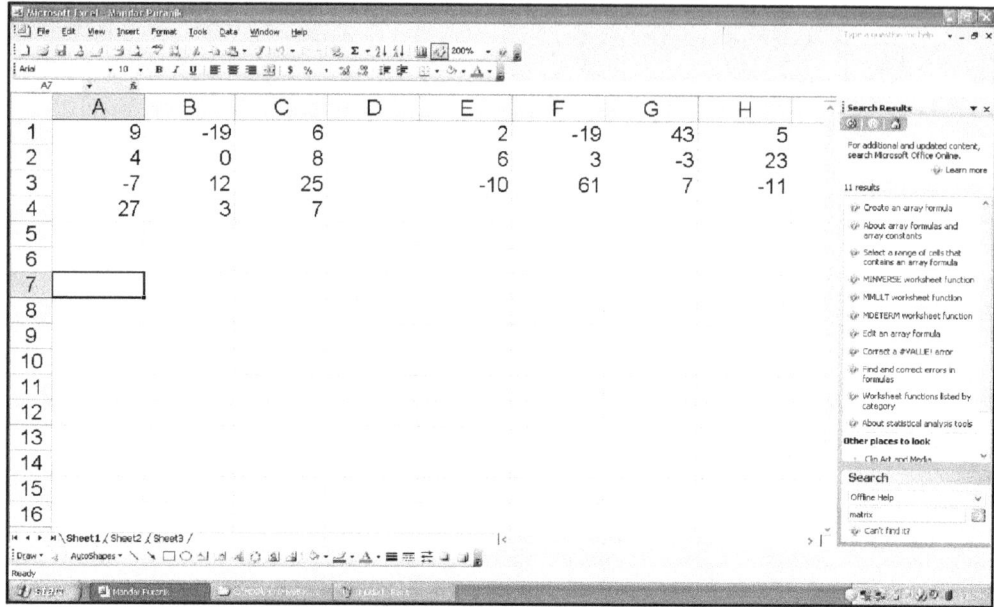

Image 1.13

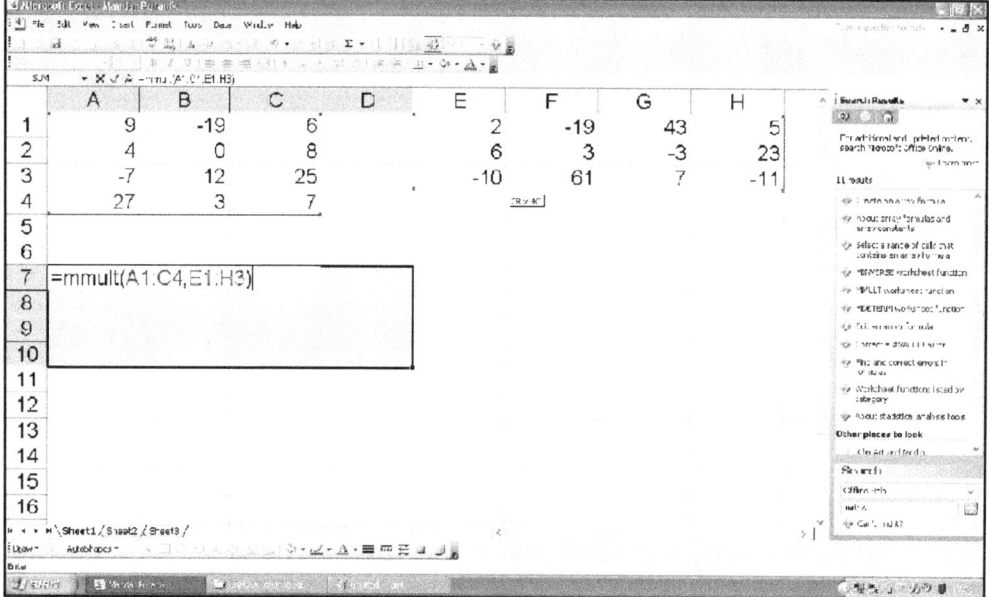

Image 1.14

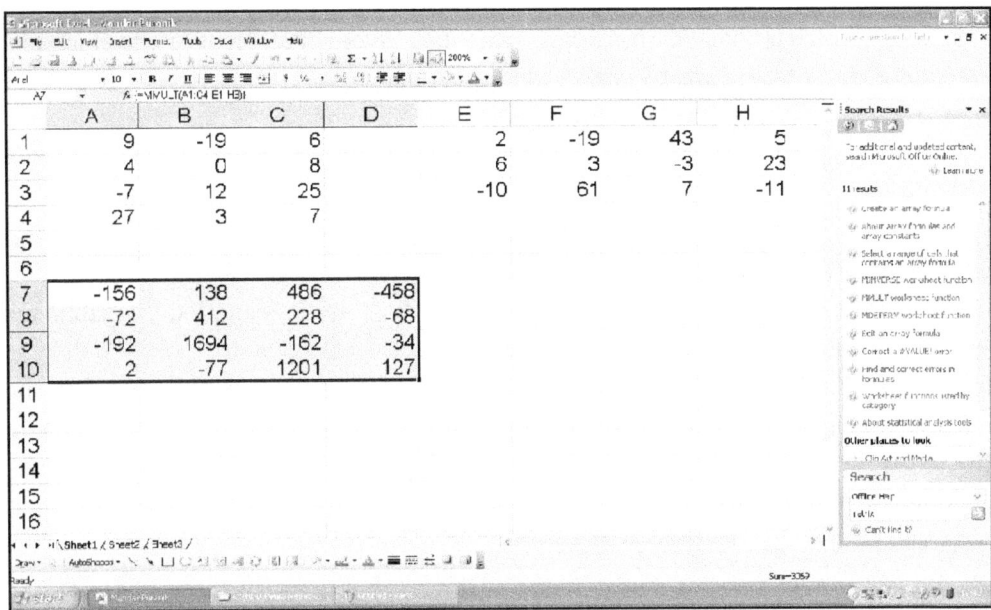

Image 1.15

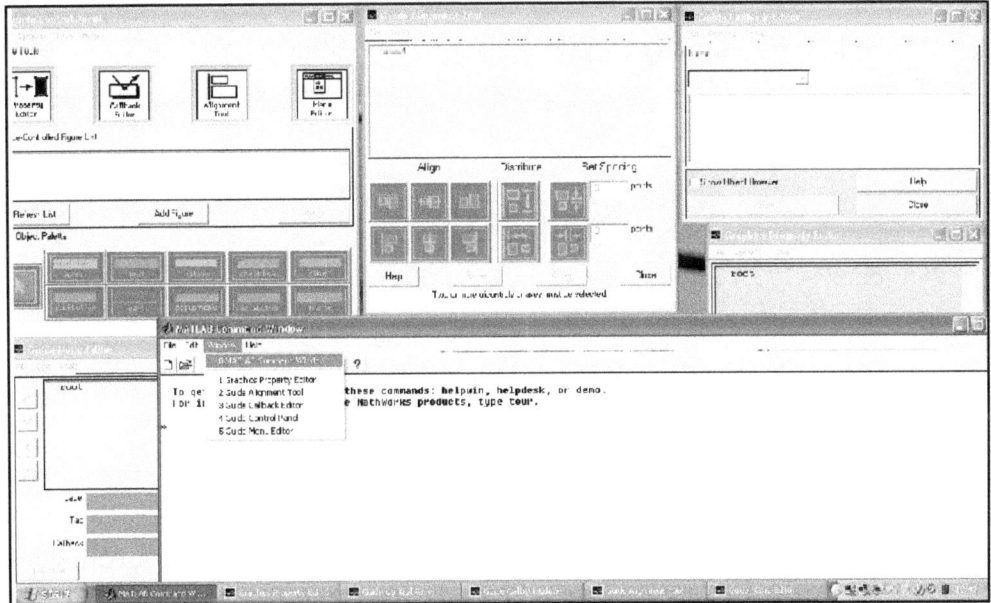

Image 1.16

Basic Arithmetic in MatLab

For solving basic arithmetic problems, we may type mathematical expression at >> prompt and the answer will be displayed as illustrated below :

>> 5 * 3 + $\frac{62}{2}$ − 24

ans =

22

>>

Similarly, other expressions also may be entered as, sin(), asin(), exp(), log(), log10(), sqrt(), abs(), ceil(), floor(), etc.

Remember, MatLab does not support fabs() function, hence abs() function is used for both integers and real numbers. Similarly, it does not support pow(x, y) function, so for x^y, we need to use carrot symbol (shift-6) as below :

>> 3 ^ 4

ans =

81

>>

In addition to ceil() and floor() functions, MatLab supports round() function which obeys the basic rounding rule as illustrated below :

>> round (5.3)

ans =

5

>> round (5.8)

ans =

6

>> round (−5.3)

ans =

− 5

>> round (−5.8)

ans =

− 6

>>

In MatLab, you may assign value to variables and use variables in expressions. For example, say we wish to generate bill for stationary items according to following prices, pencil for Rs. 2/-, pen for Rs. 5/-, notebook for Rs. 12/-. A customer has purchased 22 pencils, 17 pens and 13 notebooks. This bill may be generated as :

```
>> pencil = 2
pencil =
    2
>> pen = 5
pen =
    5
>>
```

To hide command prompt response, we may type command with semicolon as :
```
>> notebook = 12;
>>
```
Thus, response is hidden but the value is assigned to the variable. Now, we may generate bill as :
```
>> bill = 22 * pencil + 17 * pen + 13 * notebook
bill =
    285
>>
```

Using Script Files

MatLab provides us a facility to write and save a script file which may be run in MatLab environment whenever required. For example, the above problem of bill generation may be solved by a script file.

Type following lines in Notepad ;
```
pencil = 2;
pen = 5;
notebook = 12;
bill = 22 * pencil + 17 * pen + 13 * notebook
```

Save this file in "C:\MatLab\bin" folder with name say "example.m". Note extension to Notepad file is normally ".txt" but we have to take care to save this file NOT as ".txt" but as ".m" file. Now, to run this file in MatLab environment, just type the filename at >>prompt and we will get the answer as below :
```
>> example
bill =
    285
>>
```

Handling Matrices

To define a matrix in MatLab, we can write a command as below :
$$a = [3\ 4\ -2;\ 1\ 7\ 0;\ -7\ 5\ 9]$$
This generates a square matrix as below :

$$a = \begin{bmatrix} 3 & 4 & -2 \\ 1 & 7 & 0 \\ -7 & 5 & 9 \end{bmatrix}$$

The transpose of matrix can be found by command a'. Similarly, determinant and inverse can be obtained by det(a) and inv(a). All these commands and their responses are shown below :

```
>> a = [3 4 -2; 1 7 0; -7 5 9]
   a =
        3   4  -2
        1   7   0
       -7   5   9
>> a'
   ans =
        3   1  -7
        4   7   5
       -2   0   9
>> det (a)
   ans =
       45
>> inv (a)
   ans =
        1.4000  -1.0222   0.3111
       -0.2000   0.2889  -0.0444
        1.2000  -0.9556   0.3778
>>
```

Matrix multiplication is as easy as basic arithmetic multiplication. We can write command as c = a * b. If a and b variables store numeric values, it will be basic arithmetic multiplication. On the other hand, if a and b represent matrices of appropriate dimensions then MatLab performs matrix multiplication and stores the answer (matrix with relevant dimensions).

For example, see following example :

```
>> a = [1 3 5 7; 0 2 4 6; -2 1 3 5]
```

```
a =
    1    3    5    7
    0    2    4    6
   -2    1    3    5
>> b = [9 3 1; 8 2 6; 0 -5 7; 4 8 2]
b =
    9    3    1
    8    2    6
    0   -5    7
    4    8    2
>> c = a * b
c =
   61   40   68
   40   32   52
   10   21   35
>>
```

Decision Making Statements

MatLab support decision making statements like :

"if ... end", "if ... else ... end",

"if ... elseif ... else ... end" or "switch ...

case ... end"

To understand these structures, let us take different examples.

Get marks of a student from user. If user enters positive number, it is right, if it is not a positive number, generate and display error message as "Invalid marks".

Let us make script file for the solution. Hence, type following lines in Notepad and save as :

"C : \MatLab\bin\IfExample.m".

```
marks = input('Enter marks:');
if marks < 1
    disp('Invalid marks')
end
```

Its execution will be as below :

```
>>IfExample
Enter marks : -15
Invalid marks
>>IfExample
```

Enter marks : 25
>>

This program does not respond if marks are valid, so let us modify the program which will accept marks ranging from 1 to 25 and generate and display message as "Marks Accepted", otherwise "Invalid Marks". So make the Notepad as below :

```
marks = input('Enter marks:');
if marks < 1 | marks > 25
    disp('Invalid marks')
else
    disp('Marks Accepted')
end
```

Execution of this file will be[*]

>>IfExample
Enter marks : 17
Marks Accepted
>>IfExample
Enter marks : 27
Invalid marks
>>

Now, let us modify the program which will generate and display message "Invalid Marks" if the number entered by user is not ranging from 1 to 25. But will display "PASS" if number is ranging from 10 to 25 and will display "FAIL" if it is ranging from 1 to 9. The program is as below :

```
marks = input('Enter marks:');
if marks < 1 | marks > 25
    disp('Invalid marks')
elseif marks > 9
    disp('PASS')
else
    disp('FAIL')
end
```

The execution is illustrated below :

---

[*] | symbol indicates logical operator OR and & indicates logical operator AND.

```
>>IfExample
Enter marks : 0
Invalid marks
>> IfExample
Enter Marks : 7
FAIL
>> IfExample
Enter marks : 17
PASS
>>
```

To learn "switch ... case ... end", let us take a different example wherein we will also learn NESTING of various structures.*

Let us get a number from user as marks of student. If the number is not ranging from 1 to 50, it is "Invalid Marks". If the marks are ranging from 1 to 19, display message as "FAIL". If the number is ranging from 20 to 29, display "Good", if it is ranging from 30 to 39 display, "Excellent", if it is ranging from 40 to 49 display, "Outstanding", if it is equal to 50 display, "It is a University Record" The script file program will be :

```
marks = input('Enter marks:');
if marks < 1   | marks > 50
    disp('Invalid marks')
else
    Switch ceil ((marks + 1)/10)
        case {6}
            disp('It is a University Record')
        case {5}
            disp('Outstanding')
        case {4}
            disp('Excellent')
        case {3}
            disp('Good')
        Otherwise
            disp('FAIL')
    end
end
```

---

* These concepts are similar to C programming, hence not discussed in detail.

The execution of this script file program is obvious and as below :

```
>>IfExample
Enter marks : 51
Invalid marks
>> IfExample
Enter marks : 50
It is a University Record
>> IfExample
Enter marks : 49
Outstanding
>> IfExample
Enter marks : 19
FAIL
>>
```

Loop Structures

MatLab supports two loop structures, "for ... end" and "while ... end".

Let us take a simple example to display squares of odd integers from 1 to 15 and develop programs in script files using both these structures separately.

Script file – "C:\MatLab\bin\ForExample.m"

```
for n = 1:15
    x(n) = n ^ 2;
end
for n = 1:15
    if 2* round (n/2) ~ = n
        disp (x(n))
    end
end
```

The output will be as,

```
>> ForExample
    1
    9
    25
    49
    81
    121
    169
```

225
>>

The same output can be obtained by :

"C:\MatLab\bin\WhileExample.m" developed as below :

```
n = 1;
while n < 16
    x(n) = n ^ 2;
    n = n + 1;

end
n = 1;
while n < 16
    if 2 * round(n/2) ~ = n
        disp(x(n))
    end
    n = n + 1;
end
```

In these two programs, you must have observed use of '~=' operator, which is a logical operator to compare inequality.

All such logical operators supported by MatLab are as listed below :

Operator	Meaning
= =	Equality (equal to)
<	Less than
< =	Less than or equal to
>	Greater than
> =	Greater than or equal to
~ =	Not equal to
|	Or
&	And

1.4 Error

Various numerical methods are used by engineers and scientists for solving engineering problems. These numerical methods are well suited for solving mathematical problems by using modern digital computers which are very fast and efficient and reliable in performing arithmetic operations.

Approximations and errors are integral part of numerical methods. Prior to using the numerical methods it is essential to know how errors arise, how they grow during the numerical computations and how they affect the accuracy of a solution. Fig. 1.1 indicates different sources of error, which get introduced in various forms.

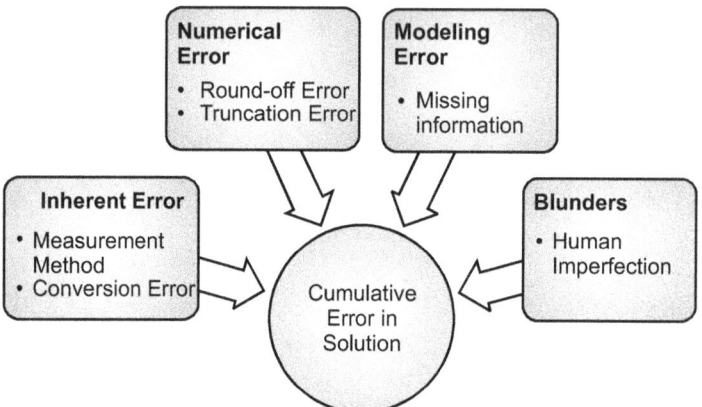

Fig. 1.1 : Sources of Errors

1.5 MEASURES OF ERROR

Actually, Error is expressed as the difference between Exact Value and Approximate or Measured Value.

The error can be measured by the following methods.

1.5.1 Absolute Error

Consider x_a denote the true or actual value and x_t denote an approximated or measured value. Then error incurred is given by,

Error, $\qquad E = x_a - x_t$ and $\qquad$ ... (1.1)

Absolute Error, $\qquad E_a = |x_a - x_t| \qquad$ ... (1.2)

For example, during the measurement of thickness of coating, actual thickness $x_a = 1.0674$ is measured as $x_t = 1.06743345$ and then the error is given by,

Error, $\qquad E = x_a - x_t$

$\qquad E = 1.06774 - 1.06743345$

$\qquad E = -0.000033345 = -3.3345 \times 10^{-5}$

Absolute Error, $\qquad E_a = |1.06774 - 1.06743345| = 3.3345 \times 10^{-5}$

Although the magnitude of error is small but in comparison with the actual thickness, 1.06774 i.e. 6.774×10^{-4}, it is very significant.

Also, while measurement of thickness of plate of 100 mm thickness is observed 99.998 mm, the absolute error is 0.002 mm, which is very large as compared to error in thickness of coating. But in case of measurement of thickness of plate it is considerably low to the actual value.

To avoid this difficulty, another measure of error is used known as Relative Error (E_R).

1.5.2 Relative Error

Relative error or normalized error E_R is representing a true value x_a by an approximate value x_t defined by,

$$E_R = \frac{\text{Absolute Error}}{|\text{True Value}|} = \frac{|x_a - x_e|}{|x_a|} \quad \ldots (1.3)$$

e.g. Measurement of thickness of Coating :

$$E_R = \frac{\text{Absolute Error}}{|\text{True Value}|} = \frac{3.3345 \times 10^{-5}}{1.0674} = 3.12 \times 10^{-5}$$

e.g. Measurement of thickness of Plate :

$$E_R = \frac{\text{Absolute Error}}{|\text{True Value}|} = \frac{|100 - 99.998|}{|100|} = 2 \times 10^{-5}$$

Comparing above two, error in measurement of thickness of coating is more than 1.5 times of the error in measurement of thickness of plate.

1.5.3 Percentage Relative Error

Also, the percentage relative error can be expressed as,

$$\text{Percentage } E_R = \frac{\text{Absolute Error}}{|\text{True Value}|} \times 100\% = \frac{|x_a - x_e|}{|x_a|} \times 100\% \quad \ldots (1.4)$$

1.6 SIGNIFICANT DIGITS

Usually, the numerical solution to a given problem is sought to a desired level of accuracy and precision wherein the error is below a set tolerance level. The idea of significant numbers is essential to understand the concept of accuracy and precision in the solution and also to designate the reliability of a numerical value.

The Significant Digits of a number are those that can be used with confidence. Suppose we seek a numerical solution to an accuracy of 10^{-3} and obtain as solution y = 12.03456789. Here the solution is reliable only upto the first three decimal places i.e. y = 12.0345 or the solution has five significant digits : 1, 2, 3, 4 and 5.

Some constant numbers like π, e, etc. have infinite number of significant digits.

e.g. π = 3.142857142857……………………

Such numbers can never be represented exactly on a computer which operates with fixed number of significant digits due to hardware limitations. The omission of certain digits from such numbers results in what is called 'round-off-error'.

Some thumb rules on the significant digits, within the desired level of accuracy are :
- All non-zero digits are significant,
- All zeros occurring between non-zero digits are significant,
- Trailing zeros following a decimal point are significant.
- Zeros between the decimal point and preceding a non-zero digit are not significant. e.g. 0.004756 (4756×10^{-6}, have four significant digits).
- Trailing zeros in large numbers without the decimal point are not significant. e.g. 28000 can be written as 2.8×10^3 and contains only two significant digits.

1.7 NUMERICAL ERRORS

Numerical errors arise during computations due to round-off errors and truncation errors.

1.7.1 Round-off Errors

Round-off error occurs because computers use fixed number of bits and hence fixed number of binary digits to represent numbers. In a numerical computation round-off errors are introduced at every stage of computation. When the number of bits required for representing a number is less than the number is usually rounded to fit the available number of bits. This is done either by chopping or by symmetric rounding.

Chopping : Rounding a number by chopping amounts to dropping the extra digits. Here the given number is truncated. Suppose that we are using a computer with a fixed word length of four digits. Then the truncated representation of the number 2.32451 will be 2.324. The digits 51 will be dropped. Now to evaluate the error due to chopping let us consider the normalized representation of the given number 'x ' i.e.

$$x = 2.32451 = 0.232451 \times 10^1$$
$$x = (0.2324 + 0.000051) \times 10^1$$

∴ Error due to Chopping is 0.000051 or 5.1×10^{-5}.

1.7.2 Truncation Errors

Often an approximation is used in place of an exact mathematical procedure. For instance consider the Taylor series expansion of say sin x i.e. $\sin x = x - \frac{x^3}{3!} + \frac{x^5}{5!} - \frac{x^7}{7!} + ...$ ... (1.5)

In practice, we cannot use all of the infinite number of terms in the series for computing the sine of angle x. We usually terminate the process after a certain number of terms. The error that results due to such a termination or truncation is called as 'Truncation Error'.

For example, let us consider evaluation of exponential function using first three terms at x = 0.2.

$$e^x = 1 + x + \frac{x^2}{2!} + \frac{x^3}{3!} + \frac{x^4}{4!} + \frac{x^5}{5!} + \ldots$$

$$e^x \approx 1 + x + \frac{x^2}{2!}$$

$$e^x \approx 1 + 0.2 + \frac{0.2^2}{2!} = 1.22$$

$$\therefore \quad \text{Truncation Error} = \frac{x^3}{3!} + \frac{x^4}{4!} + \frac{x^5}{5!} + \ldots$$

$$\therefore \quad \text{Truncation Error} = \sum_{i=3}^{\infty} \frac{x^i}{i!}$$

1.7.3 Machine Epsilon

We know that we would encounter round-off error when a number is represented in floating-point form. The relative round-off error due to chopping is defined by,

$$e_r = \left| \frac{g_x \times 10^{E-d}}{f_x \times 10^E} \right| \quad \ldots (1.6)$$

$$|g_z| < 1.0 \quad \text{and} \quad |f_x| \geq 0.1 \quad \ldots (1.7)$$

Here we know that

$$e_r < \left| \frac{1.0 \times 10^{E-d}}{0.1 \times 10^E} \right| = 10^{-d+1} \quad \ldots (1.8)$$

i.e. maximum relative round-off error due to chopping is given by 10^{-d+1}. We know that the value of 'd' i.e. the length of mantissa is machine dependent. Hence, the maximum relative round-off error due to chopping is also known as machine epsilon ($E_{chopping}$). Similarly, maximum relative round-off error due to symmetric rounding is given by

$$e_r < \left| \frac{0.5 \times 10^{E-d}}{0.1 \times 10^E} \right| = 0.5 \times 10^{-d+1}$$

Machine-Epsilon (ϵ) for symmetric rounding is given by,

$$\epsilon_{symmetric-rounding} = \frac{1}{2} \times 10^{-d+1}$$

It is important to note that the machine epsilon represents upper bound for the round-off error due to floating point representation.

For a computer system with binary representation the machine epsilon due to chopping and symmetric rounding are given by

$$\epsilon_{chopping} = 2^{-d+1} \quad \text{and} \quad \epsilon_{symmetric-rounding} = 2^{-d} \quad \text{respectively.}$$

e.g. Assume that our binary machine has 24-bit mantissa. Then $\epsilon_{symmetric-rounding} = 2^{-24}$. Say that our system can represent a q decimal digit mantissa.

$$2^{-24} = \frac{1}{2} \times 10^{-q+1}$$

Then, i.e.
$$2^{-23} = 10^{-q+1}$$
$$-23 \log_{10} 2 = -q + 1$$
$$q = 23 \log_{10} 2 + 1 \approx 7.9$$

Note that our machine can store numbers with seven significant decimal digits.

1.7.4 Algorithmic Error or Inherent Error

Error which arises from the method itself is known as inherent error.

e.g. Numerical Integration by trapezoidal method, Calculation of area of circle, etc.

REVIEW QUESTIONS

1. Explain the Algorithm of Pseudo code also Explain the standard symbols and Draw a flow chart of Pseudo code.
2. Write a short note on standard terms in C programming.
3. State and Explain the structured of C programming.
4. What are the Arithmetic operators and logical operator ?
5. Develop of a C program to display integar from 1 to 50 on separate lines.
6. Determine the permutation and combination of 3 white balls out of 10 white balls selected 3 ball.
7. Explain the solvers.
8. What are the Decision making statements.
9. Write a short note on loop statements.
10. Write a short not on measuring error also types of error.
11. Explain the Numerical Error.

Chapter 2
SOLUTION OF TRANSCENDENTAL EQUATION

2.1 ROOTS OF EQUATIONS

An architect designs a spherical overhead water tank for a residential complex. A civil engineer constructs it as shown in Fig. 2.1.

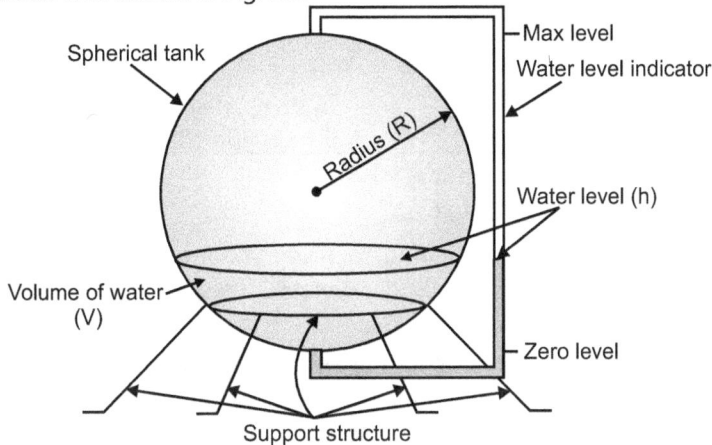

Fig. 2.1

Due to construction of a transparent glass tube level indicator, the residents can see level of water inside the tank. But problem is that, volume of water contained by the tank is never clear. Hence, a mathematician derived an equation to relate the water level to the volume of water as :

$$V = \frac{\pi h^2 (3R - h)}{3} \qquad \ldots (2.1)$$

where, V- Volume of water
          h- Water level
and   R- Inner radius of the tank

The residents of the society were happy that they can know amount of water available in the tank just by a simple calculation based on water level. But now the problem is in summer days, that a tanker is called to store water in the empty tank. Now as usual disputes water tanker owner used to say that he had poured 1000 lit of water. Here, society chairman wishes to verify that really he had poured 1000 lit. If not then tell him strongly that water must be at certain level to make volume of 1000 lit. Thus, the calculation is now in the reverse direction and the accurate calculation becomes difficult as one needs to solve a polynomial equation. This engineering problem is commonly known as finding roots of a equation.

To understand the society chairman's problems, let us assume radius of tank to be 3 m, so the capacity of tank to store water is,

$$V = \frac{\pi \times (2 \times 3000)^2 (3 \times 3000 - 2 \times 3000)}{3} \text{ mm}^3$$

Here h is taken is 2R because tank is to be fully filled with water.

$$\therefore \quad V = \frac{\pi \times 6000^2 \times 3000}{3} \times 10^{-6} \text{ lit.}$$

Remember $\quad 1 \text{ mm}^3 = 10^{-3}$ cc and 1 cc $= 1$ ml
Hence, $1 \text{ mm}^3 \quad = 10^{-6}$ lit.

$$\therefore \quad V = 113097.3355 \text{ lit.}$$

Now, volume of water can be determined corresponding to given value of water level. So assuming water level as 1 m volume,

$$V = \frac{\pi \times 1000^2 \times (3 \times 3000 - 1000)}{3 \times 10^6}$$

$$= 8377.5804 \text{ lit.}$$

But determining water level corresponding to given volume of 1000 lit. is not a straight forward. One has to assume water level and calculate corresponding volume, and iterate the procedure by judgement or guess work so that volume is near 1000 lit.

This crude approach to the solution is person dependent, so one may require 5 iterations to reach solution, other may require 15 iterations. Someone due to improper guess work may never reach the solution. So in engineering approach this is not a numerical method. One such trial and error approach is illustrated below :

Table 2.1

No. of Iterations	Assumed Level h in mm	Volume in Lit.
1	500	2225.2948
2	350	1109.6367
3	340	1048.3453
4	335	1018.3259
5	332	1000.5152
6	331	994.6118

Thus, answer is when 1000 lit. water is poured in the empty tank the water level will be 332 mm. Why guesses were done as indicated in Table 2.1 ? Truly, there is no logic, it is personal feeling that we may reach the solution.

2.2 TRANSCENDENTAL EQUATIONS

In engineering or scientific problems we may not always come across only polynomial equations. Sometimes, for example, referring Fig. 2.2 for relation between tensions in the flat belt wrapped over a pulley with wrap angle of θ radians and having coefficient of friction μ, we will write mathematical expression as :

$$\frac{T_1}{T_2} = e^{\mu\theta}$$

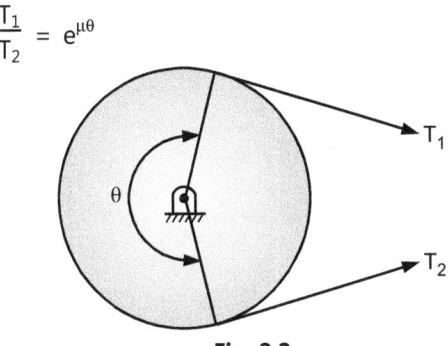

Fig. 2.2

This equation is not a polynomial equation. Such equations are called as Transcendental* equations. The transcendental equation is that equation which contains transcendental functions. And transcendental function is a function that does not satisfy a polynomial equation. In simple words, an equation that includes exponential functions, logarithms and trigonometrical functions is called as a transcendental equation.

2.3 VARIOUS METHODS

To handle such type of problems, various scientists suggested various methods as below :
1. Graphical method
2. Bisection method
3. False position method
4. Simple fixed point iteration method
5. Newton – Raphson method
6. Secant method
7. Miller's method
8. Bairstow's method

Out of these some are bracketing methods and others are non-bracketing or open methods.
- Bracketing methods are those in which two initial guesses are required.
  Bracketing methods may require more iterations to reach near desired solution but they are convergent methods. That means these methods keep on going towards the solution, and solution is guaranteed.
  For example, Bisection method, False position method, Fixed point iteration method,

---

* The dictionary meaning of Transcendental is superior or beyond ordinary. The polynomial equations are made of any functions such as addition, multiplication or power function. The exponential, logarithm and trigonometric functions are beyond these algebraic functions, hence equations containing such functions are superior than algebraic, in other words, transcendental equations.

Newton-Raphson method and Secant method require only one initial guess, hence they are called open methods.

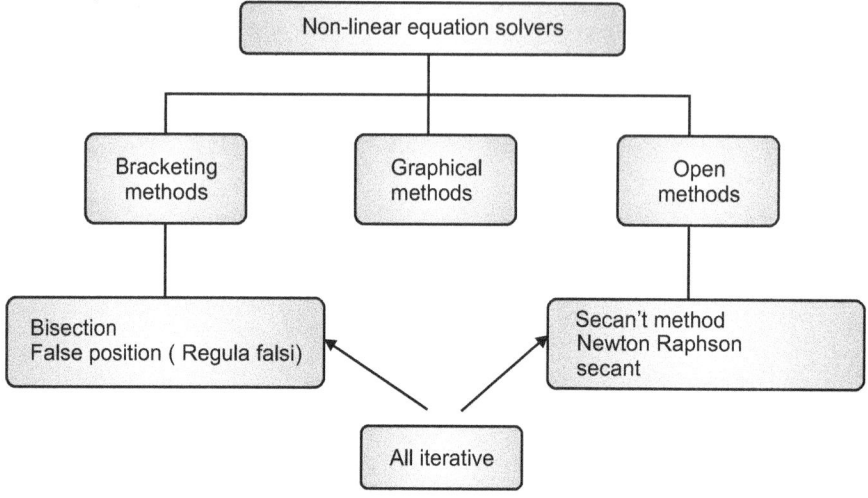

Fig. 2.3

- Open methods have risk of divergence. That means they may take you away from the desired solution. But if they are converging they take you fast near the solution.

  e.g. Newton Raphson Method, Successive Approximation method.

  Miller's method and Bairstow's methods are specially developed to handle real as well as imaginary roots. Newton's method can also find complex roots.

2.4 BRACKETING METHODS

- **Two** initial guesses for the root are required.
- The two guesses must **"bracket"** the root i.e., on either side of the root.
- Two bracketing methods to be introduced :
  1. Bisection method
  2. False position method (Regula falsi)

2.4.1 Bisection Method

Procedure :

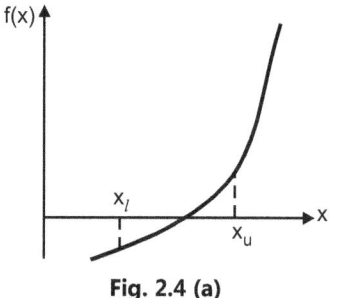

Fig. 2.4 (a)

Step 1 : Choose x_l and x_u as two guesses for the root such that

$$f(x_l) f(x_u) < 0$$

In other words, f(x) changes sign between x_l and x_u.

Step 2 : Estimate the root x_r of $f(x) = 0$ as the mid-point between x_l and x_u as:

$$x_r = \frac{x_l + x_u}{2}$$

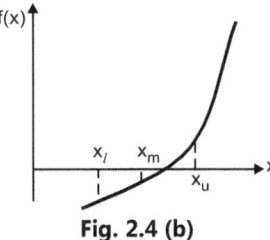

Fig. 2.4 (b)

Step 3 : Now check the following:
- If $f(x_l)f(x_r) = 0$ then the root is x_r;
- stop the algorithm.
  If $f(x_l)f(x_r) < 0$ then
- the root lies in interval (x_l, x_r); update xu as xr;
- go to step 2.
  If $f(x_l)f(x_r) > 0$ then
- the root lies in interval (x_r, x_u);
- update x_l as x_r;
- go to step 2.

Features of Bisection Method
- Guaranteed to converge: The bracket gets halved with each iteration.
- Only the signs of the computed function values are used.
- Relatively slow convergence: Each iteration gains one binary digit in accuracy. (Roughly one decimal digit per 3.3 iterations.)

2.4.2 False Position Method

- A shortcoming of the bisection method is that, in dividing the interval (x_l, x_u) into halves, no account is taken of the *magnitudes* of $f(x_l)$ and $f(x_u)$.
- The *false position method* (or *regula falsi* in Latin) exploits such information to obtain an improved estimate of the root.

Procedure

Step 1 : Join $f(x_l)$ and $f(x_u)$ by a straight line. The x-intercept of this line gives an improved estimate of the root.

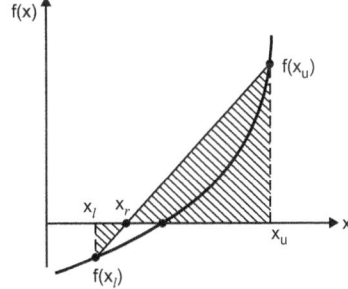

Fig. 2.5

Step 2 : Equation of the straight line (using two-point form):

$$\frac{y - f(x_u)}{x - x_u} = \frac{f(x_u) - f(x_1)}{x_u - x_l}$$

Substituting $y = 0$ and $x = x_r$,

$$x_r = x_u - \frac{x_u - x_l}{f(x_u) - f(x_l)} f(x_u)$$

Step 3 : Check the following :
If $f(x_l)f(x_r) = 0$ then x_r
If $f(x_l)f(x_r) < 0$ then Update x_u as x_r; go to step 2.
If $f(xl)f(xr) > 0$ then Update xl as xr; go to step 2.

Difference in Bisection and False Position Method
- The only difference between the two methods lies in step 2: *Mid-point vs linear interpolation*.
- False position method *generally* performs *better* than bisection method.

Flow Chart for Bisection and False Position Method

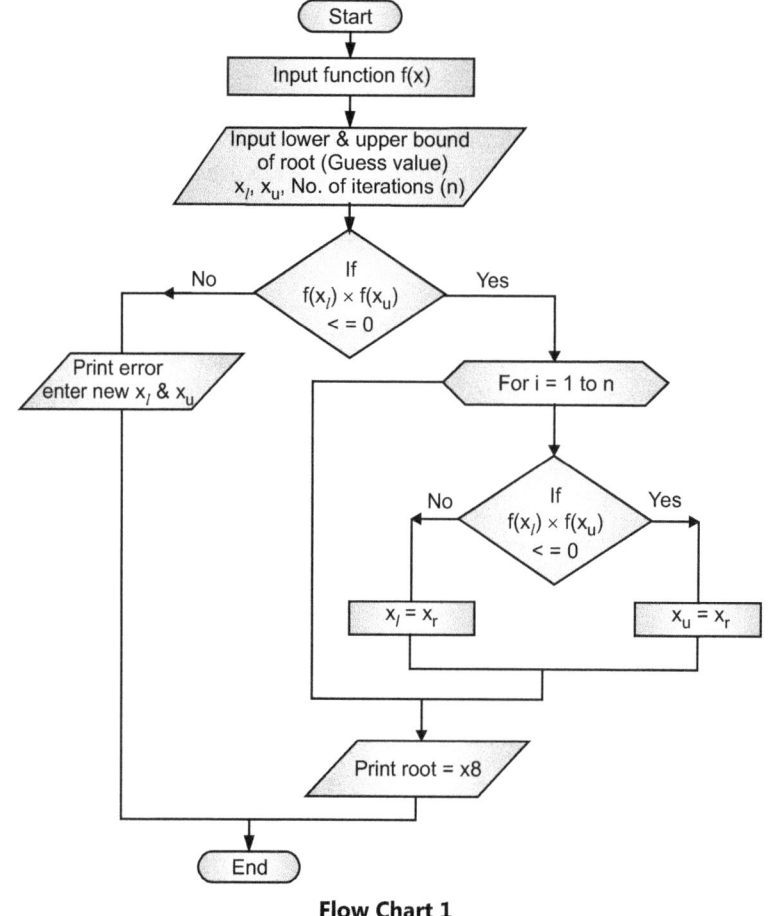

Flow Chart 1

Matlab Code :

```
fstr = input('\n Input Function String f(x) >>> ', 's');
f=inline(fstr);
disp(sprintf([ \n  y = f(x) = 'fstr]));
x1 = input('\n Input Lower Guess Value of Root (x1) = ');
xu = input('\n Input Upper Guess Value of Root (xu) = ');
n = input ('\n No. of Iteration (n) = ');
if x1*xu>0
    fprintf('\n Error, enter alternate values of x1 and xu');
end
%% BISECTION METHOD
for i=1 : n
    xr = (x1 + xu)/2;        %Bisection formula
    if x1*xr <= 0
        xu=xr
    else
        x1=xr;
    end
    fprintf('\n Root after %d iteration by Bisection Method=%f', i, x1);
end
%% FALSE POSITION METHOD
for i=1:n
    xn1 = xu - f(xu) * (xu - x1) / (f(xu) - f (x1))          %False Position formula
    ifx1*xr <= 0
        xu=xr;
    else
        x1=xr;
    end
    fprintf('\n Root after %d iteration by False Position Method =%f', i, x1);
end
```

SOLVED EXAMPLES

Example 2.1 : Find real root of the equation $e^x \cos x = 1.2$ upto 3 decimal accuracy assume root lies between 0 and 1. Use (a) Bisection Method, (b) False Position Method.

Solution :

[A] Bisection Method

$$x_l = 0 \Rightarrow f(x_l) = e^{x_l} \cdot \cos(x_l) - 1.2 = e^{(0)} \times \cos(0) - 1.2 = -0.2 \, (-ve)$$
$$x_u = 1 \Rightarrow f(x_u) = e^{(1)} \cdot \cos(1) - 1.2$$
$$= 0.2687 \, (+ve)$$

(Note : x in radians)

Since
$$f(x_l) \times f(x_u) = -0.2 \times 0.2687$$
$$= -0.0537 = (-ve) \therefore \text{ Root lies between } x_l \text{ and } x_u$$
$$x_r = \frac{x_l + x_u}{2} = \frac{0 + 1}{2} = 0.5 \quad \ldots \text{ Bisection Rule}$$
$$f(x_r) = e^{0.5} \times \cos(0.5) - 1.2$$
$$= 0.2469 \, (+ve)$$

Now, since $f(x_l) \times f(x_r)$ i.e. $(-ve) \times (+ve) \Rightarrow (-ve)$, Root lies between x_l and x_r.

$$\therefore \qquad x_r = \frac{x_l + x_u}{2}$$
$$= \frac{0 + 0.5}{2}$$
$$= 0.25$$
$$f(x_r) = e^{0.25} \cdot \cos(0.25) - 1.2$$
$$= 0.0441 \, (+ve)$$

Since, $\quad f(x_l) \times f(x_r) = (-ve)$, root lies between x_l and x_r.

This procedure is repeated upto said no. of iterations or accuracy achieved.

Accuracy $= |x_l - x_u| \quad = |0.25 - 0| = 0.25 >= 0.001$

Please refer following table of results.

Iteration No.	x_l	x_u	x_r	$f(x_l)$	$f(x_u)$	$f(x_r)$	$f(x_l)*f(x_u)$	Accuracy
0	0	1		−0.2	0.2687		−0.0537	
1	0	1	0.5	−0.2	0.2687	0.2469	−0.0494	
2	0	0.5	0.25	−0.2	0.2469	0.0441	−0.0088	0.2500
3	0	0.25	0.125	−0.2	0.0441	−0.0757	0.0151	0.1250
4	0.1250	0.2500	0.1875	−0.0757	0.0441	−0.0149	0.0011	0.0625
5	0.1875	0.2500	0.2188	−0.0149	0.0441	0.0149	−0.0002	0.0313
6	0.1875	0.2188	**0.2031**	−0.0149	0.0149	0.0000	0.0000	**0.0156**

[B] False Position Method

Note : Only difference between Bisection Method and False Position Method is formula to get intermediate value.

$$x_r = x_u - \frac{x_u - x_l}{f(x_u) - f(x_l)} \times f(x_u)$$

Refer result in following table :

SOLUTION OF TRANSCENDENTAL EQUATION

Iteration No.	x_l	x_u	x_r	$f(x_l)$	$f(x_u)$	$f(x)$	$f(x_l)*f(x_u)$	Accuracy
0	0	1		−0.2	0.2687		−0.0537	
1	0	1	0.42672	−0.2	0.2687	0.1948	−0.0390	
2	0	0.42672	0.18209	−0.2	0.1948	−0.0201	0.0040	0.2446
3	0.18209	0.42672	0.30601	−0.02011	0.19482	0.09490	−0.00191	0.1239
4	0.18209	0.30601	0.19368	−0.02011	0.09490	−0.00898	0.00018	0.1123
5	0.19368	0.30601	0.21333	−0.00898	0.09490	0.00973	−0.00009	0.0196
6	0.19368	0.21333	0.19538	−0.00898	0.00973	−0.00736	0.00007	0.0179
7	0.19538	0.21333	0.20400	−0.00736	0.00973	0.00087	−0.00001	0.0086
8	0.19538	0.20400	0.19909	−0.00736	0.00087	−0.00381	0.00003	0.0049
9	0.19909	0.20400	0.20348	−0.00381	0.00087	0.00037	0.00000	0.0044
10	0.19909	0.20348	**0.20267**	−0.00381	0.00037	−0.00040	0.00000	**0.0008**

Hence root of equation is 0.20267 by false position method.

Example 2.2 : *Find real root of the equation $x^2 - 4x + 2 = 0$ upto 3 decimal accuracy assume root lies between 0 and 1. Use (a) Bisection Method, (b) False Position Method.*

Solution :

[A] Bisection Method

$$x_l = 0 \Rightarrow f(x_l) = x_l^2 - 4x_l + 2 = 0^2 - 4 \times 0 + 2 \Rightarrow 2.0 \ (+ve)$$

$$x_u = 1 \Rightarrow f(x_u) = x_u^2 - 4x_u + 2 = 1^2 - 4 \times 1 + 2 \Rightarrow -1.0 \ (-ve)$$

Since
$$f(x_l) \times f(x_u) = 2 \times -1$$
$$= -2 \ (-ve) \therefore \text{Root lies between } x_l \text{ and } x_u$$

$$x_r = \frac{x_l + x_u}{2} = \frac{0+1}{2} = 0.5 \qquad \ldots \text{Bisection Rule}$$

$$f(x_r) = (0.5)^2 - 4 \times 0.5 + 2 = 0.25 \ (+ve)$$

Now, since $f(x_l) \times f(x_r)$ i.e. $(+ve) \times (+ve) \Rightarrow (+ve)$, Root lies between x_r and x_u.

∴ $\qquad x_l = x_r = 0.5$ and $x_u = 1.0$

∴ $\qquad x_r = \dfrac{x_l + x_u}{2}$

$$= \frac{0.5 + 1}{2}$$

$$= 0.75$$

$$f(x_r) = -0.4375 \, (-ve)$$

Since, $f(x_l) \times f(x_r) = (-ve)$, root lies between x_l and x_u.

This procedure is repeated upto said no. of iterations or accuracy achieved.

Accuracy $= |x_r - x_{r\_prev.\ itn}| = |0.75 - 0.5| = 0.25 >= 0.001$

Please refer the following table of results.

Iteration No.	x_l	x_u	x_r	$f(x_l)$	$f(x_u)$	$f(x)$	$f(x_l)*f(x_u)$	Accuracy
0	0	1		2	−1		−2.0000	
1	0	1	0.5	2	−1	0.25	0.5000	
2	0.5000	1.0000	0.7500	0.2500	−1.0000	−0.4375	−0.1094	0.2500
3	0.5000	0.7500	0.6250	0.2500	−0.4375	−0.1094	−0.0273	0.1250
4	0.5000	0.6250	0.5625	0.2500	−0.1094	0.0664	0.0166	0.0625
5	0.5625	0.6250	0.5938	0.0664	−0.1094	−0.0225	−0.0015	0.0313
6	0.5625	0.5938	0.5781	0.0664	−0.0225	0.0217	0.0014	0.0156
7	0.5781	0.5938	0.5859	0.0217	−0.0225	−0.0004	0.0000	0.0078
8	0.5938	0.5859	0.5898	−0.0225	−0.0004	−0.0115	0.0003	0.0039
9	0.5859	0.5898	0.5879	−0.0004	−0.0115	−0.0059	0.0000	0.0020
10	0.5859	0.5879	0.5869	−0.0004	−0.0059	−0.0032	0.0000	0.0010
11	0.5879	0.5869	**0.5874**	−0.0059	−0.0032	−0.0046	0.0000	**0.0005**

→ Hence Root ⇒ 0.5874

[B] False Position Method

Refer result in following table by False position method

Iteration No	x_l	x_u	x_r	$f(x_l)$	$f(x_u)$	$f(x)$	$f(x_l)*f(x_u)$	Accuracy
0	0	1		2	−1		−2.0000	
1	0	1	0.66667	2	−1	−0.22222222	−0.4444	
2	0.0000	0.6667	0.44444	2.0000	−0.2222	0.4198	0.8395	0.2222
3	0.4444	0.6667	0.64444	0.4198	−0.2222	−0.1625	−0.0682	0.2000
4	0.4444	0.6667	0.58974	0.4198	−0.2222	−0.0112	−0.0047	0.0547
5	0.4444	0.5897	0.53945	0.4198	−0.0112	0.1332	0.0559	0.0503
6	0.5394	0.5897	0.58844	0.1332	−0.0112	−0.0075	−0.0010	0.0490
7	0.5884	0.5884	**0.58844**	−0.0075	−0.0075	−0.0075	0.0001	**0.000**

→ Hence Root ⇒ 0.5884

Example 2.3 : Find real root of the equation $e^x - 3x$ upto 3 decimal accuracy assume root lies between 0 and 1. Use (a) Bisection Method, (b) False Position Method.

Solution :

[A] Bisection Method

$$x_l = 0 \Rightarrow f(x_l) = e^x - 3x = e^0 - 3 \times 0 = 1.0 \ (+ve)$$
$$x_u = 1 \Rightarrow f(x_u) = -0.2817182 \ (-ve)$$

Since $f(x_l) \times f(x_u) = (+ve) \times (-ve) \Rightarrow (-ve) \ \therefore$ Root lies between x_l and x_u

$$x_r = \frac{x_l + x_u}{2} = \frac{0 + 1}{2} = 0.5 \qquad \text{... Bisection Rule}$$

$$f(x_r) = e^{0.5} - 3 \times 0.5 = 0.148721 \ (+ve)$$

Now, since $f(x_l) \times f(x_r)$ i.e. $(+ve) \times (+ve) \Rightarrow (+ve)$, Root lies between x_r and x_u.

$\therefore \qquad x_l = x_r = 0.5$

$\therefore \qquad x_r = \dfrac{x_l + x_u}{2} = \dfrac{0.5 + 1}{2} = 0.75$

$$f(x_r) = -0.1329 \ (-ve)$$

Since, $f(x_l) \times f(x_r) = (-ve)$, root lies between x_l and x_r.

This procedure is repeated upto said no. of iterations or accuracy achieved.

Please refer following table of results.

Itr. No.	x_l	x_u	x_r	$f(x_l)$	$f(x_u)$	$f(x_r)$	$f(x_l)*f(x_u)$	Accuracy
0	0	1		1	−0.2817182		−0.2817	
1	0	1	0.5	1	−0.2817182	0.148721271	0.1487	
2	0.5000	1.0000	0.7500	0.1487213	−0.2817182	−0.13299998	−0.0198	0.2500
3	0.5000	0.7500	0.6250	0.1487213	−0.133	−0.00675404	−0.0010	0.1250
4	0.5000	0.6250	0.5625	0.1487213	−0.006754	0.067554657	0.0100	0.0625
5	0.5625	0.6250	0.5938	0.0675547	−0.006754	0.029516072	0.0020	0.0313
6	0.5938	0.6250	0.6094	0.0295161	−0.006754	0.011156489	0.0003	0.0156
7	0.6094	0.6250	0.6172	0.0111565	−0.006754	0.002144652	0.0000	0.0078
8	0.6172	0.6250	0.6211	0.0021447	−0.006754	−0.00231889	0.0000	0.0039
9	0.6172	0.6211	0.6191	0.0021447	−0.0023189	−9.0663E−05	0.0000	0.0020
10	0.6172	0.6191	0.6182	0.0021447	−9.066E−05	0.00102611	0.0000	0.0010
11	0.6182	0.6191	**0.6187**	0.0010261	−9.066E−05	0.000467502	0.0000	**0.0005**

[B] False Position Method

Refer result in following table :

Itr. No.	x_l	x_u	x_r	$f(x_l)$	$f(x_u)$	$f(x_r)$	$f(x_l)*f(x_u)$	Accuracy
0	0	1		1	−0.2817182		−0.2817	
1	0	1	0.7802	1	−0.2817182	−0.15869362	−0.1587	
2	0.0000	0.7802	0.60872	1	−0.1586936	0.011921476	0.0119	0.1715
3	0.6087	0.7802	0.75672	0.0119215	−0.1586936	−0.13888244	−0.0017	0.1480
4	0.6087	0.7567	0.61906	0.0119215	−0.1388824	4.27422E-06	0.0000	0.1377
5	0.6191	0.7567	0.62994	4.274E-06	−0.1388824	−0.0123219	0.0000	0.0109
6	0.6191	0.7567	0.61906	4.274E-06	−0.1388824	−5.6724E-07	0.0000	0.0109
7	0.6191	0.6191	**0.6190**	−5.672E-07	−5.672E-07	−5.6724E-07	0.0000	**0.0000**

Example 2.4 : *Find real root of the equation $x \sin x + \cos x$ upto 3 decimal accuracy. Use (a) Bisection Method, (b) False Position Method.*

Solution :

[A] Bisection Method : Assume root lies between 0 and 1.

$$x_l = 0 \Rightarrow f(x_l) = 1.00 \ (+ \text{ve})$$
$$x_u = 1 \Rightarrow f(x_u) = 1.3818 \ (+ \text{ve})$$

Since
$$f(x_l) \times f(x_u) = (+ \text{ve}) \times (+ \text{ve})$$
$$= (+ \text{ve}) \ \therefore \ \text{Root doesn't lie between 0 and 1}$$

Assume root lies between 2 and 3.

$$x_l = 2 \Rightarrow f(x_l) = 1.4024 \ (+ \text{ve})$$
$$x_u = 3 \Rightarrow f(x_u) = -0.5666 \ (- \text{ve})$$

Since
$$f(x_l) \times f(x_u) = (+ \text{ve}) \times (- \text{ve})$$
$$= (- \text{ve}) \ \therefore \ \text{Root lies between 2 and 3}$$

Please refer following table of results.

Itr. No	x_l	x_u	x_r	$f(x_l)$	$f(x_u)$	$f(x_r)$	$f(x_l)*f(x_u)$	Accuracy
0	0	1		1.0000	1.3818		1.3818	Since $f(X_l)*f(X_u)$ is greater than 0, root doesn't lie between X_l and X_u
1	2		1.3818	1.4024		1.9379	
2	3		1.4024	−0.5666		−0.7947	

1	2.0000	3.0000	2.5000	1.4024	−0.5666	0.6950	0.9748	
2	2.5000	3.0000	2.7500	0.6950	−0.5666	0.1253	0.0871	0.2500
3	2.7500	3.0000	2.8750	0.1253	−0.5666	−0.2073	−0.0260	0.1250
4	2.7500	2.8750	2.8125	0.1253	−0.2073	−0.0374	−0.0047	0.0625
5	2.7500	2.8125	2.7813	0.1253	−0.0374	0.0449	0.0056	0.0313
6	2.7813	2.8125	2.7969	0.0449	−0.0374	0.0040	0.0002	0.0156
7	2.7969	2.8125	2.8047	0.0040	−0.0374	−0.0166	−0.0001	0.0078
8	2.7969	2.8047	2.8008	0.0040	−0.0166	−0.0063	0.0000	0.0039
9	2.8008	2.8047	2.8027	−0.0063	−0.0166	−0.0115	0.0001	0.0020
10	2.8027	2.8047	2.8037	−0.0115	−0.0166	−0.0141	0.0002	0.0010
11	2.8037	2.8047	**2.8042**	−0.0141	−0.0166	−0.0154	0.0002	**0.0005**

[B] False Position Method : Refer result in following table :

Itr.No.	x_l	x_u	x_r	$f(x_l)$	$f(x_u)$	$f(x)$	$f(x_l)*f(x_u)$	Accuracy
	0	1		1.0000	1.3818		1.3818	Since $f(X_l)*f(X_u)$ is greater than 0, root doesn't lie between X_l and X_u
	1	2		1.3818	1.4024		1.9379	
	2	3		1.4024	−0.5666		−0.7947	
1	2.0000	3.0000	2.71223	1.4024	−0.5666	0.2198	0.3083	
2	2.7122	3.0000	2.91719	0.2198	−0.5666	−0.3258	−0.0716	0.2050
3	2.7122	2.9172	2.76952	0.2198	−0.3258	0.0753	0.0165	0.1477
4	2.7695	2.9172	2.82902	0.0753	−0.3258	−0.0816	−0.0061	0.0595
5	2.7695	2.8290	2.78069	0.0753	−0.0816	0.0463	0.0035	0.0483
6	2.7807	2.8290	2.80388	0.0463	−0.0816	−0.0145	−0.0007	0.0232
7	2.7807	2.8039	2.78909	0.0463	−0.0145	0.0244	0.0011	0.0148
8	2.7891	2.8039	2.80035	0.0244	−0.0145	−0.0052	−0.0001	0.0148
9	2.7891	2.8004	2.79616	0.0244	−0.0052	0.0059	0.0001	0.0113
10	2.7962	2.8004	2.79962	0.0059	−0.0052	−0.0032	0.0000	0.0042
11	2.7962	2.7996	**2.79799**	0.0059	−0.0032	0.0010	0.0000	**0.0035**

2.5 OPEN METHODS

Open methods are based on formulae that require either :
- Only a single starting value of x; or
- Two starting values that do not necessarily bracket a root.

2.5.1 Newton-Raphson Method

Now we know, that we find root of an equation means we find value of x where f(x) = 0. (Refer Fig. 2.10 and Fig. 2.11).

Newton-Raphson method suggests us to make an initial guess for value of x. Then locate corresponding f(x) on the graph. Draw tangent to the curve at that point. The intersection point of this tangent and X-axis is new guess value for x. Iterate this process till you reach sufficiently near the root. The above process is explained graphically in Fig. 2.6.

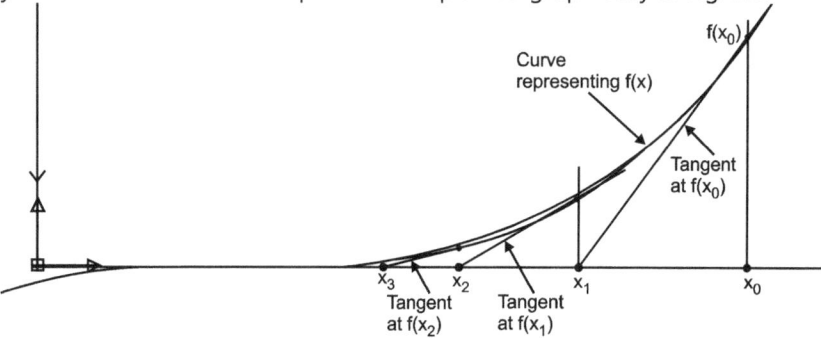

Fig. 2.6

2.5.1.1 Newton-Raphson Formulation

As initial guess value of x_0 is known, hence $f(x_0)$ is also known. To determine x_1, let us refer Fig. 2.6 again. The slope of tangent at point $(x_0, f(x_0))$ can be obtained by two ways :

1. Slope of line $= \dfrac{\Delta y}{\Delta x} = \dfrac{f(x_0) - 0}{x_0 - x_1}$

2. Slope of tangent to a curve at given point

$$= \left(\dfrac{dy}{dx}\right) = f'(x_0)$$

Now equating these two expressions,

$$f'(x_0) = \dfrac{f(x_0) - 0}{x_0 - x_1}$$

∴ $$x_0 - x_1 = \dfrac{f(x_0)}{f'(x_0)}$$

∴ $$x_1 = x_0 - \dfrac{f(x_0)}{f'(x_0)}$$

As the process is iterative, for next iteration,

$$x_2 = x_1 - \dfrac{f(x_1)}{f'(x_1)}$$

Further, $\quad x_3 = x_2 - \dfrac{f(x_2)}{f'(x_2)}$

Hence, the formula may be generalised as :

$$x_i = x_{i-1} - \dfrac{f(x_{i-1})}{f'(x_{i-1})}$$

2.5.1.2 Divergence in Newton-Raphson Method

Fig. 2.6 shows convergence of the method towards the root of equation. But this may not be the case always. If the initial guess is at wrong place with respect to the curvature of f(x) the method shows divergence as illustrated in Fig. 2.7.

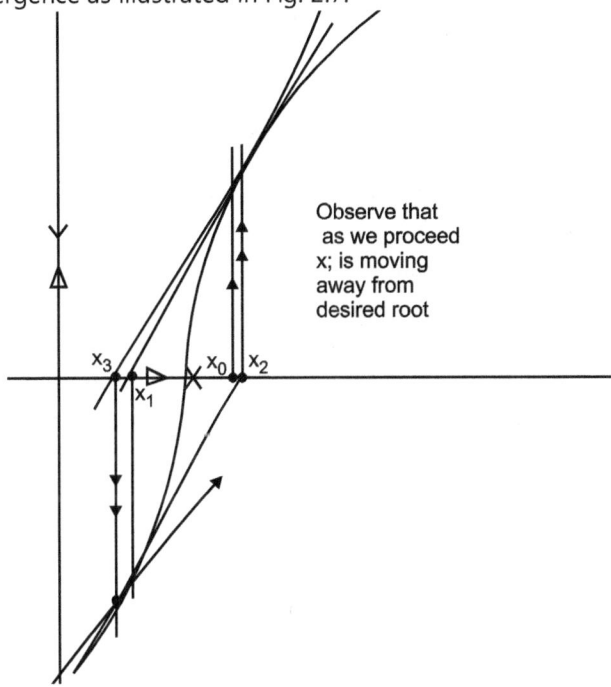

Observe that as we proceed x_i is moving away from desired root

Fig. 2.7

***Example* 2.5 :** Determine water level in mm so that the spherical tank shown in Fig. 2.1 will contain 1000 lit. water. The volume in lit. and water level in mm are related to each other as :

$$V = \dfrac{\pi h^2 (3R - h)}{3 \times 10^6}$$

where R is radius of the tank and is equal to 3000 mm.

Solution : The mathematical expression can be written as

$$f(h) = 3 \times 10^6 \, V - 3\pi h^2 R + \pi h^3$$

---

* We are repeating the same problem statement, to observe that same final answer is obtained even when the method is different.

Substituting   R = 3000 and V = 1000
$$f(h) = 3 \times 10^9 - 9000 \pi h^2 + \pi h^3$$
and $$f'(h) = 3\pi h^2 - 18000 \pi h$$

Assuming initial guess h_0 = 1000 mm
$$f(h_0) = 3 \times 10^9 - 9000 \pi \times 1000^2 + \pi \times 1000^3$$
$$= -22132741229$$

and $$f'(h_0) = 3\pi \times 1000^2 - 18000 \times \pi \times 1000$$
$$= -47123890$$

∴ $$h_1 = 1000 - \frac{22132741229}{47123890}$$
$$= 530.329 \text{ mm}$$

Now, $$f(h_1) = 3 \times 10^9 - 9000 \pi \times 530.329^2 + \pi \times 530.329^3$$
$$= -4483531672$$

and $$f'(h_1) = 3\pi \times 530.329^2 - 18000 \times \pi \times 530.329$$
$$= -27338674$$

∴ $$h_2 = 530.329 - \frac{4483531672}{27338674}$$
$$= 366.329 \text{ mm}$$

Next, $$f(h_2) = 3 \times 10^9 - 9000 \pi \times 366.329^2 + \pi \times 366.329^3$$
$$= -639888357.1$$

and $$f'(h_2) = 3\pi \times 366.329^2 - 18000 \pi \times 366.329$$
$$= -19450643$$

∴ $$h_3 = 366.329 - \frac{639888357.1}{19450643}$$
$$= 333.431$$

Further, the calculations in all iterations may be tabulated as below:

Table 2.2

Iteration No.	h_{i-1}	$f(h_{i-1})$	$f'(h_{i-1})$	h_i	Difference $h_i - h_{i-1}$
1	1000	− 22132741229	− 47123890	530.329	− 469.671
2	530.329	− 4483531672	− 27338674	366.329	− 164
3	366.329	− 639888357.1	− 19450643	333.431	− 32.8981
4	333.431	− 26976009.24	− 17807267	331.916	− 1.51489
5	331.916	− 57685.55385	− 17731101	331.913	− 0.00325

Thus, h = 331.913 mm is final solution, which fairly matches with solution of successive approximation method. The reader may try the method with changed initial guesses as $h_0 = -10000$ and $h_0 = 10000$, the method will naturally converge to other two roots which do not have physical significance.

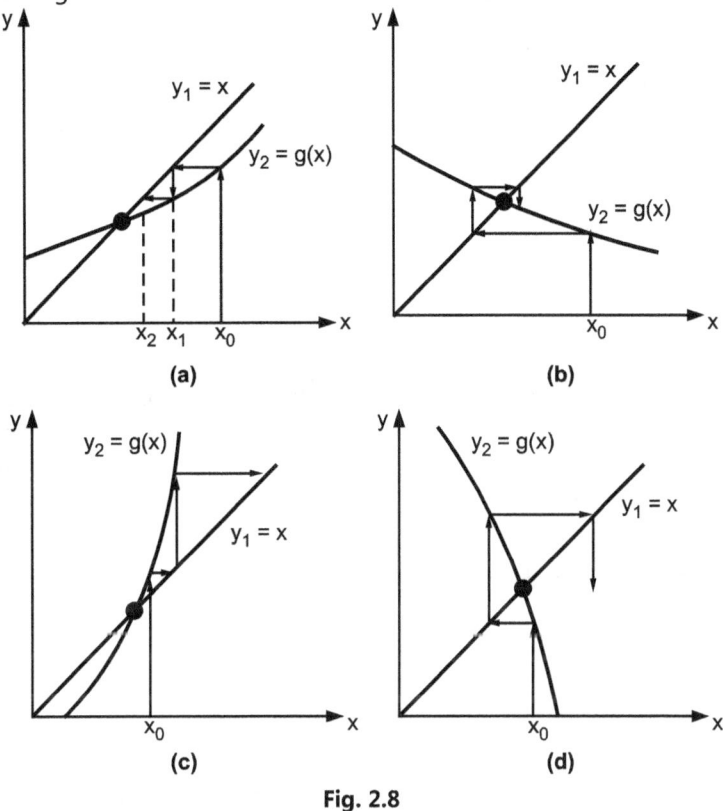

Fig. 2.8

2.5.1.3 Convergence Criteria

To understand whether the method is going to converge or not with given initial guess, we may use the following criteria.

For both the methods we have formulae as,

for successive approximation method,

$$x_i = g(x_{i-1})$$

for Newton-Raphson method,

$$x_i = x_{i-1} - \frac{f(x_{i-1})}{f'(x_{i-1})} = g(x_{i-1})$$

Now evaluate $g'(x_{i-1})$, if $|g'(x_{i-1})| < 1$ error i.e. difference between x_i and x_{i-1} reduces with each iteration.

Thus, the method will converge to the root.

If $|g'(x_{i-1})| > 1$ error increases and hence method diverges from the root.

Further if $|g'(x_{i-1})| < 1$ and $g'(x_{i-1})$ is i.e. $0 < g'(x_{i-1}) < 1$ then error will be positive and will reduce in monotonic nature as shown in Fig. 2.8 (a).

If $|g'(x_{i-1})| < 1$ and $g'(x_{i-1})$ is negative i.e. $-1 < g'(x_{i-1}) < 0$ then error will oscillate and finally reach the root as shown in Fig. 2.8 (b).

If $|g'(x_{i-1})| > 1$ and $g'(x_{i-1})$ is positive. i.e. $1 < g'(x_{i-1})$ then error will be positive and will increase in monotonic nature as shown in Image 2.8 (c).

If $|g'(x_{i-1})| > 1$ and $g'(x_{i-1})$ is negative. i.e. $g'(x_{i-1}) < -1$ then error will oscillate and will increase refer as Fig. 2.8 (d).

To summarise,

Table 2.3

Fig. 2.8	Represents the Situation	Nature of Graph	Conclusion
(a)	$0 < g'(x_{i-1}) < 1$	Monotonic	Convergent
(b)	$-1 < g'(x_{i-1}) < 0$	Oscillating	Convergent
(c)	$1 < g'(x_{i-1})$	Monotonic	Divergent
(d)	$g'(x_{i-1}) < -1$	Oscillating	Divergent

Pit falls for Newton Raphson Method

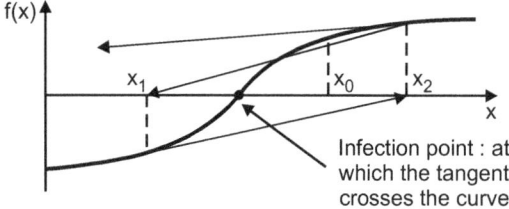

(a) An inflection point near a root causes divergence

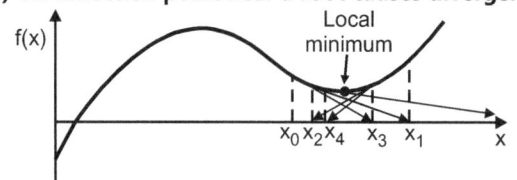

(b) A local maximum or minimum causes oscillations

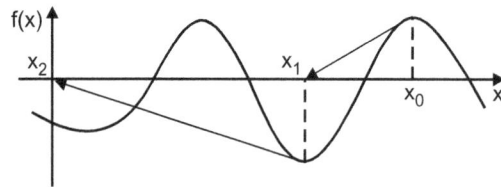

(c) Root jumping (usually due to near zero slopes)

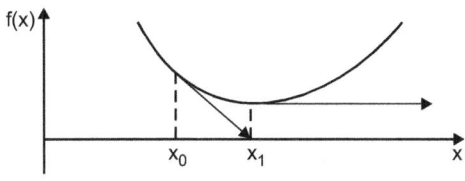

(d) Exactly zero slope

Fig. 2.9

2.5.1.4 Pseudo Code for Newton-Raphson Method

1. Define f(x) and also f'(x).
2. Get accuracy level acc from user.
3. Get initial guess x_current from user.
4. x_new = x_current
5. Do

    x_current = x_new

    x_new = x_current − f(x_current)/ f'(x_current)

    while absolute value of (x_{new} − x_current) > acc
6. Display x_new as final answer.
7. End

2.5.1.5 Flow Chart for Newton-Raphson Method

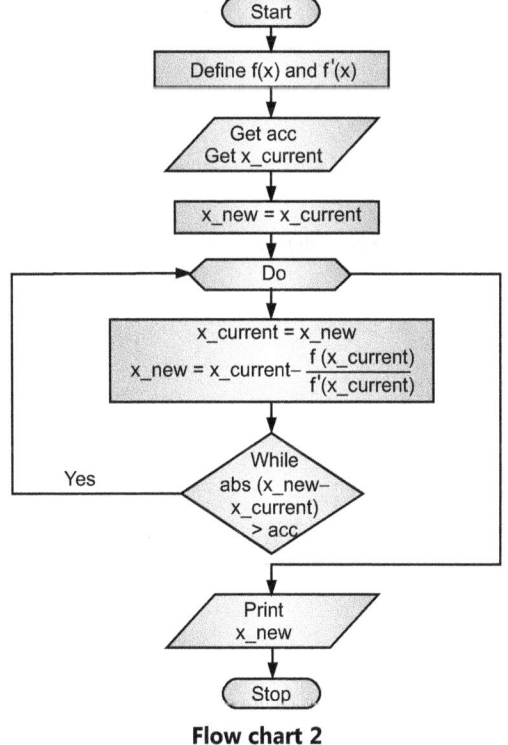

Flow chart 2

2.5.1.6 C Program for Newton-Raphson Method

```c
#include<stdio.h>
#include<conio.h>
#include<math.h>
main()
{
 float acc, x_current, x_new;
 float f(float);
 float fdash(float);
 clrscr();
 printf("****************************************************");
 printf("\n****************************************************");
 printf("\nProgram to find root of equation by Newton Raphson Method");
 printf("\n****************************************************\n\n");
 printf("Enter Accuracy Level: ");
 scanf ("%f", &acc);
 printf("Enter initial guess: ");
 scanf ("%f", &x_current);
 x_new=x_current;
 do
 {
  x_current=x_new;
  x_new = x_current - f(x_current)/fdash(x_current);
 } while(fabs(x_new-x_current)>acc);
 printf("Root of equation is %f", x_new);
 getch();
}
float f(float h)
{
 return(3*pow(10,9)-9000*3.14159*h*h+3.14159*pow(h,3));
}
float fdash(float h)
{
 return(3*3.14159*h*h-18000*3.14159*h);
}
```

2.5.1.7 MATLAB

```
fprintf('\n***************** ROOTS OF EQUATION **************');
fprintf('\n************* NEWTON-RAPHSON METHOD ************');
fstr = input('\n Input Function String f(x) >>> ','s');
f=inline(fstr);                              % Function Declaration
disp(sprintf(['\n  y = f(x) = ' fstr]));
fstr1 = input('\n Input (dy/dx) = g(x) >>> ','s');
f1=inline(fstr1);                            % Function Declaration
disp(sprintf(['\n  (dy/dx) = g(x) = ' fstr1]));
x0 = input('\n Input Initial Guess Value of Root = ');
acc = input('\n Input Accuracy = ');
x1=x0-f(x0)/f1(x0);
while abs(x1-x0)>=acc
   x0=x1;
   x1=x0-f(x0)/f1(x0);
   fprintf('\n Root = %f',x1);
end
```

2.5.1.8 Solution of Newton-Raphson Method using MS-Excel

To get solution in tabular form in MS-Excel follow the steps given below :

1. Type initial guess (say 1000) in cell A1.
2. Type formula for f(x) in cell B1 as
   = 3*10 ^ 9 – 9000*pi()*A1*A1 + pi()*A1^3
3. Type formula for f'(x) in cell C1 as
   = 3*pi()*A1*A1 – 18000*pi()*A1

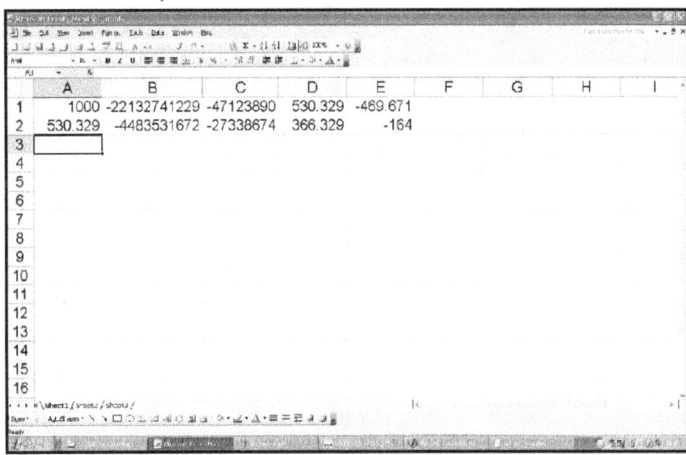

Image 2.1

4. Type formula for determining new guess value in cell D1 as
   = A1 – B1/C1
5. Type formula for difference in calculated value and current guess in cell E1 as
   = abs(D1 – A1)
   The Excel worksheet will look as shown in Image 2.1.
6. For considering calculated value as new guess for next iteration, type formula in A2 as
   = D1
7. Copy cell B1 in B2, C1 in C2, D1 in D2 and E1 in E2.
8. Thus, second iteration is completed in the excel worksheet. The sheet will look as shown in Image 2.2.

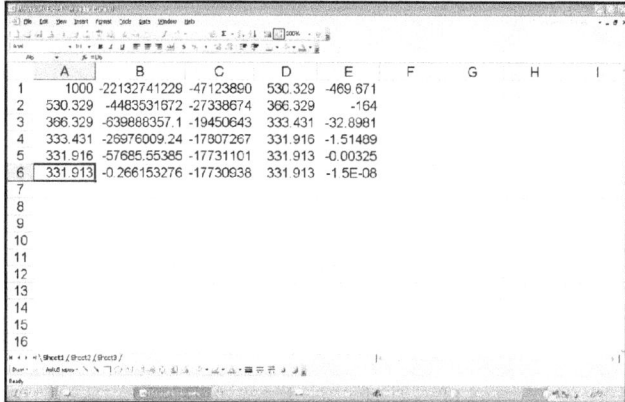

Image 2.2

9. Copy cells from A2 to E2 for generating multiple rows indicating calculations for multiple iterations. The worksheet will now look as shown in Image 2.3. The latest value of h from column 0 is the final answer. Hence, final answer is 331.913 mm.

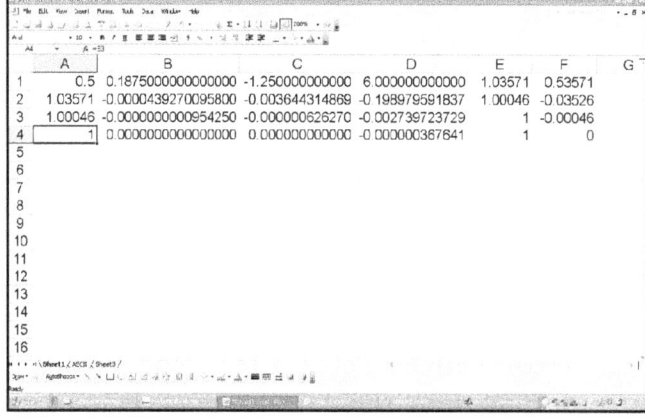

Image 2.3

Note : Column A represents current guess, column B represents f(h), column C represents f'(h), column D represents calculated value of new guess and column E represents the accuracy level of the current answer.

2.5.2 Successive Approximation Method

This is an open method which employs a formula from the given mathematical expression itself. As mentioned earlier it has risk of divergence. We will understand these concept of convergence and divergence through this text.

The method tell us to rearrange the terms of mathematical expressions in such a way that, given mathematical expression will become

$$f(x) = 0$$
$$x = g(x)$$

Thus, the step-by-step approach is

Step 1 : Rearrange terms of f(x) = 0 in such a way to get x = g(x).
Step 2 : Guess some value for x.
Step 3 : Evaluate g(x).
Step 4 : As x = g(x), the value obtained is next guess for x.
Step 5 : Again evaluate g(x).
Step 6 : Thus repeat steps 3 and 4 till difference in two successive guesses is very negligible.

2.5.2.1 Convergence and Divergence

Note, if the difference in two successive guesses is increasing, it is called divergence and we will never reach the solution. If the said difference is reducing it is called convergence and after certain number of iterations we will reach the solution.

To stop the iterations and to declare the current guess as final answer, user may define the accuracy level or tolerance error. For example, if tolerance error ϵ = 0.01 and difference between two successive guesses is greater than ϵ, the iterations are to be continued, if that difference is less than or equal to ϵ, the iterations are stopped and latest value of x is declared as final answer, i.e. root of equation.

To understand this procedure, let us solve the previous problem of water level.

Example 2.6 : Determine water level in mm so that the spherical tank refer in Fig. 2.1 will contain 1000 lit. water. The volume in lit. and water level in mm are related to each other as :

$$V = \frac{\pi h^2 (3R - h)}{3 \times 10^6}$$

where R is radius of the tank and is equal to 3000 mm.

Solution : According to successive approximation method,

$$f(h) = 3 \times 10^6 V - \pi h^2 (3R - h)$$

which is to be rearranged to get,

$$h = g(h)$$

∴ The original expression is rewritten as,
$$3 \times 10^6 \, V = \pi h^2 (3R - h)$$
∴ $$3 \times 10^6 \, V = 3\pi h^2 R - \pi h^3$$

Hence, we may rearrange and get two expressions as,

$$h = \sqrt[3]{\frac{3\pi h^2 R - 3 \times 10^6 \, V}{\pi}} \qquad \ldots (1)$$

or $$h = \sqrt{\frac{3 \times 10^6 V + \pi h^3}{3\pi R}} \qquad \ldots (2)$$

Let us use equation (1) to evaluate h.
Let the first guess to be equal to 0 mm.

∴ $$h_1 = \sqrt[3]{\frac{3\pi \times 0 \times 3000 - 3 \times 10^6 \times 1000}{\pi}}$$

$$= \sqrt[3]{\frac{-3 \times 10^6 \times 1000}{\pi}}$$

$$= -984.745 \text{ mm}$$

Difference in h_1 and h_0 is $h_1 - h_0 = -984.745$

∴ $$h_2 = \sqrt[3]{\frac{3\pi \times (-984.745)^2 \times 3000 - 3 \times 10^6 \times 1000}{\pi}}$$

$$= \sqrt[3]{\frac{24418263818}{\pi}}$$

$$= 1980.865 \text{ mm}$$

Difference in h_2 and h_1 is
$$h_2 - h_1 = 1980.865 - (-984.745)$$
$$= 2965.61$$

Further, $$h_3 = \sqrt[3]{\frac{3\pi \times 1980.865^2 \times 3000 - 3 \times 10^6 \times 1000}{\pi}}$$

$$= \sqrt[3]{\frac{107944130688}{\pi}}$$

$$= 3250.991 \text{ mm}$$

Now, difference in h_3 and h_2 is
$$h_3 - h_2 = 3250.991 - 1980.865$$
$$= 1270.125$$

Next, $$h_4 = \sqrt[3]{\frac{3\pi \times 3250.991^2 \times 3000 - 3 \times 10^6 \times 1000}{\pi}}$$

$$= \sqrt[3]{\frac{295831463076}{\pi}} = 4549.503 \text{ mm}$$

∴ $h_4 - h_3 = 4549.503 - 3250.991$
$= 1298.513$

The difference in successive guesses is not taking certain direction i.e. it is sometimes reducing and sometimes increasing. Hence, we need to perform more number of iterations. A few such iterations including earlier are tabulated below :

Table 2.4

Iteration No. i	Guess Value h_{i-1}	Calculated Value h_i	Difference $h_i - h_{i-1}$
1	0	– 984.745	– 984.745
2	– 984.745	1980.865	2965.61
3	1980.865	3250.991	1270.125
4	3250.991	4549.503	1298.513
5	4549.503	5701.373	1151.87
6	5701.373	6631.226	929.853
7	6631.226	7336.017	704.7909
8	7336.017	7848.175	512.1583
9	7848.175	8210.011	361.8351
10	8210.011	8460.875	250.864
11	8460.875	8632.626	171.7519
12	8632.626	8749.231	116.6044
13	8749.231	8827.952	78.72106
14	8827.952	8880.899	52.94676
15	8880.899	8916.421	35.52231
16	8916.421	8940.231	23.79237
17	8940.213	8956.131	15.91804
18	8956.131	8966.773	10.64188
19	8966.773	8973.884	7.111011
20	8973.884	8978.634	4.750072

From Table 2.4 it is observed that the method is converging. So we may continue iterating the procedure and at $h_{30} = 8988.012$ we observe the difference $(h_{29} - h_{30}) = 0.083573$ i.e. error has reduced below 0.1 mm. Hence, we may say that this solution is within accuracy limit of 0.1 mm.

Practical Considerations

Thus, mathematically at water level of 8988.012 mm volume of water in the spherical tank will be 1000 lit. approximately. Let us verify the answer by substitution in original expression.

∴ $$V = \frac{\pi \times 8988.012^2 \,(3 \times 3000 - 8988.012)}{3 \times 10^6} = 1014.151 \text{ lit.}$$

But, here we observe that height of spherical tank is 2R i.e. 6000 mm. That means the tank can have maximum water level of 6000 mm. Thus, the solution, is mathematically correct but has no physical significance. Hence, we reject this solution.

Now, let us use equation (2) to evaluate h. As done earlier let the first guess h_0 be 0 mm.

$$\therefore \quad h_1 = \sqrt{\frac{3 \times 10^6 \times 1000 + \pi \times 0}{3\pi \times 3000}}$$

$$= \sqrt{\frac{3 \times 10^6 \times 1000}{3 \times \pi \times 3000}}$$

$$= 325.735 \text{ mm}$$

$\therefore$ Difference between h_1 and h_0 is

$$h_1 - h_0 = 325.735$$

Iterating the procedure,

$$h_2 = \sqrt{\frac{3 \times 10^6 \times 1000 + \pi \times 325.735^3}{3\pi \times 3000}}$$

$$= \sqrt{\frac{3108578336}{3\pi \times 3000}}$$

$$= 331.5772 \text{ mm}$$

The difference, $h_2 - h_1 = 331.5772 - 325.735$

$$= 5.842236$$

Next iteration gives,

$$h_3 = \sqrt{\frac{3 \times 10^6 \times 1000 + \pi \times 331.5772^3}{3\pi \times 3000}}$$

$$= \sqrt{\frac{3114525982}{3\pi \times 3000}} = 331.8943 \text{ mm}$$

and $\quad h_3 - h_2 = 331.8943 - 331.5772$

$$= 0.317052$$

Let us tabulate the iterations as earlier.

Table 2.5

No. of Iterations 1	Guess Value h_{i-1}	Calculated Value h_i	Difference $h_i - h_{i-1}$
1	0	325.735	325.735
2	325.735	331.5772	5.842236
3	331.5772	331.8943	0.317052
4	331.8943	331.9118	0.017521

Thus, difference is reduced below 0.1 mm which is sufficient accuracy level. Hence, we can conclude that the answer is that, for water volume of 1000 lit. the water level expected is

331.9118 mm.

Let us verify by substitution in original expression.

$$\therefore \quad V = \frac{\pi \times 331.9118^2 \, (3 \times 3000 - 331.9118)}{3 \times 10^6} = 999.9938 \text{ lit.}$$

Hence, the answer can be accepted. Further, this answer is physically possible. So, this is the only desired solution.

Observations

In previous method why did we get two different solutions ? To understand this let us plot the graph of function :

$$f(h) = 3 \times 10^6 \, V - \pi h^2 \, (3R - h)$$

mentioned at start of the solution, with respect to water level, as shown in Fig. 2.10.

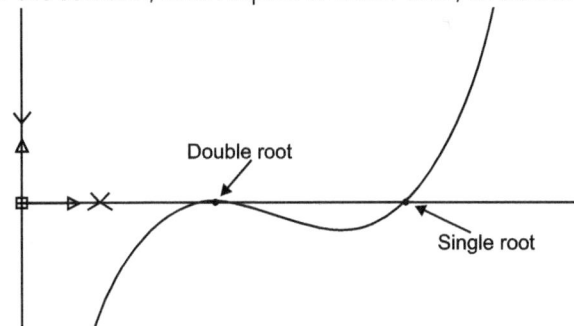

Fig. 2.10

where the curve is plotted for the range of h varying from – 500 mm to 10,000 mm. As the part of graph near the origin is not clear, Fig. 2.11 shows magnified curve near origin.

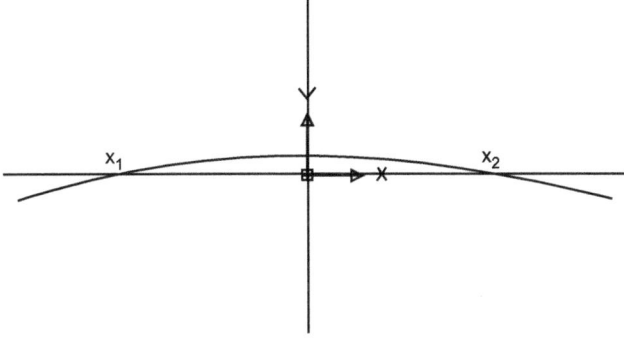

Fig. 2.11

In these figures we observe the graph intersects the X-axis at three locations marked x_1, x_2, x_3. These points are values of h where $f(h) = 0$. Thus, x_1, x_2, x_3 are roots of equation. The degree of polynomial equation is 3, hence the equation has three roots. One of these roots is negative. Physically, negative water level has no meaning, so that root is to be rejected. Further, we have already discussed regarding physical significance of rest of the two positive roots.

2.5.2.2 Algorithm* for Successive Approximation Method

1. Get x = g(x) from user. That means define g(x).
2. Get accuracy level (tolerance error) from user.
3. Get x_current from user. This is initial guess.
4. x_new = x_current. This step is must for manipulations inside the loop structure.
5. Do
   x_current = x_new
   x_new = g(x-current)
   While absolute value of difference between x_new and x_current is greater than accuracy level.
6. Display x_new as the final answer.
7. End.

2.5.2.3 Flow Chart for Successive Approximation Method

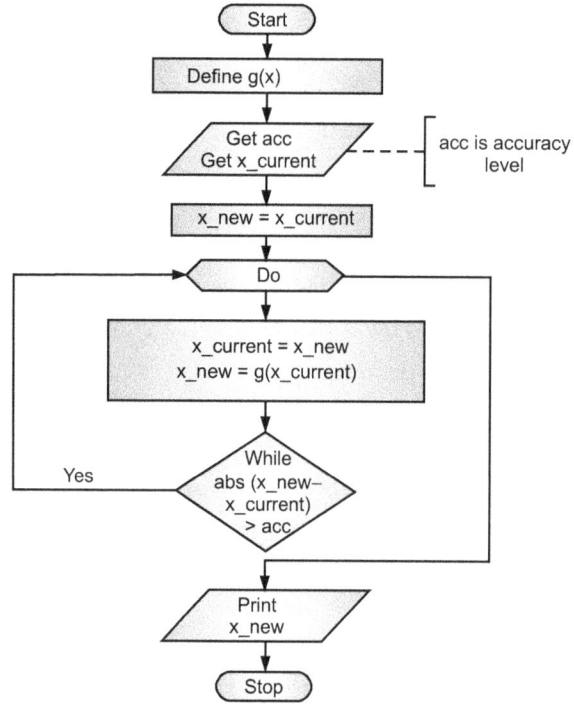

Flow chart 3

2.5.2.4 C Program for Successive Approximation Method

It is important to note that, we have indicated that x = g(x) is to be accepted from user. But, actually it will be written in the program itself as illustrated below :

---

* We can assume that Algorithm and Pseudo code are synonyms of each other.

```c
#include<stdio.h>
#include<conio.h>
#include<math.h>
main()

{
 float acc, x_current, x_new;
 float g(float);
 clrscr();
 printf("****************************************************");
 printf("\n****************************************************");
 printf("\nProgram to find root of equation by Successive Approximation Method");
 printf("\n****************************************************\n\n");
 printf("Enter Accuracy Level: ");
 scanf ("%f", &acc);
 printf("Enter initial guess: ");
 scanf ("%f", &x_current);
 x_new=x_current;
 do

 {
  x_current=x_new;
  x_new = g(x_current);
 } while(fabs(x_new-x_current)>acc);
 printf("Root of equation is %f", x_new);
 getch();

}
float g(float h)
{
 return(sqrt((3*pow(10,9)+3.14159*pow(h,3))/(9000*3.14159)));
}
```

2.5.2.5 Solution of Successive Approximation method using MS-Excel

There is no direct solution available for solving such polynomials in MS-Excel. But user can store required formulae in different cells of worksheet and copy-paste the cells to get the solution.

The solution of the same problem with

$$h = \sqrt{\frac{3 \times 10^6 \, V + \pi h^3}{3\pi R}}$$

$$= \sqrt{\frac{3 \times 10^9 + \pi h^3}{9000\, \pi}}$$

is illustrated below :

1. Type initial guess i.e. 0 in cell A1.
2. Type formula as below in cell B1,
   = sqrt((3 * 10 ^ 9 + pi() * A1^3)/(9000 * pi()))
3. For difference between calculated value and guess type formula as below in cell C1.
   = abs (B1 – A1)
4. To make currently calculated value as next iteration's guess write the following formula in cell A2;
   = B1

Here the worksheet will look as shown in Image 2.4. Note that column A represents $h_i - 1$, column B represents h_i and column C represents $h_i - h_i - 1$.

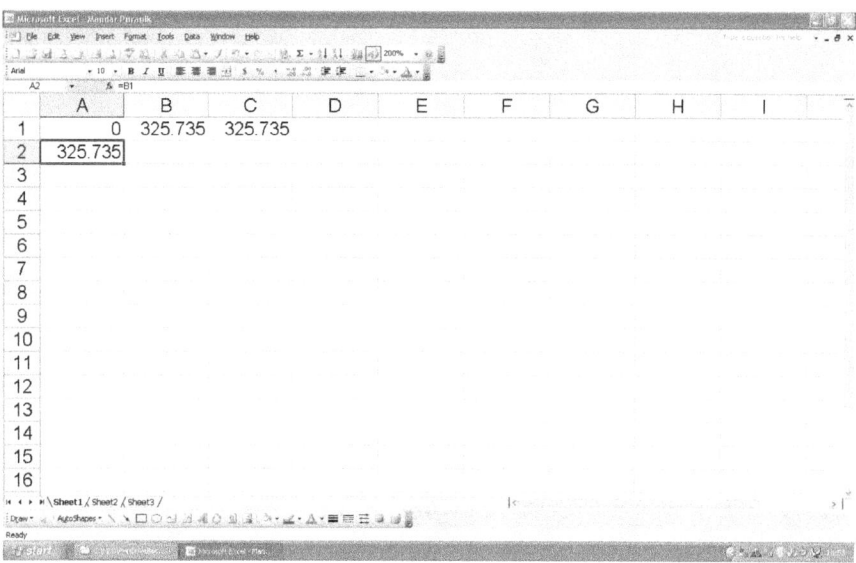

Image 2.4

5. Now copy cell A2 in multiple cells say from A3 to A10.
6. Copy cells B1 and C1 respectively from B2 to B10 and C2 to C10.

The worksheet will now look as shown in Image 2.5. The answer is obvious. It is 331.913 mm.

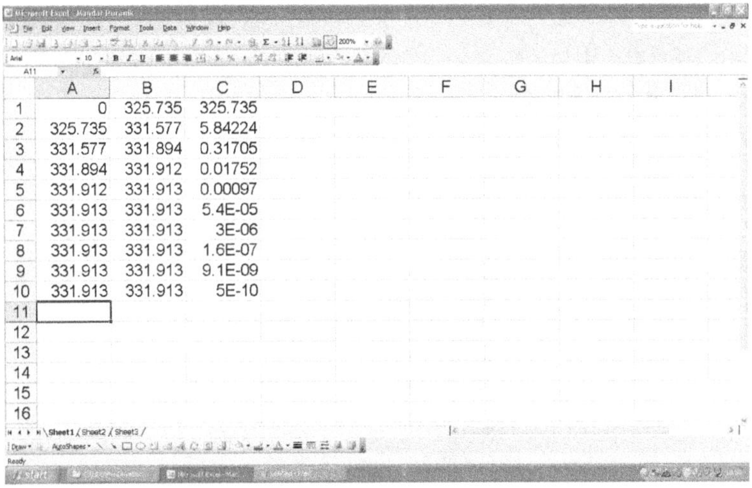

	A	B	C
1	0	325.735	325.735
2	325.735	331.577	5.84224
3	331.577	331.894	0.31705
4	331.894	331.912	0.01752
5	331.912	331.913	0.00097
6	331.913	331.913	5.4E-05
7	331.913	331.913	3E-06
8	331.913	331.913	1.6E-07
9	331.913	331.913	9.1E-09
10	331.913	331.913	5E-10

Image 2.5

2.6 COMPARISON OF SUCCESSIVE APPROXIMATION AND NEWTON-RAPHSON METHODS

Referring Table 2.8 and Table 2.9 the two distinct numbers very close to each other are obtained as root of the same equation. To understand which of them is more accurate, let us substitute the values in the equation.

Therefore, for checking accuracy of answer given by successive approximation method,

$$f(0.5788) = \ln 0.5788 + \sin 0.5788 = 0.00022150305$$

For checking accuracy of answer given by Newton-Raphson method,

$$f(0.57871) = 0.000009346152$$

Hence, it is clear that Newton-Raphson method's answer is more accurate. Furthermore, this answer is obtained with less number of iterations. In case of successive approximation method, it is observed that the difference in successive guesses is constantly reducing. Not only that, except first 2 iterations the difference is proportionately reducing. That means,

$$\frac{x_3 - x_2}{x_4 - x_3} \doteq \frac{x_4 - x_3}{x_5 - x_4} \doteq \frac{x_5 - x_4}{x_6 - x_7} \doteq \ldots\ldots$$

Hence, here this method is showing linearly convergent behaviour.

2.7 CASE OF NON-CONVERGENCE (OR DIVERGENCE)

Example 2.7 : *Determine root of*

$f(x) = x(1 - x \sin x) - 0.05$

1. *with initial guess $x_0 = 1$*
2. *with initial guess $x_0 = 1.1$*

using successive approximation method with expected accuracy level of 0.001.

Solution : We want to find root mean and we wish to determine value of x so that,

$$f(x) = 0$$
$$\therefore \quad x(1 - x \sin x) - 0.05 = 0$$
$$\therefore \quad x - x^2 \sin x - 0.05 = 0$$
$$\therefore \quad x = x^2 \sin x + 0.05$$

Thus, $\quad x = g(x) = x^2 \sin x + 0.05$

with initial guess
$$x_0 = 1$$
$$x_1 = 1^2 \sin 1 + 0.05$$
$$= 0.89147$$

$\therefore \quad x_2 = 0.89147^2 \sin 0.89147 + 0.05$
$$= 0.66829$$

$\therefore \quad x_3 = 0.66829^2 \sin 0.66829 + 0.05$
$$= 0.32674$$

$\therefore \quad x_4 = 0.32674^2 \sin 0.32674 + 0.05$
$$= 0.08427$$

$\therefore \quad x_5 = 0.08427^2 \sin 0.08427 + 0.05$
$$= 0.05060$$

$\therefore \quad x_6 = 0.05060^2 \sin 0.05060 + 0.05$
$$= 0.05013$$

The iterative calculations may be tabulated as :

Table 2.6

Iteration No. i	Guess x_{i-1}	g(x) x_i	Difference $|x_i - x_{i-1}|$
1	1	0.89147	0.10853
2	0.89147	0.66829	0.22318
3	0.66829	0.32674	0.34155
4	0.32674	0.08427	0.24247
5	0.08427	0.05060	0.03367
6	0.05060	0.05013	0.00047

Now with initial guess of $x_0 = 1.1$
$$x_1 = 1.1^2 \sin 1.1 + 0.05$$
$$= 1.12836$$

$\therefore \quad x_2 = 1.12836^2 \sin 1.12836 + 0.05$
$$= 1.200604$$

$\therefore \quad x_3 = 1.200604^2 \sin 1.200604 + 0.05$
$$= 1.3938$$

$\therefore \quad x_4 = 1.3938^2 \sin 1.3938 + 0.05$
$$= 1.96234$$

Let us tabulate all the calculations:

Table 2.7

Iteration No. i	Guess x_{i-1}	g(x) x_i	Difference $|x_i - x_{i-1}|$
1	1.1	1.12836	0.02836
2	1.12836	1.200604	0.072244
3	1.200604	1.3938	0.193196
4	1.3938	1.96234	0.56854
5	1.96234	3.60935	1.64701
6	3.60935	− 5.8239	9.43325
7	− 5.8239	15.086	20.9099
8	15.086	132.648	117.562
9	132.648	11356.107	11223.459

It is observed that the difference in successive guess is not reducing, but increasing rapidly. Thus, this is a case of non-convergence (or a case of divergence).

2.7.1 Horner's Method

This is known to be good method for finding the approximate solution either rational or irrational of numerical equation. Under Horner's method the solution of the equation is got by successive diminishing the digits occurring in root.

Suppose the root of the equation lies between a and $a + 1$, the value of the root may be something like a, bcd where b,c,d ... ... are the digits after decimal. So objective is to find the values of these digits. We proceed by following steps :

Step 1 : Diminishing the value of the root of the given equation by a, so that the root of the new equation is 0, bcd ...

Step 2 : Multiply the root of the transformed equation by 10 so that root of the equation is b. cd ...

Step 3 : Now diminish the root by b and multiply the roots of the resulting equation by 10 so root is c.d ...

Step 4 : Proceeding with similar fashion, now diminish the root by c and so on. Finally the root may be evaluated to any desired degree of accuracy and that digit by digit.

Example :

Consider the equation $x^3 + x^2 + x - 50 = 0$ whose roots are to be computed correct to three decimal places.

As per the Descarte's rule of sign number of sign changes in the equation is one and hence there is one positive root. Also f(4) is positive andm f(3) is negative, therefore root lies between 3 and 4.

Step 1 :

Now as per the first step, diminish the root of the given equation by 3 i.e. divide the $x^2 + 2x + x - 50 = 0$ successively by $x - 3$. (Equation whose roots are diminished by h of the roots of the given equation)

```
        1       1       1       -50     (3
                3       12      39
                4       13      -11
                3       21
                7       34
                3
        1       10
```

Thus, transferred equation is $x^2 + 10x^2 + 34x - 11 = 0$.

Step 2 :

The roots of this equation lie between 0 and 1. Now multiply the roots of this equation by 10, which mean second terms by 10, third term by 100 and 4th by 1000. Thus we get the new equation as $x^3 + 100x^2 + 3400x - 11000 = 0$. Its roots lie between 2 and 3.

Step 3 :

Now diminish its root by 2,

```
        1       100     3400    -11000  (2
                2       204     7208
                102     3604    -3792
                2       208
                104     3812
                2
        1       106
```

Thus, transferred equation is $x^3 + 106x^2 + 3812x - 3792 = 0$.

Step 4 :

The roots of this equation lie between 0 and 1. Now multiply the roots of this equation by 10, we get the new equation as $x^3 + 1060x^2 + 381200x - 3792000 = 0$. Its roots lie between 9 and 10.

Step 5 :

Now diminish its root by 9,

	1	1060	381200	–	(9
				3792000	
		9	9621		
				3517389	
		1069	390821	**–274611**	
		9	9702		
		1078	**400523**		
		9			
	1	**1087**			

Thus, transferred equation is $x^3 + 1087x^2 + 400523x - 274611 = 0$.

Step 6 :

The roots of this equation lie between 0 and 1. Now multiply the roots of this equation by 10, we get the new equation as $x^3 + 10870 x^2 + 40052300x - 27461000 = 0$. Its roots lie between 6 and 7.

As we required the root up to three decimal places only, our destination have reached, hence no need to proceed further. Our root up to three decimal places is 3.296

2.8 MULTIPLE ROOTS

We already know that root of equation is value of x where f(x) is zero. Referring Fig. 2.10 we may say that, graphically root is a point where the curve of f(x) intersects the X-axis.

Now let us build a function by multiplying factors as below :

$$f(x) = (x - 2)(x - 1)(x - 1)$$

It is clear that f(x) = 0 at x = 1 or x = 2.

Hence x = 1 and x = 2 are roots of equation.

After multiplication,

$$f(x) = (x - 2)(x^2 - 2x + 1)$$
$$= x^3 - 2x^2 + x - 2x^2 + 4x - 2$$
$$= x^3 - 4x^2 + 5x - 2$$

The equation is cubic polynomial, hence there are three roots. So we understand x = 1 is a double root. Thus, it is a case of multiple roots. Graphically, existence of double root will be as shown in Fig. 2.12.

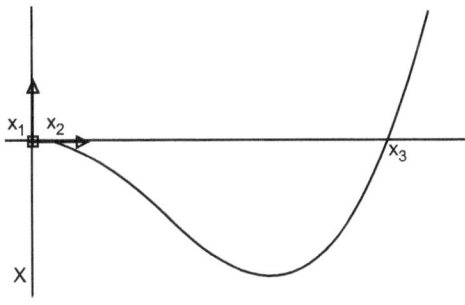

Fig. 2.12

Now let us build another fraction as :

$$f(x) = (x-2)(x-1)(x-1)(x-1)$$
$$= (x^3 - 4x^2 + 5x - 2)(x-1)$$
$$= x^4 - 4x^3 + 5x^2 - 2x - x^3 + 4x^2 - 5x + 2$$
$$= x^4 - 5x^3 + 9x^2 - 7x + 2$$

The equation will have single root at x = 2 and triple root at x = 1. Thus, at x = 1 we will have multiple roots. Graphically, these will be seen as shown in Fig. 2.13.

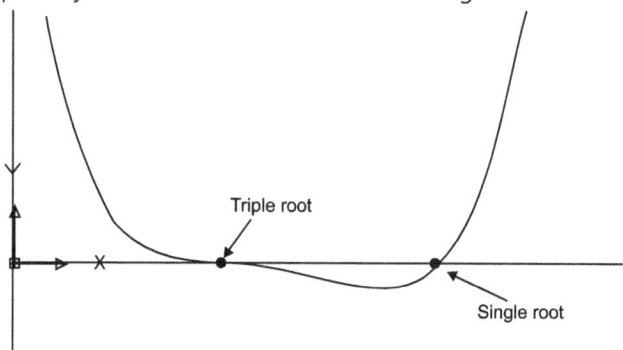

Fig. 2.13

Further readers may generate polynomial functions as :

$$f(x) = (x-2)(x-1)(x-1)(x-1)(x-1)$$
and
$$f(x) = (x-2)(x-1)(x-1)(x-1)(x-1)(x-1)$$

and so on, and plot the roots graphically.

The coinciding four roots and five roots will be seen as shown in Fig. 2.14 and Fig. 2.14 (b).

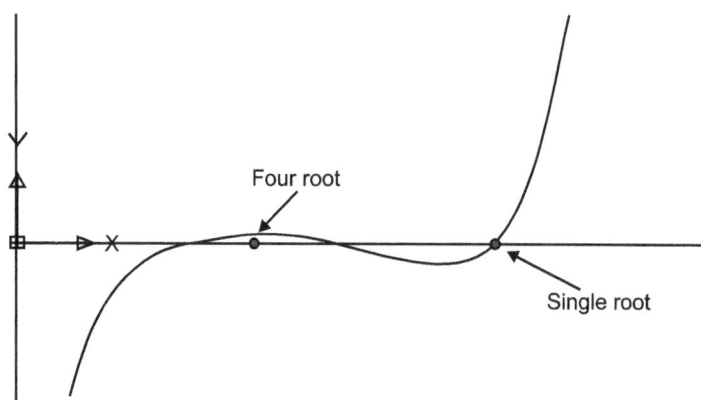

Fig. 2.14 (a)

Conclusion of this discussion is that, if curve of f(x) is tangential to X-axis and not crossing it, then there will be either 2 or 4 or 6 ... even number of multiple roots coinciding at the point of contact.

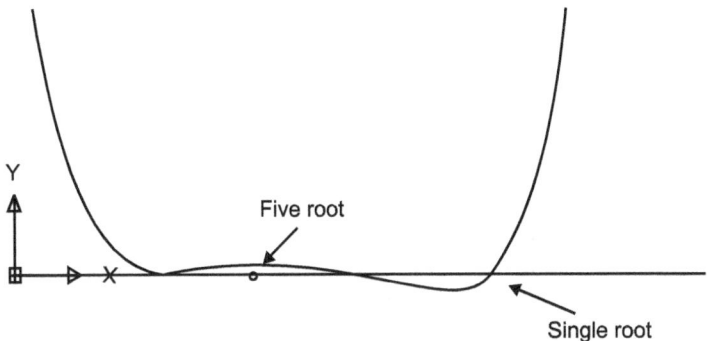

Fig. 2.14 (b)

And if the curve of f(x) is tangential to X-axis but crossing it then there will be either 3 or 5 or 7 ... odd number of multiple roots coinciding at the point of contact.

2.9 APPLICATION OF THE METHODS TO TRANSCENDENTAL EQUATIONS

The methods remain same, although the equation is changed from polynomial to transcendental. To understand application of the methods to transcendental equation, let us solve a numerical problem.

Example 2.8* : *Determine root of the following equation :*

$f(x) = \ln x + \sin x$

Assume initial guess as 1.5 and permissible error 0.0005.

Solution : (a) Using Successive Approximation Method :

The root is value of x when f(x) = 0.

∴ We need to solve the equation

$$\ln x + \sin x = 0$$

∴ $\ln x = -\sin x$

∴ $x = e^{-\sin x}$

Thus, $x = g(x)$

where $g(x) = e^{-\sin x}$

Now, $x_0 = 1.5$

∴ $x_1 = g(x_0)^*$
$= e^{-\sin 1.5}$
$= 0.3688$

∴ $x_2 = g(x_1)$
$= e^{-\sin 0.3688}$
$= 0.6973$

∴ $x_3 = g(x_2)$
$= e^{-\sin 0.6973}$
$= 0.5261$

---

* While calculating sin x, remember x is in radians. Hence while solving on calculator set calculator's angle mode to radian. Do not keep it in degree.

$$\therefore \quad x_4 = g(x_3) = e^{-\sin 0.5261} = 0.6052$$

$$\therefore \quad x_5 = g(x_4) = e^{-\sin 0.6052} = 0.5661$$

$$\therefore \quad x_6 = g(x_5) = e^{-\sin 0.5661} = 0.5849$$

$$\therefore \quad x_7 = g(x_6) = e^{-\sin 0.5849} = 0.5757$$

$$\therefore \quad x_8 = g(x_7) = e^{-\sin 0.5757} = 0.5802$$

$$\therefore \quad x_9 = g(x_8) = e^{-\sin 0.5802} = 0.5780$$

$$\therefore \quad x_{10} = g(x_9) = e^{-\sin 0.5780} = 0.5791$$

$$\therefore \quad x_{11} = g(x_{10}) = e^{-\sin 0.5791} = 0.5785$$

$$\therefore \quad x_{12} = g(x_{11}) = e^{-\sin 0.5785} = 0.5788$$

Tabulating all the results as shown in Table 2.8.

Table 2.8

Iteration No. i	Guess x_{i-1}	g(x) i.e. x_i	Difference $|x_i - x_{i-1}|$
1	1.5	0.3638	1.1312
2	0.3688	0.6973	0.3285
3	0.6973	0.5261	0.1712
4	0.5261	0.6052	0.0791
5	0.6052	0.5661	0.0391
6	0.5661	0.5849	0.0188
7	0.5849	0.5757	0.0092
8	0.5757	0.5802	0.0045
9	0.5802	0.5780	0.0022
10	0.5780	0.5791	0.0011
11	0.5791	0.5785	0.0006
12	0.5785	0.5788	0.0003

Hence root of the equation is 0.5788.

(b) Using Newton-Raphson method :

$$f(x) = \ln x + \sin x$$

Hence
$$f'(x) = \frac{1}{x} + \cos x$$

Assuming $x_0 = 1.5$, as given

$$x_1 = x_0 - \frac{f(x_0)}{f'(x_0)} = 1.5 - \frac{(\ln 1.5 + \sin 1.5)}{\frac{1}{1.5} + \cos 1.5}$$

$$= -0.4026$$

Here x_1 is negative, hence x_2 cannot be determined as natural logarithm of negative number does not exist. Hence we are forced to change the initial guess. It is observed that if initial guess is greater than 1.35 the same problem will arise. Hence assuming $x_0 = 1.35$,

$$x_1 = 1.35 - \frac{(\ln 1.35 + \sin 1.35)}{\frac{1}{1.35} + \cos 1.35}$$

$$= 0.02066$$

∴ $$x_2 = 0.02066 - \frac{(\ln 0.02066 + \sin 0.02066)}{\frac{1}{0.02066} + \cos 0.02066}$$

$$= 0.09878$$

∴ $$x_3 = 0.09878 - \frac{(\ln 0.09878 + \sin 0.09878)}{\frac{1}{0.09878} + \cos 0.09878}$$

$$= 0.29811$$

$$x_4 = 0.29811 - \frac{(\ln 0.29811 + \sin 0.29811)}{\frac{1}{0.29811} + \cos 0.29811}$$

$$= 0.51076$$

∴ $$x_5 = 0.51076 - \frac{(\ln 0.51076 + \sin 0.51076)}{\frac{1}{0.51076} + \cos 0.51076}$$

$$= 0.57542$$

∴ $$x_6 = 0.57542 - \frac{(\ln 0.57542 + \sin 0.57542)}{\frac{1}{0.57542} + \cos 0.57542}$$

$$= 0.57871$$

∴ $$x_7 = 0.57871 - \frac{(\ln 0.57871 + \sin 0.57871)}{\frac{1}{0.57871} + \cos 0.57871}$$

$$= 0.57871$$

Thus, the results may be tabulated as :

Table 2.9

Iteration No. i	Guess x_{i-1}	Calculated next guess x_i	Difference $|x_i - x_{i-1}|$
1	1.35	0.02066	1.32934
2	0.02066	0.09878	0.07812
3	0.09878	0.29811	0.19933
4	0.29811	0.51076	0.21265
5	0.51076	0.57542	0.06466
6	0.57542	0.57871	0.00329
7	0.57871	0.57871	0.00000

Hence root of equation is 0.57871.

SOLVED EXAMPLES

Example 2.9 : *Get root of following polynomial equation*

$$f(x) = x^3 + 13.2 x^2 + 12.5x - 208$$

with initial guess $x_0 = 2$ and accuracy level of 0.001 using Newton-Raphson method, in MatLab software.

Solution : For Newton-Raphson method we will require $f'(x)$. So we will first store the given polynomial in variable form. Then store its differential in other variable, then will iterate the process of determining new guess as below.

```
>> a = [1   13.2   12.5   -208];
>> b = polyder (a);
>> x = 2;
>> x = x_polyval (a, x) / polyval (b, x)
   x = 3.5809
>> x = x_polyval (a, x) / polyval (b, x)
   x = 3.2239
>> x = x_polyval (a,x) / polyval (b, x)
   x = 3.2006
>> x = x_polyval (a, x) / polyval (b, x)
>> x = 3.2005
```

Thus, we iterated the same expression till we reach the answer with expected accuracy.

Example 2.10 : *Determine the real root of the equation $e^x = 5x$ using successive approximation method. Assume initial guess $x = 0.15$ and solve upto 5 iterations.*

Solution : The given equation

$$e^x = 5x$$

can be rewritten as :

$$x = \frac{1}{5}e^x = g(x)$$

First iteration :

$$x_1 = g(x_0) = \frac{1}{5}e^{x_0} = \frac{1}{5} \times e^{0.15} = 0.2324$$

Second iteration :

$$x_2 = g(x_1) = \frac{1}{5}e^{x_1} = \frac{1}{5} \times e^{0.2324} = 0.2523$$

Third iteration :

$$x_3 = g(x_2) = \frac{1}{5}e^{x_2} = \frac{1}{5} \times e^{0.2523} = 0.2574$$

Fourth iteration :

$$x_4 = g(x_3) = \frac{1}{5}e^{x_3} = \frac{1}{5} \times e^{0.2574} = 0.2587$$

Fifth iteration :

$$x_5 = g(x_4) = \frac{1}{5}e^{x_4} = \frac{1}{5} \times e^{0.2587} = 0.2590$$

Example 2.11 : *Solve the polynomial equation.*

$x - 0.3 \cos x - 1 = 0$

by iterative method to get answer with 4 digits accuracy. Take initial guess of the root as 0.5.

Solution : The given equation can be rewritten as

$$x = \cos^{-1}\left(\frac{x-1}{0.3}\right)$$

But, with initial guess of $x = 0.5$, the equation becomes

$$x = \cos^{-1}\left(\frac{-0.5}{0.3}\right) = \cos^{-1}(-1.6667)$$

This is mathematical error, as there cannot exist any angle having cosine ratio greater than 1 in magnitude. Therefore, rewriting equation as

$$x = 1 + 0.3 \cos x$$

we get $\quad x = g(x)$

where $\quad g(x) = 1 + 0.3 \cos x$

Using the iterative method, the successive approximations are as below :

$x_1 = g(x_0) = 1 + 0.3 \cos (0.5) = 1.2633$

$x_2 = g(x_1) = 1 + 0.3 \cos (1.2633) = 1.0908$

$x_3 = g(x_2) = 1 + 0.3 \cos (1.0908) = 1.1385$

$x_4 = g(x_3) = 1 + 0.3 \cos (1.1385) = 1.1257$

$x_5 = g(x_4) = 1 + 0.3 \cos (1.1257) = 1.1292$

$x_6 = g(x_5) = 1 + 0.3 \cos(1.1292) = 1.1282$
$x_7 = g(x_6) = 1 + 0.3 \cos(1.1282) = 1.1285$
$x_8 = g(x_7) = 1 + 0.3 \cos(1.1285) = 1.1284$
$x_9 = g(x_8) = 1 + 0.3 \cos(1.1284) = 1.1284$

Thus root of the equation is $x = 1.1284$.

Example 2.12 : *The bacteria concentration (C) in a reservoir varies as*

$$C = 4e^{-2t} + e^{-0.1t}$$

Calculate time required for the bacteria concentration to be 0.5 using Newton-Raphson method, accurate upto 4 decimal places.

Solution : The given equation is

$$f(t) = 4e^{-2t} + e^{-0.1t} - 0.5$$

Newton-Raphson method required evaluation of $f'(t)$ also.

$$\therefore \quad f'(t) = -8e^{-2t} - 0.1 e^{-0.1t}$$

Now, assuming initial guess as $x_0 = 0$,

$$t_1 = t_0 - \frac{f(t_0)}{f'(t_0)}$$

$$= 0 - \frac{4e^{-2 \times 0} + e^{-0.1 \times 0} - 0.5}{-8e^{-2 \times 0} - 0.1 e^{-0.1 \times 0}}$$

$$= 0.5556$$

∴ Second iteration is,

$$t_2 = 0.5556 - \frac{4e^{-2 \times 0.5556} + e^{-0.1 \times 0.5556} - 0.5}{-8e^{-2 \times 0.5556} - 0.1e^{-0.1 \times 0.5556}}$$

$$= 1.2017$$

∴ Third iteration is,

$$t_3 = 1.2017 - \frac{4e^{-2 \times 1.2017} + e^{-0.1 \times 1.2017} - 0.5}{-8e^{-2 \times 1.2017} - 0.1e^{-0.1 \times 1.2017}}$$

Fourth iteration gives $t_4 = 2.1234$
Fifth iteration gives $t_5 = 3.9966$
Sixth iteration gives $t_6 = 6.4609$
Seventh iteration gives $t_7 = 6.9206$
Eighth iteration gives $t_8 = 6.9315$
Ninth iteration gives $t_9 = 6.9315$

Thus time for bacteria concentration of 0.5 is $t = 6.9315$.

Example 2.13 : *Find root of equation $x^3 + x - 1 = 0$ using Newton-Raphson method. Initial guess value $x_0 = 0$; accuracy desired is 4 digits accuracy.*

Solution : $\quad f(x) = x^3 + x - 1$

∴ $f'(x) = 3x^2 + 1$

According to Newton-Raphson formula,

$$x_1 = x_0 - \frac{f(x_0)}{f'(x)}$$

with initial guess of $x_0 = 0$

First iteration is

$$x_1 = 0 - \frac{-1}{1} = 1$$

Second iteration is

$$x_2 = x_1 - \frac{f(x)}{f'(x)}$$

$$= 1 - \frac{1}{4}$$

$$= 0.75$$

Third iteration is

$$x_3 = 0.75 - \frac{0.75^3 + 0.75 - 1}{3 \times 0.75^2 + 1}$$

$$= 0.6860$$

Fourth iteration gives $x_4 = 0.6823$
Fifth iteration gives $x_5 = 0.6823$
Thus desired root is $x = 0.6823$

Example 2.14 : *What is the modified Newton Raphson method. State its advantages.*

Solution : The Newton-Raphson method determines next guess value by a formula :

$$x_i = x_{i-1} - \frac{f(x_{i-1})}{f'(x_{i-1})}$$

Compared with successive approximation method or any other method Newton-Raphson method is quite fast in reaching near the desired root. But if at the location of desired root there are multiple roots existing, due to nature of curve, Newton-Raphson method reaches the root location very slowly. Example of existence of multiple root is a polynomial having factors as $(x - 1)$, $(x - 2)$ and $(x - 2)$. Thus $x = 2$ is repeated root.

To accelerate Newton-Raphson method in such cases, the polynomial function in the formula is differentiated and the formula is modified as :

$$x_i = x_{i-1} - \frac{g(x_{i-1})}{g'(x_{i-1})}$$

where, $g(x_{i-1}) = \frac{(x_{i-1})}{f'(x_{i-1})} = \frac{u}{v}$

$$\therefore \quad g'(x_{i-1}) = \frac{vu' - uv'}{v^2}$$

$$= \frac{f'(x_{i-1}) f'(x_{i-1}) - f(x_{i-1}) f''(x_{i-1})}{[f'(x_{i-1})]^2}$$

∴ Formula becomes,

$$x_i = x_{i-1} - \frac{[f(x_{i-1}) / f'(x_{i-1})] [f'(x_{i-1})]^2}{[f'(x_{i-1})]^2 - f(x_{i-1}) f''(x_{i-1})}$$

$$\therefore \quad x_i = x_{i-1} - \frac{f(x_{i-1}) f'(x_{i-1})}{[f'(x_{i-1})]^2 - f(x_{i-1}) f''(x_{i-1})}$$

Due to this double differentiation, error that is difference between two successive guesses reduces rapidly and the multiple root location is reached very fast. This is advantage of the modified Newton-Raphson method.

Example 2.15 : *Draw flowchart and write computer program for successive approximation method, to find root of an equation.*

Solution : Refer Sections 2.5.2.3 and Section 2.5.2.4. These sections are the desired answers in the examination.

Example 2.16 : *Find root of $x^3 - \cos^2 x = 0$ using Newton-Raphson method upto accuracy of 0.02. Explain convergence criteria for this method.*

Solution : The given equation is

$$f(x) = x^3 - \cos^2 x$$

$$\therefore \quad f'(x) = 3x^2 - (-2 \cos x \sin x)$$

$$\therefore \quad f'(x) = 3x^2 + \sin 2x$$

The formula for Newton-Raphson method is

$$x_i = x_{i-1} - \frac{f(x_{i-1})}{f'(x_{i-1})}$$

The convergence criteria says that absolute value of derivative of right hand side should be less than 1 for convergence.

That means

$$\left| \frac{d}{dx} \right|_{x_{i-1}} \left. - \frac{f(x_{i-1})}{f'(x_{i-1})} \right|$$

Replacing x_{i-1} by x for convenience, it becomes

$$\left| \frac{d}{dx} \right| x - \frac{f(x)}{f'(x)} \left. \right|$$

$$= \left| 1 - \frac{[f'(x)]^2 - f(x) f''(x)}{[f'(x)]^2} \right|$$

$$= \left| 1 - 1 - \frac{f(x) \, f''(x)}{[f'(x)]^2} \right|$$

$$= \left| \frac{f(x) \, f''(x)}{[f'(x)]^2} \right|$$

This derivative should be less than 1.

Let us check this criteria with given equation.

∴ $\quad f''(x) = 6x + 2(\cos^2 x - \sin^2 x)$

The derivative in convergence criteria is

$$\left| \frac{f(x) \, f''(x)}{[f'(x)]^2} \right| = \left| \frac{(x^3 - \cos^2 x)[6x + 2(\cos^2 x - \sin^2 x)]}{[3x^2 + \sin 2x]^2} \right|$$

Let us evaluate this assuming initial guess as $x_0 = 0$.

∴ $\quad \left| \dfrac{f(x_0) \, f''(x_0)}{[f'(x_0)]^2} \right| = \left| \dfrac{(0 - \cos^2 0)[0 + 2(\cos^2 0 - \sin^2 0)]}{[0 + \sin 0]^2} \right|$

$$= \left| \frac{-1 \times 2}{0} \right|$$

This is mathematical error. Hence, initial guess assumed as $x_0 = 0$ is wrong.

Let us assume initial guess as $x_0 = 1$.

∴ $\quad \left| \dfrac{f(x_0) \, f''(x_0)}{[f'(x_0)]^2} \right| = \left| \dfrac{0.7081 \times 5.1677}{15.2828} \right|$

$$= 0.2394$$

Thus it is less than 1. Hence the method will converge with $x_0 = 1$.

First iteration gives $\quad x_1 = x_0 - \dfrac{x_0^3 - \cos^2 x_0}{3x_0^2 + \sin 2x_0} = 0.8189$

Second iteration gives

$$x_2 = 0.7914; \quad |x_2 - x_1| = 0.0275$$

Third iteration gives

$$x_3 = 0.7908, \quad |x_3 - x_2| = 6 \times 10^{-4}$$

The error, that is difference in x_3 and x_2 is sufficiently smaller than 0.02. Therefore, desired root of the equation is

$$x = 0.7908$$

Example 2.17 : Determine root of the following equation using modified Newton-Raphson method with initial guess $x_0 = 3$ with 4 digit accuracy.
$$f(x) = x^3 - 6.9x^2 - 1.41x + 55.225$$

Solution : This method requires $f(x)$, $f'(x)$ and $f''(x)$.

$$\therefore \quad f(x) = x^3 - 6.9x^2 + 1.41x + 55.225$$
$$f'(x) = 3x^2 - 13.8x - 1.41$$
$$f''(x) = 6x - 13.8$$

$\therefore$ With initial guess $x_0 = 3$.
$$f(x_0) = 15.895$$
$$f'(x_0) = -15.81$$
$$f''(x_0) = 4.2$$

$$\therefore \quad x_1 = x_0 - \frac{f(x_0)\, f'(x_0)}{[f'(x_0)]^2 - f(x_0)\, f''(x_0)}$$
$$= 4.37175$$

$$\therefore \quad f(x_1) = 0.74043$$
$$f'(x_1) = -4.4036$$
$$f''(x_1) = 12.4305$$

$$\therefore \quad x_2 = x_1 - \frac{f(x_1)\, f'(x_1)}{[f'(x_1)]^2 - f(x_1)\, f''(x_1)}$$

$$\therefore \quad x_2 = 4.69179$$
$$\therefore \quad f(x_2) = 0.00048$$
$$f'(x_3) = -0.11795$$
$$f''(x_2) = 14.3508$$

$$\therefore \quad x_3 = x_2 - \frac{f(x_2)\, f'(x_2)}{[f'(x_2)]^2 - f(x_2)\, f''(x_2)}$$
$$= 4.7$$

$$\therefore \quad f(x_3) = 1.58096 \times 10^{-10}$$
$$f'(x_3) = -6.74799 \times 10^{-5}$$
$$f''(x_3) = 14.4$$

$$\therefore \quad x_4 = x_3 - \frac{f(x_3)\, f'(x_3)}{[f'(x_3)]^2 - f(x_3)\, f''(x_3)}$$
$$= 4.7$$

Thus the root exists at $x = 4.7$.

PROBLEMS FOR PRACTICE

1. Find root of the following equation using successive approximation method with initial guess of $x_0 = 1$ and accuracy upto three digits.
$$x e^x = 1$$
   Ans. : $x = 0.5671$

2. Find square root of 15 using Newton-Raphson method, correct upto two decimal places.
   [**Hint :** Write the function as $f(x) = x^2 - 15$]
   Ans. : 3.873

3. Find cube root of 6 using modified Newton-Raphson method, correct upto 4 decimal places.
   [**Hint :** Write the function as $f(x) = x^3 - 6$]
   Ans. : 1.8171

4. Using Newton-Raphson method determine root of $f(x) = 2x - 3 \cos x$ which is near 0.8. Expected accuracy level is 4 decimal places.
   Ans. : $x = 0.9149$

5. Determine positive root of the following equation using fixed point iteration method and initial guess as $x_0 = 0.1$. The root should be accurate to 4th decimal place.
$$f(x) = x^3 + 3x^2 - \sin x$$
   [**Hint :** Write all possible forms of $x = g(x)$
   i.e. $\quad x = \sin^{-1}(x^3 + 3x^2)$
   or $\quad x = \sqrt[3]{\sin x - 3x^2}$
   or $\quad x = \sqrt{\dfrac{\sin x - x^3}{3}}$
   and repeat the procedure].
   Ans. : The answers will be 0, –3.013992 and 0.2986659 respectively. The last answer is expected here.

6. Determine using bisection method, a root of the equation $\cos x - 1.3x = 0$ with accuracy of 0.01.

7. Using five iterations of bisection method determine root of the equation. Initial guesses are $x_1 = 2.8$ and $x_2 = 3$, $f(x) = -0.9x^2 + 1.7 x + 2.5$.

8. Determine using false-position method, a root of the equation. $x_u \cos 3 e^x - 0.5$ between limits of $x_1 = 0$ and $x_2 = 1$ with accuracy of 0.01.

9. Find the root of $\sin x = x - 2$ near $x = 2.5$ by Regulafalsi method x is in radians. Not more than 5 iterations are expected.

10. Solve using Newton-Raphson method, $e^x \cos x - 1.4 = 0$. Find the value of the root up to accuracy of 0.001.

11. Solve the equation $e^x \cos x - 1.4 \sin x = 0.8$ using Newton –Raphson method taking $x = 1$ and doing 3 iterations.

12. Use false-position method method to find the root of the equation $\cos x - x e^x = 0$. Use initial guesses $x_1 = 0$ and $x_2 = 1$ to obtain accuracy of 0.01.
13. Use false-position method to obtain root of equation $x e^x - \cos 3x - 0.51 = 0$. Use initial guess $x_1 = 0$ and $x_2 = 1.0$, Do 4 iterations.

REVIEW QUESTIONS

1. Solve equation $\sin x - x \cos x = 0$ using modified Newton Raphson method, with accuracy of 0.005. You may take initial guess as 0.2. Check whether with this initial guess, the solution converges.
2. Draw a flow chart for modified Newton Raphson method.
3. Solve using Newton Raphson method the equation $\sin x - x \cos x = 0$. Assume initial guess value for $x = \dfrac{3\pi}{2}$, accuracy of function should be within 0.00001.
4. Draw flow chart for solution of roots of equation using successive approximation method.
5. Draw flowchart for successive iteration method.
6. Find a real root of the equation, $e^x \cos(x) - 1.2 = 0$ by the Newton Raphson method correct to three decimal places. State how do you select initial value of x.
7. Solve using Newton Raphson method $e^x \cdot \cos(x) - 1.4 (0)$. Find the value of root up to the accuracy of 0.01.
8. Draw the flowchart for successive approximation method.
9. Find a real root of $2x - \log_{10} x = 7$ correct to four decimal places using iteration method.
10. Draw a flow chart for modified Newton Raphson method.
    A circular shaft having 1 meter length has varying radius 'r' as follows.

X (m)	0	0.25	0.5	0.75	1
r (m)	1	0.9896	0.9589	0.9089	0.8415

11. Find the positive root of $x^4 - x = 10$ by Newton-Raphson correct to three decimal places.
12. Solve the equation to isolate x on left hand side for given function $x^2 - x - 1 = 0$, also explain following statement with graphical explanation "Successive approximation is more unstable method is more unstable method compared to Newton Raphson method to estimate roots of non-linear equations."
13. Vanderwal equation for real gases is given by
    $(p + a/v^2)(v - b) = RT$ where p = Pressure = 1 N/mm² R = Gas constant = 0.082 kJ/kg K, a = Constant = 3.82, b = Constant = 0.06, v = Volume at pressure, T = Temperature in Kelvin find volume at 300 K assume initial guess volume 20 m³/kg.
14. Using Newton's Raphsons method, find the roots of the equation $e^x = x^3 + \cos 25 x$.
15. Draw the graphical representation of successive iterative method.

Unit - II

Chapter 3
NUMERICAL INTEGRATION

3.1 INTRODUCTION

In thermodynamics you must have drawn PV diagram many times. Why we need to draw such diagrams? What is their physical significance? We know that area under the PV diagram is work done, in case of closed systems.

Let us take another simple example. A vehicle is travelling with a constant speed of 75 km/hr. If we observe its speed and plot a graph as shown in Fig. 3.1, the area under the speed diagram is the distance travelled by the vehicle in the duration, when we observed the vehicle. The dashed lines indicate the duration for which we observed the vehicle. Thus vehicle has travelled,

$$\frac{75}{60} \times 10 = 12.5 \text{ km}$$

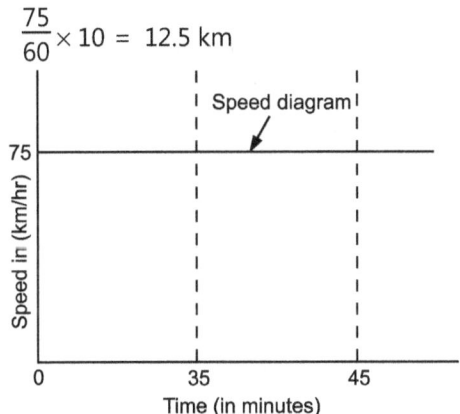

Fig. 3.1

Let us do it by making a mathematical model.
Mathematically the speed diagram can be represented as
$$x = 75/60 \qquad \ldots 75 \text{ km/hr converted to km/min}$$
and area under the curve, that is area under the speed diagram is integration of the mathematical expression between the limits. This integration represents area under the speed diagram. Area of rectangle is multiplication of height and width, in this case it is multiplication of time of travel and speed. Hence answer, we get, represents the distance travelled during observation.

Mathematically, this distance i.e. area under the speed diagram is

$$= \int_{35}^{45} x \, dx$$

where, $\quad x = 75/60$

$\therefore\quad$ Distance travelled $= \int_{35}^{45} (75/60)\, dx$

$$= (75/60) \int_{35}^{45} dx$$

$$= 75/60\, [x]_{35}^{45}$$

$$= 75/60\, (45 - 35)$$

$$= \frac{75}{60} \times 10$$

$$= 12.5 \text{ km}$$

In engineering and scientific problems, the curve for f(x) will not be always as simple as we considered in this example.

So let us go back to example of thermodynamic PV diagram. Fig. 3.2 shows nature of PV diagram for an isothermal process i.e. a process where PV = constant. Let us find the work required to be done to compress an ideal gas from pressure of 1 N/m^2 and volume of 10 m^3 to a pressure of 10 N/m^2 and volume of 1 m^3 isothermally.

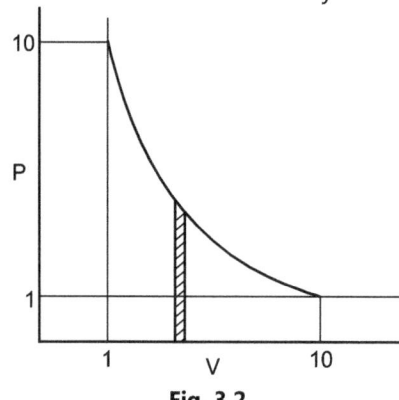

Fig. 3.2

Now the mathematical model of the thermodynamic process is

$$PV = C$$

where, $\quad C = P_1V_1 = P_2V_2 = 10$

$\therefore\quad P = \dfrac{10}{V}$

Now to determine work required to be done that means area under PV curve, let us assume a vertical strip of infinitesimal width as shown in Fig. 3.2. Let its width be dV. Now area of this strip is PdV.

Hence, to find area under the curve we need to assume many such strips and multiply their widths by corresponding pressure value.

This is represented mathematically as an integration.

∴ Area under PV diagram

$$= \int_{10}^{1} PdV \quad \text{... Integration limits indicate direction of the process}$$

$$= \int_{10}^{1} \frac{dV}{10} = [\ln V]_{10}^{1}$$

$$= [\ln 1 - \ln 10] = -2.3026 \text{ Nm}$$

Negative sign indicates that the work of 2.3026 Nm is to be performed on the system to get compression.

Further, in engineering life, you may come across some situations where the presented mathematical model may not be integrable. But your conclusions may be dependent on the integration results. For example, an object's acceleration at a given time t is represented by equation

$$f(t) = \sin^2 t \sin(t^2)$$

and you need to determine the distance travelled by the object in given observation time duration. So you need to calculate

$$\text{Distance} = \int_{t_1}^{t_2} \int_{t_1}^{t_2} \sin^2 t \sin(t^2) \, dt \, dt \quad \text{... f(t) is acceleration, hence double integration is needed}$$

In such cases, you need to solve the integrations by numerical methods.

In this chapter, we are going to learn various methods to determine value of integration numerically.

The methods we will be studying are:

1. Trapezoidal rule.
2. Simpson's 1/3rd rule.
3. Simpson's 3/8th rule.
4. Gauss Quadrature 2-point method.
5. Gauss Quadrature 3-point method.

3.2 TRAPEZOIDAL RULE

As the name suggests, this method tells us to imagine a trapezium under the given curve as shown in Fig. 3.3. The method further tells us to determine area of the trapezium.

Thus, actual area under the curve is A + B, but the method gives us the answer as A. Hence, there is error equal to area B.

Area   A = Width of the strip × Average height of the strip = $(x_1 - x_0) \times \dfrac{f(x_1) + f(x_0)}{2}$

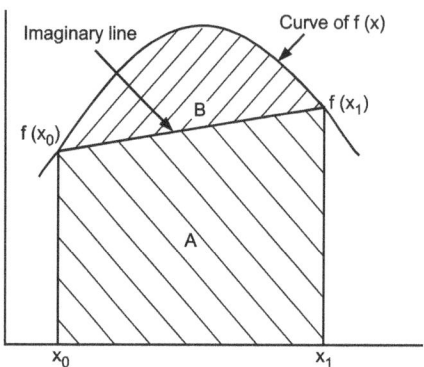

Fig. 3.3

This is the formula for Trapezoidal rule.

The error B is considerable, hence to reduce that error, we divide the big single strip into multiple strips having equal widths, as shown in Fig. 3.4. Thus, due to multiple strips the area under the curve can be calculated as

$$A = A1 + A2 + A3 + A4$$

where, net error is   B = B1 + B2 + B3 + B4

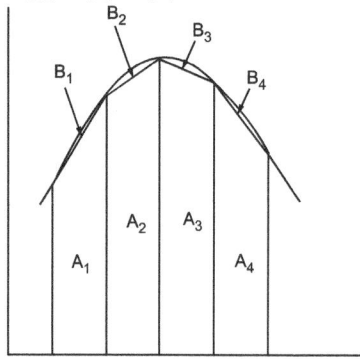

Fig. 3.4

Thus error is considerably reduced in comparison with earlier.

3.2.1 Formulation for Trapezoidal Rule

Now, area under the curve, that means integration of f(x) from x_0 to x_4 is,

$$\int_{x_0}^{x_4} f(x) = A1 + A2 + A3 + A4$$

$$= (x_1 - x_0) \times \frac{f(x_1) + f(x_0)}{2} + (x_2 - x_1) \times \frac{f(x_2) + f(x_1)}{2}$$

$$+ (x_3 - x_2) \times \frac{f(x_3) + f(x_2)}{2} + (x_4 - x_3) \times \frac{f(x_4) + f(x_3)}{2}$$

We have selected all strips in such a way that their widths are equal.

∴ $\quad x_1 - x_0 = x_2 - x_1 = x_3 - x_2 = x_4 - x_3 = h$

∴ $\quad \int_{x_0}^{x_4} f(x) = h \left[\frac{f(x_1) + f(x_0)}{2} + \frac{f(x_2) + f(x_1)}{2} + \frac{f(x_3) + f(x_2)}{2} + \frac{f(x_4) + f(x_3)}{2} \right]$

$$= \frac{h}{2} [f(x_0) + 2[f(x_1) + f(x_2) + f(x_3)] + f(x_4)]$$

Thus, a generalized formula can be written as

$$\int_{x_0}^{x_n} f(x) = \frac{h}{2} [[f(x_0) + f(x_n)] + 2[f(x_1) + f(x_2) + ... + f(x_{n-1})]]$$

For better readability, let us use notations as below,

$$f(x_0) = y_0$$
$$f(x_1) = y_1$$
$$\vdots = \vdots$$
$$f(x_n) = y_n$$

∴ The formula becomes,

$$\int_{x_0}^{x_n} f(x) = \frac{h}{2} [(y_0 + y_n) + 2(y_1 + y_2 + ... + y_{n-1})]$$

Error in the numerical integration will be reduced if more number of strips are used, in other words, error will be reduced if the strip width is reduced.

Example 3.1 : Determine the value of

$$\int_{\pi/4}^{3\pi/8} \sin x \, dx$$

using Trapezoidal rule with
1. Strip width = $\pi/32$
2. Number of strips = 6

Compare the answers with analytical answer and determine the errors.

Solution : Let us first solve it analytically.

$$I_1 = \int_{\pi/4}^{3\pi/8} \sin x \, dx$$

$$= [-\cos x]_{\pi/4}^{3\pi/8}$$

$$= \left[-\cos\frac{3\pi}{8} - \left(-\cos\frac{\pi}{4}\right)\right]$$

$$= 0.32442335$$

Now, considering strip width $h = \pi/32$

∴ $x_0 = \dfrac{\pi}{4} = \dfrac{8\pi}{32}$ ⇒ $y_0 = 0.7071$

$x_1 = \dfrac{9\pi}{32}$ ⇒ $y_1 = 0.7730$

$x_2 = \dfrac{10\pi}{32}$ ⇒ $y_2 = 0.8315$

$x_3 = \dfrac{11\pi}{32}$ ⇒ $y_3 = 0.8819$

$x_4 = \dfrac{12\pi}{32} = \dfrac{3\pi}{8}$ ⇒ $y_4 = 0.9239$

∴ $I_2 = \dfrac{(\pi/32)}{2}[(0.7071 + 0.9239) + 2(0.773 + 0.8315 + 0.8819)]$

$$= 0.32416327$$

Considering 6 strips, that means

$$h = \frac{x_n - x_0}{n} = \frac{\left(\frac{3\pi}{8} - \frac{\pi}{4}\right)}{6}$$

$$= \frac{\frac{12\pi}{32} - \frac{8\pi}{32}}{6}$$

$$= \frac{4\pi}{6 \times 32} = \frac{\pi}{48}$$

∴ $x_0 = \dfrac{\pi}{4} = \dfrac{12\pi}{48}$ ⇒ $y_0 = 0.7071$

$x_1 = \dfrac{13\pi}{48}$ ⇒ $y_1 = 0.7518$

$x_2 = \dfrac{14\pi}{48}$ ⇒ $y_2 = 0.7934$

$x_3 = \dfrac{15\pi}{48}$ ⇒ $y_3 = 0.8315$

$x_4 = \dfrac{16\pi}{48}$ ⇒ $y_4 = 0.8660$

$$x_5 = \frac{17\pi}{48} \Rightarrow y_5 = 0.8969$$

$$x_6 = \frac{18\pi}{48} \Rightarrow y_6 = 0.9239$$

$$\therefore I_3 = \frac{(\pi/48)}{2}[(0.7071 + 0.9239) + 2(0.7518 + 0.7934 + 0.8315 + 0.866 + 0.8969)]$$

$$= 0.32431053$$

% Error in numerical integration with strip width of $\pi/32$ that is with 4 strips

$$= \frac{|I_1 - I_2|}{I_1} \times 100$$

$$= \frac{0.32442335 - 0.32416327}{0.32442335} \times 100$$

$$= 0.080169\%$$

% Error in numerical integration with 6 strips that means with strip width of $\pi/48$.

$$= \frac{|I_1 - I_3|}{I_1} \times 100$$

$$= \frac{0.32442335 - 0.32431053}{0.32442335} \times 100$$

$$= 0.034776\%$$

Thus, error is reduced when we use more number of strips (in other words, we reduce width of the strips).

3.2.2 Algorithm for Numerical Integration by Trapezoidal Rule

1. Define f(x).
2. Get lower limit of integration l.
3. Get upper limit of integration u.
4. Get number of strips n.
5. Strip width h = (u − l)/n.
6. Sum = f(l) + f(u).
7. For i = 1 till i < n with increment of 1
   Sum = sum + 2 * f(l + i * h).
8. Integration = (h/2) * sum.
9. Print answer.
10. End.

3.2.3 Flow Chart for Numerical Integration by Trapezoidal Rule

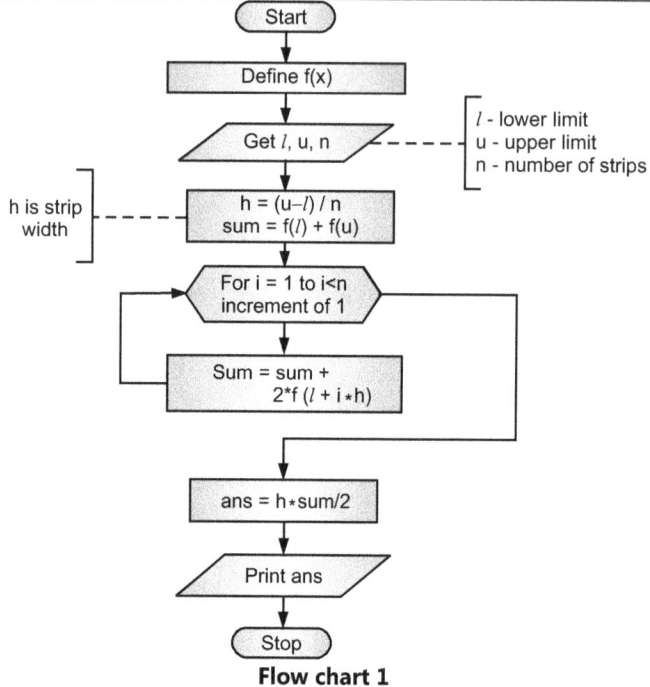

Flow chart 1

3.2.4 Matlab Code For Trapezoidal Integration

```matlab
fprintf('\n**************************************************');
fprintf('\n****************** NUMERICAL INTEGRATION ******************');
fprintf('\n********************* TRAPEZOIDAL METHOD ******************');
fprintf('\n**************************************************');
fstr = input('\n Input Function String f(x) >>> ','s');
f=inline(fstr);                                         % Function Declaration
disp(sprintf(['\n    y = f(x) = ' fstr]));
x(1) = input('\n Enter Lower Limit (x0): ');
xn  = input('\n Enter Upper Limit (xn): ');
n = input('\n Enter No. of Steps (n): ');
h = (xn-x(1))/n
area = 0;
for i = 1:n
    x(i)=x(1) + (i-1)*h;
        x(i+1) = x(i) + h;
    area = area + (h/2)*(f(x(i))+f(x(i+1)));
    fprintf('\n\t Area after %dth Strip >>> %f', i, area);
end
```

3.2.5 Numerical Integration by Trapezoidal Rule using MS-Excel

1. Type lower limit value in cell A1.
2. Type upper limit value in cell A2.
3. Type number of strips in cell A3.
4. Type formula to calculate strip width in cell A4 as
$$= \frac{(A2 - A1)}{A3}.$$
5. To generate list of all x values, type formula as
   = A1 in cell C1.

   (**Note :** Column B is kept empty for separation of numerical values.)
6. Type formula given below in cell C2,
   = C1 + $A $4.
7. Copy and paste cell C2, down in multiple cells in column C, so that list of all x values is generated in column C. For example, if n = 6, column C will contain list from C1 to C7.
8. Now type formula to calculate y_0 in cell D1 as = sin (C1).
   Or whichever function is to be integrated.
9. Copy and paste cell D1 down infront of all x list values.
10. Type formula for required summation of column D in cell F1 as,
    = D1 + D7 + 2 * sum (D2 : D6).

    [**Note :** This formula is written assuming n = 6. Hence, if n = 10, columns C and D will have list from C1 to C11 and D1 to D11. In that case, formula for required summation will be = D1 + D11 + 2 * Sum (D2 : D10)]
11. For final answer type following formula in cell F2 = A4 * F1/2.
12. Thus, cell F2 displays the answer for numerical integration by Trapezoidal rule. Image 3.1 shows solution for previous example with 6 strips.

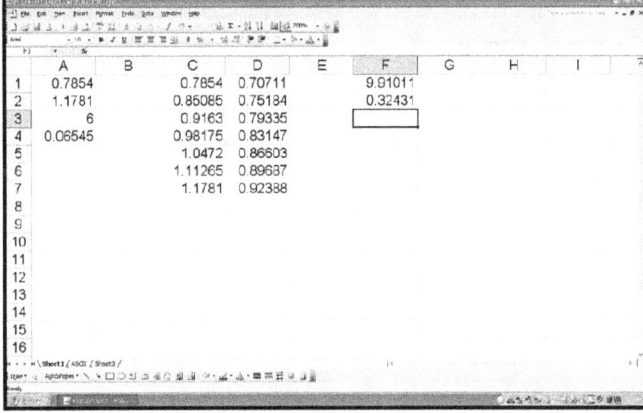

Image 3.1

3.3 SIMPSON'S 1/3RD RULE

To reduce error in numerical integration in Trapezoidal rule, one may increase number of strips or else one may consider two consecutive strips together and join their end points by a parabolic curve passing through the three points, instead of joining them by straight lines. Fig. 3.5 (a) and (b) show reduction in the error by use of parabolic curve.

Thus, considering 2 strips together and assuming parabolic curve to join the three points reduces the error drastically, but a limitation is imposed that number of strips must be divisible by 2, i.e. Simpson's 1/3rd rule can be applied only if number of strips is even.

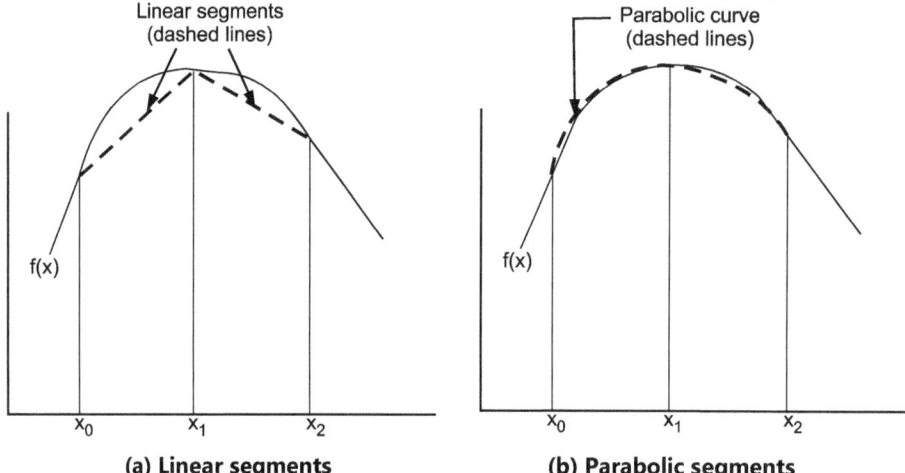

(a) Linear segments   (b) Parabolic segments

Fig. 3.5

3.3.1 Formulation for Simpson's 1/3rd Rule

In case of Trapezoidal rule, writing formula under inclined line was easier because it was equation of linear interpolation. In case of Simpson's 1/3rd rule, the curve's equation can be found by parabolic interpolation as,

Equation of parabolic curve

$$= \frac{(x-x_1)(x-x_2)}{(x_0-x_1)(x_0-x_2)} f(x_0) + \frac{(x-x_0)(x-x_2)}{(x_1-x_0)(x_1-x_2)} f(x_1) + \frac{(x-x_0)(x-x_1)}{(x_2-x_0)(x_2-x_1)} f(x_2)$$

Integrating this equation from x_0 to x_2, we get

$$I = \frac{h}{3}[f(x_0) + 4f(x_1) + f(x_2)]$$

According to notations used earlier, it becomes,

$$I = \frac{h}{3}[y_0 + 4y_1 + y_2]$$ which is formula for one set of two consecutive strips.

If there are multiple strips, the formula will take the form as

$$I = \frac{h}{3}[y_0 + 4y_1 + y_2] + \frac{h}{3}[y_2 + 4y_3 + y_4] + \frac{h}{3}[y_4 + 4y_5 + y_6] + \ldots$$

$$+ \frac{h}{3}[y_{n-2} + 4y_{n-1} + y_n]$$

$$\therefore \quad I = \frac{h}{3}[(y_0 + y_n) + 4(y_1 + y_3 + y_5 + \ldots + y_{n-1}) + 2(y_2 + y_4 + y_6 + \ldots + y_{n-2})]$$

The formula can be remembered as,

$$I = \frac{h}{3}[(y_0 + y_n) + 4(y \text{ with odd suffix}) + 2(y \text{ with even suffix})]$$

Example 3.2 : Determine integration of $f(x) = \int (x^3 - 2x^2 + 7x - 5) \, dx$, between $x = 2.2$ to 3.4 assuming 8 strips using
1. Trapezoidal rule.   2. Simpson's $1/3^{rd}$ rule.
and compare results for errors with the analytical solution.

Solution : Analytical solution is,

$$I_1 = \int_{2.2}^{3.4} (x^3 - 2x^2 + 7x - 5) \, dx$$

$$= \left[\frac{x^4}{4} - \frac{2x^3}{3} + \frac{7x^2}{2} - 5x \right]_{2.2}^{3.4}$$

$$= 25.968$$

Now, $x_0 = 2.2$, $n = 8$ and $x_8 = 3.4$

$$\therefore \quad h = \frac{x_n - x_0}{n} = \frac{x_8 - x_0}{8} = \frac{3.4 - 2.2}{8}$$

$$\therefore \quad h = 0.15$$

$\therefore$ $x_0 = 2.2$ $\Rightarrow$ $y_0 = 11.368$
$x_1 = 2.35$ $\Rightarrow$ $y_1 = 13.382875$
$x_2 = 2.5$ $\Rightarrow$ $y_2 = 15.625$
$x_3 = 2.65$ $\Rightarrow$ $y_3 = 18.114625$
$x_4 = 2.8$ $\Rightarrow$ $y_4 = 20.872$
$x_5 = 2.95$ $\Rightarrow$ $y_5 = 23.917375$
$x_6 = 3.1$ $\Rightarrow$ $y_6 = 27.271$
$x_7 = 3.25$ $\Rightarrow$ $y_7 = 30.953125$
$x_8 = 3.4$ $\Rightarrow$ $y_8 = 34.984$

Using Trapezoidal rule, $I_2 = \dfrac{h}{2}[(y_0 + y_8) + 2(y_1 + y_2 + ... + y_7)]$

$= 25.9968$

Using Simpson's $1/3^{rd}$ rule,

$I_3 = \dfrac{h}{3}[(y_0 + y_8) + 4(y_1 + y_3 + y_5 + y_7) + 2(y_2 + y_4 + y_6)]$

$= 25.968$

% Error in integration by Trapezoidal rule is,

$= \dfrac{|I_1 - I_2|}{I_1} \times 100 = 0.1109\%$

% Error in case of Simpson's $1/3^{rd}$ rule is

$= \dfrac{|I_1 - I_3|}{I_1} \times 100 = 0\%$

Note : Error is zero for this problem, but may be non-zero for other problems, depending on the nature of curve.

3.3.2 Pseudo Code for Numerical Integration by Simpson's $1/3^{rd}$ Rule

1. Define f(x).
2. Get lower limit of integration l.
3. Get upper limit of integration u.
4. Get number of strips n.
5. Strip width h = (u − l)/n.
6. Sum = f(l) + f(u).
7. For i = 1 till i < n with increment of 1

    if i is odd

    sum = sum + 4 * f(l + i * h)

    else

    sum = sum + 2 * f(l + i * h)

8. Integration = (h/3) * sum.
9. Print answer.
10. End.

3.3.3 Flow Chart for Numerical Integration by Simpson's 1/3rd Rule

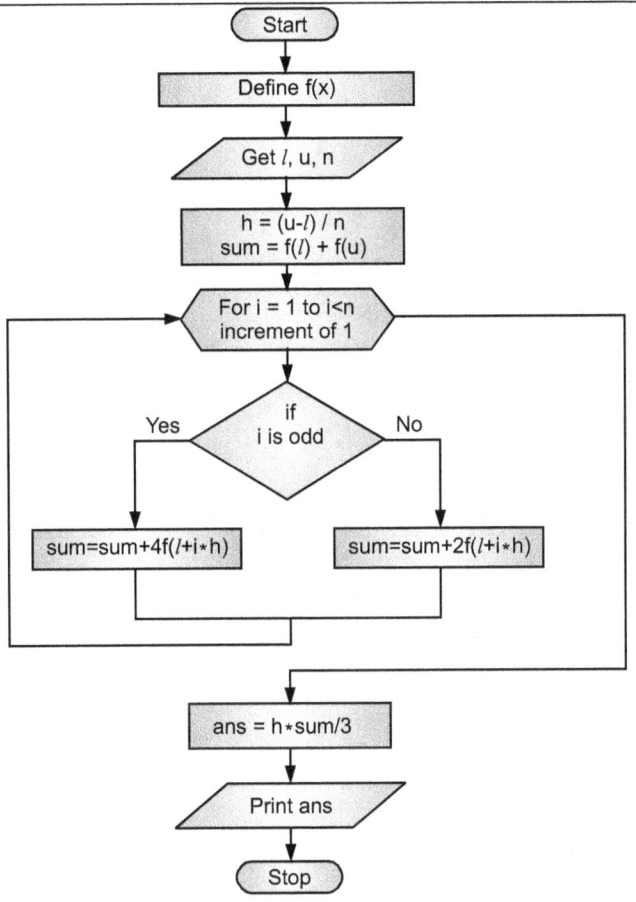

Flow chart 2

3.3.4 Matlab Code for Simpson 1/3rd Rule

```
fprintf('\n***********************************************************');
fprintf('\n******************* NUMERICAL INTEGRATION *****************');
fprintf('\n********************* SIMPSON 1/3RD RULE ******************');
fprintf('\n***********************************************************');

fstr = input('\n Input Function String f(x) >>> ','s');
f=inline(fstr);                                          % Function Declaration
disp(sprintf(['\n    y = f(x) = ' fstr]));
```

```
x(1) = input('\n Enter Lower Limit (x0): ');
xn = input('\n Enter Upper Limit (xn): ');
n = input('\n Enter No. of Steps (n): ');
h = (xn-x(1))/n

area = 0;

if rem(n,2) == 0
   for i = 1:2:n
       x(i+1) = x(i) + h;
       x(i+2) = x(i) + 2*h;
       area = area + (h/3)*(f(x(i))+4*f(x(i+1))+f(x(i+2)));
       fprintf('\n\t Area after %dth Strip >>> %f', i, area);
   end
else
   fprintf('\n\t Error, Pls input EVEN No of Steps');
end
```

3.3.5 Numerical Integration by Simpson's 1/3rd Rule using MS-Excel

1. Type lower limit value in cell A1.
2. Type upper limit value in cell A2.
3. Type number of strips in cell A3.
4. Type formula to calculate strip width in cell A4 as
$$= \frac{(A2 - A1)}{A3}$$
5. To generate list of all x values type formula as
   = A1 in cell C1
6. Type formula given below in cell C2,
   = C1 + A4
7. Copy and paste cell C2, down in multiple cells in column C, so that list of all required x values is generated.
8. Now type formula to calculate y_0 in cell D1. For previous example, it is
   = C1 ^ 3 − 2 * C1 ^ 2 + 7 * C1 − 5
9. Copy and paste cell D1 down in front of all x list values.
10. Write 1 in the cells in front of the first and the last D values i.e. in E1 and E9 and write 0 in all the cells between them.
11. Write 0 in cells F1, G1 and G2 and write 1 in cell F2.

12. Write formula as below in cell F3
    = if(F2 = 0, 1, 0)
13. Copy and paste cell F3 in columns F and G from 3rd row down infront of E column cells.
14. Replace last cell in G column by zero. (Due to "if" statement it stores 1).
15. Write formula as = D1 * E1 in cell H1.
16. Write formula as = D1 * F1 in cell J1.
17. Write formula as = D1 * G1 in cell J1.
18. Copy and paste cells H1, I1 and J1 down in respective columns for all D values.
19. Write = sum (H1 + H9) in cell next to last filled cell in column H, that is in this example's case in cell H10.
20. Write = 4 * sum (I1 : I9) in cell I10.
21. Write = 2 * sum (J1 : J9) in cell J10.
22. Write formula to get final answer in cell H11 as
    = sum (H10 : J10) * A4/3.

Thus, final answer is displayed. The Excel work sheet will look as shown in Image 3.2.

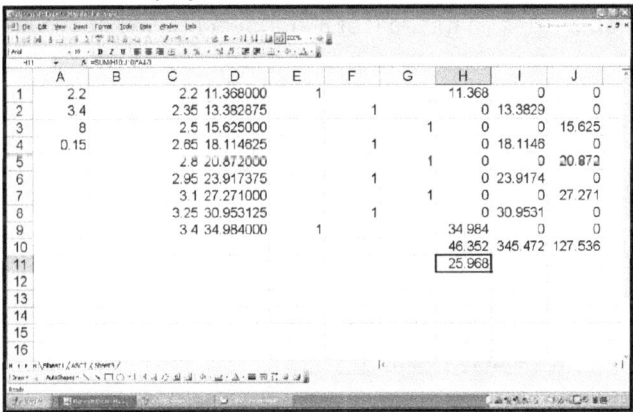

Image 3.2

3.4 SIMPSON'S 3/8TH RULE

For reduction in error that exists in evaluating numerical integrating of polynomials with higher degree or integration of transcendental equations, Simpson's 3/8th rule may also be used.

For single application of Trapezoidal rule one strip is considered. For single application of Simpson's 1/3rd rule, two strips are considered. And for single application of Simpson's 3/8th rule, three strips are considered. Hence, the limitation imposed on Simpson's 3/8th rule is that the number of strips must be divisible by 3, for multiple application of the rule.

3.4.1 Formulation for Simpson's 3/8th Rule

In this case the curve joining the four points is a polynomial with degree equal to three i.e. cubic polynomial. The equation can be found as,

$$= \frac{(x-x_1)(x-x_2)(x-x_3)}{(x_0-x_1)(x_0-x_2)(x_0-x_3)} f(x_0) + \frac{(x-x_0)(x-x_2)(x-x_3)}{(x_1-x_0)(x_1-x_2)(x_1-x_3)} f(x_1)$$

$$+ \frac{(x-x_0)(x-x_1)(x-x_3)}{(x_2-x_0)(x_2-x_1)(x_2-x_3)} f(x_2) + \frac{(x-x_0)(x-x_1)(x-x_2)}{(x_3-x_0)(x_3-x_1)(x_3-x_2)} f(x_3)$$

Integrating this equation from x_0 to x_3, we get

$$I = \frac{3h}{8}[f(x_0) + 3f(x_1) + 3f(x_2) + f(x_3)]$$

Using the earlier notations, it becomes

$$I = \frac{3h}{8}[y_0 + 3y_1 + 3y_2 + y_3]$$

which is formula for one set of three consecutive strips.

When there are multiple strips (in multiple of 3), formula will become,

$$I = \frac{3h}{8}[y_0 + 3y_1 + 3y_2 + y_3] + \frac{3h}{8}[y_3 + 3y_4 + 3y_5 + y_6] + \ldots$$

$$+ \frac{3h}{8}[y_{n-3} + 3y_{n-2} + 3y_{n-1} + y_n]$$

$$= \frac{3h}{8}[(y_0 + y_n) + 2(y_3 + y_6 + \ldots + y_{n-3})$$

$$+ 3(y_1 + y_2 + y_{n-2} + y_{n-1})$$

$$+ 4(y_4 + y_5 + y_7 + y_8 + \ldots + y_{n-5} + y_{n-4})]$$

Hence, the formula can be remembered as

$$I = \frac{3h}{8}[(y_0 + y_n) + 2(y \text{ with suffix divisible by 3})$$

$$+ 3 \, (2^{nd} \text{ and } 3^{rd} \, y \text{ from start and from end})$$

$$+ 4 \, (\text{all rest } y \text{ terms having suffix 4 to } n - 4$$

which is not divisible by 3)]

It is not practicable to remember formula as above, hence remember to repeat procedure as

$$I = \frac{3h}{8}[(y_0 + 3y_1 + 3y_2 + y_3) + \text{same set with suffixes incremented by 3}]$$

Example 3.3: Determine integration of the following functions using
1. Trapezoidal rule
2. Simpson's $3/8^{th}$ rule

Taking 12 strips between the limits

$$f(x) = \int_{1.3}^{2.5} (x + 2 \sin x) \, dx$$

Compare the errors in numerical integration with respect to analytical solution.

Solution: Analytically the integration can be determined as

$$I = \int_{1.3}^{2.5} (x + 2 \sin x) \, dx$$

$$= \left[\frac{x^2}{2} - 2 \cos x \right]_{1.3}^{2.5}$$

$$= 4.41728489$$

Now for numerical methods,

$x_0 = 1.3$, $n = 12$

$\therefore \quad x_{12} = 2.5$

The strip width $h = \dfrac{x_{12} - x_0}{n}$

$= \dfrac{2.5 - 1.3}{12}$

$= 0.1$

$\therefore$
$x_0 = 1.3$	$\Rightarrow \quad y_0 = 3.2271$
$x_1 = 1.4$	$\Rightarrow \quad y_1 = 3.3709$
$x_2 = 1.5$	$\Rightarrow \quad y_2 = 3.4950$
$x_3 = 1.6$	$\Rightarrow \quad y_3 = 3.5991$
$x_4 = 1.7$	$\Rightarrow \quad y_4 = 3.6833$
$x_5 = 1.8$	$\Rightarrow \quad y_5 = 3.7477$
$x_6 = 1.9$	$\Rightarrow \quad y_6 = 3.7926$
$x_7 = 2.0$	$\Rightarrow \quad y_7 = 3.8186$
$x_8 = 2.1$	$\Rightarrow \quad y_8 = 3.8264$
$x_9 = 2.2$	$\Rightarrow \quad y_9 = 3.8170$
$x_{10} = 2.3$	$\Rightarrow \quad y_{10} = 3.7914$
$x_{11} = 2.4$	$\Rightarrow \quad y_{11} = 3.7509$
$x_{12} = 2.5$	$\Rightarrow \quad y_{12} = 3.6969$

Using Trapezoidal rule,

$$I_2 = \frac{h}{2}[(y_0 + y_{12}) + 2(y_1 + y_2 + \ldots + y_{11})]$$

$$= 4.41550352$$

Using Simpson's 3/8th rule,

$$I_3 = \frac{3h}{8}[(y_0 + 3y_1 + 3y_2 + y_3) + (y_3 + 3y_4 + 3y_5 + y_6) + (y_6 + 3y_7 + 3y_8 + y_9)$$

$$+ (y_9 + 3y_{10} + 3y_{11} + y_{12})]$$

$$= 4.41728757$$

% Error in integration by Trapezoidal rule

$$= \frac{|I_1 - I_2|}{I_1} \times 100$$

$$= 0.04033$$

% Error in integration by Simpson's 3/8th rule

$$= \frac{|I_1 - I_3|}{I_1} \times 100$$

$$= 6.1 \times 10^{-5}$$

$$= 0.000061$$

3.4.2 Algorithm for Numerical Integration by Simpson's 3/8th Rule

1. Define function f(x).
2. Get lower limit of integration l.
3. Get upper limit of integration u.
4. Get number of strips n.
5. Strip width h = (u – l)/n.
6. Sum = 0
7. For i = 0 till i < n – 2 with increment of 3
   sum = sum + f(l + i * h) + 3 * f(l + (i + 1) * h)
   + 3 * f(l + (i + 2) * h) + f(l + (i + 3) * h)
8. Integration = $\frac{3}{8}$ h * sum.
9. Print answer.
10. End.

Note : Step 7 may be represented by nested "for" loop as

```
For i = 0 till i < n – 2 with increment of 3
{
    For j = i till j < i + 4 with increment of 1
    {
    if (j%3 == 0)
        sum = sum + f(l + j * h)
    else
        sum = sum + 3 * f(l + j * h)
    }
}
```

3.4.3 Flow Chart for Numerical Integration by Simpson's 3/8th Rule

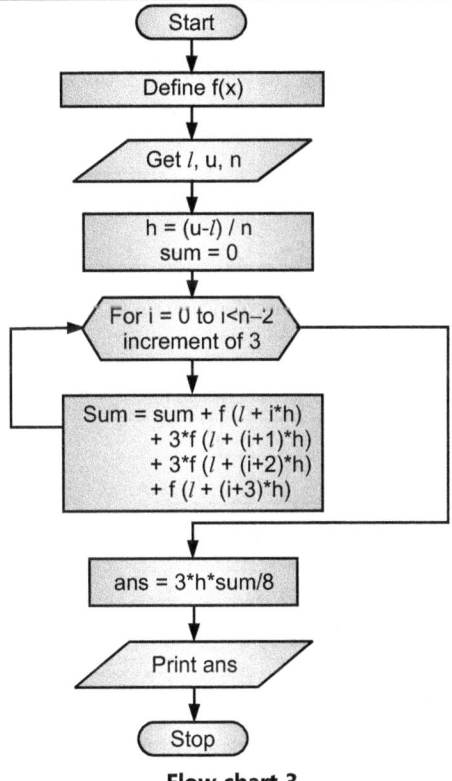

Flow chart 3

Let us make flow chart for nested "for" loops. Note that modification is done to replace too long mathematical expression of "sum". But this is not necessary. Hence, readers may neglect this modification, if they wish so. Output of both the flow charts is same.

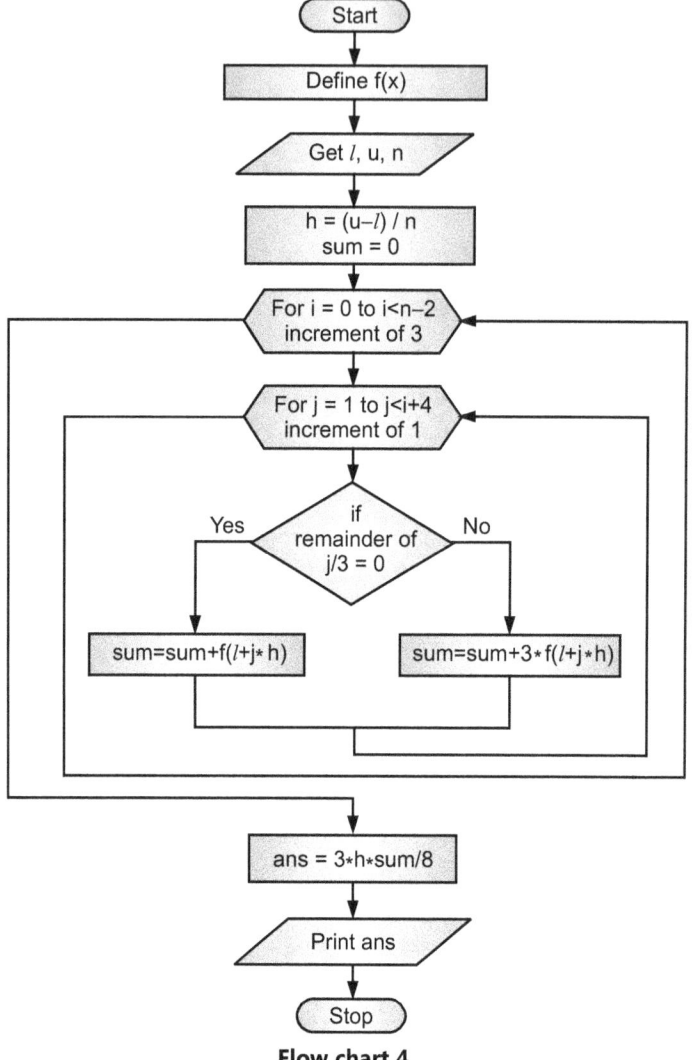

Flow chart 4

3.4.4 Matlab Code For Simpson 3/8th Rule

```
fprintf('\n*************************************************************');
fprintf('\n******************** SIMPSON 3/8th RULE ********************');
fprintf('\n*************************************************************');

%% INPUT FUNCTION IN PROGRAM
fstr = input('\n Enter FUNCTION STRING>>> ','s');
f = inline(fstr);
disp(sprintf(['\n f(x) = ' fstr]))
```

```
x(1) = input('\n Input LOWER LIMIT (X0) = ');
xn = input('\n Input UPPER LIMIT (Xn) = ');
n = input('\n Input No. of Steps (n) = ');

if rem(n,3)~=1
h = (xn-x(1))/n
area = 0;

   for i = 1:3:n
x(i+1)=x(i)+h;
x(i+2)=x(i)+2*h;
x(i+3)=x(i)+3*h;
            area=area+(3*h/8)*(f(x(i))+3*f(x(i+1))+3*f(x(i+2))+f(x(i+3)));
   end

   fprintf('\n Area is %f sq. Units', area);
else

   fprintf('\n ERROR - Enter n multiple of 3');
end
```

3.4.5 Numerical Integration by Simpson's 3/8th Rule using MS-Excel

1. Type lower limit value in cell A1.
2. Type upper limit value in cell A2.
3. Type number of strips in cell A3.
4. Type formula to calculate strip width in cell A4 as
$$= \frac{(A2 - A1)}{A3}$$
5. To generate list of all x values type formula as
   = A1 in cell C1
6. Type formula given below in cell C2,
   = C1 + $A $4
7. Copy and paste cell C2, down in multiple cells in column C, so that list of all required x values is generated. In previous example we require x_0 to x_{12} — total 13 values.
8. Now type formula to calculate y_0 in cell D1. In the example it is,

= C1 + 2 * sin (C1)

9. Copy and paste cell D1 down in front of all x list values.

   So, we get values in D column for D1 to D13.

10. Type 1, 3, 3, 2, 3, 3, 2, 3, 3, 2 ... sequentially, one number in one cell in E column, in front of D values. Replace the last cell in E column back to 1.

11. Type below given formula in cell F1,

    = D1 * E1

12. Copy and paste cell F1 down in column F infront of all E values.

13. Find sum of all numbers from F1 to F13 in cell F14 by formula

    = sum (F1 : F13)

14. Now get answer in cell F15 by formula

    = 3 * A4/8 * F14

    The excel work sheet showing the calculation and the final answer will look as shown in Image 3.3.

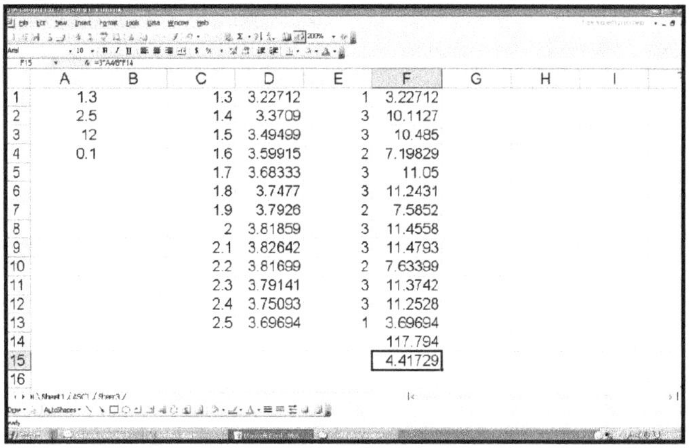

	A	B	C	D	E	F	G	H	I
1	1.3		1.3	3.22712	1	3.22712			
2	2.5		1.4	3.3709	3	10.1127			
3	12		1.5	3.49499	3	10.485			
4	0.1		1.6	3.59915	2	7.19829			
5			1.7	3.68333	3	11.05			
6			1.8	3.7477	3	11.2431			
7			1.9	3.7926	2	7.5852			
8			2	3.81859	3	11.4558			
9			2.1	3.82642	3	11.4793			
10			2.2	3.81699	2	7.63399			
11			2.3	3.79141	3	11.3742			
12			2.4	3.75093	3	11.2528			
13			2.5	3.69694	1	3.69694			
14						117.794			
15						4.41729			
16									

Image 3.3

3.5 GAUSS QUADRATURE METHODS

These methods can be understood in comparison with Trapezoidal rule. Fig. 3.6 (a) which shows application of one strip of Trapezoidal rule. If the same line is located as in Fig. 3.6 (b) parallel to earlier location, the error will be minimized due to its distribution as positive error and negative error. Gauss quadrature methods also known as Gauss Legendre method use this technique of error compensation.

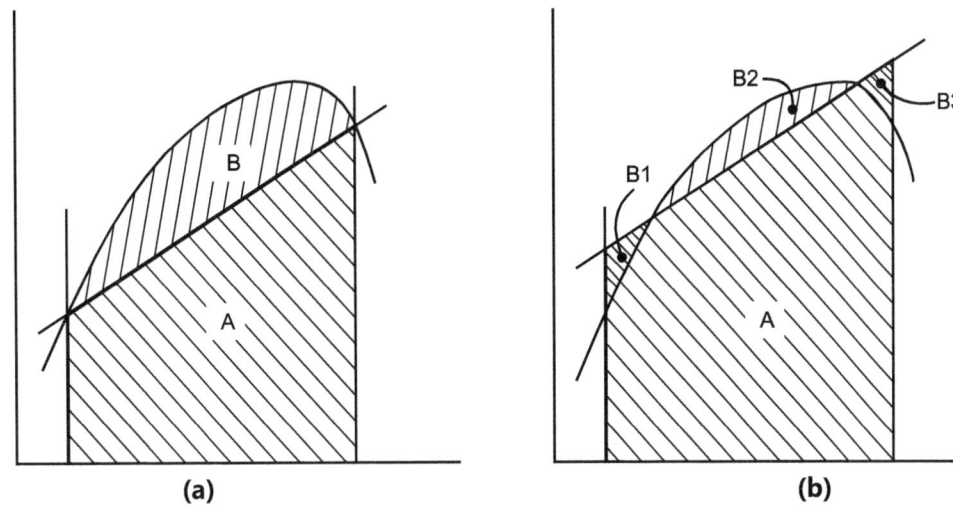

Fig. 3.6

3.5.1 Formulation of Gauss Quadrature Method

The method suggests us to change limit of integration and in turn the variable of integration as well, so that integration changes its form as below :

$$\int_a^b f(x)\, dx = \int_{-1}^{+1} f(u)\, du$$

This conversion is possible by substitution as,

$$x = \left(\frac{b-a}{2}\right) u + \left(\frac{b+a}{2}\right)$$

Thus, at $\quad x = a$

$$a = \left(\frac{b-a}{2}\right) u + \left(\frac{b+a}{2}\right)$$

$$\therefore \quad u = \frac{a - \left(\frac{b+a}{2}\right)}{\left(\frac{b-a}{2}\right)}$$

$$= \frac{2a - b - a}{b-a} = \frac{a-b}{b-a}$$

$\therefore \quad u = -1$

and at $\quad x = b$

$$b = \left(\frac{b-a}{2}\right) u + \left(\frac{b+a}{2}\right)$$

Ch. 3 | 3.23

$$\therefore \quad u = \frac{b - \left(\frac{b+a}{2}\right)}{\left(\frac{b-a}{2}\right)}$$

$$= \frac{2b - b - a}{b - a}$$

$$= \frac{b - a}{b - a}$$

$$\therefore \quad u = 1$$

Further, $\quad dx = \left(\frac{b-a}{2}\right) du$

The method then tells us to evaluate the integration

$$\int_{-1}^{1} f(u)\, du$$

by evaluating f(u) at either one, or two or three, or four or five points with respect to the following table.

Table 3.1

No. of Points	Location of Point	Weight in Calculating Integration
1.	0	2
2.	$\pm \sqrt{1/3}$	1
3.	0	8/9
	$\pm \sqrt{3/5}$	5/9
4.	$\pm \sqrt{(3 - 2\sqrt{6/5})/7}$	$\dfrac{18 + \sqrt{30}}{36}$
	$\pm \sqrt{(3 + 2\sqrt{6/5})/7}$	$\dfrac{18 - \sqrt{30}}{36}$
5.	$\pm \dfrac{1}{3}\sqrt{5 - 2\sqrt{10/7}}$	$\dfrac{332 + 13\sqrt{70}}{900}$
	$\pm \dfrac{1}{3}\sqrt{5 + 2\sqrt{10/7}}$	$\dfrac{332 - 13\sqrt{70}}{900}$

Table 3.1 describes the weightage of individual points contribution in calculating integration, i.e. area under the curve.

If we use single point the complete area will be calculated by single substitution, hence weightage is 2.

If we use two-point formula, we will have to make two substitutions, individually which will calculate left half area and right half area i.e.

$$\int_{-1}^{0} f(u)\, du \quad \text{and} \quad \int_{0}^{1} f(u)\, du$$

Hence, addition of individual weightage is 2.

If we use three-point formula, we will have to calculate f(u) at three locations out of which f(0) will have weightage as 8/9 and individually $f(\sqrt{3/5})$ and $f(-\sqrt{3/5})$ will have weightage 5/9. Therefore, total weightage will be

$$\frac{8}{9} + \frac{5}{9} + \frac{5}{9} = \frac{18}{9} = 2$$

As per our syllabus we will restrict ourselves to use two-point formula and three-point formula.

3.5.2 Procedure for Application of Two-Point Gauss Quadrature Formula

From given equation,

$$\int_{a}^{b} f(x)\, dx$$

determine f(u) and du as above.

Then evaluate f(u) for $u = \sqrt{1/3}$ and $u = -\sqrt{1/3}$

Then integration is evaluated as,

$$\int_{a}^{b} f(x)\, dx = \int_{-1}^{1} f(u)\, du = \sum \text{weight} \times f(u) = f(\sqrt{1/3}) + f(-\sqrt{1/3})$$

Physical significance of this equation is as explained by Fig. 3.6.

3.5.3 Procedure for Application of Three-Point Gauss Quadrative Formula

From given equation

$$\int_{a}^{b} f(x)\, dx$$

determine f(u) and du as above.

Then evaluate f(u)

For $\quad u = -\sqrt{3/5}$
$\quad\quad\quad u = 0$

and $\quad u = \sqrt{3/5}$

Then integration is evaluated as,

$$\int_a^b f(x)\, dx = \int_{-1}^1 f(u)\, du$$
$$= \Sigma \text{ weight} \times f(u)$$
$$= \frac{5}{9} f(-\sqrt{3/5}) + \frac{8}{9} f(0) + \frac{5}{9} f(\sqrt{3/5})$$

Similarly, the integration may be determined by one-point formula, four-point formula and five-point formula, not covered here as they are not in syllabus.

Example 3.4 : Evaluate $\displaystyle\int_0^1 \frac{1}{x+2}\, dx$ using

1. Gauss quadrature two-point formula.
2. Gauss quadrature three-point formula.

Determine error with respect to analytical integration.

Solution : To convert the integration in the form having f(u).

Let $a = 0$, $b = 1$

∴ Using conversion formula

$$x = \left(\frac{b-a}{2}\right) u + \left(\frac{b+a}{2}\right)$$

∴ $\quad x = \dfrac{u}{2} + \dfrac{1}{2}$

∴ $\quad x = \dfrac{u+1}{2}$

and differentiating both sides, we get

$$dx = \frac{du}{2}$$

∴ $\quad I = \displaystyle\int_0^1 \frac{1}{x+2}\, dx$

$$= \int_{-1}^1 \frac{1}{\left(\dfrac{u+1}{2}\right) + 2} \cdot \frac{du}{2}$$

$$= \int_{-1}^{1} \frac{2}{(u+1+4)} \frac{du}{2}$$

$$\therefore \quad I = \int_{-1}^{1} \left(\frac{1}{u+5}\right) du$$

Thus, $\quad f(u) = \dfrac{1}{u+5}$

According to two-point formula,

$$I_1 = f(-\sqrt{1/3}) + f(\sqrt{1/3})$$

$$= \frac{1}{-\sqrt{1/3}+5} + \frac{1}{\sqrt{1/3}+5}$$

$$= 0.405405405$$

According to three-point formula,

$$I_2 = \frac{5}{9} f(-\sqrt{3/5}) + \frac{8}{9} f(0) + \frac{5}{9} f(\sqrt{3/5})$$

$$= \frac{5}{9}\left(\frac{1}{-\sqrt{3/5}+5}\right) + \frac{8}{9}\left(\frac{1}{0+5}\right) + \frac{5}{9}\left(\frac{1}{\sqrt{3/5}+5}\right)$$

$$= 0.40546448$$

Analytically, $\quad I_3 = \int_{0}^{1} \frac{1}{x+2} dx$

$$= [\ln(x+2)]_0^1$$

$$= \ln 3 - \ln 2$$

$$= 0.405465108$$

% Error in numerical integration by two-point formula

$$= \frac{|I_3 - I_1|}{I_3} \times 100$$

$$= 0.014724571$$

% Error in numerical integration by three-point formula

$$= \frac{|I_3 - I_2|}{I_3} \times 100$$

$$= 1.548838575 \times 10^{-4}$$

$$= \mathbf{0.00015488} \qquad \text{... Ans.}$$

3.5.3 Algorithm for Gauss Quadrature Two-Point Formula

1. Define f(x) to be integrated.
2. Get lower limit from user *l*.
3. Get upper limit from user u.
4. c = (u − *l*)/2.
5. d = (u + *l*)/2.
6. First = f(c * −1/sqrt (3) + d);
7. Second = f(c/sqrt (3) + d);
8. Integration = c * (first + second);
9. Print integration.
10. End.

3.5.4 Flow Chart for Gauss Quadrature Two-Point Formula

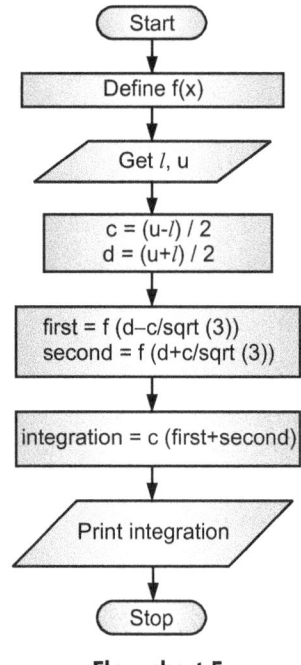

Flow chart 5

3.5.6 Algorithm for Gauss Quadrature Three-Point Formula

1. Define f(x) to be integrated.
2. Get lower limit from user *l*.
3. Get upper limit from user u.

4. c = (u − l)/2.
5. d = (u + l)/2.
6. First = f(d − c * sqrt (3/5)).
7. Second = f(0).
8. Third = f(d + c * sqrt (3/5)).
9. Integration = c/9 * (5 * first + 8 * second + 5 * third).
10. Print integration.
11. End.

3.5.7 Flow Chart for Gauss Quadrature Three-Point Formula

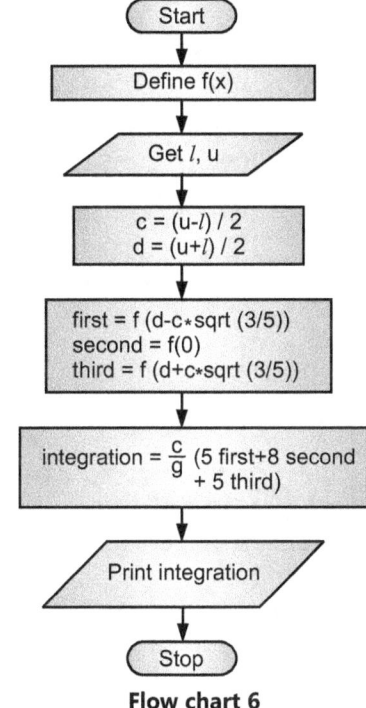

Flow chart 6

3.5.8 Matlab Code For Gauss Quadrature 2 Point and 3 Point Formula

```
fprintf('\n****************************************************');
fprintf('\n****************** NUMERICAL INTEGRATION ******************');
fprintf('\n****************** GAUSS QUADRATURE METHOD ******************');
fprintf('\n****************************************************');

fstr = input('\n Input Function String f(x) >>> ','s');
```

```
f=inline(fstr);                    % Function Declaration
disp(sprintf(['\n    y = f(x) = ' fstr]));

a = input('\n Enter Lower Limit (x0): ');
b = input('\n Enter Upper Limit (xn): ');

A = (b-a)/2;
B = (b+a)/2;

%% For Gauss 2 point formula
c1 = 1;
c2 = 1;
I = c1*f(A*(-sqrt(1/3))+B)+c2*f(A*sqrt(1/3)+B);
I1 = A*I;
fprintf('\n\t Numerical Solution for Integral >>> %f by Gauss Quadrature 2 Point Formula',I1);

%% For Gauss 3 point formula
c1 = 5/9;
c2 = 8/9;
c3 = 5/9;
I = c1*f((A*(-sqrt(3/5)))+B)+c2*f(B)+c3*f((A*sqrt(3/5))+B);
I2 = A*I;
```

3.6 MATLAB FOR NUMERICAL INTEGRATION

Matlab uses trapz (x, y) function which uses Trapezoidal rule to integrate the function y.

Following is the example to evaluate $\int_{\pi/4}^{3\pi/8} \sin x \, dx$ with strip width = $\pi/32$.

>> x = pi/4 : pi/32 : 3 * pi/8;

This defines array a with starting value $\pi/4$, ending value $3\pi/8$ and difference between two consecutive values $\pi/32$.

>> y = sin(x);

This stores all f(x) in $y_0, y_1, y_2, \ldots$

>> **trapz (x, y)**
ans =
0.3242
>>

This gives numerical integration's value. We have solved the same problem earlier using Trapezoidal rule. Readers may compare the answers.

Example 3.5 : *Evaluate the same integral with 7 data points.*

>> x = pi/4 : (3 * pi/8 − pi/4)/6 : 3 * pi/8;
>> y = sin(x);

Solution :

>> **trapz = (x, y)**
ans =
   0.3243
>>

Example 3.6 : *Determine numeric value of integration* $\int_{2.2}^{3.4} (x^3 - 2x^2 + 7x - 5)\, dx$ *assuming 8 strips for integration (in other words, 9 data points).*

Solution : Following are the steps for solution :
1. Define x values.
2. Get corresponding y values.
3. Use trapz (x, y) function.

>> x = 2.2 : (3.4 − 2.2)/8 : 3.4;

This defines all x values.

If semicolon (;) is not typed the values will be displayed as response to the command.

>> y = x ^ 3 − 2 * x ^ 2 + 7 * x − 5;

This command will result in error. Because x is not a single value. It is an array of 9 values. Hence to use one value at a time and evaluate corresponding y value type the command carefully as below.

>> y = x. ^ 3 − 2 * x. ^ 2 + 7 * x − 5;

   Observe that it is x. ^ 3 and not x ^ 3.
   Further, it is x. ^ 2 and not x ^ 2.

Now get numeric value of integration by trapz ( ) function.

>> **trapz (x, y)**
ans =
    25.9968
>>

Further, we may use cumtrapz (x, y) to see cumulative results of integration.

>> **cumtrapz (x, y)**
ans =
   Columns 1 through 7
      0   1.8563   4.0319   6.5624   9.4864   12.8456   16.6847

Columns 8 through 9
21.0515   25.9968

\>\>

These values represent numeric value of integration upto $x_0, x_1, x_2, \ldots x_8$ respectively.

Example 3.7 : Evaluate $\int_0^4 \sqrt{x}\, dx$ assuming 5 data points.

Solution : We will see a new method of defining x and f(x). Also, a new function for integration.

\>\> x = 0 : 1 : 4;

This defines $x_0 = 0, x_1 = 1, x_2 = 2, x_3 = 3, x_4 = 4$.

\>\> sqroot = inline ('x. ^0.5');

This defines a function as

sqroot (x) = x. ^ 0.5

\>\> **quad (sqroot, 0, 4)**

ans =

5.3333

\>\>

Here quad ( ) function is used to evaluate integration which work on quadrature rule.

As we have defined inline function there is no need to generate for x values. Thus, only two functions are sufficient :

1. **to define function – inline.**
2. **to evaluate integration – quad.**

SOLVED EXAMPLES

Example 3.8 : *The velocity of car running on a straight road at the interval of 2 minutes is given below.*

Time (min)	0	2	4	6	8	10	12
Velocity (km/hr)	0	22	30	27	18	7	0

Find the distance covered by the car using Simpson's $1/3^{rd}$ rule.

Solution : Distance travelled = $\int v\, dt$

where, velocity must be in km/min, so that after multiplication with time in minute it will produce answer in km.

Therefore, let us rewrite the table as,

Time (min)	0	2	4	6	8	10	12
Velocity (km/min)	0	11/30	0.5	9/20	0.3	7/60	0

According to Simpson's $1/3^{rd}$ rule,

$$I = \frac{h}{3}[(y_0 + y_6) + 4(y_1 + y_3 + y_5) + 2(y_2 + y_4)]$$

$$= \frac{2}{3}\left[(0 + 0) + 4\left(\frac{11}{30} + \frac{9}{20} + \frac{7}{60}\right) + 2(0.5 + 0.3)\right]$$

$$= \frac{2}{3}\left[4 \times \frac{56}{60} + 1.6\right] = \mathbf{3.5556 \text{ km}}$$

Thus, distance travelled by the car in these 12 minutes is 3.5556 km. ... **Ans.**

Example 3.9 : *Find the area under the curve and x-axis. Curve passes through the following points*

(1.00, 2.00), (1.50, 2.40), (2.00, 2.70), (2.50, 2.80), (3.00, 3.00), (3.50, 2.60)
(4.00, 2.10)

Solution : The above points can be written as

x	1	1.5	2	2.5	3	3.5	4
y	2	2.4	2.7	2.8	3	2.6	2.10

By Tapezoidal rule, we have

$$\int_1^4 y \cdot dx = \frac{h}{2}[(y_0 + y_n) + 2(y_1 + y_2 + y_3 + y_4 + y_5)]$$

Here, $h = 0.5$

$$= \frac{0.5}{2}[(2 + 2.10) + 2(2.4 + 2.7 + 2.8 + 3 + 2.6)]$$

$$= \mathbf{7.775} \qquad \text{... Ans.}$$

Example 3.10 : *Integrate the function*

$$f(x) = \cos(2*x)/(1 + \sin x)$$

using Gauss Legendre rule, between the limits 2 and 3.

Solution : Gauss Legendre means Gauss quadrature method requires conversion of f(x) to f(u).

∴ Substituting $x = \left(\dfrac{b-a}{2}\right)u + \left(\dfrac{b+a}{2}\right)$

where, a = 2 and b = 3

∴ $x = \left(\dfrac{3-2}{2}\right)u + \left(\dfrac{3+2}{2}\right)$

∴ $x = \dfrac{u}{2} + \dfrac{5}{2} = \dfrac{u+5}{2}$

$$\therefore \quad dx = \frac{1}{2} du$$

$$\therefore \quad I = \int_2^3 f(x)\, dx = \int_{-1}^1 \frac{\cos 2\left(\frac{u+5}{2}\right)}{1 + \sin\left(\frac{u+5}{2}\right)} \cdot \frac{1}{2} du$$

$$= \int_{-1}^1 \frac{\cos(u+5)}{2\left(1 + \sin\left(\frac{u+5}{2}\right)\right)} du$$

$$\therefore \quad f(u) = \frac{\cos(u+5)}{2\left(1 + \sin\left(\frac{u+5}{2}\right)\right)}$$

Now according to Gauss Legendre 3-point formula,

$$I = \frac{5}{9} f(-\sqrt{3/5}) + \frac{8}{9} f(0) + \frac{5}{9} f(\sqrt{3/5})$$

where, $f(-\sqrt{3/5}) = \dfrac{\cos\left(-\sqrt{3/5} + 5\right)}{2\left(1 + \sin\left(\dfrac{-\sqrt{3/5} + 5}{2}\right)\right)} = -0.12602$

$$f(0) = \frac{\cos(5)}{2(1 + \sin(5/2))} = 0.08873$$

$$f(\sqrt{3/5}) = \frac{\cos\left(\sqrt{3/5} + 5\right)}{2\left(1 + \sin\left(\dfrac{\sqrt{3/5} + 5}{2}\right)\right)}$$

$$= 0.34894$$

∴ Numerical value of integration is

$$I = \frac{5}{9}(-0.12602) + \frac{8}{9}(0.08873) + \frac{5}{9}(0.34894)$$

∴ $\quad I = 0.20272$ ... **Ans.**

Example 3.11 : *A body is in the form of a solid of revolution. The diameter D in cm of its sections at distance x cm from one end is given below. Estimate volume of the solid using Simpson's 1/3rd rule.*

x	0	2.5	5.0	7.5	10.0	12.5	15.0
D	5	5.5	6.0	6.75	6.25	5.5	4.0

Solution : The volume of the solid is given as,

$$V = \frac{\pi}{4} \cdot D^2 \times L$$

Here length of the solid is taken along x-axis. So we get,

$$V = \int_0^{15} \frac{\pi}{4} \cdot D^2 \cdot dx$$

$$\int_0^{15} \frac{\pi}{4} \cdot D^2 \cdot dx = \frac{h}{3}\left[\left(D_0^2 + D_6^2\right) + 4\left(D_1^2 + D_3^2 + D_5^2\right) + 2\left(D_2^2 + D_4^2\right)\right]$$

$$= \frac{\pi}{4} \times \frac{2.5}{3}[(25 + 16) + 4(30.25 + 45.56 + 30.25 + 2(36 + 39.06)]$$

Volume = **402.54 cm³** ... Ans.

Example 3.12 : Evaluate $\int_0^3 (2x - x^2)\, dx$, taking 6 intervals by Trapezoidal rule.

Solution : $x_0 = 3$, $x_n = x_6 = 3$ as number of intervals, n = 6.

The interval width $= \dfrac{x_n - x_0}{n} = \dfrac{3 - 0}{6} = 0.5$.

∴ Values of x and y are,

$x_0 = 0$ ⇒ $y_0 = 0$
$x_1 = 0.5$ ⇒ $y_1 = 0.75$
$x_2 = 1$ ⇒ $y_2 = 1$
$x_3 = 1.5$ ⇒ $y_3 = 0.75$
$x_4 = 2$ ⇒ $y_4 = 0$
$x_5 = 2.5$ ⇒ $y_5 = -1.25$
$x_6 = 3$ ⇒ $y_6 = -3$

According to Trapezoidal rule,

$$I = \frac{h}{2}[(y_0 + y_6) + 2(y_1 + y_2 + y_3 + y_4 + y_5)]$$

$$= \frac{0.5}{2}[(0 - 3) + 2(0.75 + 1 + 0.75 + 0 - 1.25)]$$

∴ I = **− 0.125** ... Ans.

Note : Verify the integration by analytical method. It is evaluated as zero. Hence, what we get here is an error due to Trapezoidal strips. Use Simpson's 1/3rd formula and we will observe that answer of integration comes out as zero.

Example 3.13 : Evaluate $\int_0^\pi \dfrac{\sin^2 x}{e^x + \cos x} dx$ using Simpson's 3/8th rule. Take six strips.

Solution : $\int_0^\pi \dfrac{\sin^2 x}{e^x + \cos x} \cdot dx$

By considering six strips, the corresponding values of function are obtained as follows :

$$f(x) = \dfrac{\sin^2(x)}{e^x + \cos(x)}$$

$$h = \dfrac{\text{Upper limit} - \text{Lower limit}}{\text{Number of strips}}$$

$$= \dfrac{\pi - 0}{6} = \dfrac{\pi}{6}$$

x	0	π/6	π/3	π/2	2π/3	5π/6	π
y	0	0.0979	0.2239	0.2078	0.0984	0.0195	0

According to Simpson's 3/8th rule,

$$\int_0^\pi \dfrac{\sin^2 x}{e^x + \cos x} \cdot dx = \dfrac{3h}{8}[(y_0 + y_6) + 3(y_1 + y_2 + y_4 + y_5) + 2(y_3)]$$

Here, substituting the values in above formula, we get

$$= \dfrac{3}{8} \times \dfrac{\pi}{6} [(0 + 0) + 3(0.0979 + 0.2239 + 0.0984 + 0.0195) + 2(0.2078)]$$

$$= 0.1963 [1.3191 + 0.4156] = \mathbf{0.3405} \qquad \text{... Ans.}$$

Example 3.14 : Evaluate $\int_0^1 \int_0^1 e^{(x+2y)} dx\, dy$ using Simpson's 1/3rd rule. Take h = k = 0.025.

Solution : Variables x and y both are varying from 0 to 1 with interval of 0.25.

∴ $x_0 = y_0 = 0$
$x_1 = y_1 = 0.25$
$x_2 = y_2 = 0.5$
$x_3 = y_3 = 0.75$
$x_4 = y_4 = 1$

The integration formula is,

$$I = \frac{h}{3} \cdot \frac{k}{3} \sum_{\substack{i=0 \\ j=0}}^{\substack{j=4 \\ i=4}} w_{ij}\, f(x_i, y_j)$$

where, weight matrix is written as $w_{ij} = \begin{bmatrix} 1 & 4 & 2 & 4 & 1 \\ 4 & 16 & 8 & 16 & 4 \\ 2 & 8 & 4 & 8 & 2 \\ 4 & 16 & 8 & 16 & 4 \\ 1 & 4 & 2 & 4 & 1 \end{bmatrix}$

Let us tabulate values of $f(x_i, y_j)$ alongwith multiplication factors from weight matrix.

x→ \ y↓	0	0.25	0.5	0.75	1
0	1 × 1	1.649 × 4	2.718 × 2	4.482 × 4	7.389 × 1
0.25	1.284 × 4	2.117 × 16	3.49 × 8	5.755 × 16	9.488 × 4
0.5	1.649 × 2	2.718 × 8	4.482 × 4	7.389 × 8	12.182 × 2
0.75	2.117 × 4	3.49 × 16	5.755 × 8	9.488 × 16	15.643 × 4
1	2.718 × 1	4.482 × 4	7.389 × 2	12.182 × 4	20.086 × 1

Integration = $\frac{h}{3} \times \frac{k}{3} \times$ Summation of all elements of above table.

∴ I = **5.49107** ... **Ans.**

Example 3.15 : *The velocity v(km/hr) of a vehicle which starts from rest, is given at fixed intervals of time t (min) as follows.*

Time (min)	2	4	6	8	10	12	14	16	18	20
Velocity (km/hr)	10	18	25	29	32	20	11	05	02	00

Estimate approximately the distance covered in 20 minutes.

Solution : The distance travelled is integration of velocity curve drawn with respect to time. But as units are not matching, let us rewrite the table with time in minutes and velocity in km/min.

Time (min)	2	4	6	8	10	12	14	16	18	20
Velocity (km/hr)	1/6	0.3	5/12	29/60	8/15	1/3	11/60	1/12	1/30	00

These are 10 data points, thus 9 intervals. But the description says that vehicle starts from rest i.e. at t = 0, v = 0, is the first data point. Thus, total number of intervals is 10. Hence, we can apply Simpson's 1/3rd rule.

Accordingly, integration will be

$$I = \frac{h}{3}[(y_0 + y_{10}) + 4(y_1 + y_3 + y_5 + y_7 + y_9) + 2(y_2 + y_4 + y_6 + y_8)]$$

$$= \frac{2}{3}[(0 + 0) + 4(1/6 + 5/12 + 8/15 + 11/60 + 1/30)$$

$$+ 2(0.3 + 29/60 + 1/3 + 1/2)]$$

I = **5.1556 km** ... **Ans.**

Thus distance travelled in 20 minutes is 5.1556 km.

Problems For Practice

1. A spaceship is travelling with a speed that can be expressed as

$$V = \left\{2000 \ln\left[\frac{140000}{140000 - 2100\,t}\right] - 9.8\,t\right\} \text{ m/s}$$

   Using Gauss quadrature 2-point formula determine the distance it travelled in first eight seconds of flight. Using Gauss quadrature 3-point formula determine the distance it travelled from 8th second to 30th second.

   [**Ans.** : 687.284 m, 11061 m]

2. On indicator diagram of an engine, following values of pressure and volume are recorded in power stroke.

P (mPa)	7.5	0.428	0.23	0.157	0.12	0.096	0.08
V (m³)	0.01	0.07	0.13	0.19	0.25	0.31	0.37

   Determine the work that engine has produced using Simpson's $3/8^{th}$ rule.

   [**Ans.** : 236.6162 kJ]

3. Evaluate $\int \sin^2 x \cdot \sin(x^2)/e^x \, dx$ from $x = 0.5$ to $x = 1.2$ with interval width to be 0.1.

   [**Ans.** : By Trapezoidal rule I = 0.06189]

4. Evaluate $\int_{-2.5}^{3.5} (x^3 - 7x^2 + 5x - 3) \, dx$ using Simpson's $1/3^{rd}$ rule with 6 intervals.

   [**Ans.** : 111.75]

5. A circle is drawn with centre at the origin (0, 0) with radius of 10 units. Determine area of a circle using Gauss quadrature 2-point formula.

   [**Hint** : Equation of circle $x^2 + y^2 = r^2$ must be arranged as $y = \sqrt{r^2 - x^2}$.

   Then area of circle = $4 \int_0^{10} \sqrt{r^2 - x^2} \, dx$]

   [**Ans.** : Area of circle = 318.445208]

6. Evaluate $\int_0^1 3x^2 \, dx$ with 6 intervals, using :
   (a) Trapezoidal rule.
   (b) Simpson's $1/3^{rd}$ rule.

   [**Ans.** : Trapezoidal rule – I = 1.013889, Simpson's $1/3^{rd}$ rule – I = 1.0000]

7. A cantilever beam is loaded with a varying load. The variation of the load is modeled as,

   Load per unit length = xe^x kN/m.

   Determine total load on the beam if its length is 500 mm, using Gauss Legendre's 3-point formula.

   [**Ans.** : Total load = 0.1756 kN]

9. Acceleration of an object is given by,
   $$f(t) = \sqrt{t} \cdot \sin^2 t \text{ m/s}^2.$$
   Using Simpson's $3/8^{th}$ rule for six intervals, determine distance travelled by the object in 12 seconds.

   [**Hint** : Numerical integration of $\int_0^{12} \sqrt{t} \cdot \sin^2 t \, dt$ is average speed in the span of 12 seconds. Hence, to determine distance travelled multiply the integration value by 12 seconds]

   [**Ans.** : Distance = 174.938 m]

10. Water is flowing through a channel whose shape is described by x and y coordinates as below.

x (cm)	0	10	20	30	40	50
y (cm)	0	7	18	16	4	0

Neglecting other factors, determine maximum volume flow rate of water in m^3/hr if its velocity is 2 m/s.

[**Hint** : Q = VA, where A is to be obtained by integration]
[**Ans.** : Area = 450 cm^2, Q = 324 m^3/hr]

REVIEW QUESTIONS

1. Using Gauss-Legendre three point method find $\int (x^2 - 5x + 3) \, dx$ in the limits 3 to 5.

2. The data listed in table gives measurements of heat flux q at the surface of a solar collector. Estimate the total heat absorbed by a 2×10^5 cm^2 collector panel during 14 hr period. The panel has an absorption efficiency ε = 42%. The total heat absorbed is given by

$$H = \varepsilon \int_0^t qA \, dt$$

where A is area, q is heat flux and t is time.

t (hr)	0	1	2	3	4	6	8	11	14
q (cal/cm².hr)	0.05	1.72	5.23	6.38	7.86	8.05	8.03	5.82	0.24

Use Simpson's 1/3 rd Rule.

3. Draw flow chart for Simpson's 3/8th Rule.
4. Find double integral of f (x, y) = $x^2 + y^2 + 5$ for x = 0 to 2 and y = 0 to 2 taking increments in both x and y as 0.5.
5. Write a flow chart to write a Newton's forward table.
6. Draw flow-chart for numerical integration using Simpson's 1/3rd rule, of given function y = f (x) between the limits a and b.
7. Evaluate $\int_0^1 \frac{1}{1+x^2} dx$. Use 3 point Gauss Legendre method.
8. Draw flowchart for integration by 3/8th Simpson rule.
9. Explain the trapezoidal rule, simpson's 1/3rd method and simpson's 3/8th rule, using graphical representation.
10. Draw a flowchart for Simpson's 3/8 rule of integration.
11. An axial pull of 300 KN is applied at one end of the shaft whose modulus of elasticity is $200*10^9$ N/m² .The axial elongation of the shaft (Δ) is given by,

$$\Delta x = (P/E) \int_0^1 (1/A) \times dx.$$ Where A is cross sectional area of shaft. Determine elongation of shaft over the entire length by Simpson'3 rule.

12. Use Simpson's 1/3rd rule to estimate following integration :

$$\int_1^2 \frac{e^x}{x} dx.$$

13. Explain what is meant by Simpson's strip for 1/3rd rule and 3/8th rule ? Explain why Simpson's 3/8th rule give more accuracy compared to trapezoidal and Simpson's 1/3rd rule with same number of strips.
14. Draw flow chart for Simpson's 3/8 rule.
15. Calculate the value of the following function by Simpson's 1/3rd rule usind 11 ordinates.

$$\int_0^{\pi/2} \sin x \cdot dx$$

16. Draw the flow chart for modified Newton's Raphson's method.
17. How could we improve the accuracy of a numerical integration process?
18. Explain concept used in Gauss Quadrature method.
19. Physically, integrating $\int_a^b f(x)\,dx$ means finding the

    (a) area under the curve from a to b
    (b) area to the left of point a
    (c) area to the right of point b
    (d) area above the curve from a to b

20. The mean value of a function f (x) from a to b is given by

    (a) $\dfrac{f(x) + f(b)}{2}$

    (b) $\dfrac{f(a) + 2f\left(\dfrac{a+b}{2}\right) + f(b)}{4}$

    (c) $\int_a^b f(x)\,dx$

    (d) $\dfrac{\int_a^b f(x)\,dx}{b - a}$

21. The area of a circle of radius a can be found by the following integral

    (a) $\int_0^a (a^2 - x^2)\,dx$

    (b) $\int_0^{2\pi} \sqrt{a^2 - x^2}\,dx$

    (c) $4\int_0^a (a^2 - x^2)\,dx$

    (d) $\int_0^a (a^2 - x^2)\,dx$

22. For a definite integral of any third order polynomial, the two-point Gauss quadrature rule will give the same results as the

   (i) 1-segment trapezoidal rule
   (ii) 2-segment trapezoidal rule
   (iii) 3-segment trapezoidal rule
   (iv) Simpson's 1/3 rule

23. $\int_{5}^{10} f(x)\,dx$ is exactly

   (a) $\int_{-1}^{1} f(2.5x + 7.5)\,dx$

   (b) $2.5 \int_{-1}^{1} f(2.5x + 7.5)\,dx$

   (c) $5 \int_{-1}^{1} f(5x + 5)\,dx$

   (d) $5 \int_{-1}^{1} (2.5x + 7.5) f(x)\,dx$

24. Show graphical representation of each method.

25. Write realistic applications of this experiment in brief (at least two applications).

Chapter 4
SOLUTIONS OF ORDINARY DIFFERENTIAL EQUATIONS (ODE)

4.1 INTRODUCTION

Differential equations occur in engineering and sciences as mathematical models of physical phenomenon. For example, equation of motion, Simple Harmonic Motion (SHM), deflection of beam, heat flow equations, etc. represented by differential equations.

For example, the motion of a damped spring-mass system is given by

$$m \cdot \frac{d^2x}{dt^2} + c\frac{dx}{dt} + kx = 0 \qquad \ldots (4.1)$$

where,
- x — displacement from equilibrium position (m)
- t — time (s)
- m — mass (kg)
- c — damping coefficient (N-s/m)
- k — spring stiffness (N/m)

Such equations which contain unknown functions and its derivatives are called as differential equations. These type of equations sometimes referred as **rate equations** because it expresses rate of change of a variable as a function of variables and parameters. Such equations play very important role in engineering and science applications because many physical phenomena are best formulated mathematically as rate of change.

In above equation (4.1), quantity being differentiated (x) is called as **dependent variable**. The quantity with respect to which x is differentiated, t, is called as **independent variable**.

4.2 CLASSIFICATION OF DIFFERENTIAL EQUATIONS

When function involves one independent variable, the equation is called as **Ordinary Differential Equation (ODE)**.

Example, $\quad \dfrac{d^2\theta}{dt^2} + \dfrac{g}{l}\sin\theta = 0 \qquad \ldots$ Motion of simple pendulum

When function involves two or more than two independent variables, it is called as **Partial Differential Equation**.

Example, $\quad \dfrac{\partial^2 u}{\partial x^2} + \dfrac{\partial^2 u}{\partial y^2} = f(x, y) \qquad \ldots$ Poisson's equation

Ordinary differential equations are also classified in terms of order and degree.

- **Order** is same as the *highest order derivative*.
- **Degree** is the *power of highest order derivative*.

Example, $\quad x^3 \cdot \dfrac{d^3y}{dx^3} + x\dfrac{d^2y}{dx^2} + x^2 \cdot \dfrac{dy}{dx} + xy = e^x \quad$ ... Order = 3 and Degree = 1

$\quad\quad\quad\quad \left(\dfrac{dy}{dx} + 1\right)^2 + x^2 \cdot \dfrac{dy}{dx} = \sin x \quad$ ... Order = 1 and Degree = 2

4.3 TAYLOR'S SERIES METHOD

Consider the differential equation

$$\dfrac{dy}{dx} = f(x, y) \quad\quad\quad ...(4.2)$$

which is to be solved, subjected to the initial conditions $x = x_0$ and $y = y_0$.

If $y = f(x)$ is the solution of the equation, Taylor's series expansion about $x = x_0$, gives

$$y = f(x) = f(x_0) + (x - x_0) \cdot f'(x_0) + \dfrac{(x - x_0)^2}{2!} f''(x_0) + \dfrac{(x - x_0)^3}{3!} f'''(x_0) + ...$$

Also, it can be written as

$$y = y_0 + (x - x_0) \cdot y'_0 + \dfrac{(x - x_0)^2}{2!} \cdot y''_0 + \dfrac{(x - x_0)^3}{3!} \cdot y'''_0 + ...$$

where, $\quad y'_0 = \left(\dfrac{dy}{dx}\right)_{x = x_0}, \quad y''_0 = \left(\dfrac{d^2y}{dx^2}\right)_{x = x_0}, ...$

Derivatives $y'_0, y''_0, ...$, etc. can be found from equation 4.1 while y_0 is known as initial condition.

Note :

1. Taylor's series has advantage that it is derived in any order and values of y(x) are easily obtained.
2. However, method is time consuming due to calculation of higher order derivatives.

Example 4.1 : *Find by Taylor's series method, the values of y at x = 0.1 and x = 0.2 to five decimals from* $\dfrac{dy}{dx} = x^2y - 1, y(0) = 1$.

Solution : Given data : $x = 0, y_0 = 1$ at $x = x_0$.

Equation, $\quad \dfrac{dy}{dx} = x^2y - 1$

i.e. $\quad\quad y' = x^2y - 1 \quad\quad\quad$ ... (I)

Substituting values of x_0, y_0, we get

$$y'_0 = x_0^2 y_0 - 1 = 0 - 1$$

$$\boxed{y'_0 = -1}$$

Differentiating successively and substituting, we get

$$y''_0 = 2x_0 y_0 + x_0^2 y'_0$$

$$= 2(0)(1) + (0)^2 \times 1$$

$$\therefore \boxed{y''_0 = 0}$$

$$y'''_0 = \frac{d}{dx}(2x_0 y_0) + \frac{d}{dx}\left(x_0^2 y'_0\right)$$

$$= 2y_0 + 2x_0 y'_0 + 2x_0 y'_0 + x_0^2 y''_0$$

$$= 2y_0 + 4x_0 y'_0 + x_0^2 y''_0$$

$$\therefore \quad y'''_0 = 2 \times (1) + 4 \times (0) \times (-1) + (0)^2 \cdot (0)$$

$$\therefore \boxed{y'''_0 = +2}$$

$$y^{iv}_0 = 6y'_0 + 6x_0 \cdot y''_0 + x_0^2 \cdot y'''_0$$

$$\therefore \quad y^{iv}_0 = 6 \times (-1) + 6 \times (0) \times (0) + (0)^2 \times 2$$

$$\therefore \boxed{y^{iv}_0 = -6}$$

By Taylor's series, we have

$$y = y_0 + (x - x_0) \cdot y'_0 + \frac{(x - x_0)^2}{2!} y''_0 + \frac{(x - x_0)^3}{3!} y'''_0 + \frac{(x - x_0)^4}{4!} y^{iv}_0 + \ldots$$

Substituting values of $x_0 = 0$, $y_0 = 1$ and $y'_0, y''_0, y'''_0, y^{iv}_0$, we get

$$y = y_0 + x \cdot y'_0 + \frac{x^2}{2} \cdot y''_0 + \frac{x^3}{6} \cdot y'''_0 + \frac{x^4}{24} y^{iv}_0 + \ldots$$

$$y = 1 + x \cdot (-1) + \frac{x^2}{2}(0) + \frac{x^3}{6}(2) + \frac{x^4}{24}(-6) + \ldots$$

$$\boxed{y = 1 - x + \frac{x^3}{3} - \frac{x^4}{4} + \ldots} \quad \ldots \text{(II)}$$

To find value of y at x = 0.1, substitute x = 0.1 in equation (I).

$$y(0.1) = 1 - (0.1) + \frac{(0.1)^3}{3} - \frac{(0.1)^4}{4} + ...$$

∴ $y(0.1) = 1 - 0.1 + 0.3333 - 0.025 + ...$

$\boxed{y(0.1) = 0.90030}$ ... Ans.

Also, $y(0.2) = 1 - 0.2 + \frac{(0.2)^3}{3} - \frac{(0.2)^4}{4} + ...$

$\boxed{y(0.2) = 0.80227}$ ... Ans.

Example 4.2 : *Evaluate y(0.1) correct upto four decimal places using Taylor's series method, if $\frac{dy}{dx} = x^2 + y^2, y(0) = 1$.*

Solution : Given data :

$$\frac{dy}{dx} = y' = x^2 + y^2$$

$$x_0 = 0, \; y_0 = 1$$

Differentiating given equation successively and substituting values of x_0, y_0, we get,

$$y'_0 = x_0^2 + y_0^2$$

$$y'_0 = (0)^2 + 1^2$$

∴ $\boxed{y'_0 = 1}$

$$y''_0 = 2x + 2y \cdot y'$$

∴ $y''_0 = 2x_0 + 2y_0 \cdot y'_0$

$$= 2 \times (0) + 2 \times (1) \times (1)$$

∴ $\boxed{y''_0 = 2}$

$$y'''_0 = 2 + 2(y')^2 + 2y \cdot y''$$

∴ $y'''_0 = 2 + 2 \times (1)^2 + 2 \times (1) \times (2)$

∴ $y'''_0 = 2 + 2 + 4$

∴ $\boxed{y'''_0 = 8}$

$$y_0^{iv} = 4 \cdot y' \cdot y'' + 2y \cdot y''' + 2y' \cdot y''$$
$$= 6 \cdot y'y'' + 2 \cdot y \cdot y'''$$

∴ $y_0^{iv} = 6 \times (1) \times (2) + 2 \times (1) \times (8)$

∴ $y_0^{iv} = 12 + 16$

∴ $\boxed{y_0^{iv} = 28}$

Putting these values in Taylor's series, we have

$$y = y_0 + (x - x_0)\, y_0' + \frac{(x - x_0)^2}{2!} y_0'' + \frac{(x - x_0)^3}{3!} y_0''' + \frac{(x - x_0)^4}{4!} y_0^{iv} + \ldots$$

$x = 0.1$, $x_0 = 0$, $y_0 = 1$

∴ $y(0.1) = 1 + (0.1 - 0) \times (1) + \frac{(0.1 - 0)^2}{2} \times (2) + \frac{(0.1 - 0)^3}{6} \times 8$

$\qquad + \frac{(0.1 - 0)^4}{26} \times 28 \ldots$

$\qquad = 1 + 0.1 + 0.1^2 + 1.3333 \times 0.1^3 + 1.16667 \times 0.1^4 + \ldots$

$\boxed{y(0.1) = 1.11145}$ ... Ans.

4.4 ALGORITHM - TAYLOR SERIES METHOD

1. Input initial values x_0 and y_0 and given value of x_n.
2. Calculate n.
3. Call dfun(dy/dy), d2fun(d^2y/dy^2), d3fun(d^3y/dy^3), d4fun(d^4y/dy^4).
4. Repeat, for k = 1 to n, increment k by 1.
5. z = 0.
6. Repeat, for i = 1 to 4, increment i by 1.
7. b = 1.
8. Repeat, for j = 1 to i, increment j by 1.
9. b = b × j.
10. end loop j.
11. y_1 = (pow(h, i) × A[i])/b.
12. z = z + y_1.
13. end loop i.
14. y = y_0 + z, x_0 = x_0 + h and y_0 = y.
15. end loop k.
16. print solution.

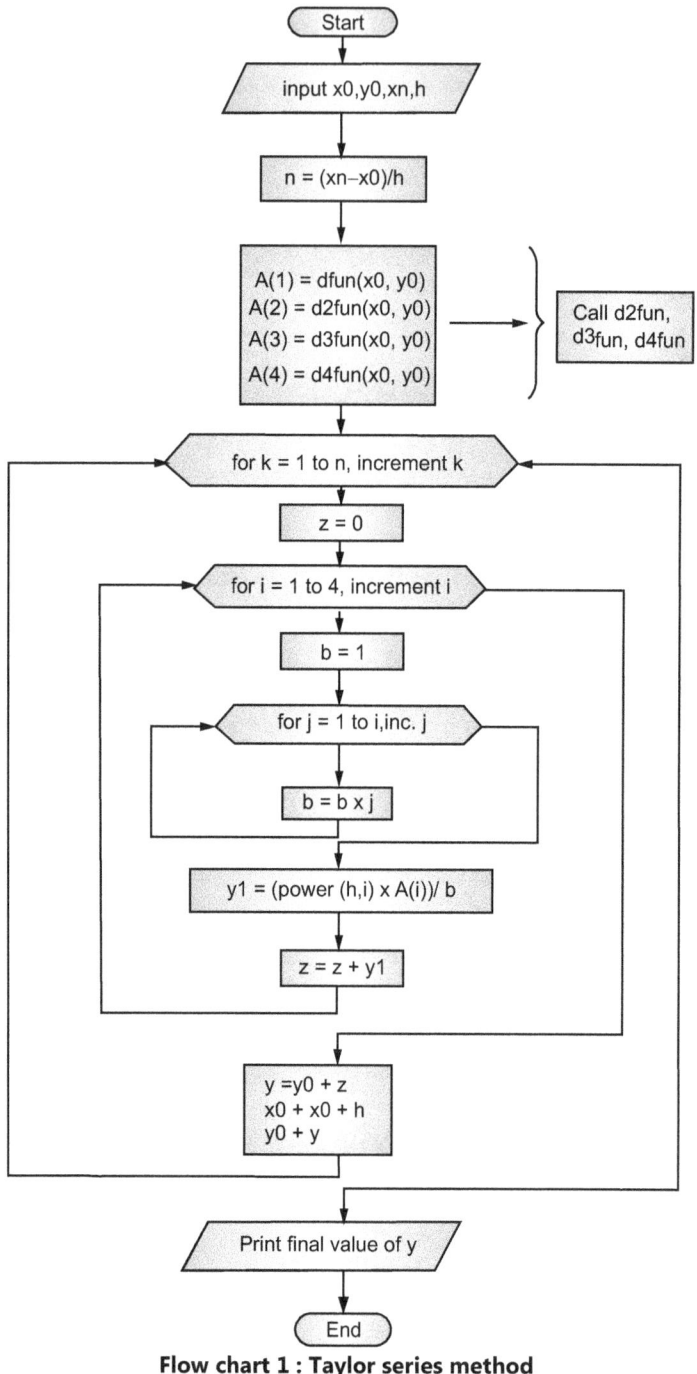

Flow chart 1 : Taylor series method

Matlab :

```matlab
% Ordinary Differential Equations
% Method - Taylor's Series
% Function dy/dx = f(x) = x² + y²

fprintf('\n*************************************************************');
fprintf('\n Ordinary Differential Equations by Taylors Series Method');
fprintf('\n*************************************************************');

x0 = input ('\n Enter Initial Value of X0 = ');
y0 = input ('\n Enter Initial Value of Y0 = ');
xn = input ('\n Enter the given value of Xn = ');
h = input ('\n Enter Interval (h) = ');

% Calculation of no. of steps >>
n=(xn-x0)/h;

x = x0;
y = y0;

for k = 1:n
    A(1)= x*x+y*y;                          % dy/dx
    A(2)= 2*x + 2*y*A(1);                   % d2y/dx2
    A(3)= 2 + 2*A(1)*A(1) + 2*y*A(2);       % d3y/dx3
    A(4)= 6*A(1)*A(2) + 2*y*A(3);           % d4y/dx4
    z=0;
    for i=1:4
        b=1;
        for j=1:i
        b=b*j;
        end
        y1=(power(h,i)*A(i));
        y1=y1/b;
        z=z+y1;
    end
```

```
    y=y+z;
    x=x+h;
    y0=y;
    fprintf('\n The value of Y(%f) = %f',x,y);
end
```

Output :

```
******************************************************************************
Numerical Solution of Ordinary Differential Equations by Taylor's Series Method
******************************************************************************
Enter Initial Value of X0 = 0
Enter Initial Value of Y0 = 1
Enter the given value of Xn = 0.1
Enter Interval (h) = 0.1
The value of Y(0.100000) = 1.111450
```

C Program :

```c
// Numerical Solution of Ordinary Differential Equations
// Program for Taylor's Series Method

#include<stdio.h>
#include<conio.h>
#include<math.h>

float dfun(float x,float y)
{
    return(x*x+y*y);
}

float d2fun(float x,float y)
{
    return(2*x+2*y*dfun(x,y));
}

float d3fun(float x,float y)
{
    return(2+2*(y*d2fun(x,y)+dfun(x,y)*dfun(x,y)));
}
float d4fun(float x,float y)
{
    return(2*(y*d3fun(x,y)+3*dfun(x,y)*d2fun(x,y)));
}
```

```c
void main()
{
    float x0,y0,x,h,y,y1,A[5],z;
    int i,j,k,n,b;
    clrscr();

    printf("\n Enter the initial value of Xo:\t");
    scanf("%f",&x0);
    printf("\n Enter initial value of Yo:\t");
    scanf("%f",&y0);
    printf("\n Enter the given value of X:\t");
    scanf("%f",&x);
    printf("\n Enter the value of step size h:\t");
    scanf("%f",&h);
    n=(x-x0)/h;
    A[1]=dfun(x0,y0);
    A[2]=d2fun(x0,y0);
    A[3]=d3fun(x0,y0);
    A[4]=d4fun(x0,y0);
    for(k=1;k<=n;k++)
    {
        z=0;
        for(i=1;i<=4;i++)
        {
            b=1;
            for(j=1;j<=i;j++)
            {
                b=b*j;
            }
            y1=(pow(h,i)*A[i]);
            y1=y1/b;
            z=z+y1;
        }
        y=y0+z;
        x0=x0+h;
        y0=y;
    }
    printf("\n The final value of Y:\t= %f",y);
    getch();
}
```

Output :
Enter the initial value of Xo: 0
Enter initial value of Yo: 1
Enter the given value of X: 0.1
Enter the value of step size h: 0.1
The final value of Y: = 1.111450

Example 4.3 : *Find the values of y at x = 0.1 and x = −0.1, using Taylor's series method of third order, given that* $\frac{dy}{dx} = \frac{1}{x+y}$, $y(0) = 2.$

Solution : Given : $y' = \frac{1}{x+y}$ ... (I)

Differentiating equation (I) successively w.r.t. x, we get,

$$y'' = -\frac{1}{(x+y)^2}(1+y') \quad \text{... (II)}$$

$$y''' = -\left[\frac{(x+y)^2 \cdot y'' - (1+y')^2 \times 2(x+y)}{(x+y)^4}\right] \quad \text{... (III)}$$

Taking $x_0 = 0$ and $y_0 = 2$ and putting in equations, (II) and (III), we have

$y'_0 = 0.5$

$y''_0 = -0.375$

$y'''_0 = 0.65625$

Now, by Taylor's series method,

$$y_{(x_0 + h)} = y_0 + (x - x_0) \cdot y'_0 + \frac{(x - x_0)^2}{2!}y''_0 + \frac{(x - x_0)^3}{3!}y'''_0$$

where, $h = x - x_0$

∴ $y_{(0.1)} = 2 + (0.1 - 0) \times 0.5 + \frac{(0.1 - 0)^2}{2} \times (-0.375) + \frac{(0.1 - 0)^3}{6} \times 0.65625$

$\boxed{y_{(0.1)} = 2.0482}$

Substituting $h = -0.1$, we get,

$y(-0.1) = 2 + (-0.1 - 0) \times 0.5 + \frac{(-0.1 - 0)^2}{2!} \times (-0.375) + \frac{(-0.1 - 0)^3}{3!}$

$\times (0.65625) + ...$

$= 2 - 0.1 \times 0.5 + \frac{0.01}{2} \times (-0.375) - \frac{0.001}{6} \times 0.65625$

$= 2 - 0.05 - 0.00188 - 0.00011$

∴ $\boxed{y(-0.1) = 1.948016}$ ... **Ans.**

4.5 EULER'S METHOD

Consider the equation $\frac{dy}{dx} = f(x, y)$, which is to be solved subjected to the initial conditions at $x = x_0, y = y_0$.

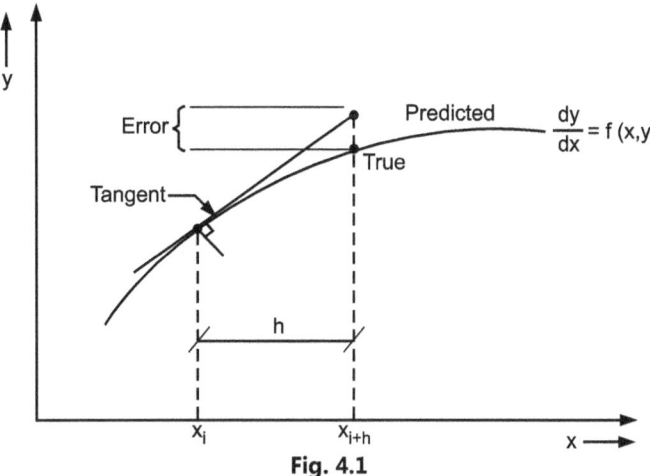

Fig. 4.1

To obtain values of y_1 at $x = x_1 = (x_0 + h)$ where h is the interval between x_0 and x_1, we have,

$$\frac{dy}{dx} = f(x, y)$$

∴ $\quad dy = f(x, y) \cdot dx$

Integrating both sides, with limits x_0 to x_1 and y_0 to y_1

$$\int_{y_0}^{y_1} dy = \int_{x_0}^{x_1} f(x, y) \cdot dx$$

∴ $\quad y_1 - y_0 = f(x_0, y_0) \times [x]_{x_0}^{x_1}$

∴ $\quad y_1 = y_0 + (x_1 - x_0) \cdot f(x_0, y_0)$

∴ $\quad y_1 = y_0 + h \cdot f(x_0, y_0)$

Similarly, $\quad y_2 = y_1 + h \cdot f(x_1, y_1)$

$\quad y_3 = y_2 + h \cdot f(x_2, y_2)$

.
.
.

$\quad y_n = y_{n-1} + h \cdot f(x_{n-1}, y_{n-1})$

Generalized formula for Euler's method can be written as

$$\boxed{y_{i+1} = y_i + h \cdot f(x_i, y_i)} \quad \text{where } i = 0, 1, 2, \ldots n.$$

Example 4.4 : Find y(2.2) by using Euler's method for $\frac{dy}{dx} = -xy^2$ where $y(2) = 1$. Consider $h = 0.1$.

Solution : Given data :

$$\frac{dy}{dx} = -x \cdot y^2$$

$$h = 0.1$$

∴ $x_1 = x_0 + h$

∴ $x_1 = 2 + 0.1$

∴ $\boxed{x_1 = 2.1}$

$x_2 = x_1 + h$ or $x_0 + n \cdot h$ ..... n – number of steps
$= 2.1 + 0.1$ or $2.2 + 2 \times 0.1$

∴ $\boxed{x_2 = 2.2}$

By using Euler's method, we have

$$y_1 = y_0 + h \cdot f(x_0, y_0)$$

We have

$$f(x_0, y_0) = -x_0 \, y_0^2$$
$$= -2 \times (1)^2$$

∴ $f(x_0, y_0) = -2$

∴ $y_1 = 1 + 0.1 \times (-2)$

∴ $y_1 = 0.8$

$f(x_1, y_1) = -x_1 \cdot y_1^2 = -(2.1) \times (0.8)^2 = -1.344$

Similarly, $y_2 = y_1 + h \cdot f(x_1, y_1)$

∴ $y_2 = 0.8 + 0.1 \times (-1.344)$

∴ $\boxed{y_2 = 0.6656}$

∴ $\boxed{y = 0.6656 \text{ at } x = 2.2}$ ... Ans.

Algorithm for Euler's Method :

1. Input x_0, y_0 and n
2. Calculate h
3. Assign $xa[1] = x_0$, $ya[1] = y_0$
4. Repeat for i – 1 to n, increment i by 1
5. Calculate $xa[i + 1]$ and $ya[i + 1]$
6. print xa and ya
7. end loop for i
8. End

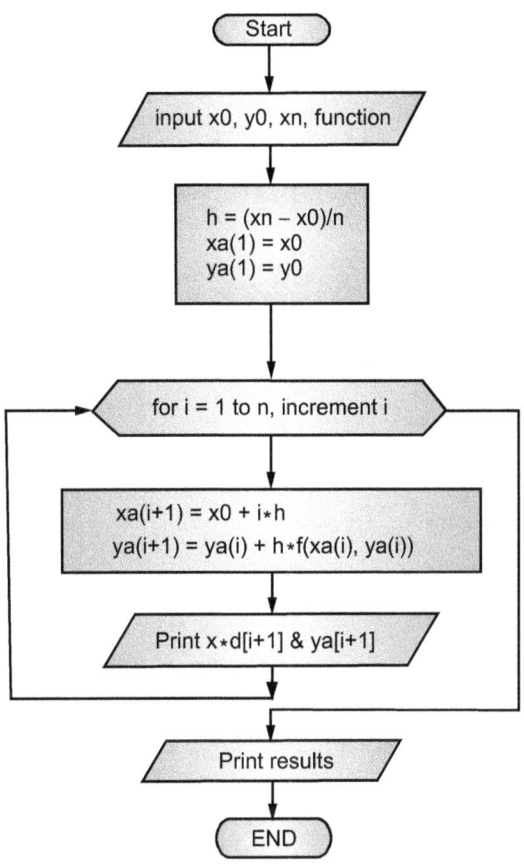

Flow chart 2 : Euler's method

Euler's Method

```
fprintf('\n***********************************************************');
fprintf('\n Ordinary Differential Equations by Eulers Method');
fprintf('\n***********************************************************');
fstr = input('\n Input Function String >>> ','s');
f=inline(fstr);  % Function Declaration
disp(sprintf(['\n    dy/dx = f(x,y) = ' fstr]))

x0 = input('\n Enter initial value of x (X0) = ');
y0 = input('\n Enter initial value of y (Y0) = ');
xn = input('\n Enter Final value of x (Xn) = ');
```

```
n = input ('\n No. of Steps (n)= ');

format short g;
h=(xn-x0)/n;
disp(sprintf('     h = ( xn - x0 ) / n '))
disp(sprintf('       = ( %g - %g ) / %g ',xn,x0,n))
disp(sprintf('       = %g',h))
xa(1)=x0 ;
ya(1)=y0 ;

fprintf('\n  X \t\t Y \t\t f(x,y)');
fprintf('\n%.2f \t %.4f \t %.4f', xa(1),ya(1),f(xa(1),ya(1)));
for i = 1:n
   xa(i+1) = x0 + i*h;
   fun=f(xa(i),ya(i));
   ya(i+1)=ya(i)+h*fun;
   fprintf('\n%.2f \t%.4f \t%.4f',xa(i+1),ya(i+1),f(xa(i+1),ya(i+1)));
end;

% To find Exact solution of dy/dx = f(x,y)
xspan = [x0 xn];
[x,y]=ode45(f,xspan,y0);

% Plotting the Exact and Approximate solution of the ODE.
hold on
xlabel('x');
ylabel('y');
title('Exact and Approximate Solution of the ODE by Euler Method');
plot(x,y,'--','LineWidth',2,'Color',[1 0 0]);
plot(xa,ya,'-','LineWidth',2,'Color',[0 0 0]);
legend('Exact','Approximation');
```

Output :
```
*******************************************************
Numerical Solution of Ordinary Differential Equations by Eulers Method
*******************************************************
```
Input Function String >>> -x*y*y
  dy/dx = f(x,y) = -x*y*y
Enter initial value of x (X0) = 2
Enter initial value of y (Y0) = 1
Enter final value of x (Xn) = 2.2
No. of steps (n) = 2
  h = (xn - x0) / n
    = (2.2 - 2) / 2
    = 0.1

X	Y	f(x,y)
2.00	1.0000	−2.0000
2.10	0.8000	−1.3440
2.20	0.6656	−0.9747

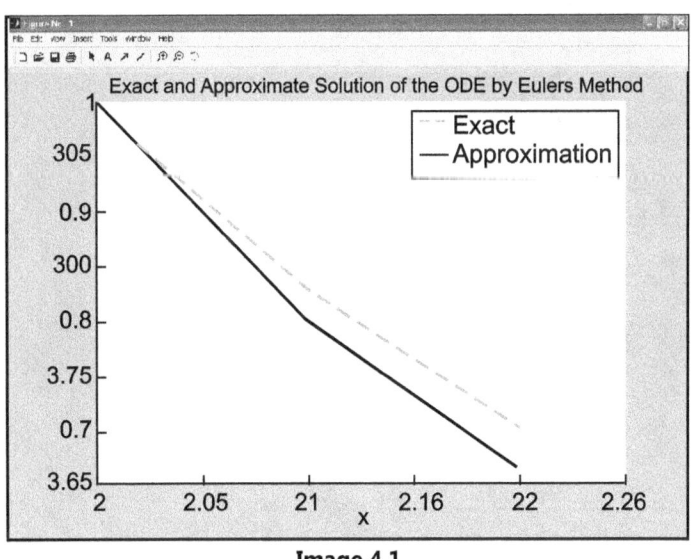

Image 4.1

Example 4.5 : Solve $\dfrac{dy}{dx} = \sqrt{x^2 + y}$ using Euler's method to find y at x = 0.4.
Given y = 1 at x = 0. Take h = 0.2.
Solution : Given data :
$$\dfrac{dy}{dx} = \sqrt{x^2 + y} \implies f(x_0, y_0) = \sqrt{x_0^2 + y_0} = \sqrt{0^2 + 1} = 1.0$$

$$h = 0.2$$
$$x_0 = 0, \quad y_0 = 1$$
$$x_1 = x_0 + h = 0 + 0.2$$
$$\therefore \quad x_1 = 0.2$$
$$x_2 = x_1 + h = 0.2 + 0.2$$
$$\therefore \quad x_2 = 0.4$$

By Euler's method,
$$y_1 = y_0 + h \cdot f(x_0, y_0)$$
$$\therefore \quad y_1 = 1 + 0.2 \times (1.0)$$
$$\therefore \quad \boxed{y_1 = 1.2} \qquad \text{... Ans.}$$

$$\therefore \quad f(x_1, y_1) = \sqrt{x_1^2 + y_1}$$
$$= \sqrt{0.2^2 + 1.2}$$
$$\therefore \quad f(x_1, y_1) = 1.113552$$
$$\Rightarrow \quad f(x_0, y_0) = \sqrt{x_0^2 + y_0}$$
$$= \sqrt{0^2 + 1}$$
$$= 1.0$$
$$y_2 = y_1 + h \cdot f(x_1, y_1)$$
$$\therefore \quad y_2 = 1.2 + 0.2 \times 1.113552$$
$$\therefore \quad y_2 = 1.42271$$
$$\therefore \quad \boxed{y = 1.42271 \text{ at } x = 0.4} \qquad \text{... Ans.}$$

Example 4.6 : Solve $\dfrac{dy}{dx} = \dfrac{y-x}{y+x}$ using Euler's method to find y at x = 0.1.
Given y(0) = 1 and h = 0.02.

Solution : Given data : $x_0 = 0$, $y_0 = 1$ $\Rightarrow$ $f(x_0, y_0) = \dfrac{y_0 - x_0}{y_0 + x_0} = \dfrac{1-0}{1+0} = 1.00$

h = 0.02, $y_{(0.1)}$ = ?
$$n = \frac{x - x_0}{h} = \frac{0.1 - 0}{0.02} = 5$$
$$\therefore \quad x_1 = x_0 + h = 0.02$$
$$\therefore \quad x_1 = 0.02, \ x_2 = 0.04, \ x_3 = 0.06, \ x_4 = 0.08, \ x_5 = 0.10.$$

By using Euler's method,
$$y_1 = y_0 + h \cdot f(x_0, y_0)$$
$$\therefore \quad y_1 = 1 + 0.02 \times 1.0$$
$$\therefore \quad y_1 = 1.02$$

$$f(x_1, y_1) = \frac{y_1 - x_1}{y_1 + x_2} = \frac{1.02 - 0.02}{1.02 + 0.02} = 0.9615$$

Repeating above step, we get,

i	x_i	y_i	$f(x_i, y_i)$
0	0	1	1.0
1	0.02	1.02	0.9615
2	0.04	1.0392	0.9259
3	0.06	1.0577	0.8926
4	0.08	1.0756	0.8615
5	0.10	1.0928	

∴ $\boxed{y_{(0.1)} = 1.0928}$ ... Ans.

Example 4.7 : Solve $5x \cdot \frac{dy}{dx} + y^2 - 2 = 0$; $y(4) = 1$ for $y(4.1)$ and $y(4.2)$, taking $h = 0.05$.

Solution : Given data :

$$5x \cdot \frac{dy}{dx} + y^2 - 2 = 0$$

∴ $$\frac{dy}{dx} = \left(\frac{2 - y^2}{5x}\right) = f(x, y)$$

$x_0 = 4, \quad y_0 = 1$
$h = 0.05$

∴ $$f(x_0, y_0) = \frac{2 - y_0^2}{5x_0}$$

$$= \frac{2 - 1^2}{5 \times 4} = \frac{1}{20} = 0.050$$

∴ $y_1 = y_0 + h \cdot f(x_0, y_0)$
$= 1 + 0.05 \times 0.05$

∴ $y_1 = 1.0025$

Similarly, we get,

i	x_i	y_i	$f(x_i, y_i)$
0	4.0	1.0	0.050
1	4.05	1.0025	0.0491
2	4.1	1.0050	0.0483
3	4.15	1.0074	0.0475
4	4.20	1.0097	–

∴ $\boxed{y_{(0.1)} = 1.0050}$

and $\boxed{y_{(0.2)} = 1.0097}$ ... Ans.

Improvements in Euler's Method

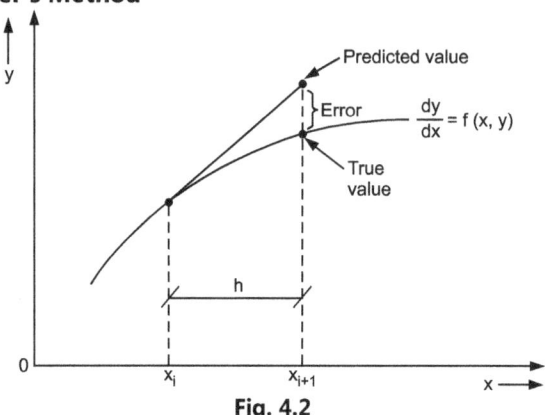

Fig. 4.2

The fundamental source of error in Euler's method is derivative taken at initial condition and it is assumed to be constant across total interval. This error can be reduced by reducing step size or interval.

Two simple modifications are available to overcome shortcomings of this method.

Method I : In this method, slope at initial point and at final point is calculated by Euler's method. Then, average of these two slopes is taken.

At the beginning of Euler's method, slope or $\dfrac{dy}{dx}$ is given by,

$$\dfrac{dy}{dx} = f(x_i, y_i)$$

Therefore, by Euler's method, we have,

$$y_{i+1}^0 = y_i + h \cdot f(x_i, y_i)$$

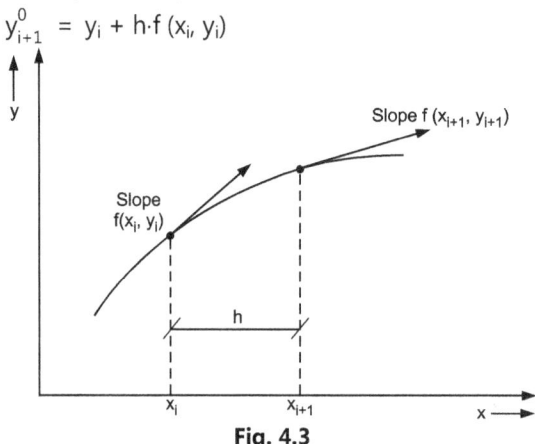

Fig. 4.3

By considering this value of y_{i+1}^0, we get slope at the end of interval given by

$$\dfrac{dy}{dx} = f(x_{i+1}, y_{i+1}^0)$$

By taking average of these two slopes, we have,

$$\left(\frac{dy}{dx}\right)_{avg} = \frac{f(x_i, y_i) + f(x_{i+1}, y_{i+1}^0)}{2}$$

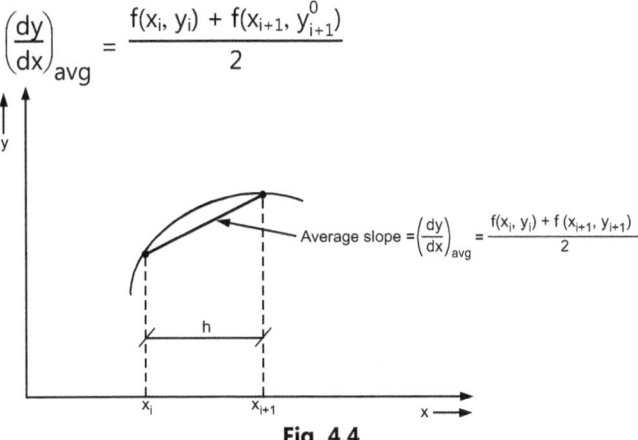

Fig. 4.4

By using this average slope and Euler's formula, we have,

$$y_{i+1} = y_i + h\left[\frac{f(x_i, y_i) + f(x_{i+1}, y_{i+1}^0)}{2}\right]$$

$$\therefore \quad y_{i+1}^{(1)} = y_i + \frac{h}{2} \cdot \left[f(x_i, y_i) + f\left(x_{i+1}, y_{i+1}^{(0)}\right)\right]$$

Similarly, $\quad y_{i+1}^{(2)} = y_i + \frac{h}{2} \cdot \left[f(x_i, y_i) + f\left(x_{i+1}, y_{i+1}^{(1)}\right)\right]$

$$\vdots$$

$$y_{i+1}^{n+1} = y_i + \frac{h}{2}\left[f(x_i, y_i) + f(x_{i+n}, y_{i+n})\right]$$

This method is called as **Improved Euler's method** or **Heun's method**.

Method II :

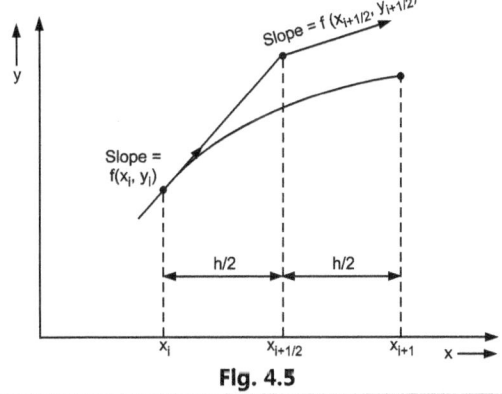

Fig. 4.5

In this method, slope at initial point and mid-point of interval is taken. Then average of these two slopes is taken.

Slope at mid-point is given by,

$$\frac{dy}{dx} = f(x_{i+1/2}, y_{i+1/2})$$

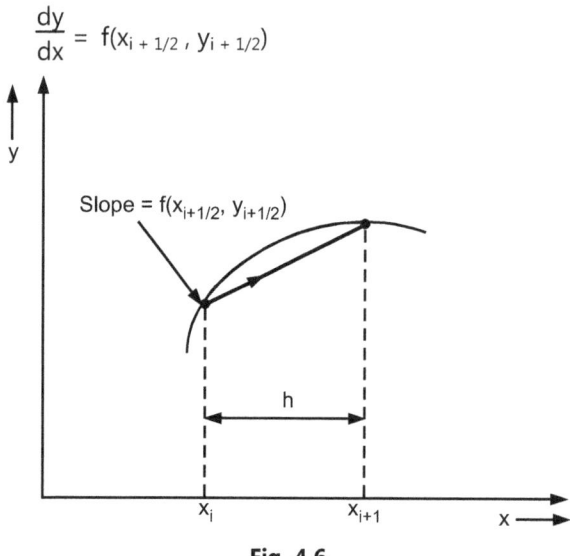

Fig. 4.6

By considering this slope value, we have,

$$y_{i+1} = y_i + h \cdot f(x_{i+1/2}, y_{i+1/2})$$

Note : Since, above formula does not contain y_{i+1}, term on both sides, it can only be used as predictor formula and not as corrector formula.

4.6 ALGORITHM FOR MODIFIED EULER'S METHOD

1. Input x_0, y_0, x_n, n and acc.
2. Calculate h $(=(x_n - x_0)/n)$.
3. Repeat loop for i = 1 to n, increment i by 1.
4. Calculate y_1 and y_2.
5. While $|y_2 - y_1|$ > acc, calculate y_1 and y_2.
6. $x_0 = x_0 + h$ and $y_0 = y_1$
7. Print results.
8. End for loop.
9. End

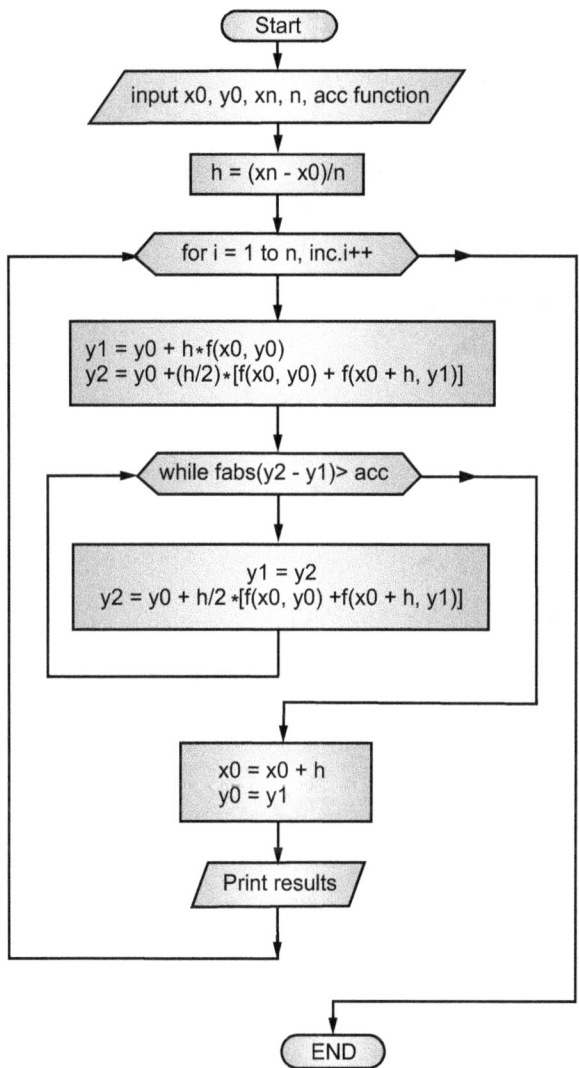

Flow chart 3 : Modified Euler's method

Matlab :

```
% Numerical Solution of Ordinary Differential Equations

fprintf('\n*************************************************************');
fprintf('\n \tNumerical Solution of ODE by Modified Eulers Method');
fprintf('\n*************************************************************');
fstr = input('\n\nInput Function String >>>','s'); %% Function definition
```

```
f=inline(fstr);
disp(sprintf(['\n    f(x,y) = dy/dx = ' fstr]))

x0 = input('\n Enter initial value of x (X0) = ');
y0 = input('\n Enter initial value of y (Y0) = ');
xn = input('\n Enter Final value of x (Xn) = ');
n = input('\n Enter No. of steps (n) = ');
acc = input ('\n Accuracy (acc)= ');

format short g;

h=(xn-x0)/n;
disp(sprintf('    h = ( xn - x0 ) / n '))
disp(sprintf('      = ( %g - %g ) / %g ',xn,x0,n))
disp(sprintf('      = %g',h))
xa(1)=x0 ;
ya(1)=y0 ;

for i=1:n
    xa(i+1)=xa(i)+h;
    y1=y0+h*f(x0,y0);
    y2=y0+((h/2)*(f(x0,y0)+f(x0+h,y1)));
    k=1;
    while abs(y2-y1)>acc
        k=k+1;
        y1=y2;
        y2=y0+((h/2)*(f(x0,y0)+f(x0+h,y1)));
        fprintf('\n itn#%d Y(%d) = %f',k,i,y2);
    end
    ya(i+1)=y2;
    x0=x0+h;
```

```
    y0=y1;
    fprintf('\nx%d = %.2f\t Y%d = %.8f',i,x0,i,y0);
end
fprintf('\n The final value of Y:\t=%.8f',y0);

% Plotting the Approximate solution of the ODE.
hold on
xspan = [x0 xn];
xlabel('X');
ylabel('Y');
title('Approximate Solution of the ODE by Modified Eulers Method');
plot(xa,ya,'-','LineWidth',2,'Color',[0 1 0]);
legend('Approximation');
```

Output :

```
**********************************************************************
    Numerical Solution of ODE by Modified Eulers Method
**********************************************************************
Input Function String >>>x+y
    f(x,y) = dy/dx = x+y
 Enter initial value of x (X0) = 0
 Enter initial value of y (Y0) = 1
 Enter Final value of x (Xn) = 0.1
 Enter No. of steps (n) = 2
 Accuracy (acc)= 0.000001
    h = ( xn - x0 ) / n
      = ( 0.1 - 0 ) / 2
      = 0.05
itn#2 Y(1) = 1.052563
 itn#3 Y(1) = 1.052564
 itn#4 Y(1) = 1.052564
 x1 = 0.05    Y1 = 1.05256406
```

itn#2 Y(2) = 1.110386

itn#3 Y(2) = 1.110388

itn#4 Y(2) = 1.110388

x2 = 0.10   Y2 = 1.11038782

The final value of Y :   = 1.11038782

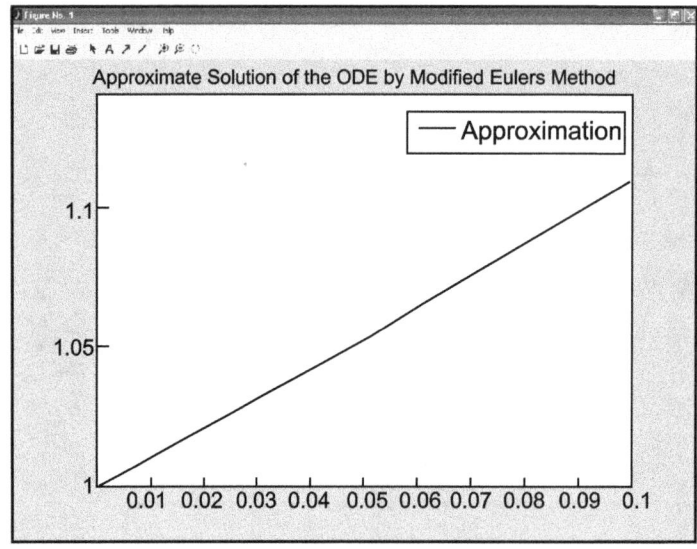

Image 4.2

Example 4.8 : Given $\dfrac{dy}{dx} = x + y$ with initial condition $y(0) = 1$. Find $y(0.05)$ and $y(0.1)$ correct upto 5 decimal places by using modified Euler's method.

Solution : Given data : $x_0 = 0$, $y_0 = 1$, $h = 0.05$.

By using Euler's method, we have

$$y_1 = y_0 + h \cdot f(x_0, y_0)$$

$\therefore \quad y_1 = 1 + 0.05 \times (x_0 + y_0)$

$\therefore \quad y_1 = 1 + 0.05 \times (0 + 1)$

$\therefore \quad \boxed{y_1 = 1.05} = y_1^{(0)}$

To improve accuracy of y_1, by using modified Euler's method, we have

$$y_1^{(1)} = y_0 + \dfrac{h}{2} [f(x_0, y_0) + f(x_1, y_1^{0})]$$

$$= 1 + \frac{0.05}{2}[(0+1) + (0.05 + 1.05)]$$

$$= 1.0525$$

$$y_1^{(2)} = y_0 + \frac{h}{2}[f(x_0, y_0) + f(x_1, y_1^1)]$$

$$= 1 + \frac{0.05}{2}[(0+1) + (0.05 + 1.0525)]$$

$$= 1.0525625$$

$$y_1^{(3)} = 1 + \frac{0.05}{2}[(0+1) + (0.05 + 1.0525625)]$$

$$= 1.052564$$

By comparing $y_1^{(2)}$ and $y_1^{(3)}$, solution is correct upto 5th decimal places.

∴ $\boxed{y_{(0.5)} = 1.052564}$ ... Ans.

Again by using Euler's method,

$$y_2 = y_1 + h \cdot f(x_1, y_1)$$

∴ $$y_2 = 1.052564 + 0.05 \times (0.05 + 1.052564)$$

$$y_2 = 1.1076922$$

By using modified Euler's method, we have

$$y_2^{(1)} = y_1 + \frac{h}{2}[f(x_1, y_1) + f(x_2, y_2^0)]$$

∴ $$y_2^{(1)} = 1.052564 + \frac{0.05}{2}[(0.05 + 1.052564) + (0.1 + 1.1076922)]$$

$$= 1.1120511$$

$$y_2^{(2)} = 1.052564 + \frac{0.05}{2}[(0.05 + 1.052564) + (0.1 + 1.1120511)]$$

$$= 1.1104294$$

$$y_2^{(3)} = 1.052564 + \frac{0.05}{2}[(0.05 + 1.052564) + (0.1 + 1.1104294)]$$

$$= 1.1103888$$

$$y_2^{(4)} = 1.052564 + \frac{0.05}{2}[(0.05 + 1.052564) + (0.1 + 1.1103888)]$$

$$= 1.1103888$$

Comparing $y_2^{(3)}$ and $y_2^{(4)}$, we have accuracy upto 5th digit.

∴ $\boxed{y_{(0.1)} = 1.1103888}$ ... Ans.

Example 4.9 : *By using modified Euler's method, find y(0.1), y(0.2), y(0.3), y(0.4) for $\frac{dy}{dx} = \log_{10}(x^2 + y)$ for y(0) = 1, h = 0.1 and accuracy upto 4th digit.*

Solution : Given data :

$$\frac{dy}{dx} = \log_{10}(x^2 + y) = f(x, y)$$

$$x_0 = 0, \quad y_0 = 1$$

$$h = 0.1$$

By using Euler's method, we have,

$$y_1 = y_0 + h \cdot f(x_0, y_0) \quad \Rightarrow \quad y_1 = 1 + 0.1 \times \log_{10}(x_0^2 + y_0)$$

$$= 1 + 0.1 \times \log_{10}(0^2 + 1)$$

$$= 1.00 = y_1^{(0)}$$

$$y_1^{(1)} = y_0 + \frac{h}{2}[f(x_0, y_0) + f(x_1, y_1^{(0)})]$$

$$= 1 + \frac{0.1}{2}[\log_{10}(0^2 + 1) + \log_{10}(0.1^2 + 1.0)]$$

$$= 1.000221$$

Similarly, $y_1^{(2)} = y_0 + \frac{h}{2}[f(x_0, y_0) + f(x_1, y_1^{(1)})]$

$$= 1 + \frac{0.1}{2}[\log_{10}(0^2 + 1) + \log_{10}(0.1^2 + 1.000221)]$$

∴ $y_1^{(2)} = 1.000216$ ..... correct upto 4th decimal place.

∴ $\boxed{y(0.1) = 1.000216}$ ... Ans.

For y_2 i.e. $y_{(0.2)}$,

$$y_2 = y_1 + h \cdot f(x_1, y_1)$$

$$= 1.000216 + 0.1 \times \log_{10}(0.1^2 + 1.000216)$$

$$y_2 = 1.000657 = y_2^{(0)}$$

By using modified Euler's method, we have,

$$y_2^{(1)} = y_1 + \frac{h}{2}[f(x_1, y_1) + f(x_2, y_2^{(0)})]$$

$$= 1.000657 + \frac{0.1}{2}[\log_{10}(0.1^2 + 1.000216) + \log_{10}(0.2^2 + 1.000657)]$$

$y_2^{(1)}$ = 1.001316

Similarly,

$y_2^{(2)}$ = 1.001316

∴ $\boxed{y(0.2) = 1.001316}$ ... Ans.

Repeating previous steps, for x = 0.3, we get,

$y_3^{(0)}$ = 1.003074

$y_3^{(1)}$ = 1.004148

$y_3^{(2)}$ = 1.004149

∴ $\boxed{y(0.3) = 1.004149}$ ... Ans.

and $\boxed{y(0.4) = 1.009501}$ ... Ans.

Example 4.10 : Solve equation $5x \cdot \frac{dy}{dx} + y^2 - 2 = 0$, $y(4) = 1$ for $y(4.1)$ and $y(4.2)$, taking $h = 0.1$ by modified Euler's method.

Solution : Given data :

$$5x \cdot \frac{dy}{dx} + y^2 - 2 = 0$$

∴ $$\frac{dy}{dx} + \frac{y^2 - 2}{5x} = 0$$

∴ $$\frac{dy}{dx} = f(x, y)$$

$$= \frac{2 - y^2}{5x}$$

$h = 0.1$

$x_0 = 4, \quad y_0 = 1$

By using Euler's method,

$y_1 = y_0 + h \cdot f(x_0, y_0)$

$= 1 + 0.1 \times \left(\dfrac{2 - 1^2}{5 \times 4}\right)$

$= 1.0050$

By using modified Euler's formula, we get,

$y_1^{(1)} = y_0 + \dfrac{h}{2} [f(x_0, y_0) + f(x_1, y_1^{(0)})]$

$= 1 + \dfrac{0.1}{2} \left[\left(\dfrac{2 - 1^2}{5 \times 4}\right) + \left(\dfrac{2 - 1.005^2}{5 \times 4.1}\right)\right]$

Similarly, $y_1^{(2)} = 1 + \dfrac{0.1}{2}\left[\left(\dfrac{2-1^2}{5\times 4}\right) + \left(\dfrac{2-1.004915^2}{5\times 4.1}\right)\right]$

$= 1.004915$

$\therefore \quad \boxed{y_{(4.1)} = 1.004915}$ ... Ans.

Similarly,

$y_2 = y_1 + h\cdot f(x_1, y_1)$ ... Euler's formula

$= 1.004915 + 0.1 \times \left(\dfrac{2-1.004915^2}{5\times 4.1}\right)$

$= 1.009745 = y_2^{(0)}$

By modified Euler's formula,

$y_2^{(1)} = y_1 + \dfrac{h}{2}[f(x_1, y_1) + f(x_2, y_2^{(0)})]$

$= 1.004915 + \dfrac{0.1}{2}\left[\left(\dfrac{2-1.004915^2}{5\times 4.1}\right) + \left(\dfrac{2-1.009745^2}{5\times 4.2}\right)\right]$

$= 1.009665$

Similarly,

$y_2^{(2)} = 1.009665$

$\therefore \quad \boxed{y_{(4.2)} = 1.009665}$ ... Ans.

4.7 RUNGE-KUTTA METHODS

Runge-Kutta method is one of the earliest and most widely used numerical methods of solving ordinary differential equations of the order. It is suitable for differential equations where the computation of higher order derivative is complicated.

These methods are distinguished by their orders in the sense they agree with Taylor's series method. These methods are developed to avoid the computation of higher order derivatives in Taylor's series. In place of these derivatives, extra values of given function f(x, y) are used.

4.7.1 Runge-Kutta 2nd Order Method

Consider differential equation $\dfrac{dy}{dx} = f(x, y)$ subjected to initial condition $y(0) = y_0$.

Let $h = x_1 - x_0$ i.e. interval between x (equidistant).

Then by Runge-Kutta 2nd order method, first increment in y is calculated as follows :

$k_1 = h\cdot f(x_0, y_0)$

$k_2 = h\cdot f(x_0 + h, y_0 + k_1)$

$\therefore \quad \Delta y = \dfrac{1}{2}(k_1 + k_2)$

Then, $x_1 = x_0 + h$
and $y_1 = y_0 + \Delta y_0$

i.e. $\boxed{y_1 = y_0 + \frac{1}{2}(k_1 + k_2)}$

Similarly, next increments of y are calculated as

$$y_2 = y_1 + \frac{1}{2}(k_1 + k_2)$$

where, $k_1 = h \cdot f(x_1, y_1)$ and
$k_2 = h \cdot f(x_1 + h, y_1 + k)$

∴ Generalized formula for Runge-Kutta 2nd order method can be written as,

$$y_{i+1} = y_i + \frac{1}{2}(k_1 + k_2)$$

where, $k_1 = h \cdot f(x_i, y_i)$
and $k_2 = h \cdot f(x_i + h, y_i + k_1)$

Note : This method coincides with Taylor's series upto terms of h^2.

4.7.2 Runge-Kutta 4th Order Method

By Runge-Kutta 4th order method, first increment in y is computed from the formulae,

$$k_1 = h \cdot f(x_0, y_0)$$
$$k_2 = h \cdot f\left(x_0 + \frac{h}{2}, y_0 + \frac{k_1}{2}\right)$$
$$k_3 = h \cdot f\left(x_0 + \frac{h}{2}, y_0 + \frac{k_2}{2}\right)$$
$$k_4 = h \cdot f(x_0 + h, y_0 + k_3)$$

∴ $\Delta y = \dfrac{k_1 + 2k_2 + 2k_3 + k_4}{6}$

Then, $y_1 = y_0 + \frac{1}{6}(k_1 + 2k_2 + 2k_3 + k_4)$ at $x_1 = x_0 + h$.

Similarly, $y_2 = y_1 + \frac{1}{6}(k_1 + 2k_2 + 2k_3 + k_4)$

where, $k_1 = h \cdot f(x_1, y_1)$
$k_2 = h \cdot f\left(x_1 + \frac{h}{2}, y_1 + \frac{k_1}{2}\right)$
$k_3 = h \cdot f\left(x_1 + \frac{h}{2}, y_1 + \frac{k_2}{2}\right)$

$$k_4 = h \cdot f(x_1 + h, y_1 + k_3)$$

Generalized formulae for Runge-Kutta's 4th order method are

$$y_{i+1} = y_i + \frac{1}{6}(k_1 + 2k_2 + 2k_3 + k_4)$$

where,
$$k_1 = h \cdot f(x_i, y_i)$$
$$k_2 = h \cdot f\left(x_i + \frac{h}{2}, y_i + \frac{k_1}{2}\right)$$
$$k_3 = h \cdot f\left(x_i + \frac{h}{2}, y_i + \frac{k_2}{2}\right)$$
$$k_4 = h \cdot f(x_i + h, y_i + k_3)$$

Note : This method coincides with the Taylor's series upto terms of h^4.

Example 4.11 : Solve $\frac{dy}{dx} = -2xy^2$ with $y(0) = 1$ and $h = 0.1$ for interval 0 to 0.5 using Runge-Kutta 2nd order and 4th order method.

Solution : Given data :
$$\frac{dy}{dx} = -2xy^2 = f(x, y)$$
$$h = 0.1$$

Runge-Kutta 2nd Order Method :

For $y(0.1) \Rightarrow x_0 = 0, y_0 = 1$
$$k_1 = h \cdot f(x_0, y_0) = 0.1 \times (-2 \times 0 \times 1^2) = 0.00$$
$$k_2 = h \cdot f(x_0 + h, y_0 + k_1) = 0.1 \times [-2 \times (0.1) \times (1)^2]$$
$$= -0.020$$

$\therefore \quad y_{(0.1)} = y_1 = y_0 + \frac{1}{2}(k_1 + k_2)$

$$= 1 + \frac{1}{2}[0 - 0.02]$$
$$= 0.9900$$

Similarly, for $y(0.2) \Rightarrow x_1 = 0.1, y_1 = 0.9900$
$$k_1 = h \cdot f(x_1, y_1) = 0.1 \times [-2 \times 0.1 \times (0.9900)^2]$$

$\therefore \quad k_1 = -0.019602$

$$k_2 = h \cdot f(x_1 + h, y_1 + k_1)$$
$$= 0.1 \times [-2 \times (0.2) \times (-0.019602)^2]$$

$\therefore \quad k_2 = -0.037667$

$\therefore \quad y_{(0.2)} = y_2 = y_1 + \frac{1}{2}[k_1 + k_2]$

∴ $y_2 = 0.961366$

Similarly, for y(0.3), we have,

$k_1 = -0.036969$, $k_2 = -0.051271$, $y_{(0.3)} = 0.917246$

For $y_{(0.4)}$ ⇒ $k_1 = -0.050480$, $k_2 = -0.060103$, $y_{(0.4)} = 0.861954$

For $y_{(0.5)}$ ⇒ $k_1 = -0.059437$, $k_2 = -0.064403$, $y_{(0.5)} = 0.800034$

Runge-Kutta 4th Order Method :

For $y_{(0.1)}$ ⇒ $x_0 = 0$, $y_0 = 1$, $h = 0.1$

$$k_1 = h \cdot f(x_0, y_0) = 0.1 \times (-2 \times 0 \times 1^2) = 0$$

$$k_2 = h \cdot f\left(x_0 + \frac{h}{2}, y_0 + \frac{k_1}{2}\right)$$

$$= 0.1 \times \left[-2 \times \left(\frac{0.1}{2}\right) \times (1)^2\right]$$

$$= -0.0100$$

$$k_3 = h \cdot f\left(x_0 + \frac{h}{2}, y_0 + \frac{k_2}{2}\right)$$

$$= 0.1 \times \left[-2 \times \left(\frac{0.1}{2}\right) \times \left(1 - \frac{0.01}{2}\right)^2\right]$$

$$= -0.009900$$

$$k_4 = h \cdot f(x_0 + h, y_0 + k_3)$$

$$= 0.1 \times [-2 \times 0.1 \times (1 - 0.0099)^2] = -0.019606$$

∴ $$y_1 = y_0 + \frac{1}{6}[k_1 + 2k_2 + 2k_3 + k_4]$$

$$= 1 + \frac{1}{6}[0 + 2 \times (-0.01) + 2 \times (-0.0099) - 0.019606]$$

$\boxed{y_1 = 0.990099 = y_{(0.1)}}$ ... Ans.

By repeating above steps for calculation of $y_{(0.2)}$, $y_{(0.3)}$, $y_{(0.4)}$ and $y_{(0.5)}$, we get,

x	k$_1$	k$_2$	k$_3$	k$_4$	y
0.1	0	− 0.01	− 0.0099	− 0.019606	0.990099
0.2	− 0.019606	− 0.028829	− 0.028559	− 0.036982	0.961538
0.3	− 0.036982	− 0.044467	− 0.044115	− 0.0505	0.917431
0.4	− 0.050501	− 0.055719	− 0.055394	− 0.059449	0.862068
0.5	− 0.059453	− 0.062351	− 0.062134	− 0.063989	0.79999

For comparison :

	Runge-Kutta 2nd order	Runge-Kutta 4th order
$y_{(0.1)}$	0.9900	0.990099
$y_{(0.2)}$	0.961366	0.961538
$y_{(0.3)}$	0.917246	0.917431
$y_{(0.4)}$	0.861954	0.862068
$y_{(0.5)}$	0.800034	0.79999

Runge-Kutta 2nd Order Method :

Algorithm :

1. Input x_0, y_0, x and h.
2. Calculate n.
3. Repeat i = 1 to n, increment i.
4. Calculate k_1 and k_2.
5. Calculate y.
6. Calculate $x_0 = x_0 + h$, $y_0 = y$.
7. End i.
8. Print results.
9. End.

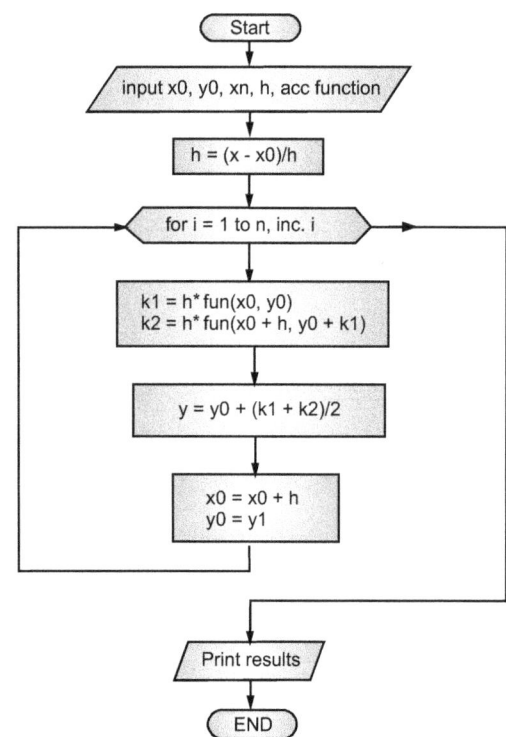

Flow chart 4 : Runge-Kutta 2nd order method

Matlab :

```
fprintf('\n***********************************************');

fprintf('\n Numerical Solution of ODE by Runge-Kutta Second Order Method');

fprintf('\n***********************************************');
fstr= input('\n Input function string >>>','s'); %% Function definition
f=inline(fstr);
disp(sprintf(['\n    f(x,y) = dy/dx = ' fstr]))

x0 = input('\n Enter Initial Value of X0 = ');
y0 = input('\n Enter Initial Value of Y0 = ');
xn = input('\n Enter the given value of Xn = ');
h = input('\n Enter Interval (h) = ');

% Calculation of no. of steps >>
n=(xn-x0)/h;
disp(sprintf('     n = ( xn - x0 ) / h '))
disp(sprintf('       = ( %g - %g ) / %g ',xn,x0,h))
disp(sprintf('       = %g',n))
xa(1)=x0 ;
ya(1)=y0 ;
for i = 2:n+1
    k1=h*f(x0,y0);
    k2=h*f(x0+h,y0+k1);
    xa(i)=x0+h;
    ya(i)=y0+(1/2)*(k1+k2);
    fprintf('\n Value of k1 = %f \t k2 = %f \t Y(%f) = %f',k1,k2,xa(i),ya(i));
    x0=xa(i);
    y0=ya(i);
end
% Plotting the Approximate solution of the ODE.
hold on
xspan = [x0 xn];
```

```
xlabel('X');
ylabel('Y');
title('Approximate Solution of the ODE by Runge-Kutta 2nd Method');
plot(xa,ya,'-','LineWidth',2,'Color',[0 1 0]);
legend('Approximation');
```

Output :

****
    Numerical Solution of ODE by Runge-Kutta Second Order Method
****

Input function string >>>-2*x*y*y
 f(x,y) = dy/dx = -2*x*y*y
Enter Initial Value of X0 = 0
Enter Initial Value of Y0 = 1
Enter the given value of Xn = 0.5
Enter Interval (h) = 0.1
   n = (xn - x0) / h
     = (0.5 - 0) / 0.1
     = 5

Value of k1 = 0.000000	k2 = −0.020000	Y(0.100000) = 0.990000
Value of k1 = −0.019602	k2 = −0.037667	Y(0.200000) = 0.961366
Value of k1 = −0.036969	k2 = −0.051271	Y(0.300000) = 0.917246
Value of k1 = −0.050480	k2 = −0.060103	Y(0.400000) = 0.861954
Value of k1 = −0.059437	k2 = −0.064403	Y(0.500000) = 0.800034

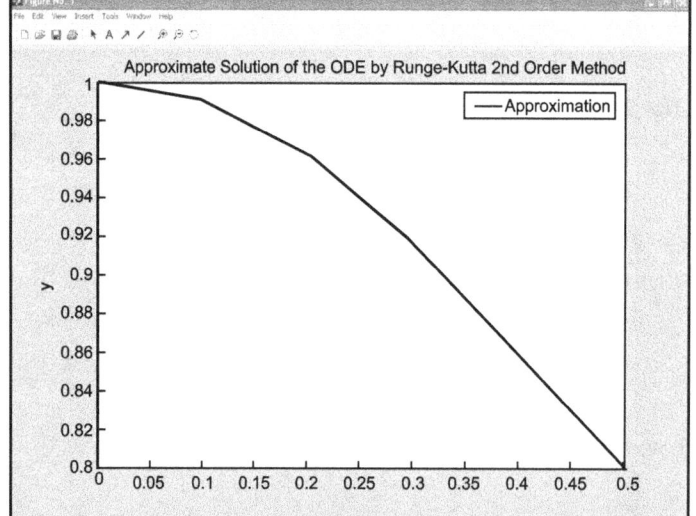

Image 4.3

Runge-Kutta 4th Order Method :
Algorithm :
1. Input x_0, y_0, x and h.
2. Calculate n.
3. Repeat i = 1 to n, inc. i.
4. Calculate k_1, k_2, k_3 and k_4.
5. Calculate y.
6. Calculate $y_0 = y_0$ and $x_0 = x_0 + h$.
7. End i.
8. Print results.
9. End.

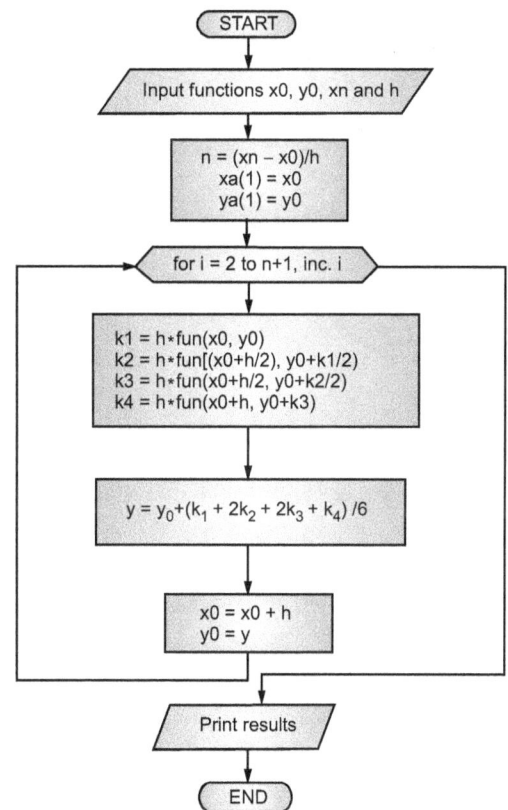

Flow chart 5 : Runge-Kutta 4th order method

Matlab :

```
% Ordinary Differential Equations
% Method - Runge-Kutta 4th Order Method

fprintf('\n***********************************************************');
fprintf('\n Numerical Solution of ODE by Runge-Kutta 4th Order Method ');
```

```
fprintf('\n************************************************************');

fstr = input('\n Input function string f(x,y) = ','s');  %% Function definition
f=inline(fstr);
disp(sprintf(['\n    f(x,y) = dy/dx = ' fstr]))

x0 = input ('\n Enter Initial Value of X0 = ');
y0 = input ('\n Enter Initial Value of Y0 = ');
xn = input ('\n Enter the given value of Xn = ');
h = input ('\n Enter Interval (h) = ');

% Calculation of no. of steps >>
n=(xn-x0)/h;
disp(sprintf('n = ( xn - x0 ) / h '))
disp(sprintf('  = ( %g - %g ) / %g ',xn,x0,h))
disp(sprintf('  = %g',n))
xa(1)=x0 ;
ya(1)=y0 ;

for i = 2:n+1
   k1= h*f(x0,y0);
   k2= h*f(x0+(h/2),y0+(k1/2));
   k3= h*f(x0+(h/2),y0+(k2/2));
   k4= h*f(x0+h,y0+k3);
   xa(i)=x0+h;
   ya(i)=y0+(1/6)*(k1+2*k2+2*k3+k4);
   fprintf('\n k1 = %.4f k2 = %.4f k3 = %.4f k4 = %.4f', k1,k2,k3,k4);
   x0=xa(i);
   y0=ya(i);
   fprintf('\t =>Y(%.2f) = %.5f',xa(i),ya(i));
end
% Plotting the Approximate solution of the ODE.
hold on
xspan = [x0 xn];
xlabel('X');
ylabel('Y');
title('Approximate Solution of the ODE by Runge-Kutta 4th Order Method');
plot(xa,ya,'-','LineWidth',2,'Color',[0 1 0]);
legend('Approximation');
```

Output :

****

    Numerical Solution of ODE by Runge - Kutta 4th Order Method

****

Input function string f(x,y) = -2*x*y*y

   f(x,y) = dy/dx = -2*x*y*y

Enter Initial Value of X0 = 0

Enter Initial Value of Y0 = 1

Enter the given value of Xn = 0.5

Enter Interval (h) = 0.1

n = (xn - x0) / h

  = (0.5 - 0) / 0.1

  = 5

k1 = 0.0000 k2 = –0.0100 k3 = –0.0099 k4 = –0.0196 =>Y(0.10) = 0.99010

k1 = –0.0196 k2 = –0.0288 k3 = –0.0286 k4 = –0.0370 =>Y(0.20) = 0.96154

k1 = –0.0370 k2 = –0.0445 k3 = –0.0441 k4 = –0.0505 =>Y(0.30) = 0.91743

k1 = –0.0505 k2 = –0.0557 k3 = –0.0554 k4 = –0.0594 =>Y(0.40) = 0.86207

k1 = –0.0595 k2 = –0.0624 k3 = –0.0621 k4 = –0.0640 =>Y(0.50) = 0.80000

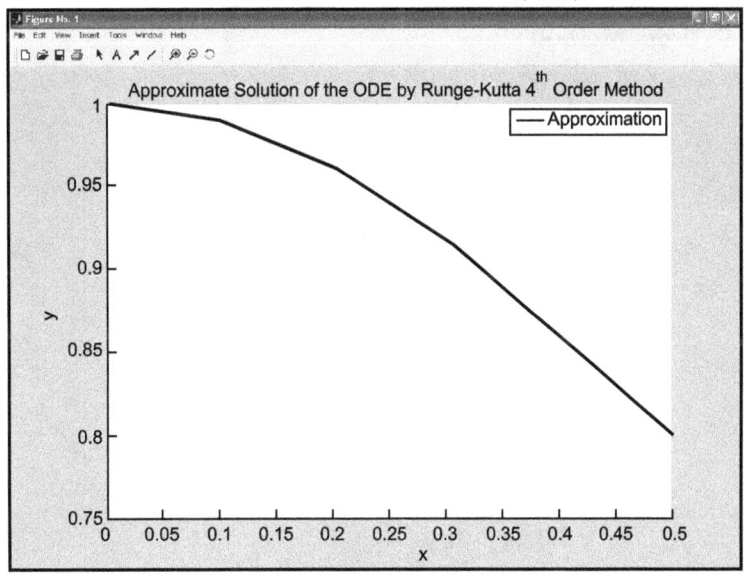

Image 4.4

Example 4.12 : Solve $\frac{dy}{dx} = 3x + \frac{1}{2}y$ with $y(0) = 1$, $h = 0.1$ by Runge-Kutta 2nd order and 4th order.

Solution : Given data :
$$\frac{dy}{dx} = 3x + \frac{y}{2}$$
$$x_0 = 0,\ y_0 = 1$$
$$h = 0.1$$
$$y(0.1) = ?$$

Runge-Kutta 2nd Order Method :

For $y(0.1) \Rightarrow x_0 = 0,\ y_0 = 1,\ h = 0.1$

$$k_1 = h \cdot f(x_0, y_0) = 0.1 \times [3 \times (0) \times 1/2]$$

$\therefore \quad k_1 = 0.0500$

$$k_2 = h \cdot f(x_0 + h, y_0 + k_1) = 0.1 \times [3 \times (0 + 0.1) \times (1 + 0.05)/2]$$

$\therefore \quad k_2 = 0.0825$

$$y_{(0.1)} = y_0 + \frac{1}{2}(k_1 + k_2) = y_1$$

$$= 1 + \frac{1}{2}(0.0500 + 0.0825)$$

$\therefore \quad \boxed{y_{(0.1)} = 1.066250}$ ... **Ans.**

Runge-Kutta 4th Order Method :

For $y_{(0.1)} \Rightarrow x_0 = 0,\ y_0 = 1,\ h = 0.1$

$$k_1 = h \cdot f(x_0, y_0) = 0.1 \times [3 \times (0) \times 1/2]$$

$\therefore \quad k_1 = 0.0500$

$$k_2 = h \cdot f\left(x_0 + \frac{h}{2}, y_0 + \frac{k_1}{2}\right)$$

$$= 0.1 \times [3 \times (0 + 0.1/2) \times (1 + (0.05/2))/2]$$

$\therefore \quad k_2 = 0.066250$

$$k_3 = h \cdot f\left(x_0 + \frac{h}{2}, y_0 + \frac{k_2}{2}\right)$$

$$= 0.1 \times [3 \times (0 + 0.1/2) \times (1 + (0.066250/2))/2]$$

$\therefore \quad k_3 = 0.066656$

$$k_4 = h \cdot f(x_0 + h, y_0 + k_3)$$

$$= 0.1 \times [3 \times (0 + 0.1) \times (1 + (0.0666506/2))/2]$$

∴ $k_4 = 0.083333$

∴ $y_1 = y_0 + \dfrac{1}{6}[k_1 + 2k_2 + 2k_3 + k_4]$

$= 1 + \dfrac{1}{6}[0.05 + 2 \times 0.066250 + 2 \times 0.066656 + 0.083333]$

∴ $\boxed{y_1 = 1.066524 = y_{(0.1)}}$ ... Ans.

Example 4.13 : Solve $\dfrac{dy}{dx} = 1 + y^2$ where $y = 0$ when $x = 0$, find $y(0.2)$, $y(0.4)$ and $y(0.6)$ using Runge-Kutta 4th order method.

Solution : Given data :

$$\dfrac{dy}{dx} = 1 + y^2$$

$x_0 = 0, \; y_0 = 0$

$h = 0.20$

$y(0.1) = ?$

For $y_{(0.2)} \Rightarrow x_0 = 0, \; y_0 = 0, \; h = 0.2$

$k_1 = h \cdot f(x_0, y_0) = 0.2 \times [1 + 0^2]$

∴ $k_1 = 0.20$

$k_2 = h \cdot f\left(x_0 + \dfrac{h}{2}, y_0 + \dfrac{k_1}{2}\right)$

$= 0.2 \times [1 + (0 + 0.2/2)^2]$

∴ $k_2 = 0.202$

$k_3 = h \cdot f\left(x_0 + \dfrac{h}{2}, y_0 + \dfrac{k_2}{2}\right)$

$= 0.2 \times [1 + (0 + 0.202/2)^2]$

∴ $k_3 = 0.20204$

$k_4 = h \cdot f(x_0 + h, y_0 + k_3)$

$= 0.2 \times [1 + (0 + 0.20204)^2]$

∴ $k_4 = 0.208164$

∴ $y_1 = y_0 + \dfrac{1}{6}[k_1 + 2k_2 + 2k_3 + k_4]$

$= 1 + \dfrac{1}{6}[0.2 + 2 \times 0.202 + 2 \times 0.20204 + 0.208164]$

∴ $\boxed{y_1 = 0.202707 = y_{(0.2)}}$ ... Ans.

For $y_{(0.4)} \Rightarrow x_1 = 0.2, \; y_1 = 0.202707, \; h = 0.2$

$$k_1 = h \cdot f(x_0, y_0) = 0.2 \times [1 + (0.202707)^2]$$

$\therefore \quad k_1 = 0.208218$

$$k_2 = h \cdot f\left(x_0 + \frac{h}{2}, y_0 + \frac{k_1}{2}\right)$$

$$= 0.2 \times [1 + (0 + 0.208218/2)^2]$$

$\therefore \quad k_2 = 0.218827$

$$k_3 = h \cdot f\left(x_0 + \frac{h}{2}, y_0 + \frac{k_2}{2}\right)$$

$$= 0.2 \times [1 + (0 + 0.218827/2)^2]$$

$\therefore \quad k_3 = 0.219484$

$$k_4 = h \cdot f(x_0 + h, y_0 + k_3)$$

$$= 0.2 \times [1 + (0.219484)^2]$$

$\therefore \quad k_4 = 0.235649$

$\therefore \quad y_1 = y_0 + \dfrac{1}{6}[k_1 + 2k_2 + 2k_3 + k_4]$

$$= 1 + \frac{1}{6}[0.208218 + 2 \times 0.218827 + 2 \times 0.219484 + 0.235649]$$

$\therefore \quad \boxed{y_2 = 0.422789 = y_{(0.4)}}$ ... **Ans.**

Similarly, for x = 0.6, we get

$k_1 = 0.235750$
$k_2 = 0.258464$
$k_3 = 0.260945$
$k_4 = 0.293499$

$\therefore \quad \boxed{y_3 = 0.0684133 = y_{(0.6)}}$ ... **Ans.**

Example 4.14 : Use Runge-Kutta 4th order to solve $10 \dfrac{dy}{dx} = x^2 + y^2$, $y(0) = 1$ for the interval $0 \leq x \leq 0.5$ with h = 0.10.

Solution : Given data : $10 \dfrac{dy}{dx} = x^2 + y^2$

$\therefore \quad \dfrac{dy}{dx} = \dfrac{x^2 + y^2}{10}$

We have, $x_0 = 0$, $y_0 = 1$, h = 0.1

$k_1 = h \cdot f(x_0, y_0) = 0.1 \times [(0^2 + 1^2)]/10$

$\therefore \quad k_1 = 0.01$

$$k_2 = h \cdot f\left(x_0 + \frac{h}{2}, y_0 + \frac{k_1}{2}\right)$$

$$= 0.1 \times [(0 + 0.1/2)^2 + (1 + 0.01/2)^2]/10$$

$\therefore$ $\quad k_2 = 0.010125$

$$k_3 = h \cdot f\left(x_0 + \frac{h}{2}, y_0 + \frac{k_2}{2}\right)$$

$$= 0.1 \times [(0 + 0.1/2)^2 + (1 + 0.010125/2)^2]/10$$

$\therefore$ $\quad k_3 = 0.010127$

$\quad k_4 = h \cdot f(x_0 + h, y_0 + k_3)$

$\quad\quad = 0.1 \times [(0 + 0.1)^2 + (1 + 0.010127)^2]/10$

$\therefore$ $\quad k_4 = 0.010304$

$\therefore$ $\quad y_1 = y_0 + \dfrac{1}{6}[k_1 + 2k_2 + 2k_3 + k_4]$

$$= 1 + \frac{1}{6}[0.01 + 2 \times 0.010125 + 2 \times 0.010127 + 0.010304]$$

$\therefore$ $\quad \boxed{y_1 = 1.010135 = y_{(0.1)}}$ ... Ans.

By repeating above steps, we get

$k_1 = 0.0103$,	$k_2 = 0.0105$,	$k_3 = 0.0105$,	$k_4 = 0.0108$	=> Y(0.20) = 1.02068
$k_1 = 0.0108$,	$k_2 = 0.0112$,	$k_3 = 0.0112$,	$k_4 = 0.0115$	=> Y(0.30) = 1.03184
$k_1 = 0.0115$,	$k_2 = 0.0120$,	$k_3 = 0.0120$,	$k_4 = 0.0125$	=> Y(0.40) = 1.04384
$k_1 = 0.0125$,	$k_2 = 0.0131$,	$k_3 = 0.0131$,	$k_4 = 0.0137$	=> Y(0.50) = 1.05691

Example 4.15 : *Find values of y(1.2) and y(1.4) using Runge-Kutta 4th order method with h = 0.2 and y(1) = 1 for* $\dfrac{dy}{dx} + \dfrac{y}{x} = y^2.$

Solution : Given data :

$$\frac{dy}{dx} + \frac{y}{x} = y^2$$

$\therefore$ $\quad \dfrac{dy}{dx} = f(x, y) = \left(y^2 - \dfrac{y}{x}\right)$

$x_0 = 1, y_0 = 1, h = 0.2$

$\quad k_1 = h \cdot f(x_0, y_0) = 0.2 \times [1^2 - (1/1)]$

$\therefore$ $\quad k_1 = 0 \quad k_2 = h \cdot f\left(x_0 + \dfrac{h}{2}, y_0 + \dfrac{k_1}{2}\right)$

$\quad\quad = 0.2 \times [(1 + 0/2)^2 - (1 + 0/2)/(1 + 0.1/2)]$

$\therefore$ $\quad k_2 = 0.0182$

$\quad k_3 = h \cdot f\left(x_0 + \dfrac{h}{2}, y_0 + \dfrac{k_2}{2}\right)$

$\quad\quad = 0.2 \times [(1 + 0.0182/2)^2 - (1 + 0.0182/2)/(1 + 0.1/2)]$

$\therefore$ $\quad k_3 = 0.0202$

$\quad k_4 = h \cdot f(x_0 + h, y_0 + k_3)$

$\quad\quad = 0.2 \times [(1 + 0.0202)^2 + (1 + 0.0202)/(1 + 0.1)]$

$\therefore$ $\quad k_4 = 0.0381$

$$\therefore \quad y_1 = y_0 + \frac{1}{6}[k_1 + 2k_2 + 2k_3 + k_4]$$

$$= 1 + \frac{1}{6}[0 + 2 \times 0.0182 + 2 \times 0.0202 + 0.0381]$$

$$\therefore \quad \boxed{y_1 = 1.01914 = y_{(1.2)}} \qquad \text{... Ans.}$$

Similarly, for x = 1.4, we get,
$k_1 = 0.0379,\quad k_2 = 0.0558,\quad k_3 = 0.0582,\quad k_4 = 0.0782 \Rightarrow Y(1.40) = 1.07649$

4.8 Runge-Kutta Method For Simultaneous Equations

For simultaneous equations of first order,

$$\frac{dy}{dx} = f(x, y, z)$$

$$\frac{dz}{dx} = \phi(x, y, z)$$

Subject to initial conditions at $x = x_0$, $y = y_0$ and $z = z_0$.
Let h, k, l be increments in x, y and z respectively.
By applying Runge-Kutta 4th order method, we have,

$k_1 = h \cdot f(x_0, y_0, z_0)$ $\qquad\qquad l_1 = h \cdot \phi(x_0, y_0, z_0)$

$k_2 = h \cdot f\left(x_0 + \frac{h}{2}, y_0 + \frac{k_1}{2}, z_0 + \frac{l_1}{2}\right),$ $\qquad l_2 = h \cdot \phi\left(x_0 + \frac{h}{2}, y_0 + \frac{k_1}{2}, z_0 + \frac{l_1}{2}\right),$

$k_3 = h \cdot f\left(x_0 + \frac{h}{2}, y_0 + \frac{k_2}{2}, z_0 + \frac{l_2}{2}\right),$ $\qquad l_3 = h \cdot \phi\left(x_0 + \frac{h}{2}, y_0 + \frac{k_2}{2}, z_0 + \frac{l_2}{2}\right),$

$k_4 = h \cdot f(x_0 + h, y_0 + k_3, z_0 + l_3),$ $\qquad l_4 = h \cdot \phi(x_0 + h, y_0 + k_3, z_0 + l_3),$

$\therefore \quad k = \frac{1}{6}(k_1 + 2k_2 + 2k_3 + k_4)$ $\qquad\qquad l = \frac{1}{6}(l_1 + 2l_2 + 2l_3 + l_4)$

Then,
$y_1 = y_0 + k$ and
$z_1 = z_0 + l$

Note :

1. For 2nd degree equations, like

$$\frac{d^2y}{dx^2} = f\left(x, y, \frac{dy}{dx}\right) \text{ can be solved by considering } z = \frac{dy}{dx} = \phi(x, y, z)$$

$$\therefore \quad \frac{d^2y}{dx^2} = \frac{dz}{dx} = f(x, y, z)$$

Therefore, second degree equations can be reduced to first degree equations and solved by Runge-Kutta 4th order method.

2. Modified Euler's method, Runge-Kutta 2nd order and 4th order methods are single step predictor-corrector formulae.

Example 4.16 : A body of mass 2 kg is attached to spring with a spring constant of 10. The differential equation governing the displacement of the body 'y' and time 't' is given by,

$$\frac{d^2y}{dt^2} + 2\frac{dy}{dt} + 5y = 0$$

Find displacement at time $t = 0.5$, given that $y_{(0)} = 2$ and $y'_{(0)} = -4$.

Solution :

$$\frac{d^2y}{dt^2} + 2\frac{dy}{dt} + 5y = 0$$

Assume

$$\frac{dy}{dt} = z \qquad \ldots (I)$$

$$\Rightarrow \quad \frac{d^2y}{dt^2} = \frac{dz}{dt}$$

$$\therefore \quad \frac{dz}{dt} + 2z + 5y = 0 \qquad \ldots (II)$$

Initial conditions :

$$x_0 = 0$$
$$y_0 = 2$$
$$z_0 = \left(\frac{dy}{dt}\right)_{t=0} = -4$$

We have

$$\frac{dy}{dt} = z = f(x_0, y, z)$$

and

$$\frac{dz}{dt} = -2z - 5y = \phi(x, y, z)$$

Considering number of steps = 1

$$h = \frac{t_n - t_0}{n}$$

$$= \frac{0.5 - 0}{1}$$

∴ $\boxed{h = 0.5}$

By Runge-Kutta 4th order method :

$k_1 = h \cdot f(x_0, y_0, z_0)$
 $= 0.5 \times z_0$
 $= 0.5 \times (-4)$
 $= -2$

$k_2 = h \cdot f\left[x_0 + \frac{h}{2}, y_0 + \frac{k_1}{2}, z_0 + \frac{l_1}{2}\right]$
 $= 0.5 \times \left(-4 + \frac{-9}{2}\right)$
 $= -4.25$

$l_1 = h \cdot \phi(x_0, y_0, z_0)$
 $= 0.5 \times (-2z_0 - 5y_0)$
 $= 0.5 \times (-2 \times -4 - 5 \times 2)$
 $= -9$

$l_2 = h \cdot \phi\left[x_0 + \frac{h}{2}, y_0 + \frac{k_1}{2}, z_0 + \frac{l_1}{2}\right]$
 $= 0.5 \times \left[-2 \times \left(z_0 + \frac{l_1}{2}\right) - 5 \times \left(y_0 + \frac{k_1}{2}\right)\right]$

$$k_3 = h \cdot f\left[x_0 + \frac{h}{2}, y_0 + \frac{k_2}{2}, z_0 + \frac{l_2}{2}\right]$$

$$= 0.5 \times \left(z_0 + \frac{l_2}{2}\right)$$

$$= 0.5 \times \left(-4 + \frac{12}{2}\right)$$

$$= 1.0$$

$$k_4 = h \cdot f(x_0 + h, y_0 + k_3, z_0 + l_3)$$

$$= 0.5 \times (z_0 + l_3)$$

$$= 0.5 \times (-4 - 2.3125)$$

$$= -3.15625$$

$$y_1 = y_0 + \frac{k_1 + 2k_2 + 2k_3 + k_4}{6}$$

$$= 2 + \frac{-2 + 2 \times (-4.25) + 2 \times 1.0 + (-3.15625)}{6}$$

$$= 2 + \frac{-2 - 8.50 + 2 - 3.15625}{6}$$

$$\boxed{y_1 = 0.0573}$$

$$= 0.5 \times \left[-2 \times \left(-4 + \frac{-9}{2}\right) - 5 \times \left(2 + \frac{-2}{2}\right)\right]$$

$$= 12$$

$$l_3 = h \cdot \phi\left[x_0 + \frac{h}{2}, y_0 + \frac{k_2}{2}, z_0 + \frac{l_2}{2}\right]$$

$$= 0.5 \times \left[-2 \times \left(z_0 + \frac{l_2}{2}\right) - 5 \times \left(y_0 + \frac{k_2}{2}\right)\right]$$

$$= 0.5 \times \left[-2 \times \left(-4 + \frac{12}{2}\right) - 5 \times \left(2 + \frac{-4.25}{2}\right)\right]$$

$$= 0.5 \times (-4 - 0.625)$$

$$= -2.3125$$

$$l_4 = h \cdot \phi(x_0 + h, y_0 + k_3, z_0 + l_3)$$

$$l_4 = h \times [-2 \times (z_0 + l_3) - 5 \times (y_0 + k_3)]$$

$$= 0.5 \times [-2 \times (-4 - 2.3125) - 5 \times (2 + 1)]$$

$$= -1.1875$$

$$z_1 = z_0 + \frac{l_1 + 2l_2 + 2l_3 + l_4}{6}$$

$$= -4 + \frac{-9 + 2 \times 12 + 2 \times (-2.3125) + (-1.1875)}{6}$$

$$\boxed{z_1 = -2.46875}$$

Example 4.17 : Solve the equation $\dfrac{d^2y}{dx^2} = x\left(\dfrac{dy}{dx}\right)^2 - y^2$, subjected to initial conditions $y(0) = 1$, $y'(0) = 0$, take $h = 0.2$.

Solution : Given :

$$\frac{d^2y}{dx^2} = x\left(\frac{dy}{dx}\right)^2 - y^2$$

Consider

$$\frac{dy}{dx} = z = f(x, y, z)$$

∴

$$\frac{d^2y}{dx^2} = \frac{dz}{dx}$$

∴

$$\frac{dz}{dx} = x \cdot z^2 - y^2 = \phi(x, y, z)$$

Initial conditions :

$$x_0 = 0$$
$$y_0 = 1$$
$$z_0 = \left(\frac{dy}{dx}\right)_{x=0} = 0, \ h = 0.2, \ n = 1$$

By Runge-Kutta 4th order method :

$k_1 = h \cdot f(x_0, y_0, z_0)$
$\quad = 0.2 \times z_0$
$\quad = 0$

$k_2 = h \cdot f \left[x_0 + \dfrac{h}{2}, y_0 + \dfrac{k_1}{2}, z_0 + \dfrac{l_1}{2} \right]$
$\quad = 0.2 \times \left(z_0 + \dfrac{l_1}{2} \right)$
$\quad = 0.2 \times \left(0 - \dfrac{0.2}{2} \right)$
$\quad = -0.02$

$k_3 = h \cdot f \left[x_0 + \dfrac{h}{2}, y_0 + \dfrac{k_2}{2}, z_0 + \dfrac{l_2}{2} \right]$
$\quad = 0.2 \times \left(z_0 + \dfrac{l_2}{2} \right)$
$\quad = 0.2 \times \left(0 - \dfrac{0.1998}{2} \right)$
$\quad = -0.020$

$k_4 = h \cdot f(x_0 + h, y_0 + k_3, z_0 + l_3)$
$\quad = 0.2 \times (z_0 + l_3)$
$\quad = 0.2 \times (0 - 0.1958)$
$\quad = -0.0392$

$y_1 = y_0 + \dfrac{k_1 + 2k_2 + 2k_3 + k_4}{6}$

$\quad = 1 + \dfrac{0 + 2 \times (-0.02) + 2 \times (-0.02) + (-0.0392)}{6}$

$\boxed{y_1 = 0.980}$ ... Ans.

$l_1 = h \cdot \phi(x_0, y_0, z_0)$
$l_1 = 0.2 \times (x_0 \cdot z_0^2 - y_0^2)$
$l_1 = 0.2 \times (0 \times 0^2 - 1^2)$
$\quad = -0.20$

$l_2 = h \cdot \phi \left[x_0 + \dfrac{h}{2}, y_0 + \dfrac{k_1}{2}, z_0 + \dfrac{l_1}{2} \right]$
$\quad = 0.2 \times \left[(0 + 0.1) \times \left(0 - \dfrac{0.2}{2} \right)^2 - \left(1 + \dfrac{0}{2} \right)^2 \right]$
$\quad = -0.1998$

$l_3 = h \cdot \phi \left[x_0 + \dfrac{h}{2}, y_0 + \dfrac{k_2}{2}, z_0 + \dfrac{l_2}{2} \right]$
$\quad = 0.2 \times$
$\left[(0 + 0.1) \times \left(0 - \dfrac{0.1998}{2} \right)^2 - \left(1 - \dfrac{0.02}{2} \right)^2 \right]$
$\quad = -0.1958$

$l_4 = h \cdot \phi(x_0 + h, y_0 + k_3, z_0 + l_3)$
$\quad = 0.2 \times [(x_0 + h) \times (z_0 + l_3)^2 - (y_0 + k_3)^2]$
$\quad = 0.2 \times [(0 + 0.2) \times (0 + (-0.1958))^2 -$
$\quad\quad (1 + (-0.02))^2]$
$\quad = -0.1906$

$z_1 = z_0 + \dfrac{l_1 + 2l_2 + 2l_3 + l_4}{6}$

$\quad = 0 + \dfrac{-0.20 + 2 \times (-0.1998) + 2 \times (-0.1958) + (-0.1906)}{6}$

$\boxed{z_1 = -0.113}$ ... Ans.

Example 4.18 : Solve $\dfrac{dy}{dx} = yz + x$, $\dfrac{dz}{dx} = xz + y$. Given $y(0) = 1$, $z(0) = -1$, for $y(0.1)$, $z(0.1)$.

Solution : We have,

$\quad\quad\quad f(x, y, z) = yz + x$

$\quad\quad\quad \phi(x, y, z) = xz + y$

$\quad\quad\quad h = 0.1, x_0 = 0, y_0 = 1, z_0 = -1$

$k_1 = h \cdot f(x_0, y_0, z_0)$

$\quad = h \times (y_0 \cdot z_0 + x_0)$

$\quad = 0.1 \times (1 \times (-1) + 0)$

$k_1 = -0.1$

$k_2 = h \cdot f\left[x_0 + \dfrac{h}{2}, y_0 + \dfrac{k_1}{2}, z_0 + \dfrac{l_1}{2}\right]$

$\quad = 0.1 \times \left[\left(y_0 + \dfrac{k_1}{2}\right) \times \left(z_0 + \dfrac{l_1}{2}\right) + \left(x_0 + \dfrac{h}{2}\right)\right]$

$\quad = 0.1 \times \left[\left(1 + \dfrac{-0.1}{2}\right) \times \left(-1 + \dfrac{0.1}{2}\right) + \left(0 + \dfrac{0.1}{2}\right)\right]$

$\quad = -0.08525$

$k_3 = h \cdot f\left[x_0 + \dfrac{h}{2}, y_0 + \dfrac{k_2}{2}, z_0 + \dfrac{l_2}{2}\right]$

$\quad = h \cdot f(0.05, 0.957375, -0.954875)$

$\quad = -0.0864173$

$k_4 = h \cdot f(x_0 + h, y_0 + k_3, z_0 + l_3)$

$\quad = -0.073048$

$l_1 = h \cdot \phi(x_0, y_0, z_0)$

$\quad = h \cdot (x_0 \cdot z_0 + y_0)$

$\quad = 0.1 \times (0 \times (-1) + 1)$

$l_1 = 0.1$

$l_2 = h \cdot \phi\left[x_0 + \dfrac{h}{2}, y_0 + \dfrac{k_1}{2}, z_0 + \dfrac{l_1}{2}\right]$

$\quad = 0.1 \times \left[\left(x_0 + \dfrac{h}{2}\right) \times \left(z_0 + \dfrac{l_1}{2}\right) + \left(y_0 + \dfrac{k_1}{2}\right)\right]$

$\quad = 0.1 \times \left[\left(0 + \dfrac{0.1}{2}\right) \times \left(-1 + \dfrac{0.1}{2}\right) + \left(1 + \dfrac{-0.1}{2}\right)\right]$

$\quad = -0.09025$

$l_3 = h \cdot \phi\left[x_0 + \dfrac{h}{2}, y_0 + \dfrac{k_2}{2}, z_0 + \dfrac{l_2}{2}\right]$

$\quad = h \cdot \phi(0.05, 0.957375, -0.954875)$

$\quad = -0.0864173$

$l_4 = h \cdot \phi(x_0 + h_1, y_0 + k_3, z_0 + l_3)$

$\quad = +0.822679$

We have $\quad k = \dfrac{1}{6}[k_1 + 2k_2 + 2k_3 + k_4] = -0.0860637$

$$l = \dfrac{1}{6}[l_1 + 2l_2 + 2l_3 + l_4]$$

$\quad = 0.0907823$

$\therefore y_1 = y_0 + k = 1 - 0.0860637 = 0.9139363 = y_{(0.1)}$

$\quad z_1 = z_0 + l = -1 + 0.0907823 = -0.9092176 = z_{(0.1)}$ ... Ans.

Matlab :

%% Ordinary Simultaneous Differential Equations

```
fprintf('\n***********************************************');
fprintf('\n*************** NIRALI PUBLICATIONS ******************');
fprintf('\n******** CONM by M. T. Puranik & V. N. Chougule ******');
fprintf('\n*************** ODE - Simultaneous Equations *********');
fprintf('\n********** Runge-Kutta Second Order Method ***********');
fprintf('\n***********************************************');
```

```
fprintf('\nNote: All terms of function i.e. x,y,z needed to specify');
fstr = input('\nEnter equation dy/dx = ','s');
%Input function as a string

f=inline(fstr);              % Function Declaration
disp(sprintf(['\n    dy/dx = f(x,y) = ' fstr]))
fstr1 = input('\nEnter equation dz/dx = ','s');

%Input function as a string f1=inline(fstr1);
% Function Declaration
disp(sprintf(['\n    dz/dx = g(x,y) = ' fstr1]))

x(1) = input('\n Enter x0 = ');
y(1) = input('\n Enter y0 = ');
z(1) = input('\n Enter z0 = ');
h = input('\n Input Step Size (h) = ');

xn = input('\n Input final value of x (xn) = ');
n=(xn-x(1))/h;
X=x(1);
Y=y(1);
Z=z(1);

for i=1:n
    K1=h*f(X,Y,Z);
    L1=h*f1(X,Y,Z);
    K2=h*f((X+h/2),(Y+K1/2),(Z+L1/2));
    L2=h*f1((X+h/2),(Y+K1/2),(Z+L1/2));
    K=(K1+K2)/2;
    L=(L1+L2)/2;
    x(i)=X+h;
    y(i)=Y+K;
    z(i)=Z+L;
```

```
X=X+h;
Y=y(i);
Z=z(i);

fprintf('\n X%d = %.2f \t Y%d = %.5f \t Z%d = %.5f',i,X,i,Y,i,Z);
end
```

Matlab Output :

```
************************************************************
****************** NIRALI PUBLICATIONS ******************
******** CONM by M. T. Puranik & V. N. Chougule *******
*************** ODE - Simultaneous Equations ************
************* Runge-Kutta Second Order Method *********
************************************************************
```

Note : All terms of function i.e. x,y,z needed to specify

Enter equation dy/dx = y*z+x
   dy/dx = f(x,y) = y*z+x

Enter equation dz/dx = x*z+y
   dz/dx = g(x,y) = x*z+y

Enter x0 = 0
Enter y0 = 1
Enter z0 = – 1
Input Step Size (h) = 0.1
Input final value of x (xn) = 1.0

X1 = 0.10	Y1 = 0.90738	Z1 = –0.90487
X2 = 0.20	Y2 = 0.84118	Z2 = –0.82694
X3 = 0.30	Y3 = 0.79652	Z3 = –0.76225
X4 = 0.40	Y4 = 0.77000	Z4 = –0.70764
X5 = 0.50	Y5 = 0.75920	Z5 = –0.66053
X6 = 0.60	Y6 = 0.76237	Z6 = –0.61870
X7 = 0.70	Y7 = 0.77825	Z7 = –0.58018
X8 = 0.80	Y8 = 0.80598	Z8 = –0.54310
X9 = 0.90	Y9 = 0.84498	Z9 = –0.50561
X10 = 1.00	Y10 = 0.89500	Z10 = –0.46577

Example 4.19 : Solve the simultaneous differential equations
$\frac{dy}{dx} = 2y + z$ and $\frac{dz}{dx} = y - 3z$, where $y(0) = 0$, $z(0) = 0.5$
for $y(0.1)$ and $z(0.1)$ using Runge-Kutta 4th order method.

Solution : Given data :
$$f(x, y, z) = 2y + z$$
$$\phi(x, y, z) = y - 3z$$
$$x_0 = 0, y_0 = 0, z_0 = 0.5$$
$$h = 0.1$$

We have

$k_1 = h \cdot f(x_0, y_0, z_0)$
$= 0.1 \times [2y_0 + z_0]$
$= 0.1 \times (2 \times 0 + 0.5)$
$k_1 = 0.05$

$l_1 = h \cdot \phi(x_0, y_0, z_0)$
$= 0.1 \times [y_0 - 3z_0]$
$= 0.1 \times [0 - 3 \times 0.5]$
$= -0.15$

$k_2 = h \cdot f\left[x_0 + \frac{h}{2}, y_0 + \frac{k_1}{2}, z_0 + \frac{l_1}{2}\right]$
$= h \times \left[2\left(y_0 + \frac{k_1}{2}\right) \times \left(z_0 + \frac{l_1}{2}\right)\right]$
$= 0.1 \times \left[2 \times \left(0 + \frac{0.05}{2}\right) + \left(0.5 + \frac{-0.15}{2}\right)\right]$
$\therefore k_2 = 0.0475$

$l_2 = h \cdot \phi\left[x_0 + \frac{h}{2}, y_0 + \frac{k_1}{2}, z_0 + \frac{l_1}{2}\right]$
$= h \times \left[\left(y_0 + \frac{k_1}{2}\right) - 3\left(z_0 + \frac{l_1}{2}\right)\right]$
$= 0.1 \times \left[\left(0 + \frac{0.05}{2}\right) - 3 \times \left(0.5 - \frac{0.15}{2}\right)\right]$
$\therefore l_2 = -0.125$

$k_3 = h \cdot f\left[x_0 + \frac{h}{2}, y_0 + \frac{k_2}{2}, z_0 + \frac{l_2}{2}\right]$
$k_3 = 0.1\, f(0.05, 0.02375, 0.4375)$
$= 0.0485$

$l_3 = h \cdot \phi\left[x_0 + \frac{h}{2}, y_0 + \frac{k_2}{2}, z_0 + \frac{l_2}{2}\right]$
$l_3 = 0.1\, \phi(0.05, 0.02375, 0.4375)$
$= -0.128875$

$k_4 = h \cdot f(x_0 + h, y_0 + k_3, z_0 + l_3)$
$= h \cdot f(0.1, 0.0485, 0.371125)$
$= 0.0468125$

$l_4 = h \cdot \phi(x_0 + h, y_0 + k_3, z_0 + l_3)$
$= h \cdot \phi(0.1, 0.0485, 0.371125)$
$= -0.1064875$

We have $k = \frac{1}{6}[k_1 + 2k_2 + 2k_3 + k_4]$

$l = \frac{1}{6}[0.05 + 2 \times 0.0475 + 2 \times 0.0485 + 0.0468125]$

$\therefore \quad k = 0.04814$
$\therefore \quad y_1 = y_0 + k$

∴ $y_1 = 0 + 0.04814$

$\boxed{y_{(0.1)} = y_1 = 0.04814}$ ... Ans.

$l = \dfrac{1}{6}[l_1 + 2l_2 + 2l_3 + l_4]$

$= \dfrac{1}{6}[-0.15 + 2 \times (-0.125) + 2 \times (-0.128875) + 0.0468125]$

$= -0.1018229$

∴ $z_1 = z_0 + l$

$= 0.5 - 0.1018229$

$\boxed{z_{(0.1)} = 0.398177}$

PROBLEMS FOR PRACTICE

1. Using Runge-Kutta 4th order method solve $\dfrac{dy}{dx} - xy = 0$, given $y_{(0)} = 2$, $h = 0.1$. Find y at $x = 0.2$. **[Ans. : $y_{(0.1)} = 2.01003$, $y_{(0.2)} = 2.04040$]**

2. Solve the following differential equation using Modified Euler's method for the given boundary condition $\dfrac{dy}{dx} = \log \dfrac{(x+y)}{y(1)} = 2$, find value at y at $x = 1.4$, upto accuracy = 0.001.

   [Ans. $y_{(1.4)} = 2.49251843$]

3. $\dfrac{dy}{dx} = x + y$, given $y(0) = 1$, $h = 0.1$, find $y(0.2)$ using Runge-Kutta 2nd order method. Write a computer program in C language for this problem.

   [Ans. : $y_{(0.1)} = 1.11034$, $y_{(0.2)} = 1.24281$]

4. Solve $\dfrac{dy}{dx} = \sqrt{(x^2 + y)}$ using Runge-Kutta 4th order method to find y at $x = 0.4$, given $y(0.0) = 1.0$. Take $h = 0.2$.

   [Ans. : $y_{(0.2)} = 1.21126$, $y_{(0.4)} = 1.44954$]

5. Solve the following differential equation to get $y(0.1)$.

   $\dfrac{dy}{dx} = x + y + xy$, $y(0) = 1$

   Use : (i) Modified Euler's method with $h = 0.05$

   (ii) Runge-Kutta 4th order with $h = 0.1$

   [Ans. : (i) $y_{(0.05)} = 1.05391$, $y_{(0.1)} = 1.11601$,

   (ii) $y_{(0.05)} = 1.05386$, $y_{(0.2)} = 1.11589$]

6. Solve the differential equation $\frac{d^2y}{dt^2} = 1.5x \frac{dy}{dx} + 4.5y = 4.5$. Using Euler's method assume at $x = 0$, $\frac{dy}{dx} = -2$ and $y = 1$. Tabulate the results for $x = 0.1, 0.2$ and 0.3.

[Ans. $x_{(0.1)} \Rightarrow y_{(0.1)} = 0.801$, $z_{(0.1)} = -0.2089$, $x_{(0.2)} \Rightarrow y_{(0.2)} = 0.596$

$z_{(0.2)} = -2.151$, $y_{(0.3)} = 0.388$, $z_{(0.3)} = -2.183$]

7. Solve the equation $\frac{d^2y}{dt^2} = e^{x^2}$. Estimate the values of y at $x = 0.25, 0.50$ and 0.75. The boundary conditions are at $x = 0$ and $y = 0$ and at $x = 1$, $y = 0$.

[Hint: $\frac{dy}{dt} = z$, $\therefore \frac{d^2y}{dt^2} = e^{x^2}$, $\frac{dz}{dt} = e^{x^2}$

Boundary conditions: $x_0 = 0$, $y_0 = 0$, $\left(\frac{dy}{dx}\right)_{x=0} = 1 = z_0$]

[Ans.: $y_{(0.25)} = 0.282$, $y_{(0.50)} = 1.272$, $y_{(0.5)} = 0.635$, $z_{(0.5)} = 1.596$]

8. Using Runge-Kutta method for 4th order, find y for $x = 0.1, 0.2$ and 0.3. Given that $\frac{dy}{dx} = xy + y^2$, $y(0) = 1$. Continue the solution at 0.4 using Milne's method.

[Ans.: $y_{(0.1)} = 1.11689$, $y_{(0.2)} = 1.27739$, $y_{(0.3)} = 1.50412$, $y_{(0.4)} = 1.83894$]

9. Find $y(1.2)$ and $y(1.4)$ taking $h = 0.1$, $y(1) = 0$ for $\frac{dy}{dx} = \frac{2xy + e^x}{x^2 + x \cdot e^x}$.

[Ans.: At $x = 1.2$, $k_1 = 0.1462$, $k_2 = 0.1402$, $k_3 = 0.1399$,

$k_4 = 0.1348 \Rightarrow Y(1.20) = 0.14021$;

At $x = 1.4$, $k_1 = 0.1348$, $k_2 = 0.1303$, $k_3 = 0.1301$, $k_4 = 0.1260 \Rightarrow Y(1.40) = 0.27050$]

Review Questions

1. Solve the equations $\frac{dy}{dx} = (x + yz)$ and $\frac{dz}{dx} = (x^2 - y^2)$ using Runge-Kutta method under the boundary conditions $x = 0.0$, $y = 1.0$ and $z = 0.5$, find y and z at $x = 1.2$.

2. Solve the differential equation $\frac{dy}{dx} = \frac{(x+y)}{(y^2 - \sqrt{xy})}$ using Euler's method under the boundary conditions $x = 1.3$ and $y = 2.0$. Find y at $x = 1.8$ in 10 steps.

3. Temperature at one surface of slab of thickness, x = 20 cm is T = 500°C. Find the temperature of other surface of slab by taking step size in thickness. Δx = 4 cm. Heat flux is 1000 W/m². Use following governing relation of heat flow,
$$\frac{dT}{dx} = -\frac{q}{A}\left[\frac{1}{0.5(0.01T+1)}\right]$$

4. Given $\frac{dy}{dx} + y + xy^2 = 0$ boundary condition, y(0) = 1.
   Find y(0.3) when step size, h = 0.1, using RK-second order method.

5. Using Runge-Kutta method of order 4, find y(0.2) with h = 0.1 for the following equation $\frac{dy}{dx} = 3x + \frac{1}{2}y$, where y(0) = 1.

6. Solve the following differential equation using Modified Euler's method for the given boundary condition $\frac{dy}{dx} = \sqrt{x+y}$, y(0) = 0.36, find y(0.2) upto accuracy = 0.001.

7. Draw a flow chart for Euler's method.

8. Solve $\frac{dy}{dx} = x + y$; y(0) = 1 by Euler's method and estimate y(1) with h = 0.5 and h = 0.25. Compare the error and comment on it if analytical solution is given by $y(x) = 2e^x - x - 1$. Also estimate y(0.5) with h = 0.25 by suitable Runge-Kutta method.

9. Draw a flow chart for Runge-Kutta second order method.

10. Write short note on :
    'Taylor series representation and its application to solution of differential equations.

11. Draw a flow chart for modified Euler's method.

12. Solve the equation
    $$2\frac{d^2y}{dx^2} = 3x\frac{dy}{dx} - 9y + 9$$
    Subjected to the conditions y(0) = 1, y'(0) = −2, using Runge-Kutta 2nd order method and compute y for x = 0.1 and 0.2.

13. Draw a flow-chart for Runge Kutta 4th order method.

14. Use Runge Kutta 4th order method to solve y' − sin(y) = 1, from r = 0 to 0.5 in steps of h = 0.1.

15. Draw a Flowchart for modified Euler's method.

16. Obtain the solution of $\frac{dy}{dx} = 3x + y^2$ using Taylor's series method. Given : y(0) = 1. Determine y(0.1).

17. An object having surface area of 0.1 m² is initially at 0°C is dipped in a hot water bath. Water is initially at 95°C. Find the temperature of object after 10 sec, taking δt = 2 sec.

    Take mass of the object 1.2 kg, Cp = 450 J/kg K, heat transfer coefficient = 1200 W/m² K
    (dT/dt = h* A (T – T$_f$) l –m* Cp)

18. Using 'Runge Kutta method of order 4, find y for x = 0.1, 0.2, 0.3 given that $\frac{dy}{dx} = xy + y^2$, y(0) = 1. Continue the solution at 0.4 using Milne's method.

19. Draw flow chart for 'Modified Euler's Method'.

20. Using Runge-Kutta method of fourth order, solve
    $\frac{dy}{dx} = y^3 - x^2/y^2 + x^2$ with y (0) = 1 at x = 0.2, 0.4.

21. The second order ODE is transformed into pair of first-order ODEs as in
    $\frac{dy}{dt} = z$ y (0) = 2
    $\frac{dz}{dt} = 0.5x - y$ z (0) = 0

    Estimate the value of z and y at x = 0.2 with step size of 0.1

22. What is meant by order of Runge -Kutta method ? And compare RK methods 2nd order, 3rd order and 4th order graphically.

23. Using 2nd order Runge Kutta method solve $\frac{dy}{dx} = \frac{y^2 - x^2}{y^2 - x^2}$ With y (0) = 1.0 at x = 0.2 and x = 0.4.

24. What do you mean by Weight Average Slope over interval method in ODE solution ? What is meant by 2nd order and 4th order Runge Kutta ODE methods ?

25. Apply Runge Kutta 2nd order method to find approximate value of y for x = 0.2 in steps of 0.1, if $\frac{dy}{dx} = x + y^2$ given that y (0) = 1.0.

26. Solve following systems of ODE and estimate values of y$_1$ (1.0) and y$_2$ (10) at with step size of 0.25.
    $\begin{cases} \frac{dy_1}{dt} = -0.5y_1 \\ \frac{dy_2}{dt} = 4 - 0.1\, y_1 - 0.3y_2 \end{cases}$ $\begin{cases} y_1(0) = 4 \\ y_2(0) = 6 \end{cases}$

27. Using Runge-Kutta method of fourth order, solve for y at x = 1.2, 1.4 form
    $\frac{dy}{dx} = \frac{2xy + e^x}{x^2 + xe^x}$ given x$_0$ = 1, y$_0$ = 0

28. Draw a flow chart for modified Euler's method.
29. Solve the differential equations $\frac{dy}{dx} = 1 + xy$, $\frac{dz}{dx} = -xy$ for $x = 0.3$ using Runge-Kutta method of fourth order with initial value $x = y = 0, z = 1$.
30. Draw flow chart for 'Modified Euler's Method'.
31. Using 'Runge Kutta method of order 4', find y at $x = 0.1$ and 0.2 for the following equation $dy/dx = x + y^2$, where $y(0) = 1$.
32. Using 'Modified Euler's Method', find y at $x = 0.2$ and 0.4 for the following equation $dy/dx = y + e^x$, where $y(0) = 0$ for 2 decimal accuracy.
33. Draw flow chart for 'Euler's method'.

Unit - III

Chapter 5
INTERPOLATION

5.1 INTRODUCTION

Interpolation is a process of determining value of a function at a location between two prescribed points, without knowing the equation of function.

Already, we have used this interpolation technique many times for example, in steam tables, where values of various properties like volume, enthalpy, entropy are listed with respect to certain values of pressure. When we need value of enthalpy corresponding to a pressure value not mentioned in the table, we use interpolation technique. Generally, we use linear interpolation technique.

Let the values of x and corresponding values of y be known at two locations say x = a and x = b. To determine value of function at a third location x = c between x = a and x = b, as the curve is neither defined mathematically nor it is drawn, we imagine a straight line joining the two known points [a, f(a)] and [b, f(b)] and actually determine y coordinate of point on the straight line corresponding to x = c.

This process is explained in Fig. 5.1.

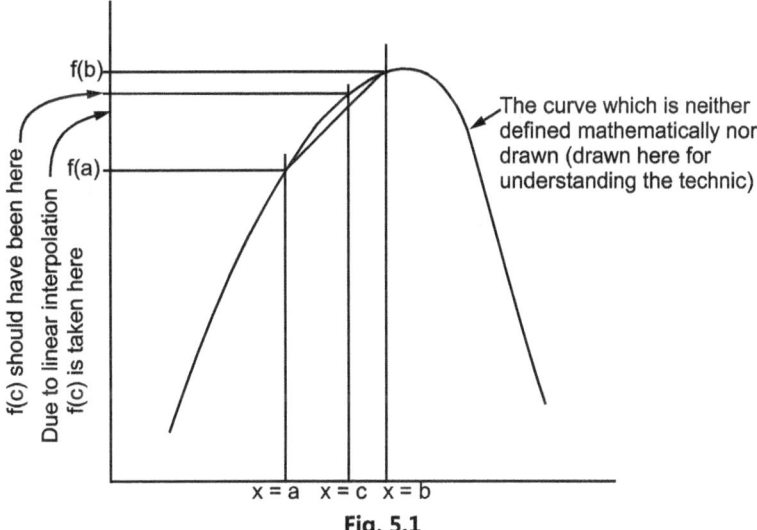

Fig. 5.1

Now, imagine that x = a and x = b are as shown in Fig. 5.2.

In this case, error in determining value of f(c) is increased drastically.

In this chapter, we are going to discuss various numerical methods which will help us in reducing the error in interpolation process.

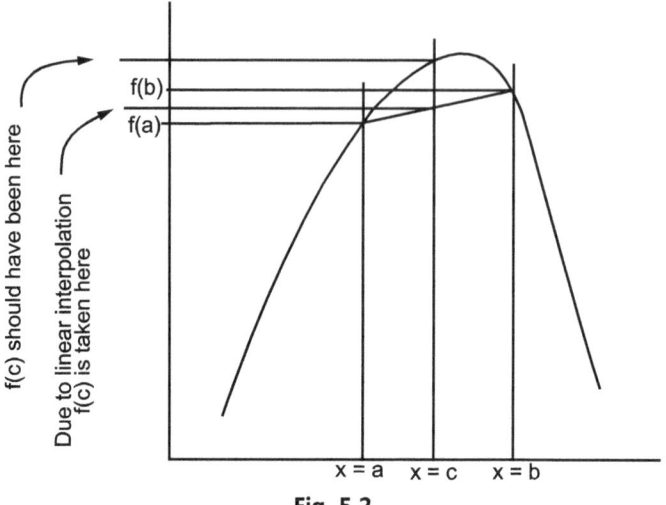

Fig. 5.2

The various methods, we will discuss are,
1. Lagrange's interpolation.
2. Newton's interpolation.
3. Hermite interpolation.
4. Spline interpolation.

5.2 LAGRANGE'S INTERPOLATION

As discussed earlier, linear interpolation is simple but inaccurate technique of interpolation. But there is no way out if function's value is known at only two points. In other words, accuracy of interpolation primarily depends on number of data points.

So to reduce the error, if multiple data points are made available, what should be the procedure to relate them with each other, so that interpolation process performance is improved? Answer to this question is given by following method which is known as Lagrange's interpolation method.

Let us say that multiple data points are available with us as

$(x_0, y_0), (x_1, y_1), (x_2, y_2), \ldots (x_n, y_n)$

where $x_0, x_1, x_2 \ldots$ are distinct values of an independent variable x and $y_0, y_1, y_2 \ldots$ are values of function f(x) corresponding to x values.

Now objective is to determine value of function at any arbitrary value x.

The Lagrange's method tells us to write the data points and the arbitrary value in a certain disciplined manner so that function's value can be easily calculated as below :

$$y = \frac{(x - x_1)(x - x_2)(x - x_3) \ldots (x - x_n)}{(x_0 - x_1)(x_0 - x_2)(x_0 - x_3) \ldots (x_0 - x_n)} f(x_0)$$

$$+ \frac{(x - x_0)(x - x_2)(x - x_3) \ldots (x - x_n)}{(x_1 - x_0)(x_1 - x_2)(x_1 - x_3) \ldots (x_1 - x_n)} f(x_1) + \ldots$$

$$+ \frac{(x-x_0)(x-x_1)(x-x_3)\ldots(x-x_n)}{(x_2-x_0)(x_2-x_1)(x_2-x_3)\ldots(x_2-x_n)} f(x_2) + \ldots$$

$$+ \frac{(x-x_0)(x-x_1)(x-x_2)\ldots(x-x_{n-1})}{(x_n-x_0)(x_n-x_1)(x_n-x_2)\ldots(x_n-x_{n-1})} f(x_n) \quad \ldots (1)$$

To remember this formula, observe that numerator of $f(x_0)$ term is product of differences between x and x-coordinate of every data point except x_0. And the denominator is product of differences between x_0 and x-coordinate of every data point except x_0.

In general, numerator of $f(x_i)$ term is product of differences between x and x-coordinate of every data point except x_i. And denominator is product of differences between x_i and x-coordinate of every data point except x_i.

Example 5.1 : *Following is the data collected for a certain process :*

x	3	4	5.5	6	7
y	1.59	2.76	3.05	2.73	1.988

Determine y at x = 5.

Solution : Usually with the known interpolation technique i.e. linear interpolation, one may consider only x = 4 and x = 5.5 as below :

By Linear Interpolation :

$$\frac{x-x_1}{x_2-x_1} = \frac{y-y_1}{y_2-y_1} \quad \text{where} \quad x_1 = 4, x_2 = 5.5, x = 5$$

$$\text{and} \quad y_1 = 2.76, y_2 = 3.05 \text{ and y is unknown.}$$

$$\therefore \quad \frac{5-4}{5.5-4} = \frac{y-2.76}{3.05-2.76}$$

$$\therefore \quad y = \frac{(3.05-2.76)(5-4)}{(5.5-4)} + 2.76$$

$$\therefore \quad y = 2.95333$$

By Lagrange's Interpolation :

$$y = \frac{(x-x_1)(x-x_2)(x-x_3)(x-x_4)}{(x_0-x_1)(x_0-x_2)(x_0-x_3)(x_0-x_4)} f(x_0)$$

$$+ \frac{(x-x_0)(x-x_2)(x-x_3)(x-x_4)}{(x_1-x_0)(x_1-x_2)(x_1-x_3)(x_1-x_4)} f(x_1)$$

$$+ \frac{(x-x_0)(x-x_1)(x-x_3)(x-x_4)}{(x_2-x_0)(x_2-x_1)(x_2-x_3)(x_2-x_4)} f(x_2)$$

$$+ \frac{(x-x_0)(x-x_1)(x-x_2)(x-x_4)}{(x_3-x_0)(x_3-x_1)(x_3-x_2)(x_3-x_4)} f(x_3)$$

$$+ \frac{(x-x_0)(x-x_1)(x-x_2)(x-x_3)}{(x_4-x_0)(x_4-x_1)(x_4-x_2)(x_4-x_3)} f(x_4) \quad \ldots (2)$$

Substituting all values from above table and x = 5 where f(x) i.e. y is to be determined,

$$y = \frac{(5-4)(5-5.5)(5-6)(5-7)}{(3-4)(3-5.5)(3-6)(3-7)} \times 1.59 + \frac{(5-3)(5-5.5)(5-6)(5-7)}{(4-3)(4-5.5)(4-6)(4-7)} \times 2.76$$

$$+ \frac{(5-3)(5-4)(5-6)(5-7)}{(5.5-3)(5.5-4)(5.5-6)(5.5-7)} \times 3.05$$

$$+ \frac{(5-3)(5-4)(5-5.5)(5-7)}{(6-3)(6-4)(6-5.5)(6-7)} \times 2.73$$

$$+ \frac{(5-3)(5-4)(5-5.5)(5-6)}{(7-3)(7-4)(7-5.5)(7-6)} \times 1.988$$

$$\therefore y = \frac{1 \times (-0.5) \times (-1) \times (-2)}{-1 \times (-2.5) \times (-3) \times (-4)} \times 1.59 + \frac{2 \times (-0.5) \times (-1) \times (-2)}{1 \times (-1.5) \times (-2) \times (-3)} \times 2.76$$

$$+ \frac{2 \times 1 \times (-1) \times (-2)}{2.5 \times 1.5 \times (-0.5) \times (-1.5)} \times 3.05 + \frac{2 \times 1 \times (-0.5) \times (-2)}{3 \times 2 \times 0.5 \times (-1)} \times 2.73$$

$$+ \frac{2 \times 1 \times (-0.5) \times (-1)}{4 \times 3 \times 1.5 \times 1} \times 1.988$$

$$\therefore y = \frac{-1}{30} \times 1.59 + \frac{-2}{-9} \times 2.76 + \frac{4}{2.8125} \times 3.05 + \frac{2}{-3} \times 2.73 + \frac{1}{18} \times 1.988$$

$\therefore y = $ **3.18856** ... Ans.

Important observations with Lagrange's interpolation : The difference in two answers is due to reasoning explained by Figs. 5.1 and 5.2.

Now what is the correct answer ? The data is actually tabulated using equation,

$$y = f(x) = \sqrt{x} - \sin x \qquad \text{... x in radians}$$

$\therefore$ At $\quad x = 5, \quad y = \sqrt{5} - \sin 5 = 3.19499$

Hence, % Error in linear interpolation $= \dfrac{|3.19499 - 2.95333|}{3.19499} \times 100$

$= 7.5637\%$

Whereas % Error in Lagrange's interpolation $= \dfrac{|3.19499 - 3.18856|}{3.19499} \times 100$

$= 0.2013\%$

The result of Lagrange's interpolation is most accurate as it is capable of handling all data points together.

What will happen if we have only two data points, say (4, 2.76) and (5.5, 3.05) and we use Lagrange's interpolation ?

The formula in that case will become,

$$y = \frac{x - x_1}{x_0 - x_1} y_0 + \frac{x - x_0}{x_1 - x_0} y_1$$

$$= \frac{x - 5.5}{4 - 5.5} \times 2.76 + \frac{x - 4}{5.5 - 4} \times 3.05 \qquad \text{... (3)}$$

To find y at x = 5,

$$y = \frac{5 - 5.5}{4 - 5.5} \times 2.76 + \frac{5 - 4}{5.5 - 4} \times 3.05$$

$$= \frac{-0.5}{-1.5} \times 2.76 + \frac{1}{1.5} \times 3.05$$

∴ y = 2.95333

This answer exactly matches with the answer we obtained using linear interpolation. Thus, as a conclusion,

Lagrange's interpolation is linear interpolation if there are 2 data points. Further, it becomes quadratic interpolation if there are 3 data points. It becomes cubic interpolation if there are 4 data points.

5.2.1 Interpolation Polynomial

In the process of interpolation, if we do not substitute value of x, we get a polynomial equation. For example, consider equation (3) from above example,

$$y = \frac{x - 5.5}{4 - 5.5} \times 2.76 + \frac{x - 4}{5.5 - 4} \times 3.05$$

which evaluates as

y = −1.84 (x − 5.5) + 2.0333 (x − 4)

∴ y = − 1.84 x + 10.12 + 2.0333x − 8.1333

∴ y = 0.1933x + 1.9867

This is a polynomial equation with single degree.

Now let us consider equation (2). Here, every term has multiplication of $(x - x_i)$ four times in the numerator. Thus, every term and in turn, finally equation for y will be a polynomial equation with degree = 4. Thus, if we have n data points, the polynomial equation will have degree (n − 1). If n is higher the polynomial will be of higher degree, hence its equation will fit the data points most accurately. Hence, interpolation is more and more accurate as we increase data points.

The equation (1) is called the Lagrange's interpolation polynomial which can be concisely given as,

$$f_n(x) = \sum_{i=0}^{n} L_i(x) f(x_i)$$

where n is degree of polynomial (in other words, n + 1 data points are used)

$L_i(x)$ is Lagrange's term and can be expressed as

$$L_i(x) = \prod_{\substack{j=0 \\ j \neq i}}^{n} \frac{x - x_j}{x_i - x_j}$$

Σ is symbol for "sum of" and $\prod$ is symbol of "product of".

Example 5.2 : *Determine interpolation polynomial for following data points. State degree of the polynomial and find value of function at x = 3.5 and x = 6.*

x	1	2	3	4
y	3.5	−5	0	24

Solution : According to Lagrange's interpolation formula [equation (1)]

$$y = \frac{(x-x_1)(x-x_2)(x-x_3)}{(x_0-x_1)(x_0-x_2)(x_0-x_3)} f(x_0) + \frac{(x-x_0)(x-x_2)(x-x_3)}{(x_1-x_0)(x_1-x_2)(x_1-x_3)} f(x_1)$$

$$+ \frac{(x-x_0)(x-x_1)(x-x_3)}{(x_2-x_0)(x_2-x_1)(x_2-x_3)} f(x_2) + \frac{(x-x_0)(x-x_1)(x-x_2)}{(x_3-x_0)(x_3-x_1)(x_3-x_2)} f(x_3)$$

$$\therefore y = \frac{3.5}{-1 \times (-2) \times (-3)} (x-2)(x-3)(x-4) + \frac{(-5)}{1 \times (-1) \times (-2)} (x-1)(x-3)(x-4) + 0$$

$$+ \frac{24}{3 \times 2 \times 1} (x-1)(x-2)(x-3)$$

$$\therefore y = 0.9167x^3 + 1.25x^2 - 18.6667x + 20$$

Thus, the interpolation polynomial is three degree polynomial. It was obvious because, we have 4 data points.

Now, at x = 3.5,

$$y = 0.9167 \times 3.5^3 + 1.25 \times 3.5^2 - 18.6667 \times 3.5 + 20$$

$$\therefore y = 9.2812$$

Also at x = 6,

$$y = 0.9167 \times 6^3 + 1.25 \times 6^2 - 18.6667 \times 6 + 20$$

$$\therefore y = \mathbf{151.007} \qquad \text{... Ans.}$$

5.2.2 Extrapolation

Similar to interpolation, this is a process where we determine value of function for x lying outside the range of data points. Here, it is important to note that, as we move away from data set, the error in calculating value of function may increase.

In the example taken above, we determined f(x) for x = 6, given the range of x from 1 to 4. Hence, this is called as 'extrapolation'.

Example 5.3 : *Determine value of y for x = 7.5 and x = 10 from the following data :*

x	3	4	5	6	7
y	1.59	2.76	3.195	2.73	1.988

Solution : Using Lagrange's interpolation formula,

$$y = \frac{(x-4)(x-5)(x-6)(x-7)}{(3-4)(3-5)(3-6)(3-7)} \times 1.59 + \frac{(x-3)(x-5)(x-6)(x-7)}{(4-3)(4-5)(4-6)(4-7)} \times 2.76$$

$$+ \frac{(x-3)(x-4)(x-6)(x-7)}{(5-3)(5-4)(5-6)(5-7)} \times 3.195 + \frac{(x-3)(x-4)(x-5)(x-7)}{(6-3)(6-4)(6-5)(6-7)} \times 2.73$$

$$+ \frac{(x-3)(x-4)(x-5)(x-6)}{(7-3)(7-4)(7-5)(7-6)} \times 1.988$$

$$\therefore y = \frac{1.59}{24}(x-4)(x-5)(x-6)(x-7) + \frac{2.76}{-6}(x-3)(x-5)(x-6)(x-7)$$

$$+ \frac{3.195}{4}(x-3)(x-4)(x-6)(x-7) + \frac{2.73}{-6}(x-3)(x-4)(x-5)(x-7)$$

$$+ \frac{1.988}{24}(x-3)(x-4)(x-5)(x-6)$$

Substituting x = 7.5 in this equation,

$$y_{7.5} = f(7.5) = \frac{1.59}{24} \times 3.5 \times 2.5 \times 1.5 \times 0.5 - \frac{2.76}{6} \times 4.5 \times 2.5 \times 1.5 \times 0.5$$

$$+ \frac{3.195}{4} \times 4.5 \times 3.5 \times 1.5 \times 0.5 - \frac{2.73}{6} \times 4.5 \times 3.5 \times 2.5 \times 0.5$$

$$+ \frac{1.988}{24} \times 4.5 \times 3.5 \times 2.5 \times 1.5$$

$\therefore y_{7.5} = 1.9233$

Similarly, substituting x = 10,

$$y_{10} = f(10) = \frac{1.59}{24} \times 6 \times 5 \times 4 \times 3 - \frac{2.76}{6} \times 7 \times 5 \times 4 \times 3 + \frac{3.195}{4} \times 7 \times 6 \times 4 \times 3$$

$$- \frac{2.73}{6} \times 7 \times 6 \times 5 \times 3 + \frac{1.988}{24} \times 7 \times 6 \times 5 \times 4$$

$\therefore \quad y_{10} = $ **16.15** ... Ans.

Important Observation : The data in the example correspond to the data given in the first example we solved in this chapter. At the end of its solution, it is mentioned that the data is actually tabulated using equation,

$$y = f(x) = \sqrt{x} - \sin x \qquad \text{... x in radians}$$

Hence, we will calculate, y at x = 7.5 and x = 10 using this equation.

$\therefore \qquad y_{7.5} = \sqrt{7.5} - \sin 7.5 = 1.8006$

and $\qquad y_{10} = \sqrt{10} - \sin 10 = 3.7063$

Thus errors in the answers are,

Result of	By Equation	By Interpolation	% Error
$y_{7.5}$	1.8006	1.9233	6.8144 %
y_{10}	3.7063	16.15	335.7445 %

As already mentioned, in extrapolation error may increase as we move away from the data set. The above example illustrates the same. In addition to understand this deeply, Fig. 5.3, which shows the difference in the imaginary curve from where data is obtained and the curve drawn using interpolation polynomial.

Fig. 5.3 demonstrates how aggressively error will grow, when we move away from data set. Hence, we should bear in mind that the polynomial can be used for extrapolation only near the end points.

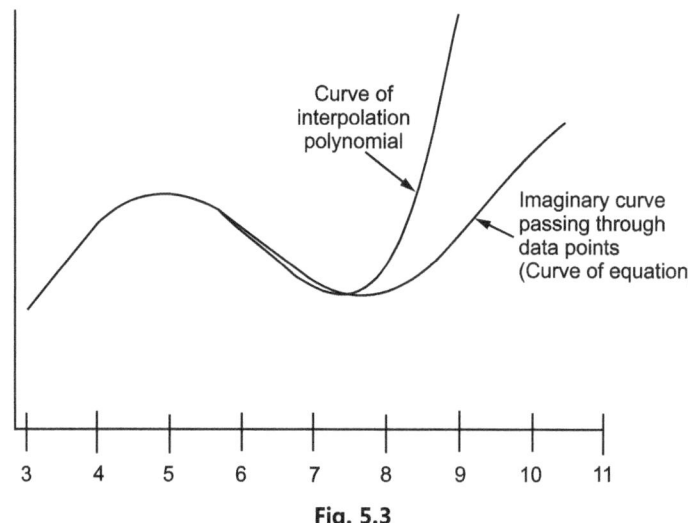

Fig. 5.3

5.2.3 Inverse Interpolation

Normally, we use the data set, and the Lagrange's interpolation formula to determine value of function f(x) at given x. But sometimes it may be required to find value of x for certain given value of f(x). This process is called 'inverse interpolation'. The method of interpolation remains same except that the positions of x values and y values are interchanged.

Example 5.4 : *Using following data, determine value of x at y = 4,*

x	2	3	5	8
y	10	6	3	2

Solution : According to Lagrange's interpolation formula,

$$x = \frac{(y-y_1)(y-y_2)(y-y_3)}{(y_0-y_1)(y_0-y_2)(y_0-y_3)} x_0 + \frac{(y-y_0)(y-y_2)(y-y_3)}{(y_1-y_0)(y_1-y_2)(y_1-y_3)} x_1$$

$$+ \frac{(y-y_0)(y-y_1)(y-y_3)}{(y_2-y_0)(y_2-y_1)(y_2-y_3)} x_3 + \frac{(y-y_0)(y-y_1)(y-y_2)}{(y_3-y_0)(y_3-y_1)(y_3-y_2)} x_4$$

$$\therefore \quad x = \frac{(4-6)(4-3)(4-2)}{(10-6)(10-3)(10-2)} \times 2 + \frac{(4-10)(4-3)(4-2)}{(6-10)(6-3)(6-2)} \times 3$$

$$+ \frac{(4-10)(4-6)(4-2)}{(3-10)(3-6)(3-2)} \times 5 + \frac{(4-10)(4-6)(4-3)}{(2-10)(2-6)(2-3)} \times 8$$

$$\therefore \quad x = \frac{(-2) \times 1 \times 2}{4 \times 7 \times 8} \times 2 + \frac{(-6) \times 1 \times 2}{(-4) \times 3 \times 4} \times 3 + \frac{(-6) \times (-2) \times 2}{(-7) \times (-3) \times 1} \times 5 + \frac{(-6) \times (-2) \times 1}{(-8) \times (-4) \times (-1)} \times 8$$

$$\therefore \quad x = 3.4286 \qquad \ldots \text{Ans.}$$

Important Observations : If the y values are oscillating as in case of earlier examples the inverse interpolation will lead to wrong results. So in that case another approach may be used, in which a polynomial of forward interpolation is determined. For example, as it is determined in Example 5.2 and roots of equation are found for given value of y. Then best suitable root is selected.

Example 5.5 : *Determine the value of x for y = 5 from the following data :*

x	1	2	3	4
y	3.5	–5	0	24

Solution : According to Lagrange's interpolation formula,

$$x = \frac{(y-y_1)(y-y_2)(y-y_3)}{(y_0-y_1)(y_0-y_2)(y_0-y_3)} x_0 + \frac{(y-y_0)(y-y_2)(y-y_3)}{(y_1-y_0)(y_1-y_2)(y_1-y_3)} x_1$$

$$+ \frac{(y-y_0)(y-y_1)(y-y_3)}{(y_2-y_0)(y_2-y_1)(y_2-y_3)} x_2 + \frac{(y-y_0)(y-y_1)(y-y_2)}{(y_3-y_0)(y_3-y_1)(y_3-y_2)} x_3$$

$$\therefore \quad x = \frac{(5-(-5))(5-0)(5-24)}{(3.5-(-5))(3.5-0)(3.5-2.4)} \times 1 + \frac{(5-3.5)(5-0)(5-24)}{(-5-3.5)(-5-0)(-5-24)} \times 2$$

$$+ \frac{(5-3.5)(5-(-5))(5-24)}{(0-3.5)(0-(-5))(0-24)} \times 3 + \frac{(5-3.5)(5-(-5))(5-0)}{(24-3.5)(24-(-5))(24-0)} \times 4$$

$$= \frac{10 \times 5 \times (-19)}{8.5 \times 3.5 \times (-20.5)} \times 1 + \frac{1.5 \times 5 \times (-19)}{(-8.5) \times (-5) \times (-29)} \times 2 + \frac{1.5 \times 10 \times (-19)}{(-3.5) \times 5 \times (-24)} \times 3$$

$$+ \frac{1.5 \times 10 \times 5}{20.5 \times 29 \times 24} \times 4$$

$$\therefore \quad x = -0.2258$$

The answer is expected between x = 3 and x = 4. But we get this illogical answer, because y values are oscillating. Hence, in this case we must use the forward interpolation polynomial, already determined in Example 5.2.

$$y = f(x) = 0.9167x^3 + 1.25x^2 - 18.6667x + 20$$

To determine value of x at y = 5, that means,

$$5 = 0.9167x^3 + 1.25x^2 - 18.6667x + 20$$

$$\therefore 0.9167x^3 + 1.25x^2 - 18.6667x + 15 = 0$$

This equation must be used to find all possible roots.

Now, using any one numerical method discussed in chapter 2 or using MatLab we can get roots of the equation.

>> roots ([0.9167 1.25 −18.6667 15])

ans =

   − 5.5575

   3.3023

   0.8916

>>

Thus x = 3.3023 which is lying between x = 3 and x = 4 is the desired answer of x for y = 5.

5.2.4 Pseudo Code for Lagrange's Interpolation Method

1. Get number of data points, n.
2. Get x and y values for all data points. Store them in arrays,
   x[0] to x[n − 1] and y[0] to y[n − 1].
3. Get x for which y is to be determined.
4. Sum = 0, mult1 = 1, mult2 = 1.
5. for i = 0 to n − 1

```
    {   for j = 0 to n−1
        {   if (i! = j)
            {   mult1 = mult1 * (x − x_j)
                mult2 = mult2 * (x_i − x_j)
            }
        }
        sum = sum + mult1/mult2 * y_i
        mult1 = 1, mult2 = 1
    }
```

6. Print sum, which is value of y for given value of x.
7. End.

5.2.5 Flow chart for Lagrange's Interpolation Method

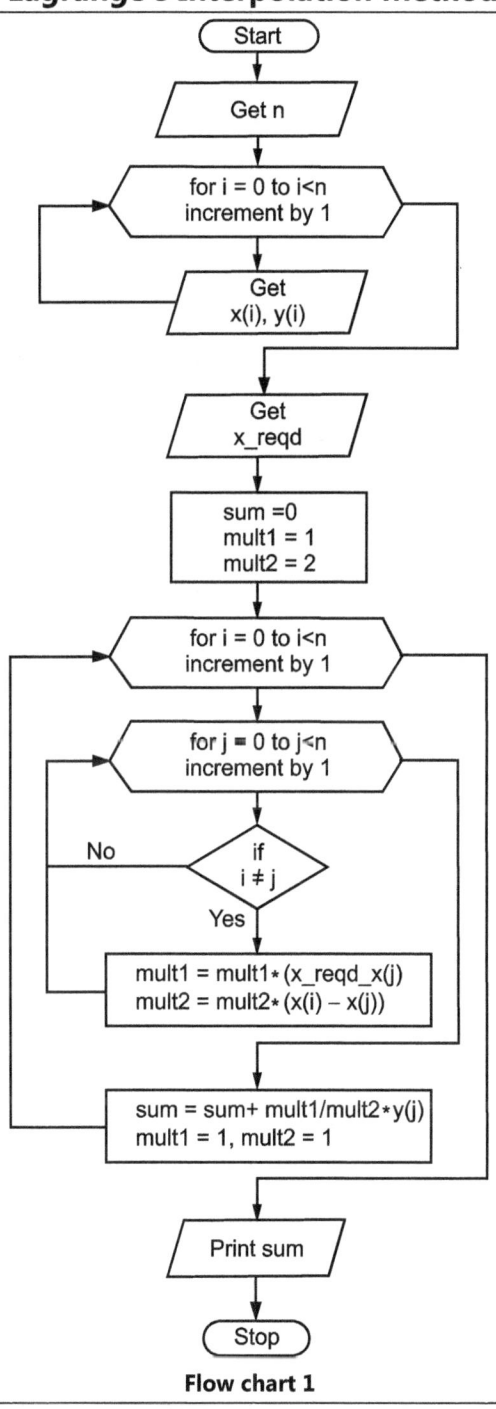

Flow chart 1

5.2.6 MATLAB Code for Lagrange's Interpolation Method

```
fprintf('\n\n*****************************************')
fprintf('\nProgram for Interpolation by Lagrange Method')
fprintf('\n*****************************************\n\n')
n=input('No. of data points= ');
for i=1:n
    x(i)=input('X= ');
    y(i)=input('Y= ');
end
x_reqd = input('Enter value of X for which Y is to be determined: ');
mult1=1;
mult2=1;
ans=0;
for j=1:n
    for k=1:n
        if (k~=j)
            mult1 = mult1 * (x_reqd-x(k));
            mult2 = mult2 * (x(j)-x(k));
        end
    end
    ans = ans + mult1/mult2*y(j);
    mult1=1;
    mult2=1;
end
fprintf('Answer is ...')
ans
```

5.2.7 Assistance of MS-Excel for Lagrange's Interpolation

1. Fill x values in Row 1. Considering Example 5.1, fill x values in cells from A1 to E1.
2. Type value of x for interpolation, somewhere away, say in cell G1.
3. Type formula as = $G $1/A1 in cell A3.
4. Copy and paste cell A3 in cells from B3 to E3.
5. Type formulae in given cells as below :
   in cell A5 formula as = A1 – A1
   in cell A6 formula as = B1 – A1
   in cell A7 formula as = C1 – A1

NA & CM (TE MECH. SEM. VI NMU)   INTERPOLATION

        in cell A8 formula as = \$D\$1 – A1
        in cell A9 formula as = \$E\$1 – A1
6. Copy and paste cells A5 to A9 in cells B5 to E5.
7. Type formulae in given cells as below :
        in cell A11 formula as = \$A\$3/A5
        in cell B11 formula as = \$B\$3/B5
        in cell C11 formula as = \$C\$3/C5
        in cell D11 formula as = \$D\$3/D5
        in cell E11 formula as = \$E\$3/E5
8. Copy and paste cells A11 to E11 in cells A12 to A15.
9. Note we get # DIV/0! error message in cells A11, B12, C13, D14 and E15 because of division by zero. Replace those cells by 1, individually.
10. Type formula as = A11 * B11 * C11 * D11 * E11 in cell G11.
11. Copy and paste cell G11 in cells from G12 to G15.
    Thus, cells G11 to G15 show multiplying factors of y_0, y_1, y_2, y_3 and y_4.
12. Now, fill in y values in H11 to H15.
13. Type formula as = G11 * H11 in cell I11.
14. Copy and paste cell I11 in cells from I12 to I15.
15. Type formula as = sum (I11 : I15) in cell I16.

The value in cell I16 is the required answer of interpolation. The worksheet will look as shown in Image 5.1.

	A	B	C	D	E	F	G	H	I
1	3	4	5.5	6	7		5		
2									
3	2	1	-0.5	-1	-2				
4									
5	0	-1	-2.5	-3	-4				
6	1	0	-1.5	-2	-3				
7	2.5	1.5	0	-0.5	-1.5				
8	3	2	0.5	0	-1				
9	4	3	1.5	1	0				
10									
11	1	-1	0.2	0.33333	0.5		-0.03333	1.59	-0.053
12	2	1	0.33333	0.5	0.66667		0.22222	2.76	0.61333
13	0.8	0.66667	1	2	1.33333		1.42222	3.05	4.33778
14	0.66667	0.5	-1	1	2		-0.66667	2.73	-1.82
15	0.5	0.33333	-0.33333	-1	1		0.05556	1.988	0.11044
16									3.18856

Image 5.1

5.3 Newton's Interpolation Methods

When the interpolation points are equally spaces, the values of the interpolation polynomial can be expressed in terms of finite differences.

Suppose that for $x_i = x_0 + ih$, where h is grid size, the values $f_0, f_1, f_2 \ldots \ldots \ldots f_n$, of the function f(x) are known. The difference $f_0, f_1, f_2 \ldots \ldots \ldots f_n$, are then called finite differences of first order.

Furthermore, we define the differences of order *k + 1* inductively by

$$\Delta^{k+1} f_i = \Delta^k f_{i+1} - f_i$$

There are three methods according to Newton's Interpolation scheme :

1. Forward difference interpolation (Δ- Forward Difference operator)
2. Backward difference interpolation (∇ - Backward Difference operator)
3. Central difference interpolation (δ - Central Difference operator)

We will discuss the first two methods. The third is not included in our syllabus, hence not included in this book.

These methods require knowledge about forward difference operator and backward difference operator.

5.3.1 Forward Difference Operator

After writing the x values and y values in two separate columns, third, fourth, fifth, ... columns are generated by writing difference in successive values in earlier column. The third column which represents difference in y values is denoted by Δy.

$$\Delta y = \Delta f(x) = f(x + h) - f(x)$$

where, h is the distance between successive values of x.

Here we will understand an important point that due to existence of this 'h' term Newton's Forward and Backward difference methods can interpolate the data set having equal interval width for independent variable. Thus, Example 5.1 cannot be solved by these methods. Examples 5.2 and 5.3 can be solved.

Further, it is important to note that usually, although x is evenly spaced, y may not be evenly spaced. This is called non-linear relation between x and y. If the relation between x and y is linear then only y values also will be evenly spaced.

Newton's forward and backward difference methods, are hence, incompetent in handling inverse interpolation problems for non-linear functions.

Coming back to the Forward Difference operator, the fourth column is denoted by $\Delta^2 y$ as it gives difference between successive differences of y values.

$$\begin{aligned}
\Delta^2 y &= \Delta(\Delta f(x)) \\
&= \Delta(f(x + h) - f(x)) \\
&= [f(x + 2h) - f(x + h)] - [f(x + h) - f(x)] \\
&= f(x + 2h) - 2f(x + h) + f(x)
\end{aligned}$$

Thus, Δ is first order forward difference
Δ^2 is second order forward difference
Δ^3 is third order forward difference
and so on, till $(n-1)^{th}$ column.

Example 5.6 : *Prepare forward difference table for the following data :*

x	1	3	5	7	9	11	13
y	–40	–64	–72	–16	152	480	1016

Solution: The table will have 6 columns for differences because data set has 7 data points.

x	y	Δy	$\Delta^2 y$	$\Delta^3 y$	$\Delta^4 y$	$\Delta^5 y$	$\Delta^6 y$
1	–40	–24	16	48	0	0	0
3	–64	–8	64	48	0	0	
5	–72	56	112	48	0		
7	–16	168	160	48			
9	152	328	208				
11	480	536					
13	1016						

Depending on degree of polynomial used for data acquisition at certain column, we will find the differences to be equal to each other and next column onwards all elements equal to zero.

Topmost element in every column is taken as 0th element, hence first column shows differences from Δy_0 to Δy_5. Second column shows second order differences from $\Delta^2 y_0$ to $\Delta^2 y_4$.

5.3.2 Backward Difference Operator

Forward difference is finding difference between current and its next term. Similarly, backward difference means finding difference between the current and earlier term. It is denoted by ∇.

Thus, $\nabla y = \nabla f(x)$
$= f(x) - f(x - h)$

Like forward difference, this will also have higher orders of differences.

Example 5.7 : *Prepare backward difference table for the following data :*

x	2	5	8	11	14
y	13.8	19.5	−1.8	−33.9	−60.6

Solution : The data set has 5 data points, hence the difference table will have 4 difference columns from ∇ to ∇^4.

x	y	∇y	$\nabla^2 y$	$\nabla^3 y$	$\nabla^4 y$
2	13.8				
5	19.5	5.7			
8	−1.8	−21.3	−2.7		
11	−33.9	−32.1	−10.8	16.2	
14	−60.6	−26.7	5.4	16.2	0

At this level, for there is no difference between forward difference table and backward difference table, we may realize their utility after solving a few problems.

5.3.3 Formulation for Interpolation using Forward Differences

Formula for interpolation using forward difference method is,

$$y = y_0 + u\Delta y_0 + \frac{u(u-1)}{2!}\Delta^2 y_0 + \frac{u(u-1)(u-2)}{3!}\Delta^3 y_0 + \ldots$$
$$+ \frac{u(u-1)(u-2)\ldots(u-(n-1))}{n!}\Delta^n y_0$$

where, $u = \dfrac{x - x_0}{h}$

Example 5.8 : *Determine value of y for x = 1.2 from the following data :*

x	0	2	4	6	8
y	−77.5	−69.7	−51.5	15.5	169.7

Solution : The forward difference table is,

x	y	Δy	$\Delta^2 y$	$\Delta^3 y$	$\Delta^4 y$
0	−77.5	7.8	10.4	38.4	0
2	−69.7	18.2	48.8	38.4	
4	−51.5	67	87.2		
6	15.5	154.2			
8	169.7				

Here, $h = 2$ and $u = \dfrac{x - x_0}{h} = \dfrac{1.2 - 0}{2} = 0.6$

According to forward difference formula,

$$y = y_0 + u\Delta y_0 + \dfrac{u(u-1)}{2!}\Delta^2 y_0 + \dfrac{u(u-1)(u-2)}{3!}\Delta^3 y_0$$

$$+ \dfrac{u(u-1)(u-2)(u-3)}{4!}\Delta^4 y_0$$

$$= -77.5 + 0.6 \times 7.8 + \dfrac{0.6 \times (0.6-1)}{1 \times 2} \times 10.4$$

$$+ \dfrac{0.6 \times (0.6-1)(0.6-2)}{1 \times 2 \times 3} \times 38.4 + 0$$

$$= -77.5 + 4.68 - 1.248 + 2.1504$$

∴ $y = -71.9176$ ... Ans.

Example 5.9 : Determine interpolation polynomial for following data and then determine $f(3.4)$.

x	2	4	6	8	10	12	14	16
y	−14	40	190	484	970	1696	2710	4060

Solution : As there are 8 data points, there will be 7 difference columns in the forward difference table.

x	y	Δy	Δ²y	Δ³y	Δ⁴y	Δ⁵y	Δ⁶y	Δ⁷y
2	−14	54	96	48	0	0	0	0
4	40	150	144	48	0	0	0	
6	190	294	192	48	0	0		
8	484	486	240	48	0			
10	970	726	288	48				
12	1696	1014	336					
14	2710	1350						
16	4060							

Here, $h = 2$ and $u = \dfrac{x - x_0}{h} = \dfrac{3.4 - 2}{2} = 0.7$

But we will not substitute value of u, because we want to get interpolation polynomial. Also we will write formula upto $\Delta^3 y$ term, because next all terms will be zero.

$$\therefore \quad y = y_0 + u\Delta y_0 + \dfrac{u(u-1)}{2!}\Delta^2 y_0 + \dfrac{u(u-1)(u-2)}{3!}\Delta^3 y_0$$

$$\therefore \quad y = -14 + \dfrac{x-2}{2} \times 54 + \left(\dfrac{x-2}{2}\right)\left(\dfrac{x-2}{2} - 1\right) \times \dfrac{96}{2} +$$
$$\left(\dfrac{x-2}{2}\right)\left(\dfrac{x-2}{2} - 1\right)\left(\dfrac{x-2}{2} - 2\right) \times \dfrac{48}{6}$$

$$= -14 + 27x - 54 + (x-2)(x-4) \times \dfrac{96}{2 \times 2 \times 2} + (x-2)(x-4)(x-6)$$
$$\times \dfrac{48}{6 \times 2 \times 2 \times 2}$$

$$= 27x - 68 + 12(x^2 - 6x + 8) + (x^2 - 6x + 8)(x - 6)$$
$$= 27x - 68 + 12x^2 - 72x + 96 + x^3 - 6x^2 + 8x - 6x^2 + 36x - 48$$

$$\therefore \quad y = x^3 - x - 20$$

Now at $x = 3.4$,

$$y = f(3.4) = (3.4)^3 - 3.4 - 20 = \mathbf{15.904} \qquad \text{... Ans.}$$

Example 5.10 : *Determine value of y for x = 8.2 using following data and forward difference formula.*

x	2	3	4	5	6	7	8	9
y	−14	4	40	100	190	316	484	700

Solution : The difference table is as below :

x	y	Δy	$\Delta^2 y$	$\Delta^3 y$	$\Delta^4 y$	$\Delta^5 y$	$\Delta^6 y$	$\Delta^7 y$
2	−14	18	18	6	0	0	0	0
3	4	36	24	6	0	0	0	
4	40	60	30	6	0	0		
5	100	90	36	6	0			
6	190	126	42	6				
7	316	168	48					
8	484	216						
9	700							

Here, $h = 1$ and $u = \dfrac{x - x_0}{h} = \dfrac{8.2 - 2}{1} = 6.2$

$\therefore \quad y = y_0 + u\Delta y_0 + \dfrac{u(u-1)}{2!}\Delta^2 y_0 + \dfrac{u(u-1)(u-2)}{3!}\Delta^3 y_0$

$\quad = -14 + 6.2 \times 18 + \dfrac{6.2 \times 5.2}{2} \times 18 + \dfrac{6.2 \times 5.2 \times 4.2}{6} \times 6$

$\therefore \quad y = 523.168$ ... Ans.

5.3.4 Formulation for Newton's Backward Difference Interpolation

Formula for interpolation using backward differences is,

$$y = y_n + s\nabla y_n + \dfrac{s(s+1)}{2!}\nabla^2 y_n + \dfrac{s(s+1)(s+2)}{3!}\nabla^3 y_n + \ldots$$
$$+ \dfrac{s(s+1)(s+2)\ldots(s+(n-1))}{n!}\nabla^n y_n$$

where, $s = \dfrac{x - x_n}{h}$

Example 5.11 : Solve Example 5.10 using backward difference formula.

Solution : The backward difference table is,

x	y	∇y	$\nabla^2 y$	$\nabla^3 y$	$\nabla^4 y$	$\nabla^5 y$	$\nabla^6 y$	$\nabla^7 y$
2	−14							
3	4	18						
4	40	36	18					
5	100	60	24	6				
6	190	90	30	6	0			
7	316	126	36	6	0	0		
8	484	168	42	6	0	0	0	
9	700	216	48	6	0	0	0	0

Here, $h = 1$ and $s = \dfrac{x - x_n}{h} = \dfrac{8.2 - 9}{1} = -0.8$

$\therefore \quad y = 700 + (-0.8) \times 216 + \dfrac{(-0.8) \times 0.2}{2} \times 48 + \dfrac{(-0.8) \times 0.2 \times 1.2}{6} \times 6$

$\quad = 700 - 172.8 - 3.84 - 0.192$

$\therefore \quad y = 523.168$ ... Ans.

5.3.5 Choice of Interpolation Method

From Example 5.10 and Example 5.11, we observe that there is no difference in the answers, although the difference operator and substituted numbers are changed. Then how to decide which method to use in which case ?

Now-a-days, due to fast computing facilities and large memory devices, we may not appreciate this difference, but physical we will notice that calculation of 'u' terms in Example 5.10 involved comparatively big numbers than those in calculation of 's' terms in Example 5.11 i.e. Example 5.10 involved calculations like $6.2 \times 5.2 \times 4.2$. On the other hand, Example 5.11 involved calculations like $(-0.8) \times 0.2 \times 1.2$, which can be performed without calculator easily. Now imagine a difference table having hundreds of x values starting from 0 to 900 say with interval of 5. Now for interpolation at $x = 897$ if we use forward difference formula, it will involve calculations like $u = \dfrac{897 - 0}{5} = 179.4$ and due to $u(u - 1)(u - 2)$ ... calculations like $179.4 \times 178.4 \times 177.4$ ... On the other hand, if we use backward difference method, it will involve calculations like $s = \dfrac{897 - 900}{5} = -0.6$ and due to $s(s + 1)(s + 2)$ .... calculations like $(-0.6) \times 0.4 \times 1.4$ ... In general, choice of forward or backward is made according to convenience in such a way that if x for which y is sought, lies near x_0 we will use forward difference method, and if it lies near x_n, we will use backward difference. Remember that there will not be difference in the final answer if choice of method is wrong.

5.3.6 Algorithm for Newton's Forward Difference Interpolation Method

1. Get number of data points, n.
2. Get x and y values for all data points. Store them in arrays x[0] to x[n – 1] and y[0] to y[n – 1].
3. Get x for which y is to be obtained.
4. Calculate h and u.
5. Sum = 0, mult = 1.
6. Store y values in first column of diff [n – 1] [n – 1] array.
7. Calculate differences and store them in diff [n – 1] [n – 1].
8. For i = 0 to i = n – 2
   {   for j = 0 to j = i
       {mult = mult * (u–j)}
       sum = sum + mult*diff[0][i+1]/factorial (i+1)
       mult = 1
   }
9. ans = sum + y[0]
10. Print ans as final answer.
11. End
12. Define function for factorial.

5.3.7 Flow Chart for Newton's Forward Difference Interpolation Method

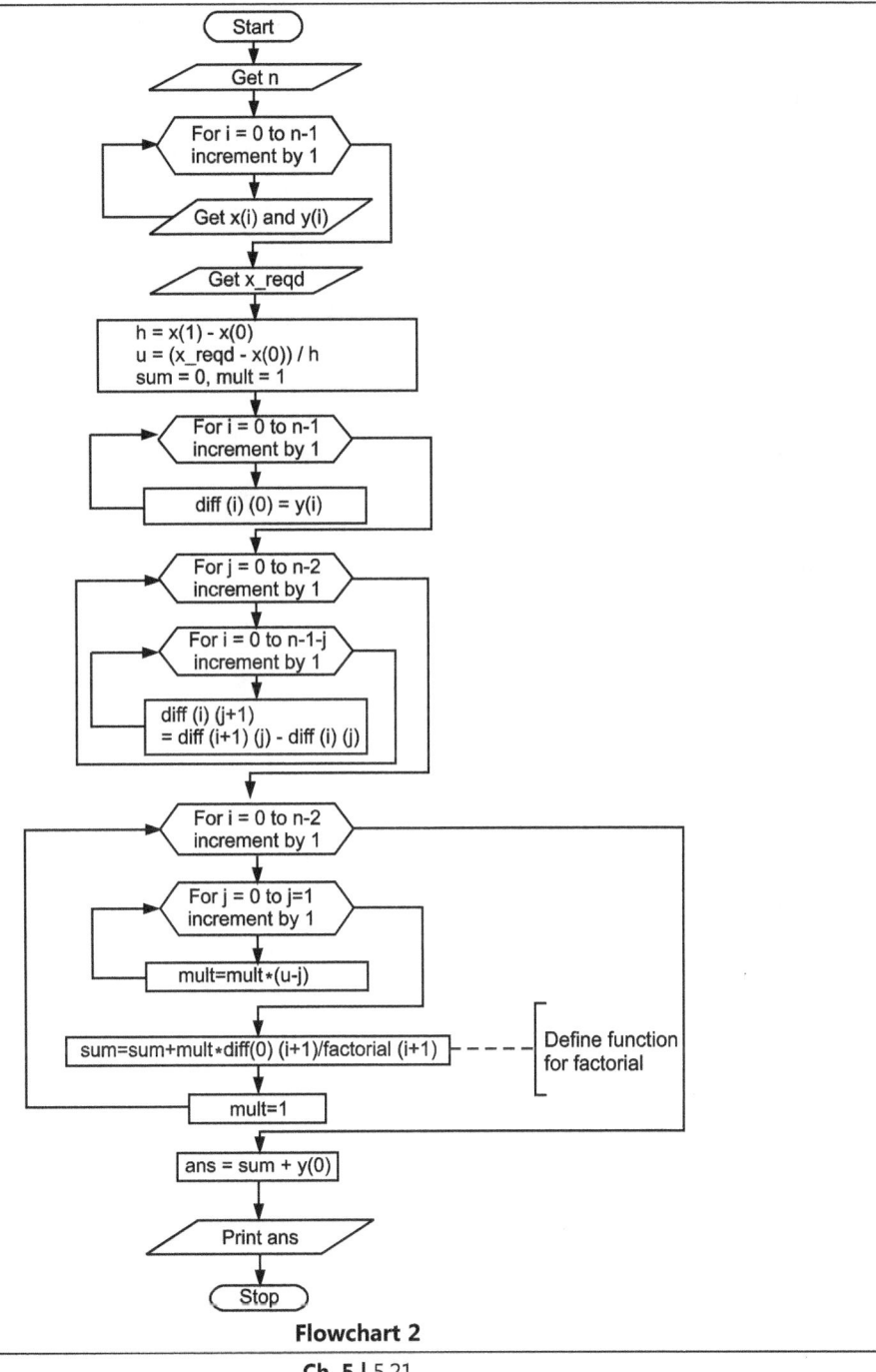

Flowchart 2

5.3.8 MATLAB Code for Newton's Forward Difference Interpolation Method

```
fprintf('\n\n*************************************************')
fprintf('\nProgram for Interpolation by NFD Method')
fprintf('\n*************************************************\n\n')
ans=0
mult=1;
n=input('No. of data points= ');
for i=1:n
        x(i)=input('X= ');
        y(i)=input('Y= ');
end
x_reqd = input ('Enter value of X for which Y is to be determined: ');
h=x(2)- x(1);
u=(x_reqd-x(1))/h;
for i=1:n
    diff(i,1)=y(i);
end
for j=1:n-1
    for i=1:n-j
        diff(i,j+1)=diff(i+1,j)-diff(i,j);
    end
end
for i=1:n-1
    factorial=1;
    for j=1:i
        mult=mult*(u-j+1);
    end
    for k=1:i
        factorial= factorial*k;
    end
    ans=ans+mult*diff(1,i+1)/factorial;
    mult=1;
end
ans=ans+y(1);
fprintf('Answer is ...')
ans
```

5.3.9 Assistance of MS-Excel for Newton's Forward Difference Interpolation Method

Construction of complete solution in MS-Excel is not an effective exercise, as it would require a lot of individual calculations. Hence, it would be a time consuming process. So, we will take assistance of MS-Excel in constructing the forward difference table. Then results of the table may be further used for calculations on calculator.

Steps for Constructing Forward Difference Table (Consider Example 5.9):
1. Fill in the first value of x (= 2) in cell A1.
2. Type formula as = A1 + 2 in cell A2, so that x is incremented by 2.
3. Copy and paste cell A2 in cells from A3 to A8, so that complete list of x values is obtained.
4. Fill in corresponding values of y in column B.
5. Type formula as = B2 – B1 in cell C2.
6. Copy and paste this formula i.e. cell C2 for all rows corresponding to x values and (n – 1) = 7 columns, that means in cell from C2 to I8.

The worksheet looks as shown in Image 5.2.

	A	B	C	D	E	F	G	H	I
1	2	-14							
2	4	40	54	54	54	54	54	54	54
3	6	190	150	96	42	-12	-66	-120	-174
4	8	484	294	144	48	6	18	84	204
5	10	970	486	192	48	0	-6	-24	-108
6	12	1696	726	240	48	0	0	6	30
7	14	2710	1014	288	48	0	0	0	-6
8	16	4060	1350	336	48	0	0	0	0

Image 5.2

7. Now to keep the horizontally repeating difference only once, that means as the number 54 is repeated in all columns from C to I, to eliminate it from D to I and keep it only in cell C2, select and delete cells from D2 to I2.
8. Repeat the same procedure down for all rows.

9. The forward difference table will look as shown in Image 5.3. The cells C2, D3, E4, F5, G6, H7 and I8 are the forward differences required in interpolation formula.

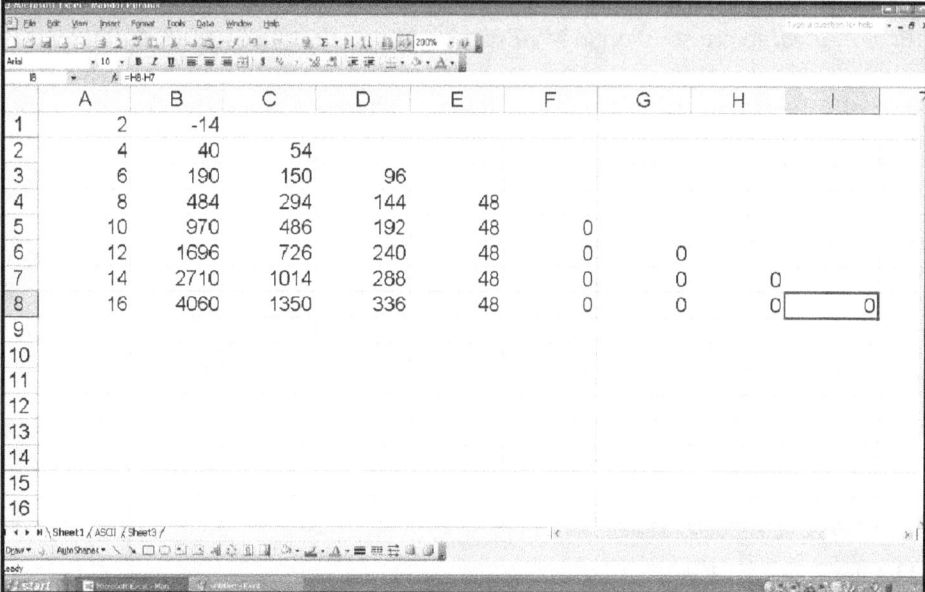

Image 5.3

5.3.10 Pseudo Code for Newton's Backward Difference Method of Interpolation

1. Get number of data points, n.
2. Get x and y values for all data points. Store them in arrays x[0] to x[n – 1] and y[0] to y[n – 1].
3. Get x for which y value is to be obtained.
4. Calculate h and s.
5. Sum = 0, mult = 1.
6. Store y values in first column of diff [n – 1] [n – 1] array.
7. Calculate differences and store them in diff [n – 1] [n – 1].
8. For i = 0 to i = n – 2
   ```
   {   for j = 0 to j = i
       {mult = mult * (s+j)}
       sum = sum + mult*diff[n–2–i][i+1]/factorial(i+1)
       mult = 1
   }
   ```
9. ans = sum + y[n–1]
10. Print ans as final answer.
11. End
12. Define function for factorial.

5.3.11 Flow Chart for Newton's Backward Difference Interpolation Method

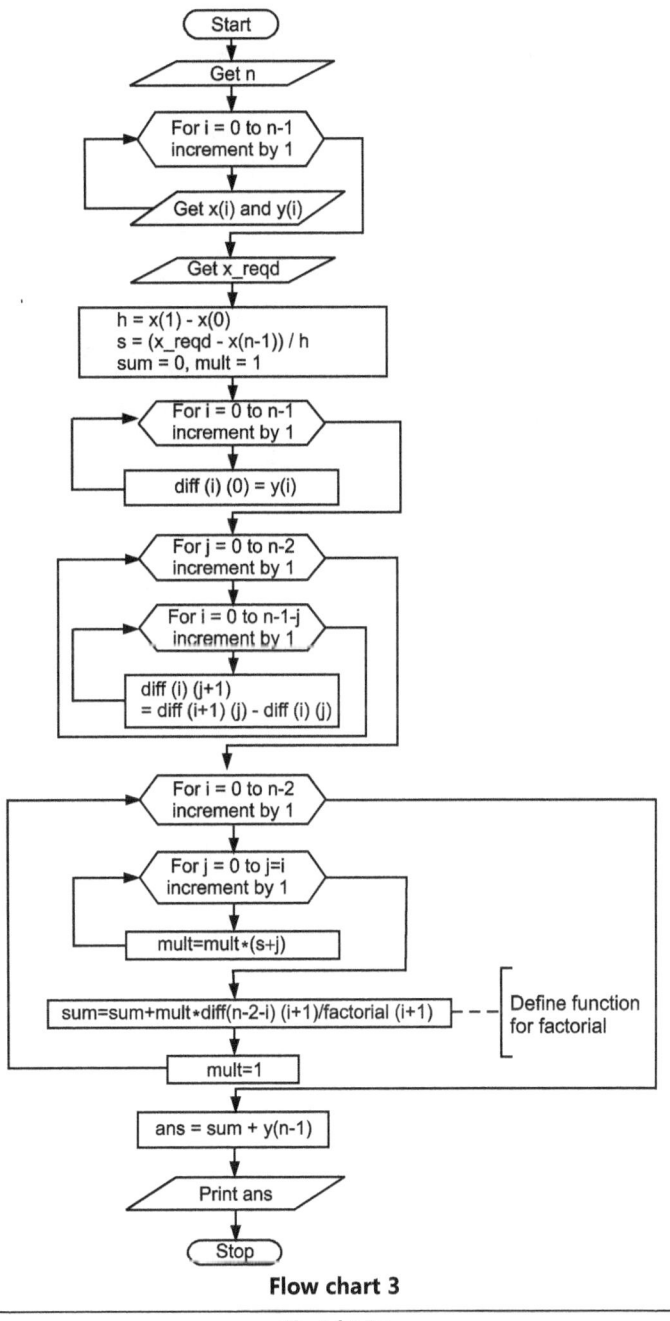

Flow chart 3

5.3.12 MATLAB Code for Newton's Backward Difference Interpolation Method

```
fprintf('\n\n****************************************************')
fprintf('\nInterpolation by Newton Backward Difference Method')
fprintf('\n****************************************************\n\n')
ans=0
mult=1;
n=input('No. of data points= ');
for i=1:n
        x(i)=input('X= ');
        y(i)=input('Y= ');
end
x_reqd = input ('Enter value of X for which Y is to be determined: ');
h=x(2)-x(1);
s=(x_reqd-x(n))/h;
for i=1:n
    diff(i,1)=y(i);
end
for j=1:n-1
    for i=1:n-j
        diff(i,j+1)=diff(i+1,j)-diff(i,j);
    end
end
for i=1:n-1
    factorial=1;
    for j=1:i
        mult=mult*(s+j-1);
    end
    for k=1:i
        factorial = factorial*k;
    end
    ans=ans+mult*diff(n-i,i+1)/factorial;
    mult=1;
end
ans=ans+y(n);
fprintf('Answer is ...')
ans
```

5.3.13 Assistance of MS-Excel for Newton's Backward Difference Interpolation Method

As mentioned earlier, we will use MS-Excel only to prepare backward difference table.

Example 5.11 is considered for following steps :

1. Fill in the first value of x (= 2) in cell A1.
2. Type formula as = A1 + 1 in cell A2, so that x is incremented by 1.
3. Copy and paste cell A2 in cells from A3 to A8.
4. Fill in corresponding values of y in column B.
5. Type formula as = B8 – B7 in cell C7.
6. Copy and paste this formula i.e. cell C7 for all rows corresponding to x values and (n – 1) = 7 columns, that means in cells from C7 to I1.

The worksheet will look as shown in Image 5.4.

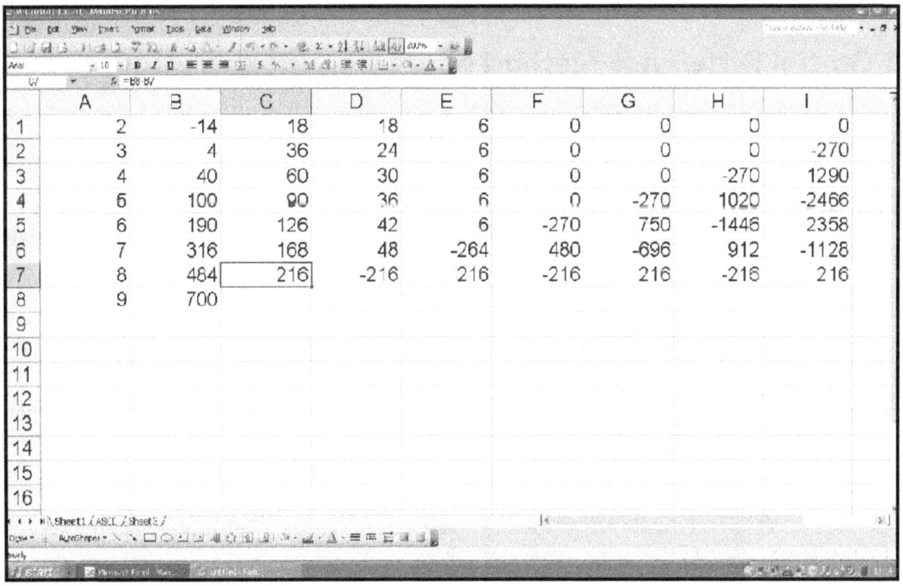

	A	B	C	D	E	F	G	H	I
1	2	-14	18	18	6	0	0	0	0
2	3	4	36	24	6	0	0	0	-270
3	4	40	60	30	6	0	0	-270	1290
4	5	100	90	36	6	0	-270	1020	-2466
5	6	190	126	42	6	-270	750	-1446	2358
6	7	316	168	48	-264	480	-696	912	-1128
7	8	464	216	-216	216	-216	216	-216	216
8	9	700							

Image 5.4

7. Now to keep the horizontally repeating difference only once, that means as the number 216 is repeated in all columns from C to I, to eliminate it from D to I and keep it only in cell C7, select and delete cells from D7 to I7.
8. Repeat the same procedure down for all rows.
9. The backward difference table will look as shown in Image 5.5.

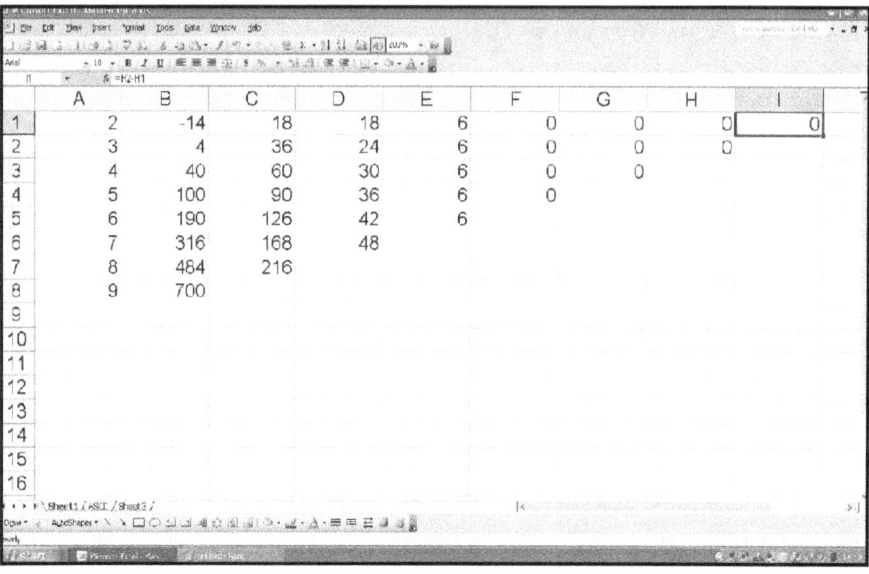

Image 5.5

5.3.14 Central Difference Method or Sterling Interpolation

Central difference formulae are best suited for interpolation near middle of the table.

Central Difference Table :

Case 1 : No. of data points (n) = ODD

X	Y	1st Difference	2nd Difference	3rd Difference	4th Difference
x_{-2}	y_{-2}				
		Δy_{-2}			
x_{-1}	y_{-1}		$\Delta^2 y_{-2}$		
		Δy_{-1}		$\Delta^3 y_{-2}$	
x_0	y_0		$\Delta^2 y_{-1}$		$\Delta^4 y_{-2}$
		Δy_0		$\Delta^3 y_{-1}$	
x_1	y_1		$\Delta^2 y_0$		
		Δy_1			
x_2	y_2				

Stirling's Formula

$$y_g = y_0 + u\left[\frac{\Delta y_0 + \Delta y_{-1}}{2}\right] + \frac{u^2}{2!}\Delta^2 y_{-1} + \frac{(u-1)u(u+1)}{3!}\left[\frac{\Delta^3 y_{-1} + \Delta^3 y_{-2}}{2}\right] + \frac{(u-1)u^2(u+1)}{4!}\Delta^4 y_{-2} + \ldots\ldots$$

where $u = \dfrac{x_q - x_0}{h}$

Note :
1. Above said formula derived by taking mean of Gauss Forward and Backward Difference Formula.
2. Stirling's Formula is to be used when number of data points is ODD.
3. Useful for $|u| < \dfrac{1}{3}$ or $-\dfrac{1}{2} < u < \dfrac{1}{2}$
4. Gives best results when $-\dfrac{1}{4} < u < \dfrac{1}{4}$

Case 2 : When n = EVEN

X	Y	1st Difference	2nd Difference	3rd Difference	4th Difference	5th Difference
x_{-2}	y_{-2}					
		Δy_{-2}				
x_{-1}	y_{-1}		$\Delta^2 y_{-2}$			
		Δy_{-1}		$\Delta^3 y_{-2}$		
x_0	y_0		$\Delta^2 y_{-1}$		$\Delta^4 y_{-2}$	
		Δy_0		$\Delta^3 y_{-1}$		$\Delta^5 y_{-2}$
x_1	y_1		$\Delta^2 y_0$		$\Delta^4 y_{-1}$	
		Δy_1		$\Delta^3 y_0$		
x_2	y_2		$\Delta^2 y_1$			
		Δy_2				
x_3	y_3					

Bessel's Formula :

$$y_g = \dfrac{y_0 + y_1}{2} + \left[u - \dfrac{1}{2}\right]\Delta y_0 + \dfrac{u(u-1)}{2!}\left[\dfrac{\Delta^2 y_0 + \Delta^2 y_{-1}}{2}\right] + \dfrac{u(u-1)\left(u - \dfrac{1}{2}\right)}{3!}\Delta^3 y_{-1}$$

$$+ \dfrac{(u+1)u(u-1)(u-2)}{4!}\left\{\dfrac{\Delta^4 y_{-1} + \Delta^4 y_{-2}}{2}\right\}$$

$$+ \dfrac{(u+1)u(u-1)(u-2)\left(u - \dfrac{1}{2}\right)}{5!}\Delta^5 y_{-2} + \ldots\ldots$$

where $u = \dfrac{x_q - x_0}{h}$

Note :
Stirling's Formula is to be used when number of data points is EVEN.
Useful for $u = \frac{1}{2}$, gives best results when $\frac{1}{4} < u < \frac{3}{4}$

Example 5.12 : Using Stirling's formula, find y(6.2) from following table:

x	2	4	6	8	10
y	30	43	64	87	104

Solution : Since we require y at x=6.4, origin for central difference method i.e. $x_0 = 6$ and
$u = \frac{x_g - x_0}{h}$

$$u = \frac{(6.2 - 6.0)}{(4 - 2)} \rightarrow u = 0.1$$

Central difference table as follows:

x	X	y	Δy	Δ²y	Δ³y	Δ⁴y
2	–4	30				
			13			
4	–2	43		8		
			Δy₋₁ = 21		Δ³y₋₂ = –6	
6	0	y₀ = 64		Δ²y₋₁ = 2		Δ⁴y₋₂ = –2
			Δy₀ = 23		Δ³y₋₁ = –8	
8	2	87		–6		
			17			
10	4	104				

By Stirling's formula, we have

$$y_g = y_0 + u\left[\frac{\Delta y_0 + \Delta y_{-1}}{2}\right] + \frac{u^2}{2!}\Delta^2 y_{-1} + \frac{(u-1)u(u+1)}{3!}$$
$$+ \left[\frac{\Delta^3 y_{-1} + \Delta^3 y_{-2}}{2}\right] + \frac{(u-1)u^2(u+1)}{4!}\Delta^4 y_{-2}$$

$$y_g = 64 + (0.1) \times \left[\frac{(21+23)}{2}\right] + \left(\frac{0.1}{4}\right)^2 \times 2 + \left(\frac{0.1 \times (0.1-1)^2}{6}\right)$$
$$\times \left[\frac{(-6-8)}{2}\right] + \left[\frac{0.1^2 + (0.1^2 - 1)}{24}\right] \times 2$$

$$y_g = 64 + 2.2 + 0.010 + 0.116 + 0.001 = 66.326 \quad \text{...Ans}$$

Example 5.13 : Using Stirling's formula, find y(1.22) from following table :

x	1	1.1	1.2	1.3	1.4
y	0.84147	0.89121	0.93204	0.96356	0.98545

Solution : Since we require y at x = 1.22, origin for central difference method i.e. $x_0 = 1.2$ and

$$u = \frac{x_g - x_0}{h}$$

$$u = \frac{(1.22 - 1.2)}{(1.1 - 1)} \to u = 0.2$$

Central difference table as follows :

x	X	y	Δy	Δ²y	Δ³y	Δ⁴y
1	−0.2	0.84147				
			0.04974			
1.1	−0.1	0.89121		−0.00891		
			Δy₋₁ = 0.04083		Δ³y₋₂ = −0.0004	
1.2	0	y₀ = 0.93204		Δ²y₋₁ = −0.00931		Δ⁴y₋₂ = 0.00008
			Δy₀ = 0.03152		Δ³y₋₁ = −0.00032	
1.3	0.1	0.96356		−0.00963		
			0.02189			
1.4	0.2	0.98545				

By Stirling's formula, we have

$$y_g = y_0 + u\left[\frac{\Delta y_0 + \Delta y_{-1}}{2}\right] + \frac{u^2}{2!}\Delta^2 y_{-1} + \frac{(u-1)u(u+1)}{3!}\left[\frac{\Delta^3 y_{-1} + \Delta^3 y_{-2}}{2}\right] + \frac{(u-1)u^2(u+1)}{4!}\Delta^4 y_{-2} + \ldots$$

$$y_g = 0.93204 + (0.2) \times \left[\frac{(0.04083 + 0.03152)}{2}\right] + \left(\frac{0.2}{4}\right)^2 \times (-0.00931) + \left(\frac{0.2 \times (0.2 - 1)2}{6}\right) \times \left[\frac{(-0.0004 - 0.00032)}{2}\right] + \left[\frac{0.2^2 + (0.2^2 - 1)}{24}\right] \times (0.00008)$$

$y_g = 0.939100$ ...**Ans**

5.4 Divided Difference Method

The Langrange's formula has the drawback that if another interpolation value were inserted then the interpolation coefficients are required to be calculated. This labor of recomputing the interpolation coefficient is saved by using Newton's General Interpolation which employs what are called "Divided Difference".

Divided Difference Table

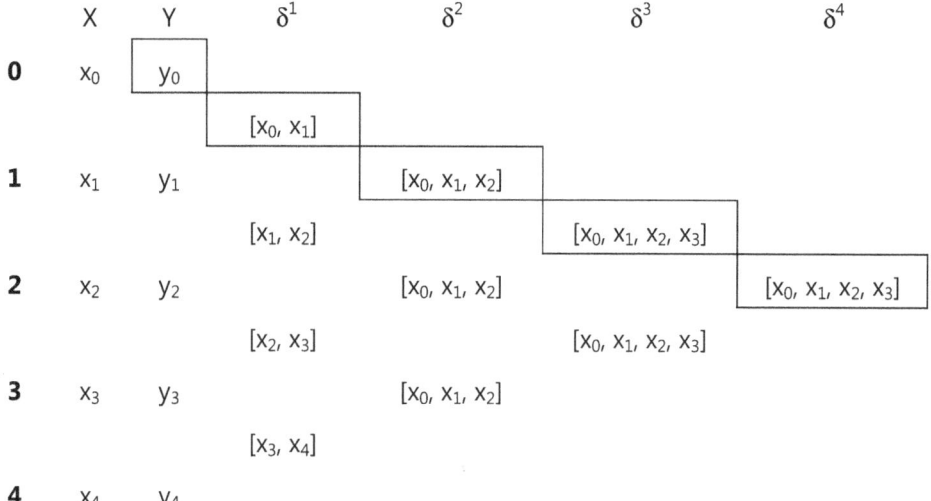

If (x_0, y_0), (x_1, y_1), (x_2, y_2), ... be given points then first divided difference for the argument x_0, x_1 is defined by the relation

$$[x_0, x_1] = \frac{y_1 - y_0}{x_4 - x_0}$$

Similarly,

$$[x_1, x_2] = \frac{y_2 - y_1}{x_2 - x_1}$$

Second divided difference for x_0, x_1, x_2 is defined as:

$$[x_0, x_1, x_2] = \frac{[x_1, x_2] - [x_0, x_1]}{x_2 - x_0}$$

Third divided difference for x_0, x_1, x_2, x_3 is defined as:

$$[x_0, x_1, x_2, x_3] = \frac{[x_1, x_2, x_3] - [x_0, x_1, x_3]}{x_3 - x_0}$$

Divided Difference formula is given by,

$$y_g = y_0 + (x_g - x_0)[x_0, x_1] + (x_g - x_0)(x_g - x_1)[x_0, x_1, x_2] + (x_g - x_0)(x_g - x_1)(x_g - x_2)[x_0, x_1, x_2, x_3] + \ldots$$

Example 5.14 : Using Newton's divided difference formula, find y(8) from following table :

x	4	5	7	10	11	13
y	48	100	294	900	1210	2028

Solution :
We have, $x_g = 8$
Newton's divided difference as follows :

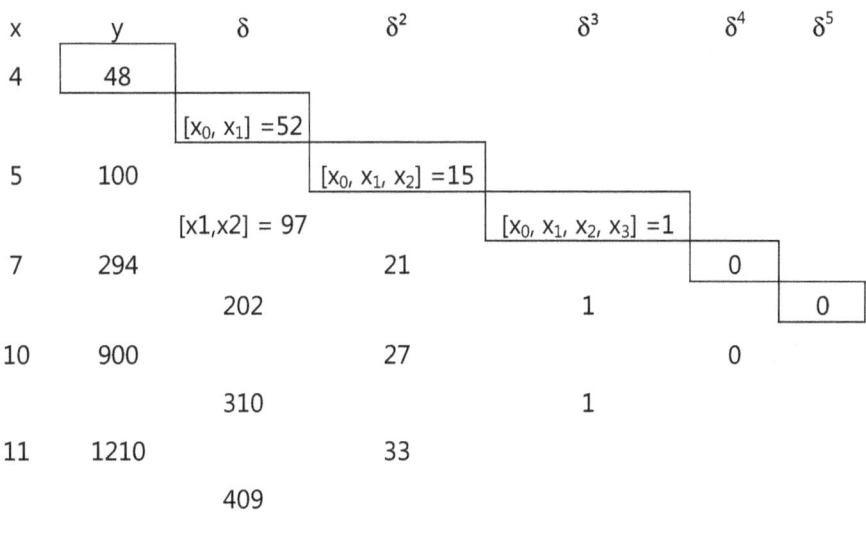

Divided Difference formula is given by,

$$y_g = y_0 + (x_g - x_0)[x_0, x_1] + (x_g - x_0)(x_g - x_1)[x_0, x_1, x_2] + (x_g - x_0)(x_g - x_1)(x_g - x_2)[x_0, x_1, x_2, x_3] + \ldots$$

Where,

$$[x_0, x_1] = \frac{y_1 - y_0}{x_1 - x_0} = 52$$

$$[x_0, x_1, x_2] = \frac{[x_1, x_2] - [x_0, x_1]}{x_2 - x_0} = 15$$

Therefore,

$$y_g = 48 + (8-4) \times 52 + (8-4) \times (8-5) \times 15 + (8-4) \times (8-5) \times (8-7) \times 1 = 448$$

5.5 MATLAB FOR INTERPOLATION

We have already seen that MatLab stores data in array form. Hence, we may prepare forward and backward difference tables as we can prepare them in MS-Excel. But this won't give us the final solution.

We may solve Lagrange's interpolation problem in MatLab as per its method. Let us consider Example 5.2, where we have determined equation of interpolating polynomial and then found f(y) as per equation. Let us use MatLab to get the interpolation polynomial equation. We need to multiply some numbers and brackets as (x – 1) (x – 2) ….

The first term of the equation in Example 5.2 is stored in MatLab as,
>> a = 3.5/(-1 * -2 * -3) * conv ([1 - 2], conv ([1 -3], [1 -4]));
Similarly second, third and fourth terms are constructed as below,
>> b = -5/(1 * -1 * -2) * conv ([1 -1], conv [1 -3], [1 -4]));
>> c = 0;
>> d = 24/(3 * 2 * 1) * conv ([1 -1], conv ([1 -2], [1 -3]));
Now to get and store polynomial equation,
>> y = a + b + c + d
y =
    0.9167   1.2500   -18.6667   20.000
>>
Thus, interpolation polynomial equation,
$$y = 0.9167x^3 + 1.25x^2 - 18.6667x + 20$$
is generated.
Now to determine its value at any given x,
For example say at x = 3.5, use polyval ( ) function.
>> polyval (y, 3.5)
ans =
    9.2812
>>
Thus, once equation is obtained, it can be used for interpolation or extrapolation as well. Similarly, with certain modifications, the same polynomial equation will help us in inverse interpolation.
Let it be required to determine x at y = 10.
Then we need to write equation as,
$$10 = 0.9167x^3 + 1.25x^2 - 18.6667x + 20$$
$$\therefore \quad 0.9167x^3 + 1.25x^2 - 18.6667x + 10 = 0.$$
The roots of this equation can be found.
Let us do all this in MatLab.
>> a = y - [0 0 0 10];
>> roots (a)
ans =
   -5.4595
    3.5298
    0.5661
>>
Looking at the data set we understand that 3.5298 must be the desired root. Rest of the two roots are lying outside the range of data set.

MatLab provides a very smart function which eliminates all efforts required for constructing the polynomial discussed above. The function is polyfit ( ).

Let us take another example where x values are varying from 1 to 10 and corresponding y values are as below :

x	1	2	3	4	5	6	7	8	9	10
y	3	10	15	24	43	78	135	220	339	498

We only know that there can be a polynomial function fitting this data. But do not know degree of polynomial, we can iteratively use polyfit ( ) function as below,

>> a = polyfit (x, y, 2)

where number 2 indicates the degree of polynomial.

The answer returned will be

ans = 9.5000   −55.1000   73.8000

Thus, MatLab says the best fitting quadratic equation is

$$f(x) = 9.5x^2 - 55.1x + 73.8$$

To verify whether equation fits the data or not, use polyval ( ) function as,

>> poly val (a, x);

ans =

columns 1 through 7
28.2000   1.6000   −6.000   5.4000   35.8000   85.2000   153.6000
columns 8 through 10
241.0000   347.4000   472.8000

>>

We observe that any data point is not satisfying the equation. That means the curve does not pass through any of the points. Hence, let us increase the degree of polynomial and try to fit a higher degree polynomial.

>> a = polyfit (x, y, 3)

ans =

1.0000   −7.0000   21.0000   −12.0000

>>

That means $f(x) = x^3 - 7x^2 + 21x - 12$ is a best fitting cubic equation. And we observe that the equation perfectly fits the data set as below.

>> polyval (a, x)

ans =

columns 1 through 7
3.0000   10.0000   15.0000   24.0000   43.0000   78.0000   135.0000
columns 8 through 10
220.0000   339.0000   498.0000

SOLVED EXAMPLES

Example 5.15 : Following data is given for a spring with hinged ends.

L_F/D	1	2	3	4	5	6	7	8
K_L	0.72	0.63	0.38	0.20	0.11	0.07	0.05	0.04

where K_L - factor depending on the ratio (L_F/D).
L_F – Free length of spring
D – Outer diameter of spring.
Find K_L at $(L_F/D) = 7.2$ using suitable method of interpolation.

Solution : As the independent variable L_F/D is equally spaced and we need dependent variable's value near end of data set, Newton's backward difference method is suitable. The difference table will have $\nabla y, \nabla^2 y, ... \nabla^7 y$ such 7 difference columns. Let $(L_F/D) = x$ and $K_L = y$. Therefore, the table becomes,

x	y	∇y	$\nabla^2 y$	$\nabla^3 y$	$\nabla^4 y$	$\nabla^5 y$	$\nabla^6 y$	$\nabla^7 y$
1	0.72							
2	0.63	−0.09						
3	0.38	−0.25	0.16					
4	0.20	−0.18	0.07	0.23				
5	0.11	−0.09	0.09	0.02	−0.21			
6	0.07	−0.04	0.05	−0.04	−0.06	0.15		
7	0.05	−0.02	0.02	−0.03	0.01	0.07	−0.08	
8	0.04	−0.01	0.01	−0.01	0.02	0.01	−0.06	0.02

Here, $h = (x_1 - x_0) = 1$ and $s = \dfrac{x - x_n}{h} = \dfrac{7.2 - 8}{1} = -0.8$

$$y = y_n + s\nabla y_n + \dfrac{s(s+1)}{2!}\nabla^2 y_n + \dfrac{s(s+1)(s+2)}{3!}\nabla^3 y_n + ...$$

$$\dfrac{s(s+1)(s+2).....(s+6)}{7!}\nabla^7 y_n$$

$$\therefore\ y = f(0.72) = 0.04 + (-0.8) \times (-0.01) + \frac{(-0.8) \times 0.2}{2} \times 0.01 + \frac{(-0.8) \times 0.2 \times 1.2}{6}$$

$$\times (-0.01) + \frac{(-0.8) \times 0.2 \times 1.2 \times 2.2}{24} \times 0.02 + \frac{(-0.8) \times 0.2 \times 1.2 \times 2.2 \times 3.2}{120} \times 0.01$$

$$+ \frac{(-0.8) \times 0.2 \times 1.2 \times 2.2 \times 3.2 \times 4.2}{720} \times (-0.06)$$

$$+ \frac{(-0.8) \times 0.2 \times 1.2 \times 2.2 \times 3.2 \times 4.2 \times 5.2}{5040} \times 0.02$$

$\therefore\ y = \mathbf{0.047411302}$ ... **Ans.**

Thus K_L will be 0.047411302 at $(L_F/D) = 7.2$.

Example 5.16 : *From the tabulated values of x and y given below, prepare forward difference table. Estimate value of y when x = 3.*

x	2	4	6	8	10
y	30	43	64	87	104

Solution : The forward difference table is,

x	y	Δy	Δ²y	Δ³y	Δ⁴y
2	30	13	8	−6	−2
4	43	21	2	−8	
6	64	23	−6		
8	87	17			
10	104				

Here, $\quad h = (x_1 - x_0) = 4 - 2 = 2$

and $\quad u = \dfrac{(x - x_0)}{h} = \dfrac{3-2}{2} = 0.5$

$$\therefore\ y = f(3) = y_0 + u\Delta y + \frac{u(u-1)}{2!}\Delta^2 y + \frac{u(u-1)(u-2)}{3!}\Delta^3 y$$

$$+ \frac{u(u-1)(u-2)(u-3)}{4!}\Delta^4 y$$

$$= 30 + 0.5 \times 13 + \frac{0.5 \times (-0.5)}{2} \times 8 + \frac{0.5 \times (-0.5) \times (-1.5)}{6} \times (-6)$$

$$+ \frac{0.5 \times (-0.5) \times (-1.5) \times (-2.5)}{24} \times (-2)$$

$\therefore\quad y = \mathbf{35.203125}$ ... **Ans.**

Example 5.17 : Using Lagrange's method fit a polynomial through following points and find value of y at x = 2.7.

x	2.1	2.5	3.1	3.5
y	5.14	6.78	10.29	13.58

Solution : According to Lagrange's formula,

$$y = \frac{(x-x_1)(x-x_2)(x-x_3)}{(x_0-x_1)(x_0-x_2)(x_0-x_3)} y_0 + \frac{(x-x_0)(x-x_2)(x-x_3)}{(x_1-x_0)(x_1-x_2)(x_1-x_3)} y_1$$

$$+ \frac{(x-x_0)(x-x_1)(x-x_3)}{(x_2-x_0)(x_2-x_1)(x_2-x_3)} y_2 + \frac{(x-x_0)(x-x_1)(x-x_2)}{(x_3-x_0)(x_3-x_1)(x_3-x_2)} y_3$$

$$= \frac{(x-2.5)(x-3.1)(x-3.5)}{(2.1-2.5)(2.1-3.1)(2.1-3.5)} \times 5.14$$

$$+ \frac{(x-2.1)(x-3.1)(x-3.5)}{(2.5-2.1)(2.5-3.1)(2.5-3.5)} \times 6.78$$

$$+ \frac{(x-2.1)(x-2.5)(x-3.5)}{(3.1-2.1)(3.1-2.5)(3.1-3.5)} \times 10.29$$

$$+ \frac{(x-2.1)(x-2.5)(x-3.1)}{(3.5-2.1)(3.5-2.5)(3.5-3.1)} \times 13.58$$

Thus, the cubic polynomial is,

$$y = -9.1786(x-2.5)(x^2-6.6x+10.85) + 28.25(x-2.1)(x^2-6.6x+10.85)$$
$$-42.875(x^2-4.6x+5.25)(x-3.5) + 24.25(x^2-4.6x+5.25)(x-3.1)$$

$$= -9.1786(x^3-9.1x^2+27.35x-27.125)$$
$$+ 28.25(x^3-8.7x^2+24.71x-22.785) - 42.875(x^3-8.1x^2+21.35x-18.375)$$
$$+ 24.25(x^3-7.7x^2+19.51x-16.275)$$

$$\therefore \quad y = 0.4464x^3 - 1.68724x^2 + 4.75904x - 1.54735$$

This is the desired polynomial.

Further, y at x = 2.7 is,

$$y = f(2.7) = 0.4464 \times 2.7^3 - 1.68724 \times 2.7^2 + 4.75904 \times 2.7 - 1.54735$$
$$= \mathbf{7.7885696} \qquad \ldots \text{Ans.}$$

Example 5.18 : The following table gives the values of x and y.

x	1.2	2.1	2.8	4.1
y	4.2	6.8	9.8	13.4

Find the value of x corresponding to y = 12 using suitable method.

Solution : This is a case of inverse interpolation, where y values are not oscillating. Hence, using Lagrange's method, with direct substitutions,

$$x = \frac{(y-y_1)(y-y_2)(y-y_3)}{(y_0-y_1)(y_0-y_2)(y_0-y_3)} x_0 + \frac{(y-y_0)(y-y_2)(y-y_3)}{(y_1-y_0)(y_1-y_2)(y_1-y_3)} x_1$$

$$+ \frac{(y-y_0)(y-y_1)(y-y_3)}{(y_2-y_0)(y_2-y_1)(y_2-y_3)} x_2 + \frac{(y-y_0)(y-y_1)(y-y_2)}{(y_3-y_0)(y_3-y_1)(y_3-y_2)} x_3$$

$$\therefore \quad x = \frac{(12-6.8)(12-9.8)(12-13.4)}{(4.2-6.8)(4.2-9.8)(4.2-13.4)} \times 1.2 + \frac{(12-4.2)(12-9.8)(12-13.4)}{(6.8-4.2)(6.8-9.8)(6.8-13.4)} \times 2.1$$

$$+ \frac{(12-4.2)(12-6.8)(12-13.4)}{(9.8-4.2)(9.8-6.8)(9.8-13.4)} \times 2.8 + \frac{(12-4.2)(12-6.8)(12-9.8)}{(13.4-4.2)(13.4-6.8)(13.4-9.8)} \times 4.1$$

$\therefore \quad x = f(12) = 0.143478 - 0.98 + 2.628889 + 1.673671$

$\therefore \quad \mathbf{x = 3.46604}$ ... **Ans.**

Example 5.19 : *Using backward difference formula for following data, estimate the number of persons earning wages between Rs. 100 and Rs. 110.*

Wages (Rs.)	Below 40	40 to 60	60 to 80	80 to 100	100 to 120
No. of Persons	250	120	100	70	50

Solution : From the data one can understand that there will be more than $(250 + 120 + 100 + 70) = 540$ persons, earning less than Rs. 110.

To calculate that number we need to convert the table to cumulative data table as

Wages (Rs.) Less Than	40	60	80	100	120
No. of Persons Earning	250	370	470	540	590

Consider wages = x and no. of persons = y.

As x is equally spaced and y at x = 110 is required, we can use the suggested backward difference method. The difference table is as,

x	y	∇y	$\nabla^2 y$	$\nabla^3 y$	$\nabla^4 y$
40	250				
60	370	120			
80	470	100	–20		
100	540	70	–30	–10	
120	590	50	–20	10	20

Here, $h = x_1 - x_0 = 60 - 40 = 20$

and $s = \dfrac{x - x_n}{h} = \dfrac{110 - 120}{20} = -0.5$

Now,

$$y = f(x) = y_n + s\nabla y_n + \frac{s(s+1)}{2!}\nabla^2 y_n + \frac{s(s+1)(s+2)}{3!}\nabla^3 y_n + \frac{s(s+1)(s+2)(s+3)}{4!}\nabla^4 y_n$$

$$\therefore \quad y = f(110) = 590 + (-0.5) \times 50 + \frac{(-0.5) \times 0.5}{2} \times (-20) + \frac{(-0.5) \times 0.5 \times 1.5}{6} \times 10$$
$$+ \frac{(-0.5) \times 0.5 \times 1.5 \times 2.5}{24} \times 20$$

$\therefore \quad y = \mathbf{566.09375}$ ... **Ans.**

Thus, 557 persons earn wages less than Rs. 110.

Example 5.20 : *Use suitable method and find out interpolating polynomial*

x	1	2	3	4	5	6
y	3.5	5	6.5	8	9.5	11

Solution : As the x values are equispaced we may use any method. So using forward difference method,

x	y	Δy	Δ²y	Δ³y	Δ⁴y	Δ⁵y
1	3.5	1.5	0	0	0	0
2	5	1.5	0	0	0	
3	6.5	1.5	0	0		
4	8	1.5	0			
5	9.5	1.5				
6	11					

Here, $h = x_1 - x_0 = 1$

and $u = \frac{x - x_0}{h} = \frac{x - 1}{1} = x - 1$

$\therefore \quad y = f(x) = y_0 + u\Delta y_0 + \frac{u(u-1)}{2!} \Delta^2 y_0 + ...$

But as $\Delta^2 y, \Delta^3 y$ .... are zeros.

$y = y_0 + u\Delta y_0$
$= 3.5 + (x - 1) \times 1.5$

$\therefore \quad y = 3.5 + 1.5x - 1.5$

Thus, equation of polynomial passing through all points is

$y = \mathbf{1.5x + 2}$ ... **Ans.**

Example 5.21 : Obtain value of t where A = 85, from following table using suitable method.

t	2	5	8	14
A	94.8	87.9	81.3	68.7

Solution : As this is problem on inverse interpolation using Lagrange's method,

$$t = \frac{(A-A_1)(A-A_2)(A-A_3)}{(A_0-A_1)(A_0-A_2)(A_0-A_3)} t_0 + \frac{(A-A_0)(A-A_2)(A-A_3)}{(A_1-A_0)(A_1-A_2)(A_1-A_3)} t_1$$

$$+ \frac{(A-A_0)(A-A_1)(A-A_3)}{(A_2-A_0)(A_2-A_1)(A_2-A_3)} t_2 + \frac{(A-A_0)(A-A_1)(A-A_2)}{(A_3-A_0)(A_3-A_1)(A_3-A_2)} t_3$$

$$\therefore \quad t = \frac{(85-87.9)(85-81.3)(85-68.7)}{(94.8-87.9)(94.8-81.3)(94.8-68.7)} \times 2$$

$$+ \frac{(85-94.8)(85-81.3)(85-68.7)}{(87.9-94.8)(87.9-81.3)(87.9-68.7)} \times 5$$

$$+ \frac{(85-94.8)(85-87.9)(85-68.7)}{(81.3-94.8)(81.3-87.9)(81.3-68.7)} \times 8$$

$$+ \frac{(85-94.8)(85-87.9)(85-81.3)}{(68.7-94.8)(68.7-87.9)(68.7-81.3)} \times 14$$

$\therefore \quad t = -0.143878 + 3.379801 + 3.30106 - 0.233153$

$\therefore \quad t = \mathbf{6.30383}$ ... **Ans.**

Thus, for A = 85 variable t must be equal to 6.30383.

Example 5.22 : Following data is taken from steam table. Find pressure at temperature t = 142°C. Use suitable method of interpolation.

Temperature, °C	140	150	160	170	180
Pressure, kgf/cm²	3.685	4.854	6.302	8.076	10.225

Solution : As pressure at t = 142°C which is near to sought, we will use Newton's forward difference method. The difference table is as,

t	P	ΔP	Δ²P	Δ³P	Δ⁴P
140	3.685	1.169	0.279	0.047	0.002
150	4.854	1.448	0.326	0.049	
160	6.302	1.774	0.375		
170	8.076	2.149			
180	10.225				

Here, $h = t_1 - t_0 = 150 - 140 = 10$

and $u = \dfrac{t - t_0}{h} = \dfrac{142 - 140}{10} = 0.2$

According to forward difference interpolation formula,

$$P = f(t) = P_0 + u\Delta P_0 + \dfrac{u(u-1)}{2!}\Delta^2 P_0 + \dfrac{u(u-1)(u-2)}{3!}\Delta^3 P_0$$
$$+ \dfrac{u(u-1)(u-2)(u-3)}{4!}\Delta^3 P_0$$

$\therefore\quad P = f(142) = 3.685 - 0.2 \times 1.169 + \dfrac{(-0.2) \times (-1.2)}{2} \times 0.279$

$\quad + \dfrac{(-0.2) \times (-1.2) \times (-2.2)}{6} \times 0.047 + \dfrac{(-0.2) \times (-1.2) \times (-2.2) \times (-3.2)}{24} \times 0.002$

$\quad = 3.4806848$ kgf/cm². ... **Ans.**

Example 5.23 : *Following data refers to a certain process. Find the cubic spline curve equations fitting the data. Further find f(2.5) and f(5.7).*

x	0	1	3	7
y	−3	4.5	0	−1

Solution : As x = 0 and x = 7 are end points, taking

$\quad f''(0) = f''(7) = 0$ we will find $f''(1)$ and $f''(3)$

Using following equation,

$(x_i - x_{i-1}) f''(x_{i-1}) + 2(x_{i+1} - x_{i-1}) f''(x_i) + (x_{i+1} - x_i) f''(x_{i+1})$

$= \dfrac{6}{x_{i+1} - x_i}[f(x_{i+1}) - f(x_i)] - \dfrac{6}{x_i - x_{i-1}}[f(x_{i-1}) - f(x_i)]$

$\therefore$ Considering x = 0, x = 1 and x = 3, first three data points, above equation gives,

$(1 - 0) f''(0) + 2(3 - 0) f''(1) + (3 - 1) f''(3) = \dfrac{6}{3 - 1}[0 - 4.5] - \dfrac{6}{1 - 0}[-3 - 4.5]$

Substituting $f''(0) = 0$, we get,

$\quad 6f''(1) + 2f''(3) = -9 - 45 = -54$ ... (i)

Considering x = 1, x = 3 and x = 7, the last three data points, the above equation gives,

$(3 - 1) f''(1) + 2(7 - 1) f''(3) + (7 - 3) f''(7) = \dfrac{6}{7 - 3}[-1 - 0] - \dfrac{6}{3 - 1}[4.5 - 0]$

Substituting $f''(7) = 0$, we get

$\quad 2f''(1) + 12f''(3) = -1.5 - 9 = -10.5$ ...(ii)

Solving equations (i) and (ii) simultaneously, we get

$\quad f''(1) = -9.2206$ and $f''(3) = 0.6618$

Now, to find $f_1(x)$, $f_2(x)$ and $f_3(x)$ the equations of curves between x_0 and x_1; x_1 and x_2; x_2 and x_3 respectively, we will use following equation,

$$f_i(x) = \frac{f''(x_{i-1})}{6(x_i - x_{i-1})}(x_i - x)^3 + \frac{f''(x_i)}{6(x_i - x_{i-1})}(x - x_{i-1})^3$$
$$+ \left[\frac{f(x_{i-1})}{x_i - x_{i-1}} - \frac{f''(x_{i-1})(x_i - x_{i-1})}{6}\right](x_i - x)$$
$$+ \left[\frac{f(x_i)}{x_i - x_{i-1}} - \frac{f''(x_i)(x_i - x_{i-1})}{6}\right](x - x_{i-1})$$

∴ Equation of curve between $x = 0$ and $x = 1$ is

$$f_1(x) = \frac{f''(0)}{6(1-0)}(1-x)^3 + \frac{f''(1)}{6(1-0)}(x-0)^3 + \left[\frac{f(0)}{1-0} - \frac{f''(0)(1-0)}{6}\right](1-x)$$
$$+ \left[\frac{f(1)}{1-0} - \frac{f''(1)(1-0)}{6}\right](x-0)$$

$$= 0 + \frac{(-9.2206)}{6}x^3 + [-3-0](1-x) + \left[4.5 - \frac{(-9.2206)}{6}\right]x$$

∴ $f_1(x) = -1.5368x^3 - 3 + 3x + 6.0368x$
$= -1.5368x^3 + 9.0368x - 3$

Further, curve between $x = 1$ and $x = 3$ is

$$f_2(x) = \frac{f''(1)}{6(3-1)}(3-x)^3 + \frac{f''(3)}{6(3-1)}(x-1)^3 + \left[\frac{f(1)}{3-1} - \frac{f''(1)(3-1)}{6}\right](3-x)$$
$$+ \left[\frac{f(3)}{3-1} - \frac{f''(3)(3-1)}{6}\right](x-1)$$

$$= \frac{(-9.2206)}{12}(27 - 27x + 9x^2 - x^3) + \frac{0.6618}{12}(x^3 - 3x^2 + 3x - 1)$$
$$+ \left[\frac{4.5}{2} - \frac{-9.2206 \times 2}{6}\right](3-x) + \left[\frac{0}{2} - \frac{0.6618 \times 2}{6}\right](x-1)$$

$= -20.7464 + 20.7464x - 6.9155x^2 + 0.7684x^3 + 0.0552x^3 - 0.1655x^2$
$+ 0.1655x - 0.0552 + 15.9706 - 5.3235x - 0.2206x + 0.2206$

∴ $f_2(x) = 0.8236x^3 - 7.081x^2 + 15.3678x - 4.6104$

And lastly curve between $x = 3$ and $x = 7$,

$$f_3(x) = \frac{f''(3)}{6(7-3)}(7-x)^3 + \frac{f''(7)}{6(7-3)}(x-3)^3 + \left[\frac{f(3)}{7-3} - \frac{f''(3)(7-3)}{6}\right](7-x)$$
$$+ \left[\frac{f(7)}{7-3} - \frac{f''(7)(7-3)}{6}\right](x-3)$$

$$= \frac{0.6618}{24}(343 - 147x + 21x^2 - x^3) + 0 + \left[\frac{0}{4} - \frac{0.6618 \times 4}{6}\right](7 - x)$$

$$+ \left[\frac{-1}{4} - 0\right](x - 3)$$

$$= 9.4582 - 4.0535x + 0.5791x^2 - 0.0276x^3 - 3.0884$$
$$+ 0.4412x - 0.25x + 0.75$$

$$\therefore \quad f_3(x) = -0.0276x^3 + 0.5791x^2 - 3.8623x + 7.1198$$

Thus, the full curve is represented as

$$f(x) = \begin{cases} -1.5368x^3 + 9.0368x - 3 & \text{x from 0 to 1} \\ 0.8236x^3 - 7.081x^2 + 15.3678x - 4.6104 & \text{x from 1 to 3} \\ -0.0276x^3 + 0.5791x^2 - 3.8623x + 7.1198 & \text{x from 3 to 7} \end{cases}$$

To determine f(2.5) using $f_2(x)$ and f(5.7) using $f_3(x)$

$$f(2.5) = 0.8236 \times 2.5^3 - 7.081 \times 2.5^2 + 15.3678 \times 2.5 - 4.6104 = 2.4216$$
$$f(5.7) = -0.0276 \times 5.7^3 + 0.5791 \times 5.7^2 - 3.8623 \times 5.7 + 7.1198 = \mathbf{-1.1917} \quad \text{... Ans.}$$

Example 5.24 : Determine x at y = 1.25 from the following data :

x	1	2	3	4
y	0.84147	1.28594	0.24443	−1.5136

Solution : This is the problem of inverse interpolation. But y values are oscillating. Hence, we cannot get value of x by direct substitution. We need to find the interpolation polynomial and find roots of the polynomial for given y. Then select appropriate root.

Hence,

$$y = \frac{(x-x_1)(x-x_2)(x-x_3)}{(x_0-x_1)(x_0-x_2)(x_0-x_3)}y_0 + \frac{(x-x_0)(x-x_2)(x-x_3)}{(x_1-x_0)(x_1-x_2)(x_1-x_3)}y_1$$

$$+ \frac{(x-x_0)(x-x_1)(x-x_3)}{(x_2-x_0)(x_2-x_1)(x_2-x_3)}y_2 + \frac{(x-x_0)(x-x_1)(x-x_2)}{(x_3-x_0)(x_3-x_1)(x_3-x_2)}y_3$$

$$= \frac{(x-2)(x-3)(x-4)}{(-1)\times(-2)\times(-3)}\times 0.84147 + \frac{(x-1)(x-3)(x-4)}{1\times(-1)\times(-2)}\times 1.28594$$

$$+ \frac{(x-1)(x-2)(x-4)}{2\times 1\times(-1)}\times 0.24443 + \frac{(x-1)(x-2)(x-3)}{3\times 2\times 1}\times(-1.5136)$$

$$= -0.140245(x-2)(x^2-7x+12) + 0.64297(x-1)(x^2-7x+12)$$
$$-0.122215(x^2-3x+2)(x-4) - 0.252266(x^2-3x+2)(x-3)$$

$$= -0.140245(x^3-9x^2+26x-24) + 0.64297(x^3-8x^2+19x-12)$$
$$-0.122215(x^3-7x^2+14x-8) - 0.252266(x^3-6x^2+11x-6)$$

$$\therefore \quad y = 0.1282x^3 - 1.5125x^2 + 4.0841x - 1.8584$$

Now substituting y = 1.25, we get,

$$f(x) = 0.1282x^3 - 1.5125x^2 + 4.0841x - 3.1084 = 0$$

Finding roots of this equation by any method, we observe that

x = 8.3136, x = 2.0746 and x = 1.4053

are the roots of equation. The data set is ranging from x = 1 to x = 4, hence x = 2.0746 and x = 1.4053, both answers are acceptable. The third answer x = 8.3136 is far away from data set, hence rejected.

PROBLEMS FOR PRACTICE

1. Given log 2 = 0.3010, log 3 = 0.4771, log 5 = 0.6990 and log 7 = 0.8451.
   Determine log 4.7 using suitable interpolation method. Determine error in the answer.
   Ans.: Lagrange's method log 4.7 = 0.67342, analytically log 4.7 = 0.6721
   % Error = 0.1964%.

2. In a laboratory a scientist conducted an experiment, where he recorded temperatures in day time as below,

At	10 : 00 am	12 : 00 noon	12 : 30 pm	2 : 00 pm
Temperature, °C	127	111	95	29

   Estimate what would be the temperature at 1 : 30 pm ? Also estimate timing when the temperature was 100°C.
   [**Hint :** 10 : 00 am is start of duration of experiment, hence take t = 0, at 12 : 00 noon, take t = 120 min, at 12 : 30 pm, t = 150 min. and at 2 : 00 pm, t = 240 min]
   Ans. : At 1 : 30 pm, temperature = 53.325°C, 100°C temperature at 12 : 28 pm.

3. Prepare forward difference table for y = 100 sin x · ln (x + 1)/$\sqrt{x + 1}$ rounded to nearest integer where x is varying from 0 to 5. From this table determine a cubic interpolation polynomial.
   [**Hint :** The table has columns upto $\Delta^5 y$ but for equation use columns upto $\Delta^3 y$)
   Ans. : $- 6.8333x^3 - 32.5x^2 + 66.6667x$.

4. Determine y at x = 3 using suitable method for the following data :

x	2.5	4	5.5	7	8.5	10	11.5
y	−62.25	−135	−189.75	−186	−83.25	159	581.25

   Ans. : Newton's forward difference method, y = −86.

5. Determine y at x = 11 using suitable method for data given in problem 4.
   Ans. : Newton's backward difference method, y = 418.

6. Using data in problem 4, determine value of x for y = 100.
   [**Hint :** Lagrange's method will be too lengthy. You may derive interpolation polynomial by Newton's difference method and find root of (f(y) − 100)]
   Ans. : 9.7132

Review Questions

1. For following data calculate difference and obtain forward and backward difference polynomials. Interpolate at x = 0.25 and x = 0.35.

x	0.1	0.2	0.3	0.4	0.5
f(x)	1.4	1.56	1.76	2.00	2.28

2. The velocity distribution of a fluid near a flat surface is given below.

x	0.1	0.3	0.6	0.8
v	0.72	1.81	2.73	3.47

    x is the distance from the surface (mm) and v is the velocity (mm/sec)

    Use Lagrange's interpolation polynomial to obtain the velocity at x = 0.4.

3. Given the table of square roots. Calculate the values of $\sqrt{151}$ and $\sqrt{155}$ by Newton's interpolation formula :

x	150	152	154	156
$y = \sqrt{x}$	12.247	12.329	12.410	12.490

4. Following data is given for the springs with hinged ends.

L_F/D	1	2	3	4	5	6	7	8
K_L	0.72	0.63	0.38	0.20	0.11	0.07	0.05	0.04

    Find K_L at (L_F/D) = 7.2, using suitable method of interpolation.

Chapter 6
CURVE FITTING

6.1 INTRODUCTION

Generally, scientists and engineers are required to obtain data involving two variables from experimental observations. It often becomes necessary to establish a mathematical relationship between experimental values. This relationship may be used for either testing existing mathematical models or establishing new relationships. These mathematical models or equations can be used to predict or forecast values of dependent variables.

The process of establishing relationships in the form of mathematical equation is known as regression analysis or curve fitting. Suppose the values of y for the different values of x are given. If we want to know the effect of x on y, then we may write a functional relationship as $y = f(x)$, where variable x is independent variable and y is dependent variable. The relationship may be linear or non-linear as shown in Fig. 6.1.

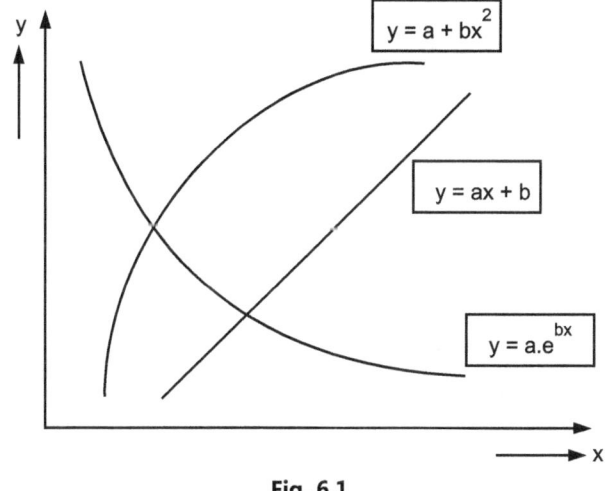

Fig. 6.1

6.2 PRINCIPLE OF LEAST SQUARE CRITERION

Let the set of data points be (x_i, y_i), where $i = 1, 2, 3, ..., n$ and the curve $y = f(x)$ be fitted through these data points.

To determine the equation of curve which very nearly passes through the set of points, we assume some form of relation between x and y as a straight line or a parabola of second degree. We assume relationship between x and y as a straight line, $y = ax + b$.

If point (x_i, y_i) is on the line then,

$$y_i = y'_i \text{ i.e.}$$

$$y'_i = ax_i + b$$

Otherwise, deviation $(y_i - y'_i)$ is observed between observed value and plotted value. It can be both +ve and −ve. In method of least squares, we take sum of squares of these deviations to neglect effect of +ve and −ve deviation. We try to minimize this sum by using the principle of maxima and minima. This is called as Least Square Criterion. This criterion can be used to fit curve of any degree.

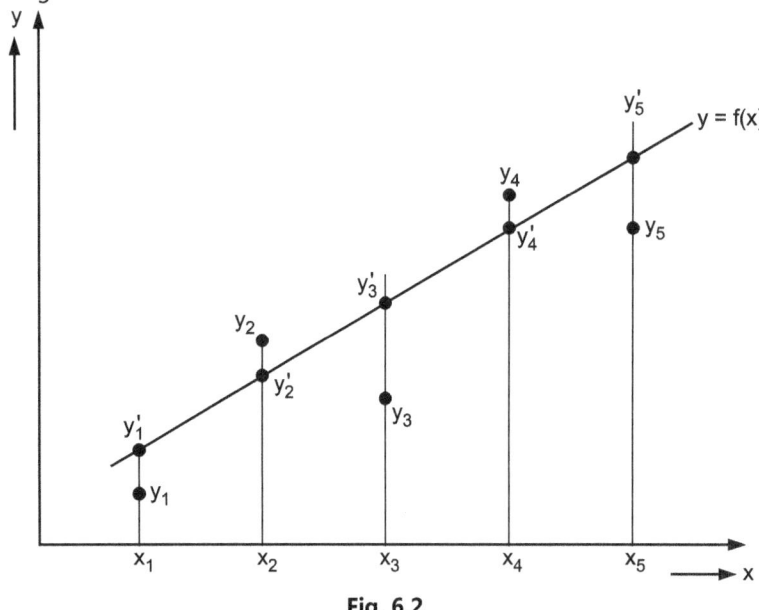

Fig. 6.2

6.3 FITTING A STRAIGHT LINE (Y = AX + B)

Let (x_i, y_i) be the observed values of x and y.

$$i = 1, 2, 3, \ldots, n$$

To fit straight line, y = ax + b using least square criterion, consider y'_i are values corresponding to x_i on a straight line. Deviations $(y_1 - y'_1), (y_2 - y'_2), \ldots, (y_n - y'_n)$ are observed.

By Least Square Criteria,

$$\text{let } S = (y_1 - y'_1)^2 + (y_2 - y'_2)^2 + \ldots + (y_n - y'_n)^2$$
$$= (y_1 - ax_1 - b)^2 + (y_2 - ax_2 - b)^2 + \ldots + (y_n - ax_n - b)^2$$

For minimum S,

$$\frac{\partial S}{\partial b} = 0, \quad \frac{\partial S}{\partial a} = 0$$

$$\frac{\partial S}{\partial b} = 0 \text{ gives}$$

$2(y_1 - ax_1 - b) + 2(y_2 - ax_2 - b) + \ldots + 2(y_n - ax_n - b) = 0$

$\therefore (y_1 + y_2 + \ldots + y_n) - a(x_1 + x_2 + \ldots + x_n) - nb = 0$

$\therefore \sum_{i=0}^{n} y_i - a \sum_{i=0}^{n} x_i - nb = 0$

$\therefore \sum_{i=0}^{n} y_i = a \sum_{i=0}^{n} x_i + nb$ ... (I)

$\dfrac{\partial S}{\partial a} = 0$ gives

$-2(y_1 - ax_1 - b)x_1 - 2(y_2 - ax_2 - b)x_2 - \ldots - 2(y_n - ax_n - b)x_n = 0$

$\therefore -(x_1y_1 + x_2y_2 + \ldots + x_ny_n) + a(x_1^2 + x_2^2 + \ldots + x_n^2) + b(x_1 + x_2 + \ldots + x_n) = 0$

$\therefore -\sum_{i=0}^{n} x_iy_i + a \sum_{i=0}^{n} x_i^2 + b \sum_{i=0}^{n} x_i = 0$

$\therefore \sum_{i=0}^{n} x_iy_i = a \sum_{i=0}^{n} x_i^2 + b \sum_{i=0}^{n} x_i$ ... (II)

Solving equations (I) and (II) simultaneously, we determine the values of a and b.

Example 6.1 : The straight line is $y = ax + b$
Given the table of points :

x	0	2	4	6	8	12	20
y	10	12	18	22	20	30	30

Use least square method to fit a straight line to the data and find the value of y (22).

Solution :

x	y	xy	x^2
0	10	0	0
2	12	24	4
4	18	72	16
6	22	132	36
8	20	160	64
12	30	360	144
20	30	600	400
$\Sigma x = 52$	$\Sigma y = 142$	$\Sigma xy = 1348$	$\Sigma x^2 = 664$

To fit a curve as y = ax + b, we have

$$\Sigma y = a\Sigma x + nb$$
$$\Sigma xy = a\Sigma x^2 + b\Sigma x$$

∴   142 = 52a + 7.b   ... (I)

and   1348 = 664 a + 54 b   ... (II)

∴ $a = \dfrac{142 - 7b}{52}$ from equation (I)

                $a = \dfrac{1348 - 52b}{664}$ from equation (II)

Comparing values of a, we get

∴ $\dfrac{142 - 7b}{52} = \dfrac{1348 - 52b}{664}$

∴   664(142 − 7b) = 52(1348 − 52b)

∴   94288 − 4648b = 70096 − 2704b

∴   94288 − 70096 = (4648 − 2704) b

∴ $b = \dfrac{24192}{194}$

∴   b = 12.4444

and substituting in equation (I), we get

$$a = \dfrac{142 - 7 \times 12.4444}{52}$$

= 1.0555

Equation of line is   **y = 1.0555.x + 12.4444**   ... Ans.

6.3.1 Algorithms

- Input number of data points (n).
- Initialize sumx, sumy, sumxy and sumx2 as 0.
- For n = 1 to n, increment i by 1.
- Input 'x' and 'y' values.
- Calculate sum x, sum y, sum x y and sum x 2.
- End loop.
- Construct coefficient matrix and solution matrix.
- Find solution matrix.
- Print results.

6.3.2 Flow Chart

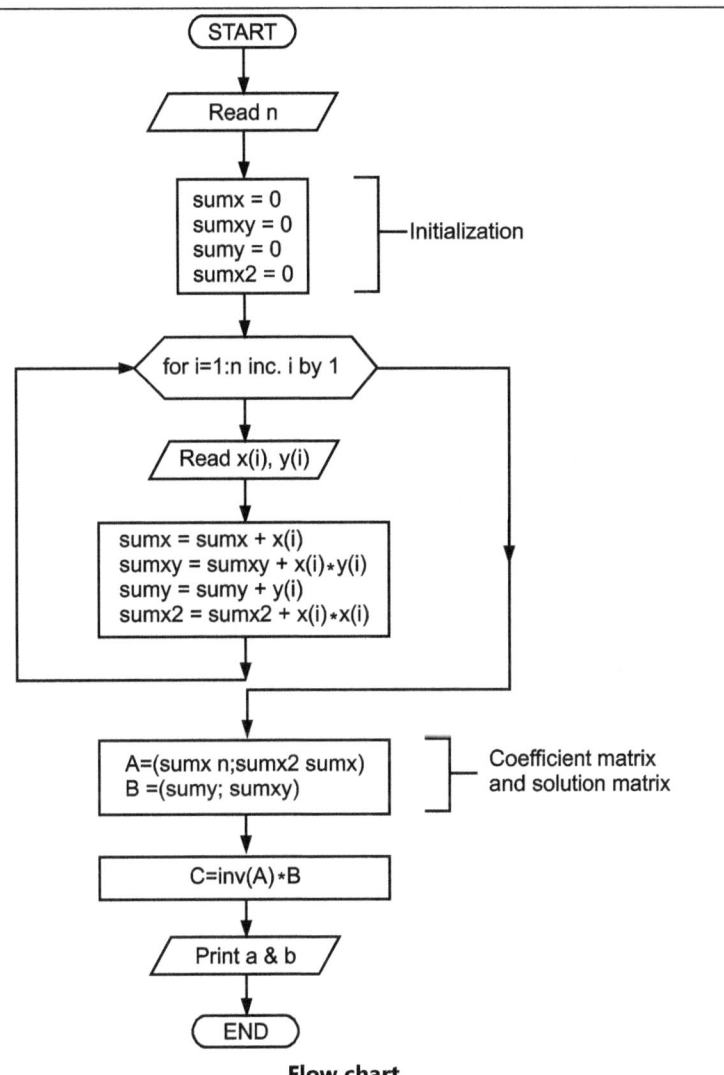

Flow chart

6.3.3 Matlab

clc;	% CLC - clears the command window and homes the cursor
clf;	% CLF - Clear current figure
close all;	% CLOSE - ALL closes all the open figure windows
clear all;	% CLEAR - ALL removes all variables, functions
%% CURVE FITTING	

```matlab
%% LEAST SQUARE CRITERION FOR STRAIGHT LINE (y = Ax + B)
fprintf('\n**********************************************************');
fprintf('\n************ CURVE FITTING: STRAIGHT LINE ************');
fprintf('\n**********************************************************');

n = input('\n\n Enter No. of DATA POINTS (n): ');
sumx = 0;
sumy = 0;
sumxy = 0;
sumx2 =0;

for i = 1:n
    fprintf('\n Point#%d >>>',i);
    x(i) = input('\nX = '); %Input Data
    y(i) = input('%Y = ');
    sumx = sumx + x(i);
    sumy = sumy + y(i);
    sumx2 = sumx2 + x(i)*x(i);
    sumxy = sumxy + x(i)*y(i);
end

fprintf('\n sumx  = %f',sumx);
fprintf('\n sumy  = %f',sumy);
fprintf('\n sumxy = %f',sumxy);
fprintf('\n sumx2 = %f',sumx2);

A = [sumx n; sumx2 sumx];          %% Coefficient Matrix
B = [sumy; sumxy];                 %% Solution Matrix
C = inv(A)*B;                      %% Solutions of A and B

fprintf('\n\n Equation of Line>>> y = (%.4f)x + (%.4f) ',C(1),C(2));

% Plotting the Actual Data and by Least Square Criteria
for i=1:n
    ya(i)=C(1)*x(i)+C(2);    %%Calculation of y as per solution
```

end

hold on
xlabel('X');
ylabel('Y');
title('Least Square Criteria');
plot(x,y,'*','LineWidth',2,'Color',[1 0 0]);
plot(x,ya,'-','LineWidth',2,'Color',[0 1 0]);

Enter No. of DATA POINTS (n): 7

Point#1 >>>
X = 0
Y = 10

Point#2 >>>
X = 2
Y = 12

Point#3 >>>
X = 4
Y = 18

Point#4 >>>
X = 6
Y = 22

Point#5 >>>
X = 8
Y = 20

Point#6 >>>
X = 12
Y = 30

Point#7 >>>
X = 20
Y = 30

sumx = 52.000000
sumy = 142.000000
sumxy = 1348.000000
sumx2 = 664.000000
Equation of Line>>> y = (1.0556)x + (12.4444)

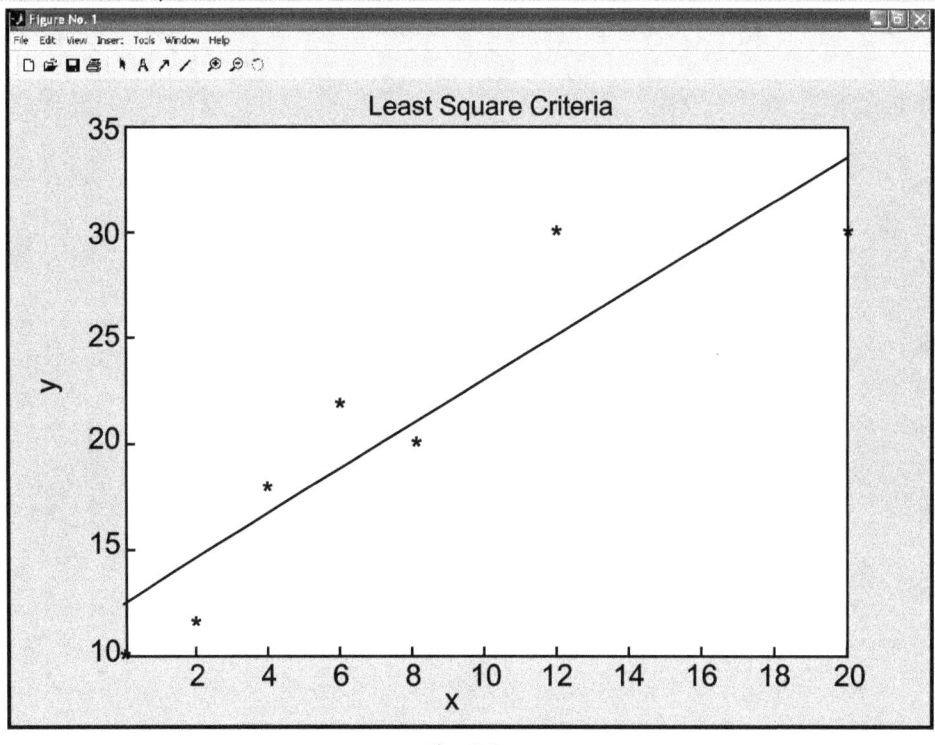

Fig. 6.3

Example 6.2 : If 'F' is the force required to lift weight 'W' by means of pulley block, find the linear law in the form of F = aW + b for following observations :

W (kg)	1000	1200	1400	1600	1800	2000
F (N)	240	260	300	330	370	420

Solution : Given Data : No. of data points (n) : 6

Assume X = 100x

x	X	y	Xy	X²
1000	10	240	2400	100
1200	12	260	3120	144
1400	14	300	4200	196
1600	16	330	5280	256
1800	18	370	6660	324
2000	20	420	8400	400
	ΣX = 90	Σy = 1920	ΣXy = 30060	ΣX² = 1420

By using least square criteria, we get

$$\Sigma y = a\Sigma X + nb \qquad \ldots (I)$$
$$\Sigma Xy = a\Sigma X^2 + b\Sigma X \qquad \ldots (II)$$

Therefore, substituting values in above equations, we get

$$1920 = 90a + 6b \qquad \ldots (III)$$
$$30060 = 1420a + 90b \qquad \ldots (IV)$$

Solving above equations simultaneously, we get, a = 18 and b = 50

Therefore, equation can be written as,

$$y = 18X + 50, \text{ but } X = 100x$$
$$\mathbf{y = 0.18x + 50} \qquad \ldots \mathbf{Ans.}$$

Alternative Method :

Assume X = x − 1500

x	X	y	Xy	X²
1000	−500	240	−120000	250000
1200	−300	260	−78000	90000
1400	−100	300	−30000	10000
1600	100	330	33000	10000
1800	300	370	111000	90000
2000	500	420	210000	250000
	ΣX = 0	Σy = 1920	ΣXy = 126000	ΣX² = 700000

By using least square criteria, we get

$$\Sigma y = a\Sigma X + nb \qquad \ldots (I)$$
$$\Sigma Xy = a\Sigma X^2 + b\Sigma X \qquad \ldots (II)$$

Therefore, substituting values in above equations, we get

$$1920 = 0 + 6b \quad \ldots (III)$$
$$126000 = 700000 a + 0 \quad \ldots (IV)$$

Solving above equations simultaneously, we get, a = 18 and b = 320

Therefore, equation can be written as,

$$y = 0.18 X + 320, \text{ but } X = x - 1500 x$$
$$y = 0.18 (x - 1500) + 320$$
$$y = 0.18 x + 50 \quad \ldots \text{Ans.}$$

Example 6.3 : *Use least square regression to fit a straight line to the data given below.*

x	1	2	3	4	5	6	8
y	0.5	2.5	2.0	4.0	3.5	6.0	5.5

Solution : Given Data : No. of Data points (n) : 7.

x	y	xy	x^2
1	0.5	0.5	1
2	2.5	5	4
3	2.0	6	9
4	4.0	16	16
5	3.5	18	25
6	6.0	36	36
8	5.5	44	64
$\Sigma x = 29$	$\Sigma y = 24$	$\Sigma xy = 125$	$\Sigma x^2 = 155$

By using least square criteria, we get

$$\Sigma y = a\Sigma x + nb \quad \ldots (I)$$
$$\Sigma xy = a\Sigma x^2 + b\Sigma x \quad \ldots (II)$$

Therefore, substituting values in above equations, we get

$$24 = 29 a + 7 b \quad \ldots (III)$$
$$125 = 155 a + 29 b \quad \ldots (IV)$$

Solving above equations simultaneously, we get, a = 0.7336 and b = 0.3893

Therefore, equation can be written as,

$$y = 0.73336 x + 0.3893 \quad \ldots \text{Ans.}$$

Example 6.4 : *Following data refers to the load lifted and corresponding force applied in a pulley system. If the load lifted and effort required are related to equation.*

Effort = a · (load lifted) + b, where a and b are constants. Evaluate a and b by lines as curve fitting.

Load lifted in kN	10.0	15.0	20.0	25.0	30.0
Effort applied in kN	0.750	0.935	1.100	1.200	1.300

Solution : Consider

x = Load lifted in kN

and y = Effort applied in kN

Effort = $a \cdot x$ (load lifted) + b

∴ $y = ax + b$

Given data : n = 5

x	y	xy	x^2
10.0	0.750	7.50	100
15.0	0.935	14.025	225
20.0	1.100	22.0	400
25.0	1.200	30.0	625
30.0	1.300	39.0	900
$\Sigma x = 100$	$\Sigma y = 5.285$	$\Sigma xy = 112.525$	$\Sigma x^2 = 2250$

By using equations (I) and (II),

$$\Sigma y = a\Sigma x + n \cdot b$$
$$\Sigma xy = a\Sigma x^2 + b\Sigma x$$

∴ $\quad 5.285 = 100a + 5 \cdot b$ ... (I)

and $\quad 112.525 = 2250 a + 100 b$ ... (II)

Multiply equation (I) by 20, we get

∴ $\quad 105.7 = 2000 a + 100 b$

$\quad\underline{112.525 = 2250 a + 100 b}$

$\quad -6.825 = -250 a$

∴ $\quad a = 0.0273$

Substituting value of a in equation (I), we get

$\quad 5.285 = 100 \times 0.0273 + 5b$

∴ $\quad b = 0.511$

∴ Equation can be written as

$\quad y = 0.0273 \times 0.511$ OR

Effort = 0.0273 × (load lifted) + 0.511 ...Ans.

6.4 Fitting an Exponential Curve $Y = A \cdot e^{BX}$

Consider equation $\quad y = a \cdot e^{bx}$

Taking natural log (ln) on both sides,

$$\ln(y) = \ln(a) + bx \cdot \ln(e)$$
$$Y = A + Bx$$

where, $\quad Y = \ln(y)$,
$\quad\quad A = \ln(a)$,
$\quad\quad B = b$

∴ $\quad Y = A + Bx$

This equation is for a straight line, therefore

$$\boxed{\begin{aligned}\Sigma Y &= n \cdot A + B \Sigma x \\ \Sigma xY &= A \Sigma x + B \Sigma x^2\end{aligned}}$$

Solving these two equations simultaneously, we get A and B

$$a = e^A \text{ and } b = B$$

Example 6.5 : *The values of x and y obtained in the experiment are as follows, the law controlling them is $y = a \cdot e^{bx}$, find the best values of the constants.*

x	2.30	3.10	4.0	4.92	5.91	7.20
y	33.00	39.10	50.36	67.20	85.60	125.0

Solution : Given data : n = 6.

Equation $y = a \cdot e^{bx}$

Taking natural log on both sides,

$$\ln(y) = \ln(a) + b \cdot x \cdot \ln(e)$$

∴ $\quad Y = A + b \cdot x$

∴ $\quad \ln(e) = 1$

where, $\quad Y = \ln(y)$ and $A = \ln(a)$

x	y	Y = ln(y)	xY	x^2
2.30	33.00	3.496508	8.041967	5.29
3.10	39.10	3.666122	11.36498	9.61
4.00	50.36	3.919197	15.67679	16
4.92	67.20	4.207673	20.70175	24.2064
5.91	85.60	4.449685	26.29764	34.9281
7.20	125.00	4.828314	34.76386	51.84
$\Sigma x = 27.43$		$\Sigma Y = 24.5675$	$\Sigma xY = 116.847$	$\Sigma x^2 = 141.8745$

By using least square criteria,

$$\Sigma y = n \cdot A + b \Sigma x$$

$\Rightarrow \quad 24.5675 = 6A + 27.43\, b$ ... (I)

$$\Sigma xY = A \cdot \Sigma x + b \Sigma x^2$$

$\Rightarrow \quad 116.847 = 27.43A + 141.8745\, b$ ... (II)

Divide equation (I) by 6, we get

$\quad 4.09458 = A + 4.571667\, b$ ... (III)

Divide equation (II) by 27.43, we get

$\quad 4.259825 = A + 5.172238\, b$ ... (IV)

Solving equations (III) and (IV) simultaneously, we get

$\quad 0.600571\, b = 0.165245$

$\therefore \quad b = 0.27514$

Substituting in equation (III), we get

$\quad A = 2.83673$

$\Rightarrow \quad a = 17.0599 = 17$ (Approx.)

$\Rightarrow$ Therefore relation between x and y, **y = 17 $e^{0.27x}$** ... Ans.

6.4.1 Algorithm

1. Input number of data points (n)
2. Initialize sumx, sumy, sumxy and sumx2 as 0.
3. For n = 1 to n, increment i by 1
4. Input 'x' and 'y' values
5. Calculate Y = log10y
6. Calculate sumx, sumY, sumxY and sumx2
7. End loop
8. Construct coefficient matrix and solution matrix
9. Find solution matrix
10. Print results

6.4.2 Matlab

```
clc;
close all;
clear all;

%% CURVE FITTING
```

```matlab
%% LEAST SQUARE CRITERION FOR EQUATION (y = A*e^Bx)
fprintf('\n*********************************************************');
fprintf('\n************** NIRALI PUBLICATIONS *********************');
fprintf('\n********* CONM by M. T. Puranik & V. N. Chougule ********');
fprintf('\n*************** CURVE FITTING: y = A*e^Bx **************');
fprintf('\n*********************************************************');

n = input('\n Enter No. of DATA POINTS (n): ');
sumx  = 0;
sumY  = 0;
sumxY = 0;
sumx2 = 0;

% Type of Equation>>> y = A*e^Bx
% Therefor taking log on both sides, we get>>> log(y)=log(A)+Bx.log(e)
% i.e log(y)=log(A)+Bx, then, Y=Bx+C, where Y=log(y), C=log(A)

for i = 1:n
    fprintf('\n Point#%d >>>',i);
    x(i) = input('\nX = ');
    y(i) = input('Y = ');
    Y(i) = log(y(i));
    sumx = sumx + x(i);
    sumY = sumY + Y(i);
    sumx2 = sumx2 + x(i)*x(i);
    sumxY = sumxY + x(i)*Y(i);
end

fprintf('\n sumx  = %f',sumx);
fprintf('\n sumY  = %f',sumY);
fprintf('\n sumxY = %f',sumxY);
fprintf('\n sumx2 = %f',sumx2);

A = [sumx n; sumx2 sumx];     %% Coefficient Matrix
B = [sumY; sumxY];            %% Solution Matrix
C = inv(A)*B;                 %% Solutions of A and B
A = exp(C(2));
```

```
B = C(1);
fprintf('\n Equation of Curve>>> y = (%.4f)*e^(%.4fx)',A,B);
% Plotting the Actual Data and by Least Square Criteria
for i=1:n
   ya(i)=A*exp(B*x(i));
end

hold on
xlabel('x');
ylabel('y');
title('Least Square Criteria');
plot(x,y,'*','LineWidth',2,'Color',[1 0 0]);
plot(x,ya,'--','LineWidth',2,'Color',[0 0 0]);
```

Output :

```
*************************************************************
****************** NIRALI PUBLICATIONS *********************
******** CONM by M. T. Puranik & V. N. Chougule ************
****************** CURVE FITTING: y = A*e^Bx ****************
*************************************************************
Enter No. of DATA POINTS (n): 6

Point#1 >>>
X = 2.3
Y = 33

Point#2 >>>
X = 3.1
Y = 39.1

Point#3 >>>
X = 4
Y = 50.36
Point#4 >>>
X = 4.92
Y = 67.2
```

Point#5 >>>
X = 5.91
Y = 85.6

Point#6 >>>
X = 7.2
Y = 125

sumx = 27.430000
sumY = 24.567500
sumxY = 116.846987
sumx2 = 141.874500
Equation of Curve>>> y = (17.0600)*e^(0.2751x)

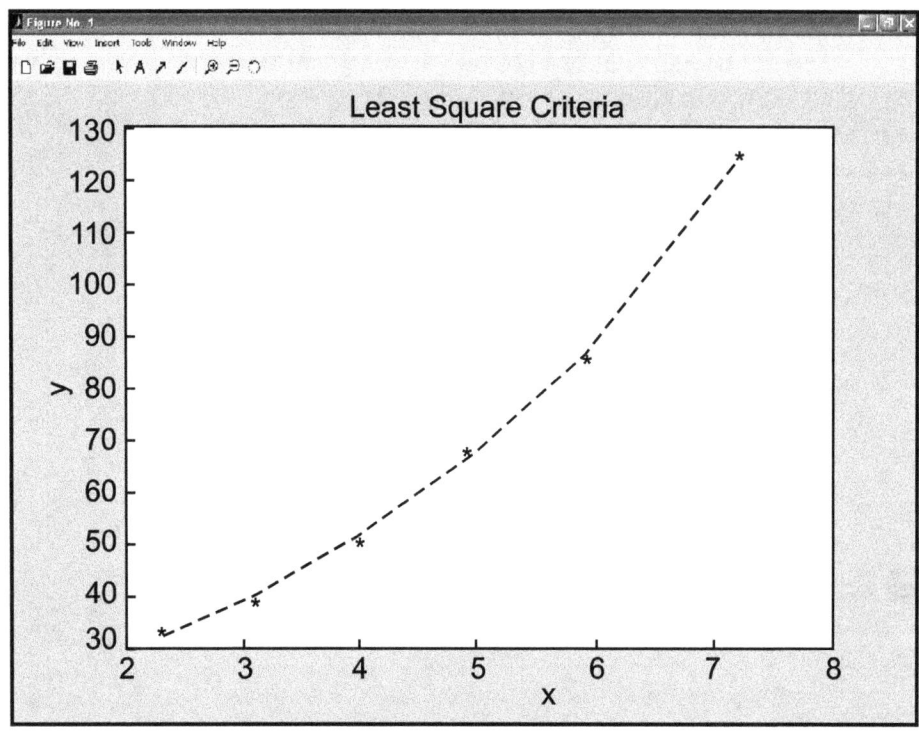

Fig. 6.4

6.5 Fitting The Curve Y = AX^B

Consider equation $y = ax^b$

$$\log_{10}(y) = \log_{10}(a) + b \cdot \log_{10}(x)$$

$\therefore \quad Y = A + B \cdot X$

where,
$Y = \log_{10}(y)$
$A = \log_{10}(a)$
$B = b$
$X = \log_{10}(x)$

This equation is for a straight line, therefore

$$\Sigma Y = n \cdot A + B \Sigma X$$
$$\Sigma XY = A \Sigma X + B \Sigma X^2$$

Solving these equations simultaneously, we get A and B.

$\therefore \quad a = \text{antilog}(A)$
$\therefore \quad b = B$

Example 6.6 : *The value of Nusselt number (y) and Reynold's number (x) found experimentally are given below. If the relation between x and y of the type $y = a \cdot x^b$*

1. Derive the formula for finding out values of a and b.
2. Find the values of a and b for given values of x and y.

Reynold's No. (x)	3000	4000	5000	6000	7000
Nusselt's No. (y)	14.3575	15.6517	16.7353	17.6762	18.5128

Solution : Given data : n = 5

Equation $\Rightarrow \quad y = a \cdot x^b$

$\log_{10}(y) = \log_{10}(a) + b \cdot \log_{10}(x)$
$Y = A + b \cdot X$

reduced to straight line equation

where,
$Y = \log_{10}(y)$
$A = \log_{10}(a)$
$X = \log_{10}(x)$

x	$X = \log_{10} x$	y	$Y = \log_{10} y$	XY	X^2
3000	3.477121	14.3575	1.157079	4.023303	12.09037
4000	3.60206	15.6517	1.194511	4.304082	12.97484
5000	3.69897	16.7353	1.223634	4.526184	13.68238
6000	3.778151	17.6762	1.247389	4.712824	14.27443
7000	3.845098	18.5128	1.267472	4.873555	14.78478
	$\Sigma X = 18.4014$		$\Sigma Y = 6.090135$	$\Sigma XY = 22.43875$	$\Sigma X^2 = 67.80679$

By using least square criteria,

$$\Sigma Y = nA + b\Sigma X$$
$$\Sigma XY = A\Sigma X + B\Sigma X^2$$

∴ $6.090135 = 5 \cdot A + 18.4014\, b$ ... (I)

and $22.43875 = 18.4014 A + 67.80679\, b$ ... (II)

Dividing equation (I) by 5 and (II) by 18.4014

$$1.218027 = A + 3.68028\, b$$

⇒ $A = 1.218027 - 3.68028\, b$

$$1.219404 = A + 3.68487126\, b$$

⇒ $A = 1.219404 - 3.6848712\, b$

∴ $0.0045912\, b = 0.001377$

By substituting in equation (I),

$$A = 0.11393$$

∴ $a = \text{antilog}(A)$
           $= 1.2999 = 1.3\ (\text{Approx})$

∴   Relation between Reynold's number and Nusselt's number is given by

$$y = 1.3\, x^{0.3} \quad \text{... Ans.}$$

6.5.1 Matlab

```
clc;
close all;
clear all;

%% CURVE FITTING
%% LEAST SQUARE CRITERION FOR EQUATION (y = A*B^x)

fprintf('\n***********************************************************');
fprintf('\n*************** CURVE FITTING: y = A*x^B ***************');
fprintf('\n***********************************************************');

n = input('\n Enter No. of DATA POINTS (n): ');
sumX  = 0;
sumY  = 0;
sumXY = 0;
sumX2 = 0;
```

```
% Type of Equation>>> y = A*x^B
% Therefore taking log on both sides, we get>>> log(y)=log(A)+B.log(x)
% i.e log(y)=log(A)+B.log(x), then, Y=BX+A', where Y=log(y) and
%                                                                        X = log(x)
for i = 1:n
    fprintf('\n Point#%d >>>',i);
    x(i) = input('\nX = ');
    X(i) = log10(x(i));
    y(i) = input('Y = ');
    Y(i) = log10(y(i));
    sumX = sumX + X(i);
    sumY = sumY + Y(i);
    sumX2 = sumX2 + X(i)*X(i);
    sumXY = sumXY + X(i)*Y(i);
end
fprintf('\n sumx  = %f',sumX);
fprintf('\n sumY  = %f',sumY);
fprintf('\n sumxY = %f',sumXY);
fprintf('\n sumx2 = %f',sumX2);

A = [sumX n; sumX2 sumX];              %% Coefficient Matrix
B = [sumY; sumXY];                     %% Solution Matrix
C = inv(A)*B;                          %% Solutions of A and B

a = power(10,C(2));
b = C(1);

fprintf('\n Equation of Curve>>> y=(%f)*x^(%f)',a,b);

% Plotting the Actual Data and by Least Square Criteria
for i=1:n
    ya(i)=a*power(x(i),b);
end

hold on
```

```
xlabel('x');
ylabel('y');
title('Least Square Criteria');
plot(x,y,'*','LineWidth',2,'Color',[1 0 0]);
plot(x,ya,'--','LineWidth',2,'Color',[0 0 0]);
```

Output :

```
*************************************************************
****************** NIRALI PUBLICATIONS **********************
******** CONM by M. T. Puranik & V. N. Chougule ************
***************** CURVE FITTING: y = A*x^B ****************
*************************************************************
 Enter No. of DATA POINTS (n): 5
 Point#1 >>>
 X = 3000
 Y = 14.3575

 Point#2 >>>
 X = 4000
 Y = 15.6517

 Point#3 >>>
 X = 5000
 Y = 16.7353

 Point#4 >>>
 X = 6000
 Y = 17.6762

 Point#5 >>>
 X = 7000
 Y = 18.5128

 sumx = 18.401401
```

sumY = 6.090135
sumxY = 22.438748
sumx2 = 67.806793

Equation of Curve>>> y=(1.299990)*x^(0.300001)

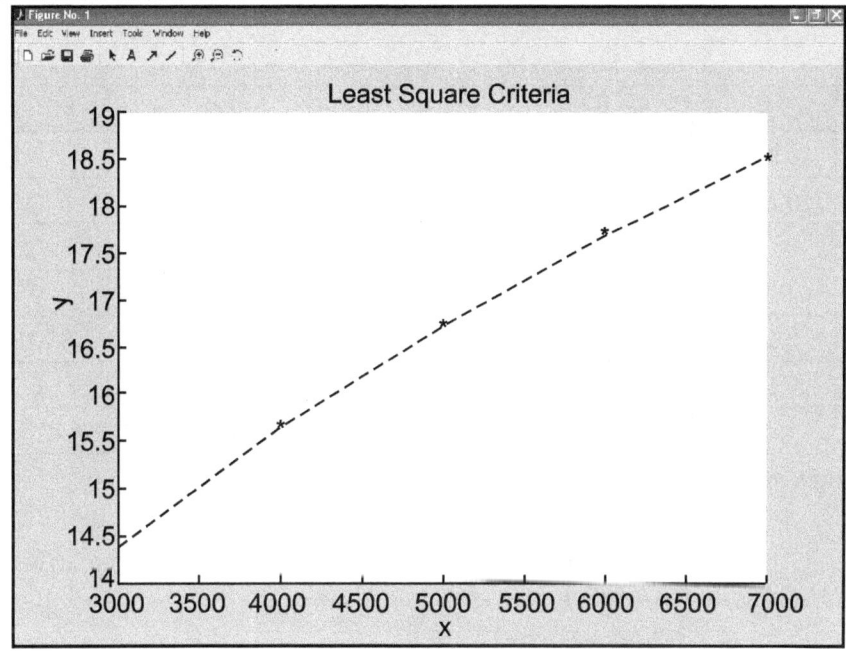

Fig. 6.5

Example 6.7 : An experiment is conducted on expansion of steam in a cylinder having 100 mm diameter and 200 mm length. Find equation of curve in P (bar) = cV^{-n} form for following observations.

P	V
5	0.3714
10	0.2264
15	0.1694
20	0.1380
25	0.1176
30	0.1033

Solution : Given data : No. of points, n = 6

$$P \text{ (bar)} = cV^{-n}$$

Taking log to the base of 10, we get

$$\log_{10}(P) = \log_{10}(c) - n\log_{10}(V)$$
$$y = ax + b, \text{ where } y = \log_{10}(P)$$
$$b = \log_{10}(c)$$
$$a = -n$$
$$x = \log_{10}(V)$$

P	V	y	X	Xy	X²
5	0.3714	0.6990	−0.4302	−0.3007	0.1850
10	0.2264	1.0000	−0.6451	−0.6451	0.4162
15	0.1694	1.1761	−0.7711	−0.9069	0.5946
20	0.138	1.3010	−0.8601	−1.1190	0.7398
25	0.1176	1.3979	−0.9296	−1.2995	0.8641
30	0.1033	1.4771	−0.9859	−1.4563	0.9720
		Σy = 7.0512	ΣX = −4.6220	ΣXy = −5.7275	ΣX² = 3.7717

By using least square criteria, we get

$$\Sigma y = a\Sigma X + nb \qquad \ldots (I)$$
$$\Sigma Xy = a\Sigma X^2 + b\Sigma X \qquad \ldots (II)$$

Therefore, substituting values in above equations, we get

$$7.0512 = -4.622\, a + 6\, b \qquad \ldots (III)$$
$$-5.7275 = 3.7717 \pm 4.6220 \qquad \ldots (IV)$$

Solving above equations simultaneously, we get,

$$a = -1.5220\, x$$

and

$$b = 0.0028$$

Therefore, equation can be written as,

$$y = 1.5220\, x + 0.0028$$

But we have

$$y = \log_{10}(P)$$
$$b = \log_{10}(c)$$
$$a = -n$$
$$x = \log_{10}(V)$$

Therefore,

$$\log_{10}(P) = -1.5220 \log_{10}(V) + \log_{10}(c)$$

i.e.

$$b = \log_{10}(c),$$
$$c = \text{antilog}(b)$$

$$c = 1.006468$$

Therefore equation can be written as

$$P = (1.006468) \times V^{-1.5220} \qquad \text{... Ans.}$$

Example 6.8 : *Following data gives corresponding values of pressure and specific volume of superheated steam :*

V	P
2	105
4	42.7
6	25.3
8	16.7
10	13

Find the equation of best fit curve passing through these points by law $PV^n = C$.

Solution : Given Data : No. of points, n = 5

$$P \text{ (bar)} = CV^{-n}$$

Taking log to the base of 10, we get

$$\log_{10}(P) = \log_{10}(C) - n \log_{10}(V)$$
$$y = ax + b, \text{ where } y = \log_{10}(P),$$
$$b = \log_{10}(C)$$
$$a = -n$$
$$x = \log_{10}(V)$$

V	P	x	y	xy	x^2
2	105	0.3010	2.0212	0.6084	0.0906
4	42.7	0.6021	1.6304	0.9816	0.3625
6	25.3	0.7782	1.4031	1.0918	0.6055
8	16.7	0.9031	1.2227	1.1042	0.8156
10	13	1.0000	1.1139	1.1139	1.0000
		$\Sigma x = 3.5843$	$\Sigma y = 7.3914$	$\Sigma xy = 4.9001$	$\Sigma x^2 = 2.8742$

By using least square criteria, we get

$$\Sigma y = a\Sigma x + nb \qquad \text{... (I)}$$
$$\Sigma xy = a\Sigma x^2 + b\Sigma x \qquad \text{... (II)}$$

Therefore, substituting values in above equations, we get

$$7.3914 = 3.5843 a + 5 b \qquad \text{... (III)}$$
$$4.9001 = 2.8742 a + 3.5843 b \qquad \text{... (IV)}$$

Solving above equations simultaneously, we get,

$$a = -1.3076$$
and
$$b = 2.4156$$

Therefore, equation can be written as,

$$y = 1.3076\, x + 2.4156$$

But we have

$$y = \log_{10}(P)$$
$$b = \log_{10}(c)$$
$$a = -n$$
$$x = \log_{10}(V)$$

Therefore, $\log_{10}(P) = -1.3076 \log_{10}(V) + \log_{10}(c)$

i.e.
$$b = \log_{10}(c),$$
$$c = \text{antilog}(b)$$
$$c = 260.3754$$

Therefore equation can be written as

$$P = (260.3754) \times V^{-1.3076} \qquad \ldots \text{Ans.}$$

6.6 Fitting the Curve Y = A·B^x

Consider $\quad y = ab^x$

Taking log on both sides,

$$\log y = \log(a) + x \cdot \log(b)$$

∴ $\quad Y = A + x \cdot B$

where,
$$A = \log(a)$$
$$B = \log(b)$$

By using equations and solving them simultaneously,

$$\Sigma Y = n \cdot A + B \Sigma x$$
$$\Sigma xY = A \cdot \Sigma x + B \Sigma x^2$$

We can get values of A and B.

$$a = \text{antilog}(A) \text{ and } b = \text{antilog}(B)$$

Example 6.9 : If the relation between, x and y is of the type $y = a \cdot b^x$, using following values of x and y, find the values of constants a and b for the best fitting curve.

x	2.1	2.5	3.1	3.5	4.1
y	5.14	6.708	10.29	13.58	20.578

Solution : Given data : n = 5,

Data points are required to be fitted in the form

$$y = a \cdot b^x$$

Taking log on both sides,

$$\log y = \log a + x \cdot \log b$$

∴ $\quad y = A + B \cdot x \quad$ ...(I)

where, $\quad y = \log_{10} y$

$A = \log_{10} A$

$B = \log_{10} B$

Equation (I) is reduced to straight line form.

x	y	Y = $\log_{10} y$	xY	x^2
2.1	5.14	0.710963	1.493023	4.41
2.5	6.788	0.831742	2.079355	6.25
3.1	10.29	1.012415	3.138488	9.61
3.5	13.58	1.1329	3.965149	12.25
4.1	20.578	1.313403	5.384953	16.81
Σx = 15.3		ΣY = 5.001423	ΣxY = 16.06097	Σx^2 = 49.33

$$y = A + Bx$$

∴ $\quad \Sigma y = n \cdot A + B \Sigma x \quad \Rightarrow \quad 5.0013423 = 5A + 15.3 B$

$\quad \Sigma xy = A \Sigma x + B \Sigma x^2 \quad \Rightarrow \quad 16.06097 = 15.3 A + 49.33 B$

Solving these two equations simultaneously,

$A = 0.078616$

$B = 0.301199$

$a = \text{antilog}(A)$

$b = \text{antilog}(B)$

∴ $\quad a = 1.198439$

and $\quad b = 2.000778$

∴ Equation $\quad \mathbf{y = 1.1984 \times 2^x} \quad$ ... Ans.

6.6.1 Algorithm

- Input number of data points (n).
- Initialize sumx, sumy, sumxy and sumx2 as 0.
- For n = 1 to n, increment i by 1.
- Input 'x' and 'y' values.
- Calculate Y = $\log_{10} y$.
- Calculate sumx, sumY, sumxY and sumx2.
- End loop.

- Construct coefficient matrix and solution matrix.
- Find solution matrix.
- Print results.

6.6.2 Matlab

```
clc;
close all;
clear all;

%% CURVE FITTING
%% LEAST SQUARE CRITERION FOR EQUATION (y = A*B^x)

fprintf('\n*************************************************************');
fprintf('\n**************** NIRALI PUBLICATIONS ********************');
fprintf('\n********* CONM by M. T. Puranik & V. N. Chougule *********');
fprintf('\n**************** CURVE FITTING: y = A*B^x ***************');
fprintf('\n*************************************************************');

n = input('\n Enter No. of DATA POINTS (n): ');
sumx  = 0;
sumY  = 0;
sumxY = 0;
sumx2 = 0;

% Type of Equation>>> y = A*B^x
% Therefore taking log on both sides, we get>>> log(y)=log(A)+x.log(B)
% i.e. log(y)=log(A)+x.log(B), then, Y=Px+Q, where P=log(B), Q=log(A)

for i = 1:n
    fprintf('\n Point#%d >>>',i);
    x(i) = input('\nX = ');
    y(i) = input('\nY = ');
    Y(i) = log10(y(i));
    sumx = sumx + x(i);
```

```
    sumY = sumY + Y(i);
    sumx2 = sumx2 + x(i)*x(i);
    sumxY = sumxY + x(i)*Y(i);
end

fprintf('\n sumx  = %f',sumx);
fprintf('\n sumY  = %f',sumY);
fprintf('\n sumxY = %f',sumxY);
fprintf('\n sumx2 = %f',sumx2);

A = [sumx n; sumx2 sumx];      %% Coefficient Matrix
B = [sumY; sumxY];             %% Solution Matrix
C = inv(A)*B;                  %% Solutions of A and B

A = power(10,C(2));
B = power(10,C(1));
fprintf('\n Equation of Curve>>> y = (%.4f)*(%.4f)^x',A,B);

% Plotting the Actual Data and by Least Square Criteria
for i=1:n
    ya(i)=A*power(B,x(i));
end
hold on
xlabel('x');
ylabel('y');
title('Least Square Criteria');
plot(x,y,'*','LineWidth',2,'Color',[1 0 0]);
plot(x,ya,'--','LineWidth',2,'Color',[0 0 0]);
```

Output :

****

****************** NIRALI PUBLICATIONS *********************

```
******** CONM by M. T. Puranik & V. N. Chougule *************
***************** CURVE FITTING: y = A*B^x *****************
************************************************************
Enter No. of DATA POINTS (n): 5

Point#1 >>>
X = 2.1

Y = 5.14

Point#2 >>>
X = 2.5

Y = 6.708

Point#3 >>>
X = 3.1

Y = 10.29

Point#4 >>>
X = 3.5

Y = 13.58

Point#5 >>>
X = 4.1
Y = 20.578
 sumx  = 15.300000
 sumY  = 4.996274
 sumxY = 16.048095
 sumx2 = 49.330000
 Equation of Curve>>> y = (1.1860)*(2.0061)^x
```

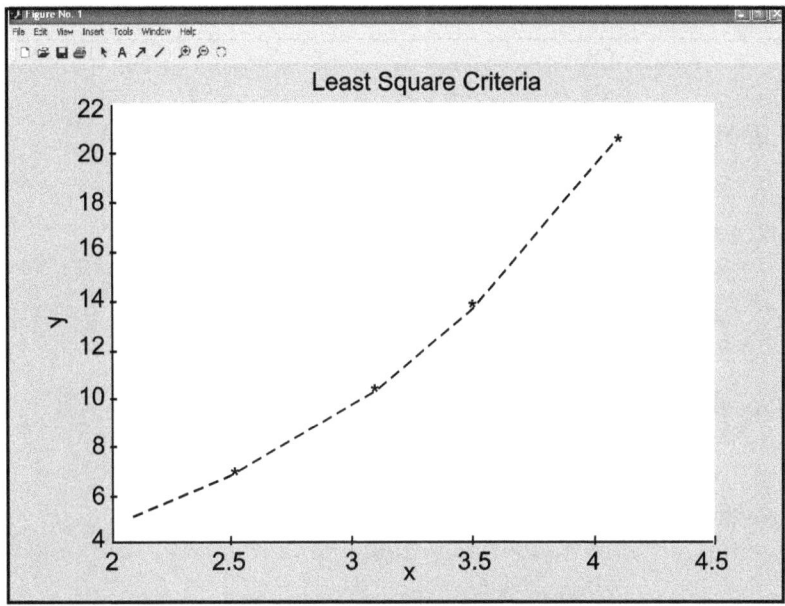

Fig. 6.6

Example 6.10 : The equation of the best curve fit is of the type $y = ab^x$. Find the values of constants a and b by fitting curve through these points.

X	2	3	4	5	6
Y	144	172.8	207.4	248.8	298.5

Solution : Given data : n = 5.

Type of equation $\Rightarrow$

$$y = a \cdot b^x$$

Taking log on both sides,

$$\log_{10}(y) = \log_{10}(a) + x \log_{10}(b)$$

$\therefore \qquad Y = A + B \cdot x \qquad \qquad \ldots \text{(I)}$

where,

$Y = \log_{10} y$

$A = \log_{10} a$

$B = \log_{10} b$

x	y	$Y = \log_{10} y$	x·Y	x^2
2	144	2.158362	4.316725	4
3	172.8	2.237544	6.712631	9
4	207.4	2.316809	9.267235	16
5	248.8	2.39585	11.97925	25
6	298.5	2.474944	14.84967	36
$\Sigma x = 20$		$\Sigma Y = 11.58351$	$\Sigma x \cdot Y = 47.12551$	$\Sigma x^2 = 90$

By using least square criteria,
$$\Sigma Y = n \cdot A + B\Sigma x$$
$$\Sigma xY = A \cdot \Sigma x + B\Sigma x^2$$
Substituting values, we get
$$11.58351 = 5A + 20B \qquad \ldots (I)$$
$$47.12551 = 20A + 90B \qquad \ldots (II)$$
Multiplying equation (I) by 4
$$\therefore \quad 46.33404 = 20A + 80B$$
$$\underline{\;47.12551\; = \;20A\; + 90B\;}$$
$$-0.79147 = -10B$$
$$\therefore \quad B = 0.079147$$
Substituting value of B in equation (I),
$$\therefore \quad A \Rightarrow 11.58351 = 5A + 20 \times 0.079147$$
$$\therefore \quad A = 2.000144$$
By taking antilog of A and B,
$$a = 100.0262 \approx 100$$
$$b = 1.99905 \approx 2$$
$$\therefore \quad \textbf{Equation is } y = 100 \times 2^x \Rightarrow y = 100 \times 2^x \qquad \ldots \textbf{Ans.}$$

6.7 FITTING A PARABOLA ($Y = AX^2 + BX + C$)

Let $y = ax^2 + bx + c$ be a parabola to be fitted for the data (x_i, y_i), where $i = 1, 2 \ldots n$.
Deviation at $x = x_i$ is given by,
$$S_i = y_i - y_i' = y_i - (ax_i^2 + bx_i + c)$$
By least square criteria, sum of squares is given by,
$$S = \sum_{i=1}^{n} S_i = \sum_{i=1}^{n} [y_i - (ax_i^2 + bx_i + c)]^2 \qquad \ldots (A)$$

Sum of least square of deviations will be less for best values of a, b and c if $\dfrac{\partial S}{\partial c} = 0$.

$$\therefore \quad \sum \{2[y_i - (ax_i^2 + bx_i + c)] \times (-1)\} = 0$$

$$\therefore \quad \sum y_i = a\sum x_i^2 + b\sum x_i + nc = 0 \qquad \ldots (I)$$

By $\dfrac{\partial S}{\partial C} = 0$, $\sum \{2[y_i - (ax_i^2 + bx_i + c)](-x_i)\} = 0$

$$\therefore \quad \sum x_i y_i = a\sum x_i^3 + b\sum x_i^2 + c\sum x_i \qquad \ldots (II)$$

By $\dfrac{\partial S}{\partial a} = 0$, $\sum \{2[y_i - (ax_i^2 + bx_i + c)](-x_i^2)\} = 0$

$$\therefore \quad \sum x_i^2 \cdot y_i = a\sum x_i^4 + b\sum x_i^3 + c\sum x_i^2 \qquad \ldots (III)$$

From equations (I), (II) and (III), generalised equations can be written as follows :

$$\Sigma y = a\Sigma x^2 + b\Sigma x + nc$$
$$\Sigma xy = a\Sigma x^3 + b\Sigma x^2 + c\Sigma x$$
$$\Sigma x^2 y = a\Sigma x^4 + b\Sigma x^3 + c\Sigma x^2$$

Example 6.11 : Fit a second degree parabola ($y = ax^2 + bx + c$) to the following data taking y as dependent variable.

X	1	2	3	4	5	6	7	8	9
Y	2	6	7	8	9	10	11	10	9

Solution : Consider $X = x - 5$
$Y = y - 7$

Also, let curve fit be

x	y	X = x – 5	Y = y – 7	XY	X²	X²Y	X³	X⁴
1	2	–4	–5	20	16	–80	–64	256
2	6	–3	–1	3	9	–9	–27	81
3	7	–2	0	0	4	0	–8	16
4	8	–1	1	–1	1	1	–1	1
5	10	0	3	0	0	0	0	0
6	11	1	4	4	1	4	1	1
7	11	2	4	8	4	16	8	16
8	10	3	3	9	9	27	27	81
9	9	4	2	8	16	32	64	256
		ΣX = 0	ΣY = 11	ΣXY = 51	ΣX² = 60	ΣX²Y = –9	ΣX³ = 0	ΣX⁴ = 608

By using least square criteria for parabolic equations, we have

$$\Sigma Y = a\Sigma X^2 + b\Sigma X + nC$$
$$\Sigma XY = a\Sigma X^3 + b\Sigma X^2 + c\Sigma X$$
$$\Sigma X^2 Y = a\Sigma X^4 + b\Sigma X^3 + c\Sigma X^2$$

Substituting values from table, we have

$60·a + 0·b + 9·c = 11$ ... (I)
$0·a + 60·b + 0·c = 51$ ... (II)
$708·a + 0·b + 60·c = -9$ ... (III)

Solving equations (I), (II) and (III) simultaneously, we can get values of a, b, c.

From equation (II), $b = \dfrac{51}{60} = 0.85$

From equations (I) and (III),

$60a + 9c = 11 \Rightarrow 1200a + 180c = 200$
$708a + 60c = -9 \Rightarrow \underline{-2124a + -180c = +-27}$
$\qquad\qquad\qquad\qquad\qquad -924a = 247$

∴ $\qquad a = -0.267$

Substituting in equation (I)
$$60x - 0.267 + 9C = 11$$
$$\therefore \quad C = 3.002$$

Hence, the curve of fit is
$$Y = aX^2 + bX + c$$
$$Y = -0.267X^2 + 0.85X + 3.00$$
$$\therefore \quad y - 7 = -0.267(x-5)^2 + 0.85(x-5) + 3$$
$$\therefore \quad y = -0.267(x^2 + 10x + 25) + 0.85(x-5) + 3 + 7$$
$$\therefore \quad \mathbf{y = -0.27\,x^2 + 3.55x - 1} \qquad \text{... Ans.}$$

6.7.1 Algorithm

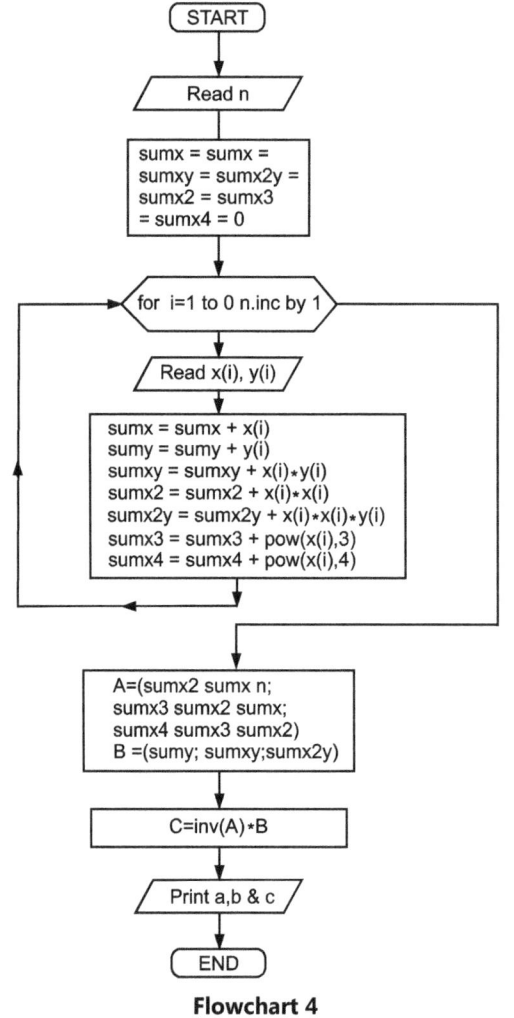

Flowchart 4

- Input number of data points (n).
- Initialize sumx, sumy, sumxy, sumx2, sumx3, sumx2y and sumx4 as 0.
- For n = 1 to n, increment i by 1.
- Input 'x' and 'y' values.
- Calculate sumx, sumy, sumxy, sumx2, sumx3, sumx2y and sumx4.
- End loop.
- Construct coefficient matrix and solution matrix.
- Find solution matrix.
- Print results.

6.7.2 Matlab

```
clc;
clf;
close all;
clear all;

%% CURVE FITTING
%% LEAST SQUARE CRITERION FOR PARABOLIC EQUATION (y = Ax^2 + Bx + C)

fprintf('\n***************************************************');
fprintf('\n****************** NIRALI PUBLICATIONS ******************');
fprintf('\n******** CONM by M. T. Puranik & V. N. Chougule *********');
fprintf('\n********** CURVE FITTING: PARABOLIC EQUATION ************');
fprintf('\n***************************************************');

n = input('\n\n Enter No. of DATA POINTS (n): ');
sumx = 0;
sumy = 0;
sumxy = 0;
sumx2 = 0;
sumx3 = 0;
sumx2y = 0;
sumx4 = 0;

for i = 1:n
    fprintf('\n Point#%d >>>',i);
```

```
    x(i) = input('\nX = ');
    y(i) = input('Y = ');
    sumx = sumx + x(i);
    sumy = sumy + y(i);
    sumx2 = sumx2 + x(i)*x(i);
    sumxy = sumxy + x(i)*y(i);
    sumx3 = sumx3 + x(i)*x(i)*x(i);
    sumx2y = sumx2y + x(i)*x(i)*y(i);
    sumx4 = sumx4 + x(i)*x(i)*x(i)*x(i);
end

fprintf('\n sumx  = %.2f',sumx);
fprintf('\t sumy  = %.2f',sumy);
fprintf('\t sumxy = %.2f',sumxy);
fprintf('\t sumx2 = %.2f',sumx2);
fprintf('\n sumx3 = %.2f',sumx3);
fprintf('\t sumx2y = %.2f',sumx2y);
fprintf('\t sumx4 = %.2f',sumx4);
A = [sumx2 sumx n; sumx3 sumx2 sumx; sumx4 sumx3 sumx2];       %% Coefficient Matrix
B = [sumy; sumxy; sumx2y];                                      %% Solution Matrix
C = inv(A)*B;                                                   %% Solutions of A, B, C

fprintf('\n\n Equation of Curve>>> y = (%.4f)x^2 + (%.4f)x + (%.4f) ',C(1),C(2),C(3));

% Plotting the Actual Data and by Least Square Criteria
for i=1:n
  ya(i)=C(1)*x(i)*x(i)+C(2)*x(i)+C(3);  %Calculation of y as per solution
end

hold on
xlabel('x');
ylabel('y');
title('Least Square Criteria');
plot(x,y,'*','LineWidth',2,'Color',[1 0 0]);
```

```
plot(x,ya,'-','LineWidth',2,'Color',[0 0 0]);
```
Output :

```
*************************************************************
***************** NIRALI PUBLICATIONS ********************
******** CONM by M. T. Puranik & V. N. Chougule ***********
*********** CURVE FITTING: PARABOLIC EQUATION *************
*************************************************************

Enter No. of DATA POINTS (n): 5
 Point#1 >>>
X = 1
Y = 1090

 Point#2 >>>
X = 2
Y = 1220

 Point#3 >>>
X = 3
Y = 1390

 Point#4 >>>
X = 4
Y = 1625

 Point#5 >>>
X = 5
Y = 1915
sumx = 15.00    sumy = 7240.00      sumxy = 23775.00      sumx2 = 55.00
sumx3 = 225.00       sumx2y = 92355.00     sumx4 = 979.00

Equation of Curve>>> y = (27.5000)x^2 + (40.5000)x + (1024.0000)
```

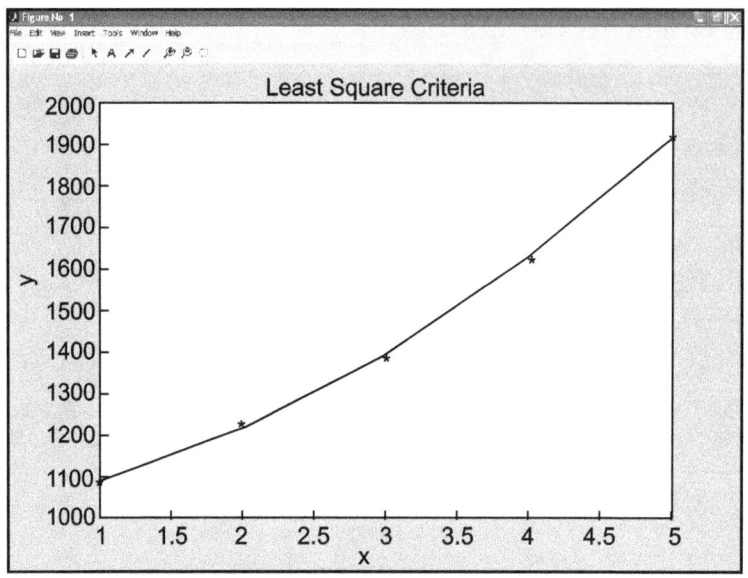

Fig. 6.7

Example 6.12 : Following is the data given for values of x and y. Fit a second degree polynomial of type $y = ax^2 + bx + c$ where a, b, c are constants.

X	−3	−2	−1	0	1	2	3
Y	12	4	1	2	7	15	30

Solution : Given data $\Rightarrow$ n = 7

X	Y	XY	X^2	X^2Y	X^3	X^4
−3	12	−36	9	108	−27	81
−2	4	−8	4	16	−8	16
−1	1	−1	1	1	−1	1
0	2	0	0	0	0	0
1	7	7	1	7	1	1
2	15	30	4	60	8	16
3	30	90	9	20	27	81
$\Sigma X = 0$	$\Sigma Y = 71$	$\Sigma XY = 82$	$\Sigma X^2 = 28$	$\Sigma X^2Y = 462$	$\Sigma X^3 = 0$	$\Sigma X^4 = 196$

By using least square criteria for parabolic equations, we have

$$\Sigma Y = a\Sigma x^2 + b\Sigma X + nC$$

$\Rightarrow \qquad 71 = 28 \cdot a + 0 \cdot b + 7 \cdot c$ ... (I)

$$\Sigma XY = a\Sigma x^3 + b\Sigma x^2 + c\Sigma x$$

$\Rightarrow \qquad 82 = 0 \cdot a + 28 \cdot b + 0 \cdot c$ ... (II)

$$\Sigma x^2 y = a\Sigma x^4 + b\Sigma x^3 + c\Sigma x^2$$
⇒ $\quad 462 = 196 \cdot a + 0 \cdot b + 28 \cdot c \qquad \ldots \text{(III)}$

Algorithm for matrix formation is as follows :

$$\begin{bmatrix} 28 & 0 & 7 \\ 0 & 28 & 0 \\ 196 & 0 & 28 \end{bmatrix} \begin{bmatrix} a \\ b \\ c \end{bmatrix} = \begin{bmatrix} 7 \\ 0 \\ 28 \end{bmatrix}$$

By using Gauss-Jordan method, matrix reduces to

$$\begin{bmatrix} 1 & 0 & 0 \\ 0 & 1 & 0 \\ 0 & 0 & 1 \end{bmatrix} \begin{bmatrix} a \\ b \\ c \end{bmatrix} = \begin{bmatrix} 2.1190 \\ 2.9286 \\ 1.6667 \end{bmatrix}$$

∴ $\quad a = 2.1190$
$\quad b = 2.9286$
$\quad c = 1.6667$

∴ Equation for curve is
$$y = 2.1190 \cdot x^2 + 2.9286 \cdot x + 1.6667 \qquad \ldots \text{Ans.}$$

Example 6.13 : Fit second degree parabola to the following :

X	0	1	2	3	4
Y	1	1.8	1.3	2.5	6.3

Solution : Consider $X = x - 2$.
$n = 5$.

x	X = x − 2	y	Xy	X^2	X^2y	X^3	X^4
0	− 2	1	− 2	4	4	− 8	16
1	− 1	1.8	− 1.8	1	1.8	− 1	1
2	0	1.3	9	0	0	0	0
3	1	2.5	2.5	1	2.5	1	1
4	2	6.3	12.6	4	25.2	8	16
	ΣX = 0	Σy = 12.9	ΣXy = 11.3	ΣX² = 10	ΣX²y = 33.5	ΣX³ = 0	ΣX⁴ = 34

Type of the curve is $y = ax^2 + bx + c$

Equation by Least Square Criteria, is
$$\Sigma Y = a\Sigma X^2 + b\Sigma X + nC$$
∴ $\quad 12.9 = 10 \cdot a + 0 \cdot b + 5 \cdot c \qquad \ldots \text{(I)}$
$$\Sigma Xy = a\Sigma x^3 + b\Sigma x^2 + c\Sigma x$$
∴ $\quad 11.3 = 0 \cdot a + 10 \cdot b + 0 \cdot c \qquad \ldots \text{(II)}$
$$\Sigma x^2 y = a\Sigma x^4 + b\Sigma x^3 + c\Sigma x^2$$
∴ $\quad 33.5 = 34 \cdot a + 0 \cdot b + 10 \cdot c \qquad \ldots \text{(III)}$

To solve simultaneous equation by Gauss Jordon method,

Augmented matrix is given by :

$$\begin{bmatrix} 10 & 0 & 5 \\ 0 & 10 & 0 \\ 34 & 0 & 10 \end{bmatrix} \begin{bmatrix} a \\ b \\ c \end{bmatrix} = \begin{bmatrix} 12.9 \\ 11.3 \\ 33.5 \end{bmatrix}$$

We get, a = 0.55, b = 1.13 and c = 1.48.

Equation of curve is given by

$$Y = 0.55 X^2 + 1.13 X + 1.48$$

∴ $Y = 0.55 (x - 2)^2 + 1.13 (x - 2) + 1.48$

$= 0.55 (x^2 - 4x + 4) + 1.13x - 2.26 + 1.48$

∴ **Y = 0.55 x^2 − 1.07 x + 1.42** ... Ans.

Example 6.14 : Fit second degree parabola to the following data by the least square method.

x	1	2	3	4	5
y	1090	1220	1390	1625	1915

Solution : n = 5. Put X = x − 3 and Y = y − 1390.

x	y	X = (x − 3)	Y = (x − 1390)	XY	X²	X²Y	X³	X⁴
1	1090	− 2	− 300	600	4	—	− 8	16
2	1220	− 1	− 170	170	1	1200	− 1	1
3	1390	0	0	0	0	− 170	0	0
4	1625	1	235	235	1	0	1	1
5	1915	2	525	1050	4	235 2100	8	16
		ΣX = 0	ΣY = 290	ΣXY = 2055	ΣX² = 10	ΣX²Y = 965	ΣX³ = 0	ΣX⁴ = 34

By using least square criteria, non parabola, we get

$$10·a + 0·b + 5·c = 290$$
$$0·a + 10·b + 0·c = 2055$$
$$34·a + 0·b + 10·c = 965$$

By using Gauss-Jordon's method, we get

a = 27.5, b = 205.5 and c = 3.0.

∴ $Y = 27.5 X^2 + 205.5X + 3$

∴ $y - 1390 = 27.4 (x - 3)^2 + 205.5 (x - 3) + 3$

∴ $y - 1390 = 27.5 (x^2 - 6x + 9) + 205.5 x - 616.5 + 3$

∴ $y = 27.5 x^2 - 165 x + 247.5 + 205.5 x + 616.5 + 3 + 1390$

∴ **y = 27.5 x^2 + 40.5 x + 1024** ... Ans.

6.8 CURVE FITTING BY USING MATLAB TOOLBOX

Step 1 : Start>>Toolboxes>>Curve Fitting>>Curve Fitting Tool as shown in Fig. 6.8.

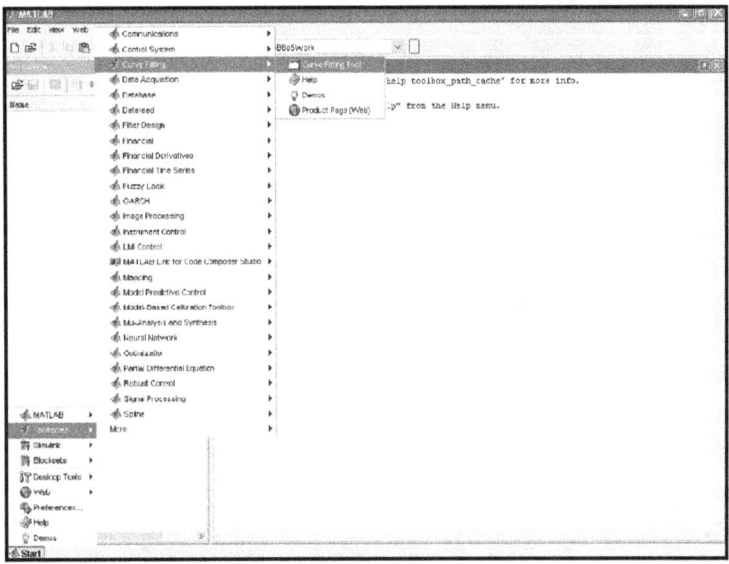

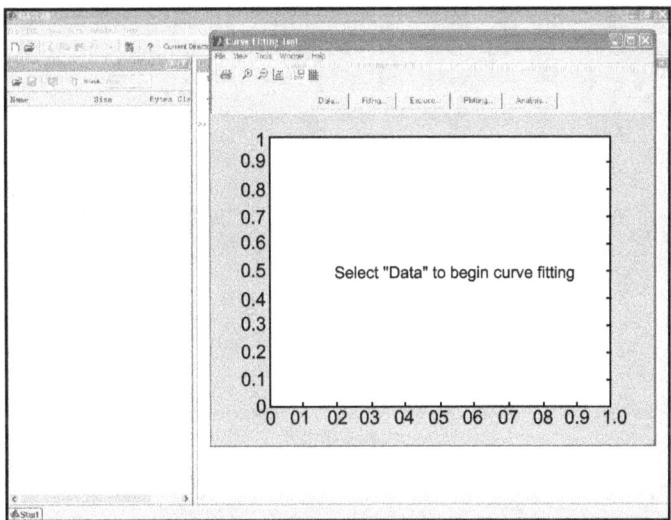

Fig. 6.8

Step 2 : Data Input : In MATLAB Command window, declare two variables as shown below :

>> x = [2 3 4 5 6 7 8 9];
>> y = [19 48 99 178 291 444 643 894];

As shown in Fig. 6.9.

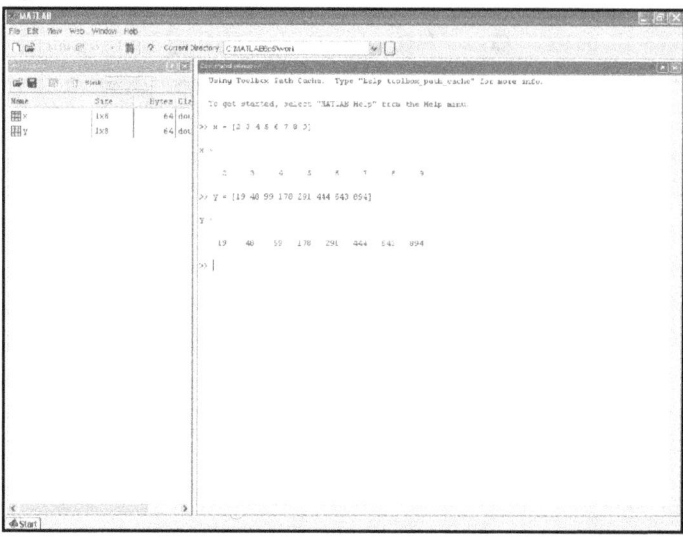

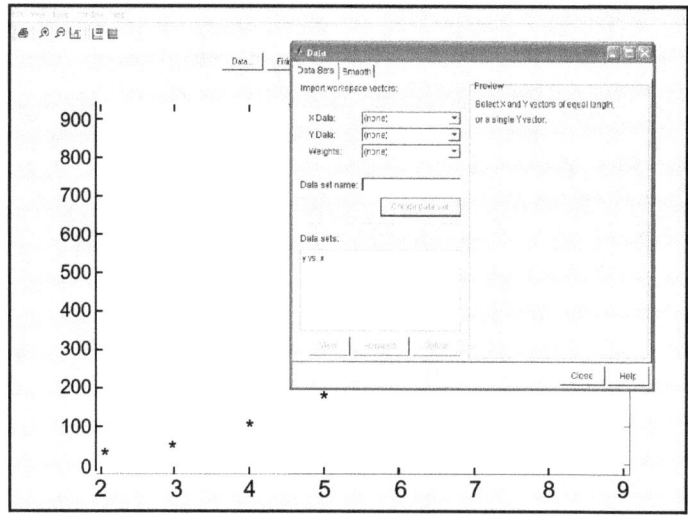

Fig. 6.9

In curve fitting Toolbox, Click on **DATA** button. Select **X Data** as x and **Y Data** as y and then select Create Data Range and select Close. (as shown in Fig. 6.10).

Step 3 : Click Fitting>>>in fit Editor>>>New Fitting>>>

    Select Fit Name – Linear Fit

    Select Type of Fit – Polynomial

    Click Apply

Results>
Linear model Poly1:
f(x) = p1*x + p2
Coefficients (with 95% confidence bounds) :
p1 = 122 (84.85, 159.2)
p2 = − 344 (− 565.4, − 122.6)
Goodness of fit :
SSE: 5.809e + 004
R-square: 0.915
Adjusted R-square: 0.9008
RMSE: 98.4

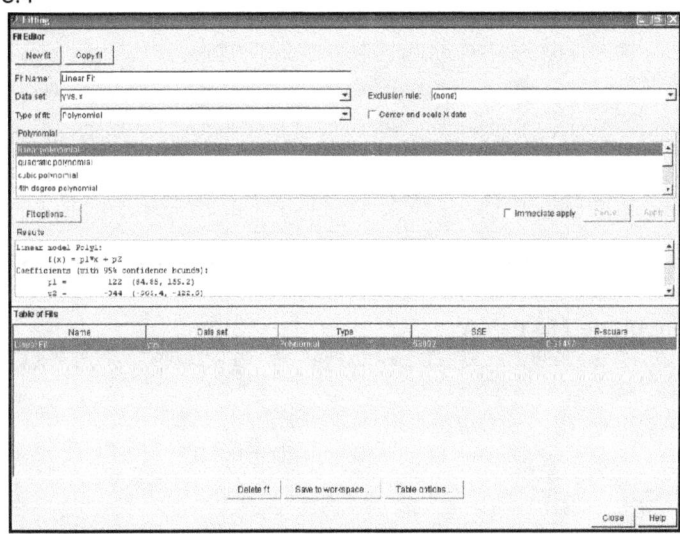

Fig. 6.10

Select Fit Name – Linear Fit
Select Type of Fit – Polynomial
Click Apply

Results>
Linear model Poly2 : f(x) = p1*x^2 + p2*x + p3
Coefficients (with 95% confidence bounds):
p1 = 18.5 (16.34, 20.66)
p2 = − 81.5 (− 105.7, − 57.33)
p3 = 118.5 (58.63, 178.4)
Goodness of fit : SSE: 594
R-square: 0.9991

Adjusted R-square: 0.9988
RMSE: 10.9

Similarly, exponential, power fits, etc. can be used for various types of fits.

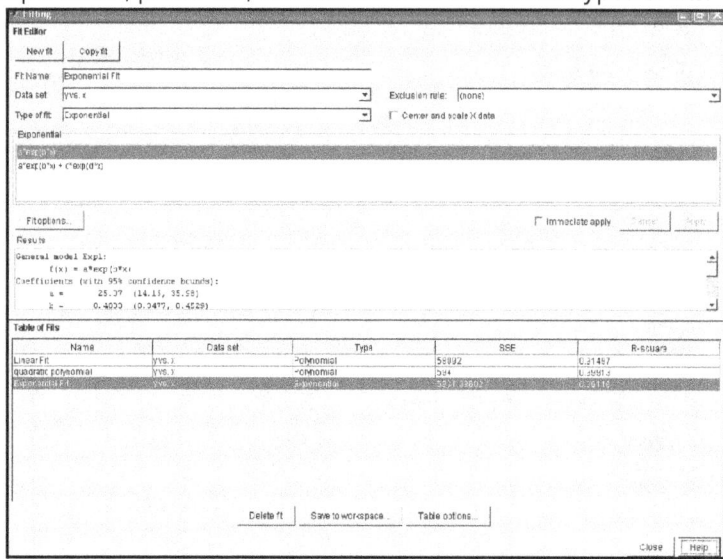

Fig. 6.11

Final results are plotted as below :

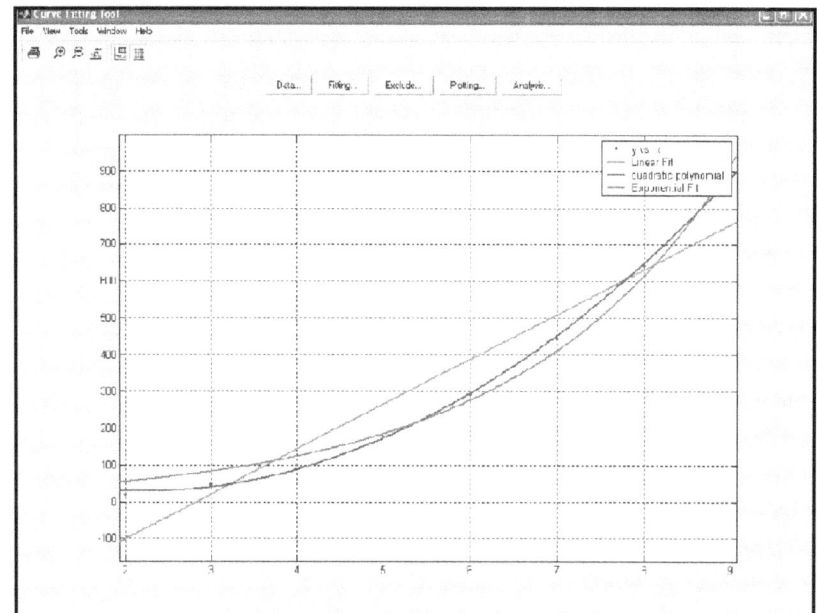

Fig. 6.12

6.9 Curve Fitting by Using Excel

Step 1 : Input data is as shown in Fig. 6.13.

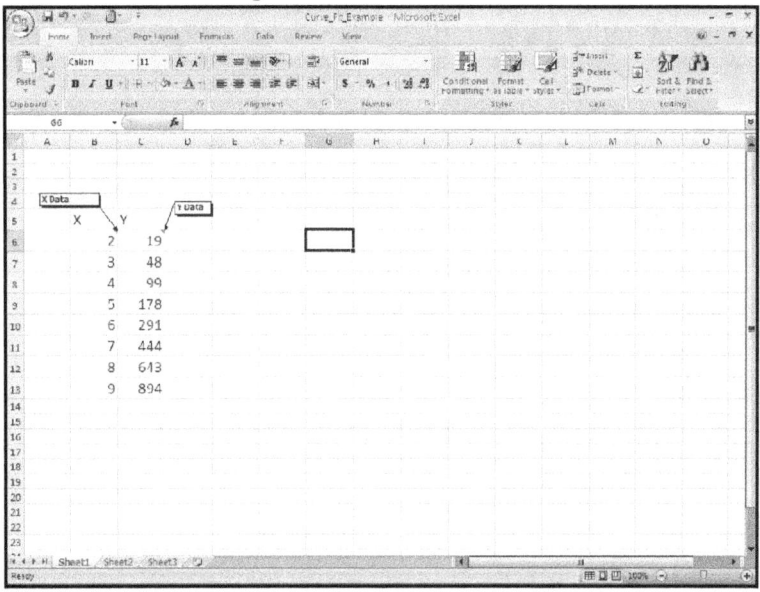

Fig. 6.13

Step 2 : Select Data>>> Data Analysis Toolbox>>>Regression, Click OK

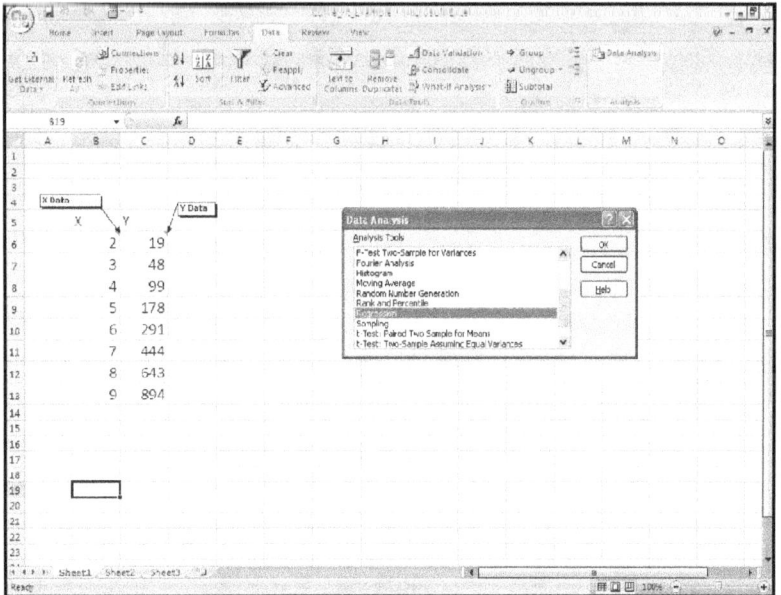

Fig. 6.14

Step 3 : Select Y Input Range and X input range. Select New Worksheet Ply and Line Fit Plots and click 'OK' button.

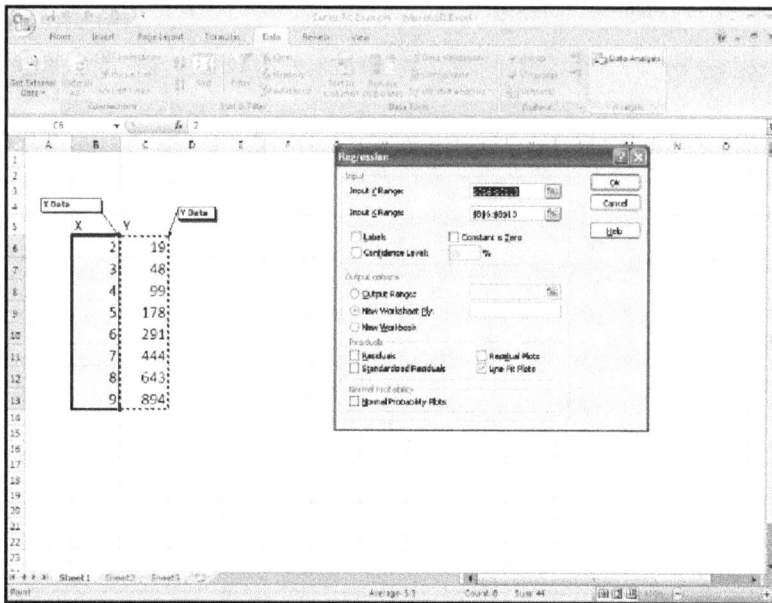

Fig. 6.15

Step 4 :

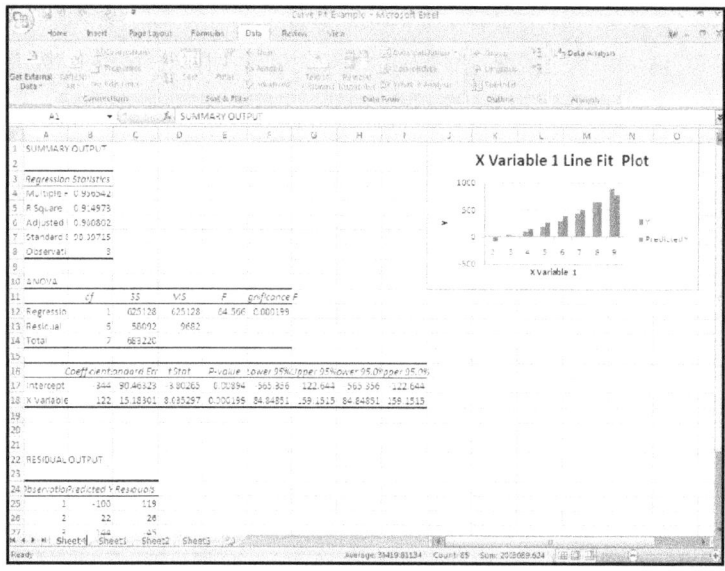

Fig. 6.16

Step 5 : Select graph, Change Chart type to Lines.

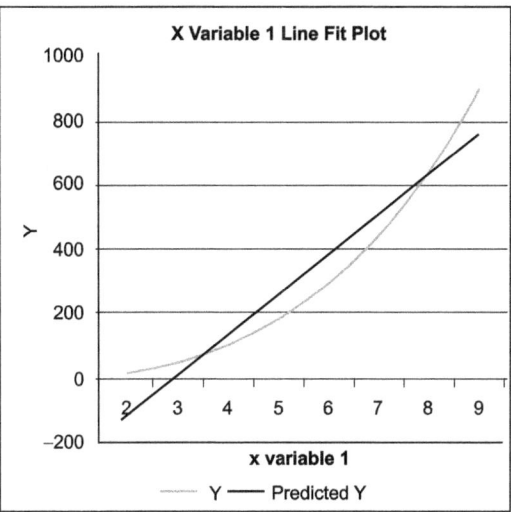

Fig. 6.17

Example 6.15 : For the tabulated values of x and y given below, fit a linear curve of type $y = mx + c$.

x	1	3	5	7	9
y	1.5	2.8	4	4.7	6

Solution : Given data : Number of points (n) = 5.

x	y	xy	x^2
1	1.5	1.5	1
3	2.8	8.4	9
5	4.0	20.0	25
7	4.7	32.9	49
9	6.0	54.0	81
$\Sigma x = 25$	$\Sigma y = 19$	$\Sigma xy = 116.8$	$\Sigma x^2 = 165$

By using least square criteria for straight line ($y = mx + c$), we get

$$\Sigma y = m\Sigma x + nc \quad \ldots \text{(I)}$$
$$\Sigma xy = m\Sigma x^2 + c\Sigma x \quad \ldots \text{(II)}$$

Therefore, substituting values in above equations, we get

$$19 = 25m + 5c \quad \ldots \text{(III)}$$
$$116.8 = 165m + 25c \quad \ldots \text{(IV)}$$

Solving above equations simultaneously, we get,

$$m = 0.5450 \text{ and } b = 1.0750$$

Therefore, equation can be written as,

$$y = 0.545 x + 1.075 \quad \ldots \text{Ans.}$$

Example 6.16 : It is known that tensile strength of plastic increases as a function of time when it is heat treated. The following data is collected :

Time (min.)	10	20	30	40	50	60
Tensile strength (N/mm^2)	4.2	17.8	49.6	48.6	64.4	104.8

Use the least square criterion to fit a straight line to this data and use the equation to determine the tensile strength at time 70 min.

Solution : Number of data points (n) = 6.

x	y	xy	x^2
10	4.2	42	100
20	17.8	356	400
30	49.6	1488	900
40	48.6	1944	1600
50	64.4	3220	2500
60	104.8	6288	3600
$\Sigma x = 210$	$\Sigma y = 289.4$	$\Sigma xy = 13338$	$\Sigma x^2 = 9100$

By using least square criteria for straight line (y = ax + b), we get

$$\Sigma y = a\Sigma x + nb \qquad \ldots (I)$$
$$\Sigma xy = a\Sigma x^2 + b\Sigma x \qquad \ldots (II)$$

Therefore, substituting values in above equations, we get

$$289.4 = 210a + 6b \qquad \ldots (III)$$
$$13338 = 9100a + 210b \qquad \ldots (IV)$$

Solving above equations simultaneously, we get,

$$a = 1.8337 \text{ and } b = -15.9467$$

Therefore, equation can be written as,

$$y = 1.8337 x - 15.9467 \qquad \ldots \text{Ans.}$$

Value of tensile strength (y) at x = 70 min is given by

$$y = 1.8337 \times 70 - 15.9467$$
$$y = 112.4123 \text{ N/mm}^2 \qquad \ldots \text{Ans.}$$

Alternative Method :

Number of data points (n) = 6

Assume X = x − 35

x	X(= x − 35)	y	Xy	X²
10	− 25	4.2	− 105	625
20	− 15	17.8	− 267	225
30	− 5	49.6	− 248	25
40	5	48.6	243	25
50	15	64.4	966	225
60	25	104.8	2620	625
	ΣX = 0	Σy = 289.4	ΣXy = 3209	ΣX² = 1750

By using least square criteria for straight line (y = ax + b), we get

$\qquad$ Σy = aΣX + nb $\qquad$ ... (I)

$\qquad$ ΣXy = aΣX² + bΣX $\qquad$ ... (II)

Therefore, substituting values in above equations, we get

$\qquad$ 289.4 = 0a + 6b $\qquad$ ... (III)

$\qquad$ 3209 = 1750a + 0b $\qquad$ ... (IV)

∴ $\qquad$ b = 48.2333 and a = 1.8337 $\qquad$ ... from equations (III) and (IV)

∴ Equation of line is

$\qquad$ y = 1.8337 X + 48.2333

∴ $\qquad$ y = 1.8337 (x − 35) + 48.2333

∴ $\qquad$ y = 1.8337 x − 64.1795 + 48.233

∴ $\qquad$ **y = 1.8336x − 15.9465** $\qquad$ ...Ans.

Value of tensile strength (y) at x = 70 min is given by

$\qquad$ y = 1.8337 × 70 − 15.9465

$\qquad$ **y = 112.4125 N/mm²** $\qquad$ ... Ans.

Example 6.17 : *A set of values of x and y are given below using least square technique, for a curve $y = a \cdot e^{bx}$. Find the values of a and b.*

x	0.1	0.2	0.3	0.4
y	1.832	2.238	2.733	3.338

Solution : Given data : Number of points (n) = 4

Consider equation, $y = a \cdot e^{bx}$

Taking natural log of equation, we get

$\qquad$ ln y = ln a + bx ln e

∴ $\qquad$ ln y = ln a + bx

∴ $\qquad$ Y = A + bx, where Y = ln y, A = ln a

x	y	Y	xY	x²
0.1	1.832	0.6054	0.06054	0.01
0.2	2.238	0.8056	0.16112	0.04
0.3	2.733	1.0054	0.30162	0.09
0.4	3.338	1.2054	0.48216	0.16
$\Sigma x = 1.0$		$\Sigma Y = 3.6218$	$\Sigma xY = 1.00544$	$\Sigma x^2 = 0.3$

By using least square criteria for straight line (Y = A + bx), we get

$$\Sigma Y = nA + b\Sigma x \qquad \ldots (I)$$
$$\Sigma xY = A\Sigma x + b\Sigma x^2 \qquad \ldots (II)$$

Therefore, substituting values in above equations, we get

$$3.6218 = 4A + b \qquad \ldots (III)$$
$$1.00544 = A + 0.3b \qquad \ldots (IV)$$

Solving above equations simultaneously, we get,

$$A = 0.4055 \text{ and } b = 1.9998 = 2$$

∴ $\quad a = e^A$

∴ $\quad a = e^{0.4055} = 1.50$

∴ Equation of curve is **y = 1.5 e^{2x}** ... Ans.

Example 6.18 : Fit the curve $y = a \cdot x^b$ using following data :

x	2000	3000	4000	5000	6000
y	15	15.5	16	17	18

Find the values of a and b.

Solution : Given data : Number of data points (n) = 5.

Consider equation, $y = a \cdot x^b$

Taking natural log of equation, we get

$$\log y = \log a + b \log x$$

∴ $\quad Y = A + bX$, where $Y = \log(y)$, $A = \log(a)$ and $X = \log(x)$

x	y	X	Y	XY	X²
2000	15	3.3010	1.1761	3.8823	10.8966
3000	15.5	3.4771	1.1903	4.1388	12.0902
4000	16	3.6021	1.2041	4.3373	12.9751
5000	17	3.6989	1.2304	4.5511	13.6819
6000	18	3.7782	1.2553	4.7428	14.2748
		$\Sigma X = 17.8573$	$\Sigma Y = 6.0562$	$\Sigma XY = 21.6523$	$\Sigma X^2 = 63.9186$

By using least square criteria for straight line (Y = A + bX), we get

$$\Sigma Y = nA + b\Sigma X \quad \ldots (I)$$
$$\Sigma XY = A\Sigma X + b\Sigma X^2 \quad \ldots (II)$$

Therefore, substituting values in above equations, we get

$$6.0562 = 5A + 17.8573b \quad \ldots (III)$$
$$21.6523 = 17.8573A + 63.9186b \quad \ldots (IV)$$

Solving above equations simultaneously, we get,

$$A = 0.6371 \text{ and } b = 0.1608$$

∴   a = antilog (A) = antilog (0.6371)
∴   a = 4.3361
∴ **Equation of curve, y = 4.3361 $x^{0.1608}$**   ... Ans.

Example 6.19 : *Using least square technique, fit a curve $y = a \cdot x^b$ for a set of points given below and find the values of a and b.*

x	0.5	1.5	2.0	2.5	3.0
y	0.7425	3.8579	5.9397	8.301	10.912

Solution : Given data : Number of points (n) = 5.

Consider equation, $y = a \cdot x^b$

Taking natural log of equation, we get

$$\log y = \log a + b \log x$$

∴   Y = A + bX, where Y = log (y), A = log (a) and X = log (x)

x	y	X	Y	XY	X²
0.5	0.7425	− 0.3010	− 0.1293	0.0389	0.0906
1.5	3.8579	0.1761	0.5864	0.1033	0.0310
2.0	5.9397	0.3010	0.7738	0.2329	0.0906
2.5	8.3010	0.3979	0.9191	0.3658	0.1584
3.0	10.912	0.4771	1.0379	0.4952	0.2276
		ΣX = 1.0512	ΣY = 3.1878	ΣXY = 1.2361	ΣX² = 0.5982

By using least square criteria for straight line (Y = A + bX), we get

$$\Sigma Y = nA + b\Sigma X \quad \ldots (I)$$
$$\Sigma XY = A\Sigma X + b\Sigma X^2 \quad \ldots (II)$$

Therefore, substituting values in above equations, we get

$$3.1878 = 5A + 1.0512b \quad \ldots (III)$$
$$1.2361 = 1.0512A + 0.5982b \quad \ldots (IV)$$

Solving above equations simultaneously, we get,

$$A = 0.3221 \text{ and } b = 1.5$$

∴   a = antilog (A) = antilog (0.3221)
∴   a = 2.0994 = 2.1 (Approx.)
∴ **Equation of curve = y = 2.1 $x^{1.5}$**   ... Ans.

Example 6.20 : Using the following points, fit the exponential curve of the type $y = ae^{bx}$ using least square method, through given points :

x	0	1	2	3
y	2	2.2103	2.4428	2.6997

Solution : Given data : Number of points (n) = 4

Consider equation, $y = a.e^{bx}$

Taking natural log of equation, we get

$\ln y = \ln a + bx \ln e$

∴ $\ln y = \ln a + bx$

∴ $Y = A + bx,$ where $Y = \ln y,$ $A = \ln a$

x	y	Y	xY	x²
0	2	0.6931	0	0
1	2.2103	0.7931	0.7931	1
2	2.4428	0.8931	1.7862	4
3	2.6997	0.9931	2.9793	9
Σx = 6.0		ΣY = 3.3724	ΣxY = 5.5586	Σx² = 14

By using least square criteria for straight line (Y = A + bx), we get

$\Sigma Y = nA + b\Sigma x$ ... (I)

$\Sigma xY = A\Sigma x + b\Sigma x^2$ ... (II)

Therefore, substituting values in above equations, we get

$3.3724 = 4A + 6b$ ... (III)

$5.5586 = 6A + 14b$ ... (IV)

Solving above equations simultaneously, we get,

A = 0.6931 and b = 0.1

∴ $a = e^A$

∴ $a = e^{0.6931} = 1.9999 = 2$ (Approx.)

∴ **Equation of curve is $y = 2e^{0.1x}$** ... Ans.

Example 6.21 : Fit the exponential curve $y = ae^{bx}$ to the following data :

t	0	1	2	3	4	5	6
N	32	47	65	92	132	190	275

Solution : Given data : Number of points (n) = 7

Consider equation, $y = a.e^{bx}$

Taking natural log of equation, we get

$\ln y = \ln a + bx \ln e$

∴ $\ln y = \ln a + bx$

∴ $Y = A + bx,$

where $Y = \ln y,$ $A = \ln a$

x	y	Y	xY	x^2
0	32	3.4657	0.0000	0
1	47	3.8501	3.8501	1
2	65	4.1744	8.3488	4
3	92	4.5218	13.5654	9
4	132	4.8828	19.5312	16
5	190	5.2470	26.2351	25
6	275	5.6168	33.7006	36
$\Sigma x = 21$		$\Sigma Y = 31.7587$	$\Sigma xY = 105.2312$	$\Sigma x^2 = 91$

By using least square criteria for straight line (Y = A + bx), we get

$$\Sigma Y = nA + b\Sigma x \quad \ldots \text{(I)}$$
$$\Sigma xY = A\Sigma x + b\Sigma x^2 \quad \ldots \text{(II)}$$

Therefore, substituting values in above equations, we get

$$31.7587 = 7A + 21b \quad \ldots \text{(III)}$$
$$105.2312 = 21A + 91b \quad \ldots \text{(IV)}$$

Solving above equations simultaneously, we get,

$$A = 3.4703 \text{ and } b = 0.3555$$

∴ $\quad a = e^A = e^{3.4703} = 32.1464$

∴ **Equation of curve is $y = 32.146\, e^{0.3555x}$** ... Ans.

PROBLEMS FOR PRACTICE

1. An experiment has been conducted on friction of bearing by keeping speed constant. Experimental results have been tabulated as follows:
2.

T	μ
120	0.0051
110	0.0059
100	0.0071
90	0.0085
80	0.0102
70	0.0124
60	0.0148

If μ and t follows the law $\mu = a \cdot e^{bT}$, find the values of a and b by using least square criterion. **[Ans.: $\mu = (0.043367)e^{(-0.018014)T}$]**

3. Dynamic viscosity of water μ (10^{-3} Ns/m^2) is related to the temperature T (°C) in the following manner:

T	μ
0	1.787
5	1.519
10	1.307
15	1.170
20	1.002
25	0.8990
30	0.7975

By using least square criteria fit above data points in parabolic equation.

[Ans. : $Y = (0.0006) x^2 - (0.0510) x + 1.7735$**]**

4. In an experiment on superheated steam, following data is recorded as follows. By using least square criteria fit above data points as exponential equation ($y = ae^x$).

P	V
10	1.00
15	0.67
20	0.50
25	0.40
30	0.33
35	0.29
40	0.25

[Ans. : $y = 1.34385 \, e^{-0.044637x}$**]**

5. The velocity of water 'u' flowing over flat surface is measured by at several distances 'y' away from the surface. Fit the curve $u = ay^2 + by + c$ by using least square criteria.

y (cm)	u (m/s)
0	0
1	5
2	15
3	30
4	50

[Ans. : $y = 2.5x^2 + 2.5x$**]**

6. A slider of machine moves along a straight rod. Its distance 'x' cm along the rod is given below for various values at time 't' seconds. Fit data by using least square criteria (i) a straight line, (ii) parabolic equation :

t	x
0	30.13
0.1	31.62
0.2	32.87
0.3	33.64
0.4	33.95
0.5	33.81
0.6	33.24

[Ans. : Straight Line : y = 5.282x + 31.167**]**

[Ans. : Parabolic Equation : –y = – 21.6312x^2 + 18.2609x + 30.0852**]**

7. A rod is rotating in a plane. The following table gives the angle Θ (radians), through which the rod has turned for various values of time t (sec).

t	x
0	0
0.2	0.12
0.4	0.49
0.6	1.12

8. Fit data by using least square criteria (i) a straight line, (ii) parabolic equation.

[Ans. : Straight Line : – y = 1.865 x – 0.127**]**

[Ans. : Parabolic Equation : y = 3.1875x^2 – 0.0475 x + 0.0005**]**

9. The upward velocity of a vehicle is given as a function of time in table below :

Velocity as a Function of Time

t(s)	v(t) (km/s)
5	1.0
10	2.25
15	13.60
20	25.10
22.5	30.0
30	40.0

Fit data by using least square criteria if above data satisfies y = ax + b

[Ans. : y = (1.7177) x – 10.6855**]**

Fit a curve y = ax^b using the following data :

x	2000	3000	4000	5000	6000
y	15	15.5	16	17	18

[Ans. : y = (4.338491) $x^{0.160694}$**]**

10. Following is the data given for values of x and y. Fit a second degree polynomial of the type y = ax^b + bx + c where a, b, c are constants.

x	− 3	− 2	− 1	0	1	2	3
y	12	4	1	2	7	15	30

[**Ans.:** $y = (2.1190)x^2 + (2.9286)x + (1.6667)$]

REVIEW QUESTIONS

1. The equation of the best fit curve is of the type $y = ab^x$. Find the values of constants a and b fitting the curve through the points

x	2	3	4	5	6
y	144	172.8	207.4	248.8	298.5

2. It is known that tensile strength of plastic increases as a function of the time when it is heat treated. The following data is collected.

Time (min)	10	20	30	40	50	60
Tensile strength (N/mm^2)	4.2	17.8	49.6	48.6	64.4	104.8

   Use least square technique to fit a straight line to this data and use the equation to determine the tensile strength at time of 70 min.

3. Using the following points, fit a exponential curve of the type $y = A e^{bx}$ using least square method, through the given points :

x	0	1	2	3
y	2.00	2.2103	2.4428	2.6997

4. Fit the exponential curve $y = ae^{bx}$ to the following data :

t	0	1	2	3	4	5	6
N	32	47	65	92	132	190	275

5. Growth of bacteria (N) in a culture after t hrs. is given in table below :

x	0	1	2	3
y	2.00	2.2103	2.4428	2.6997

   Fit a curve of the form $N = ab^t$ and estimate N when t = 7.

6. The value of Nusselt numbers (Nu) and Reynolds numbers (Re) found experimentally are given below. If the relation between Nu and Re is of the type $Nu = a \cdot Re^b$, find the values of a and b for the given values of Nu and Re.

Re	3000	4000	5000	6000	7000
Nu	14.3575	16.6517	16.7353	17.6762	18.5128

7. Explain principle of least square criteria.
8. Show that the linear regression of line of y on x passes through the point, which represents mean of x and y.
9. Draw flowchart for
   (a) A straight line, (b) Parabolic equation.

Unit - IV

Chapter 7
SOLUTION OF LINEAR ALGEBRAIC EQUATION AND ITERATIVE METHOD

7.1 INTRODUCTION

A set of linear simultaneous equation contains multiple equations with two or more variables as below :

$$ax + by + cz = d$$
$$ex + fy + gz = h$$
$$ix + jy + kz = l$$

where, x, y and z are numeric variables and a, b, c, d, e, f, g, h, i, j, k and l are numeric constants. Right sides of equations i.e. numeric constants d, h and l are called as constant terms of the equation. And rest of the numeric constants are called as coefficients of respective variables. In routine daily life or in engineering problems we may many times come across such sets of equations. Let us take an example from routine life.

- A person wishes to shift his domestic furniture from one place to another. He enquires about goods carriers and gets information that he will have to book multiple trips of two types of carriers A and B, where A is a three wheeler vehicle having load carrying capacity of 25 kg. Carrier B is four wheeler vehicle and can take load of 40 kg. The person has furniture weighing about 155 kg. Hence, he decides to book three trips of carrier A and two trips of carrier B.

How did he take this decision ? At back of his mind he must have written a mathematical model of event of furniture shifting as

$$25x + 40y = 155 \qquad \ldots (7.1)$$

where, x and y are number of trips of individual carrier.

The person would have gone wrong by selecting only one type of vehicle. That means with only carrier A, all furniture except 5 kg may be shifted in six trips and the seventh trip will be required for only 5 kg. Similarly, all furniture may be shifted in only four trips of carrier B, but the last trip is underutilized by 5 kg. So decision is made looking at both variables simultaneously and hence the furniture is shifted in less number of trips of individual carrier with proper utilization of each trip. The equation is linear equation and the situation is simple, so without any other equation appearing simultaneously, he could take the decision.

- Now take example of a factory, where a maintenance engineer is trying to determine cost of repairs of a particular machine under various heads viz. electrical repairs, mechanical repairs and miscellaneous repairs. The data he has collected is as below :

- In January, the machine had 3 electrical, 5 mechanical and 2 miscellaneous repairs costing Rs. 34,000/-.
- In February, repairs cost was Rs. 46,000/- due to 6 electrical, 2 mechanical and 5 miscellaneous repairs.
- In March, due to 1 electrical repair, 4 mechanical and 3 miscellaneous repairs, the cost of repairing was Rs. 23,000/-.

This data looks so abstract and absurd, that a layman may not draw any conclusion from it. But the engineer will convert the data into mathematical form as ;

For January $3x + 5y + 2z = 34000$
For February $6x + 2y + 5z = 46000$
For March $x + 4y + 3z = 23000$

where, x is cost of electrical repair.
      y is cost of mechanical repair.
      z is cost of miscellaneous repair.

Now the engineer has to solve all the three equations simultaneously, so that the values obtained for x, y and z will satisfy all the three equations. The set of these values is called as the Solution of Linear Simultaneous Equations.

7.2 Numerical Methods for Solution of Linear Simultaneous Equations

There are various methods for finding solution of such set of equations. These methods are classified under two types :

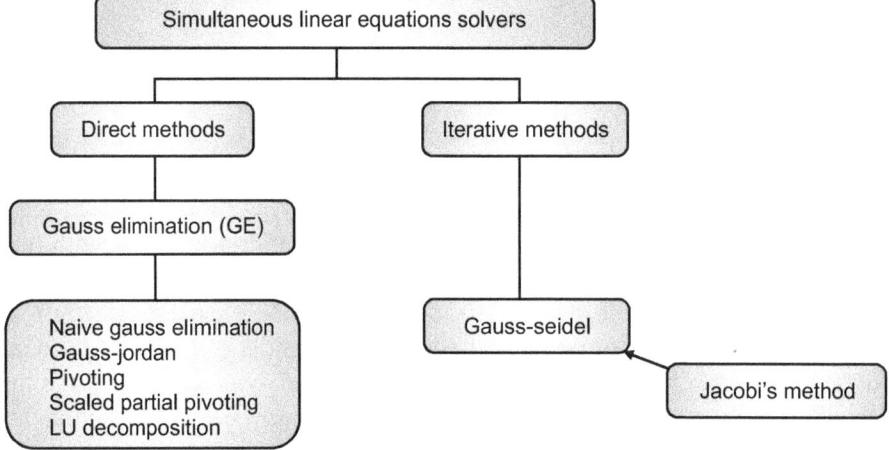

Fig. 7.1

- Direct methods, which produce exact solution after finite number of steps.

- Iterative methods which start with a trial solution go through sequence of approximate solutions and finally may converge to the most accurate solution.

Following are various methods for solutions of linear simultaneous equations :

Direct Methods
- Crammer's Rule and Matrix Inversion Method.
- Gauss Elimination Method.
- Gauss Jordan Method.

Iterative Methods
- Jacobi's Method.
- Gauss – Seidel Method.
- Triangular Factorization.
- Cholesky method.

7.3 SUFFICIENCY OF SET

Consider the example of booking carrier for furniture shifting. One may rewrite equation 7.1 as :

$$y = \frac{155 - 25x}{40}$$

For various values of x, value of y can be obtained.

x =	0	1	2	3	4	5	6	7	8
y =	3.875	3.25	2.625	2	1.375	0.75	0.125	−0.5	−1.125

All above values are solutions of the equation. But practically fraction or negative trips of a vehicle has no meaning, so the person must have decided to select solution as x = 3 and y = 2 on practical considerations. But in engineering problems, the variables may have any numerical value such as positive, negative, or fractions. Hence, only one equation for two variables is insufficient data for getting the solution. Similarly for a certain application, if we have multiple equations as below;

$$x - 3y = 2; \quad 2x + y = 11; \quad x - 2y = 2$$

There will not be a single set of solution for the three equations. On the other hand, we will have three sets of equations considering two equations at a time. Thus, this is a situation of redundant number of equations. If we look back to the example of maintenance engineer, the set contains three equations and each equation contains three variables, hence that is a case of sufficient data. As a conclusion, we may say that the set must contain number of equations exactly equal to number of variables.

Example 7.1 : *Determine sufficiency of data in each of the following examples.*

(a) The set of equations is

$$3x + 2y - z = 17$$

(b) The set of equations is
$$5x - 3y + 2z = 28$$
$$x + 2y = 3$$
$$x - 3z = -6$$
$$y + 3z = 17$$

(c) The set of equations is
$$3x + 2y = 20$$
$$x - y = 12$$
$$x = 5$$

Solution: In case of (a), there are only two equations but number of variables is three, so it is a case of insufficient data.

In case of (b), there are, in total, three variables and number of equations also is three, hence it is a case of sufficient data.

In case of (c), there are three equations, whereas number of variables is only two. Thus, it is a case of redundant data.

7.4 CONDITION OF SET

Consider a set of equations as below.

$$3x + 7y = 18; \quad 5x - 3y = 8$$

Here, coefficients of x are clearly distinct in both equations. Similarly, coefficients of y are also clearly distinct in both equations. Also ratio of coefficients of x (i.e. 3/5) and that of y (i.e. –7/3) are clearly distinct.

Hence, finding solution of such set of equations is not difficult. Further, in iterative methods, convergence to most accurate solution will require a finite (considerably small) number of iterations and in direct methods the accuracy will not be much challenged due to rounding errors. The solution of above set is $x = 2.5$ and $y = 1.5$.

Now consider a set as below;

$$3x + 7y = 18; \quad 3.1x + 6.9y = 18.1$$

where, the second equation is satisfied by the same solution.

Here, we observe that the coefficients of x i.e. 3 and 3.1 and coefficients of y i.e. 7 and 6.9 are very close to each other. Also the ratios are almost equal to 1. This set may lead to inaccurate solution due to rounding error such as :

$$\frac{3.1}{3} = 1.033333 \, \nabla \text{ and } \frac{6.9}{7} = 0.9857 \, \nabla \, 1$$

and in iterative method may require a large number of iterations to converge to most accurate solution. The earlier set (from where we started this discussion) is hence called as well-conditioned set and the later is called as ill-conditioned set.

7.5 GAUSS ELIMINATION METHOD

This is the simplest method where, using one equation, we eliminate one variable from other equations.

Assume initially we have 'n' simultaneous equations, then due to above elimination process; we will have n – 1 equations and n – 1 unknowns. We will go on repeating the above mentioned elimination process till we have two or more equations. So finally we will be left with only one equation and one variable (unknown).

Thus, that unknown is evaluated. Now, we will go on substituting values of variable in backward direction so that one by one variables will be evaluated in the reverse direction of elimination.

To understand this process, let us solve an example.

Example 7.2 : Determine values of x, y, z from the given set of equations

$$12x - 5y + 7z = 65.4$$
$$3x + 7y - 2z = -10.5$$
$$-7x + 2y - 4z = -36.6$$

Solution : From first equation, we can write,

$$x = \frac{65.4 + 5y - 7z}{12}$$

and substitute this expression for x in second and third equations.

∴ The set of equations will reduce to two equations with two unknowns, as

$$3\left(\frac{65.4 + 5y - 7z}{12}\right) + 7y - 2z = -10.5$$

$$-7\left(\frac{65.4 + 5y - 7z}{12}\right) + 2y - 4z = -36.6$$

On rearrangement of terms, we get,

$$33y - 15z = -107.4$$
$$-11y + z = 18.6$$

From the top equation, we can write,

$$y = \frac{15z - 107.4}{33}$$

and substitute this expression in the remaining equations. Thus, the set of equations now reduces down to only one equation as,

$$-11\left(\frac{15z - 107.4}{3}\right) + z = 18.6$$

On rearranging the terms, we get,

$$12z - 51.6$$

Thus, we are now left with only one equation having only one variable. Thus, we can evaluate z as,

$$z = \frac{51.6}{12} = 4.3$$

Now, we will substitute this value back in the expression of y.

$$\therefore \quad y = \frac{15 \times 4.3 - 107.4}{33} = -1.3$$

Now values of y and z will be substituted in expression for x.

$$\therefore \quad x = \frac{65.4 + 5 \times (-1.3) - 7 \times 4.3}{12} = 2.4$$

Thus, elimination sequence was,

$$x \longrightarrow \text{then} \longrightarrow y \longrightarrow \text{then } z$$

Variable z cannot be eliminated, so it is evaluated. Hence, evaluation sequence was,

$$z \longrightarrow \text{then} \longrightarrow y \longrightarrow \text{then } x$$

We go on substituting in backward direction, hence the method is called backward substitution.

7.5.1 Formulation

Imagine that there are 10 equations and 10 variables. Now the work of elimination and evaluation as discussed above will be voluminous. Hence, Gauss elimination method suggests us to arrange all equations in the matrix form as,

$$\begin{bmatrix} a_{0,0} & a_{0,1} & a_{0,2} & \cdots & a_{0,n-1} \\ a_{1,0} & a_{1,1} & a_{1,2} & \cdots & a_{1,n-1} \\ a_{2,0} & a_{2,1} & a_{2,2} & \cdots & a_{2,n-1} \\ \vdots & \vdots & \vdots & \cdots & \vdots \\ a_{n-1,0} & a_{n-1,1} & a_{n-1,2} & \cdots & a_{n-1,n-1} \end{bmatrix} \begin{bmatrix} x_0 \\ x_1 \\ x_2 \\ \vdots \\ x_{n-1} \end{bmatrix} = \begin{bmatrix} b_0 \\ b_1 \\ b_2 \\ \vdots \\ b_{n-1} \end{bmatrix}$$

Then by performing row transformation (row operations) on both A and B matrices, convert matrix A to an upper triangular matrix. Then evaluate X matrix by back substitution.

Example 7.3 : Solve the set of equations given in earlier example by Gauss elimination method.

$$12x - 5y + 7z = 65.4$$
$$3x + 7y - 2z = -10.5$$
$$-7x + 2y - 4z = -36.6$$

Solution : The set of equations in the matrix form is,

$$\begin{bmatrix} 12 & -5 & 7 \\ 3 & 7 & -2 \\ -7 & 2 & -4 \end{bmatrix} \begin{bmatrix} x \\ y \\ z \end{bmatrix} = \begin{bmatrix} 65.4 \\ -10.5 \\ -36.6 \end{bmatrix}$$

Perform row operations as $R_1 - R_0/4$ and $R_2 + 7R_0/12$

$$\begin{bmatrix} 12 & -5 & 7 \\ 3 - \dfrac{12}{4} & 7 + \dfrac{5}{4} & -2 - \dfrac{7}{4} \\ -7 + \dfrac{7 \times 12}{12} & 2 + \dfrac{7 \times (-5)}{12} & -4 + \dfrac{7 \times 7}{12} \end{bmatrix} \begin{bmatrix} x \\ y \\ z \end{bmatrix} = \begin{bmatrix} 65.4 \\ -10.5 - \dfrac{65.4}{4} \\ -36.6 + \dfrac{7 \times 65.4}{12} \end{bmatrix}$$

Thus, on simplification of numerical expressions, we get,

$$\begin{bmatrix} 12 & -5 & 7 \\ 0 & \dfrac{33}{4} & \dfrac{-15}{4} \\ 0 & \dfrac{-11}{12} & \dfrac{1}{12} \end{bmatrix} \begin{bmatrix} x \\ y \\ z \end{bmatrix} = \begin{bmatrix} 65.4 \\ \dfrac{-107.4}{4} \\ \dfrac{18.6}{12} \end{bmatrix}$$

Now perform $R_2 + R_1/9$

$$\begin{bmatrix} 12 & -5 & 7 \\ 0 & \dfrac{33}{4} & \dfrac{-15}{4} \\ 0 & \dfrac{-11}{12} + \dfrac{33}{36} & \dfrac{1}{12} - \dfrac{15}{36} \end{bmatrix} \begin{bmatrix} x \\ y \\ z \end{bmatrix} = \begin{bmatrix} 65.4 \\ \dfrac{-107.4}{4} \\ \dfrac{18.6}{12} - \dfrac{107.4}{36} \end{bmatrix}$$

On simplification, we get,

$$\begin{bmatrix} 12 & -5 & 7 \\ 0 & \dfrac{33}{4} & \dfrac{-15}{4} \\ 0 & 0 & \dfrac{-1}{3} \end{bmatrix} \begin{bmatrix} x \\ y \\ z \end{bmatrix} = \begin{bmatrix} 65.4 \\ \dfrac{-107.4}{4} \\ \dfrac{-51.6}{36} \end{bmatrix}$$

From row no. 2,

$$-\frac{1}{3}z = \frac{-51.6}{36}$$

Thus z is evaluated as,

$$z = 4.3$$

Substitute this back in row no. 1, which is,

$$\frac{33}{4}y - \frac{15}{4}z = \frac{-107.4}{4}$$

$$\therefore \quad \frac{33}{4}y - \frac{15}{4} \times 4.3 = \frac{-107.4}{4}$$

Now, y is evaluated as, $\quad y = -1.3$

Lastly, substitute y and z in row no. 0, which is,

$$12x - 5y + 7z = 65.4$$

$$\therefore \quad 12x - 5 \times (-1.3) + 7 \times 4.3 = 65.4$$

Thus x is evaluated as,

$$x = 2.4 \quad \text{... Ans.}$$

7.5.2 Standardization of Gauss Elimination Method

From previous example, we must have observed that when there are n equations for n variables ($x_0, x_1, x_2, ..., x_{n-1}$),

we perform (n − 1) row operations with respect to R_0 (first row) then;

we perform (n − 2) row operations with respect to R_1 (second row) then;

we perform (n − 3) row operations with respect to R_2 (third row) and so on;

Lastly we perform 1 row operation with respect to R_{n-2} (second row from last).

The sequence of operation being :

1. $R_1 - a_{1,0}/a_{0,0} * R_0, R_2 - a_{2,0}/a_{0,0} * R_0, ..., R_{n-1} - a_{n-1,0}/a_{0,0} * R_0$
2. $R_2 - a_{2,1}/a_{1,1} * R_1, R_3 - a_{3,1}/a_{1,1} * R_1, ..., R_{n-1} - a_{n-1,1}/a_{1,1} * R_1$

and so on for (n−2) times.

The last that is (n−2)th step being $R_{n-1} - a_{n-1,2}/a_{n-2,n-2} * R_{n-2}$.

This standardization not only helps us in problem solving but will also help in developing computer program.

Example 7.4 : Four robots A, B, C and D are placed near corners of a container for either placing objects in the container or removing objects from the container.

A supervisor observed performance of robots for four days and made the following observation table.

Table 7.1

Day	No. of Objects in the Container at Start	Robot and its Application on Objects	Duration of Working (in Hours)	No. of Objects in the Container at End
1	9	A – to place	1	30
		B – to remove	3	
		C – to place	5	
		D – to place	3	
2	12	A – to place	2	19
		B – to place	5	
		C – to remove	4	
		D – to remove	6	
3	5	A – to place	1	29
		B – to remove	2	
		C – to place	7	
		D – to remove	5	
4	16	A – to place	1	33
		B – to place	4	
		C – to remove	1	
		D – to place	2	

Example 7.5 : Determine material handling capacity of each robot in objects/hour.

Solution : Let us construct mathematical model as below,

$$a - 3b + 5c + 3d = (30 - 9) = 21$$
$$2a + 5b - 4c - 6d = (19 - 12) = 7$$
$$a - 2b + 7c - 5d = (29 - 5) = 24$$
$$a + 4b - c + 2d = (33 - 16) = 17$$

where a, b, c and d denote material handing capacities of robots A, B, C and D respectively. The equations can be written in the matrix form as,

$$\begin{bmatrix} 1 & -3 & 5 & 3 \\ 2 & 5 & -4 & -6 \\ 1 & -2 & 7 & -5 \\ 1 & 4 & -1 & 2 \end{bmatrix} \begin{bmatrix} a \\ b \\ c \\ d \end{bmatrix} = \begin{bmatrix} 21 \\ 7 \\ 24 \\ 17 \end{bmatrix}$$

As there are 4 rows R_0 to R_3, we need to perform $(4-1) = 3$ sequences of row operations as,

Sequence 1 : $R_1 - \left(\frac{2}{1}\right) R_0$, $R_2 - \left(\frac{1}{1}\right) R_0$, $R_3 - \left(\frac{1}{1}\right) R_0$

$$\begin{bmatrix} 1 & -3 & 5 & 3 \\ 0 & 11 & -14 & -12 \\ 0 & 1 & 2 & -8 \\ 0 & 7 & -6 & -1 \end{bmatrix} \begin{bmatrix} a \\ b \\ c \\ d \end{bmatrix} = \begin{bmatrix} 21 \\ -35 \\ 3 \\ -4 \end{bmatrix}$$

Sequence 2 : $R_2 - \left(\frac{1}{11}\right) R_1$, $R_3 - \left(\frac{7}{11}\right) R_1$

$$\begin{bmatrix} 1 & -3 & 5 & 3 \\ 0 & 11 & -14 & -12 \\ 0 & 0 & \frac{36}{11} & \frac{-76}{11} \\ 0 & 0 & \frac{32}{11} & \frac{73}{11} \end{bmatrix} \begin{bmatrix} a \\ b \\ c \\ d \end{bmatrix} = \begin{bmatrix} 21 \\ -35 \\ \frac{68}{11} \\ +\frac{201}{11} \end{bmatrix}$$

Sequence 3 : $R_3 - \left(\frac{(32/11)}{(36/11)}\right) R_2$ that means $R - \frac{8}{9} R_2$

$$\begin{bmatrix} 1 & -3 & 5 & 3 \\ 0 & 11 & -14 & -12 \\ 0 & 0 & \frac{36}{11} & \frac{-76}{11} \\ 0 & 0 & 0 & +\frac{1265}{99} \end{bmatrix} \begin{bmatrix} a \\ b \\ c \\ d \end{bmatrix} = \begin{bmatrix} 21 \\ -35 \\ \frac{68}{11} \\ \frac{1265}{99} \end{bmatrix}$$

Thus, from row R_3, $d = 1$

From row R_2, $\frac{36}{11} c - \frac{76}{11} = \frac{68}{11}$

Hence, $c = 4$

From row R_1, $11b - 14 \times 4 - 12 \times 1 = -35$

Therefore, $b = 3$

and from row R_0, $a - 3 \times 3 + 5 \times 4 + 3 \times 1 = 21$

Hence, $a = 7$

Thus, material handling capacity of robot A is 7 objects/hour, that for robot B is 3 objects/hour, that for robot C is 4 objects/hour and that for robot D is 1 object/hour.

Note : Here, we maintained all elements of matrices A and B either in integers or fractions*. But it is always difficult to handle numbers in the form of fractions. Hence, we convert them to decimals. Also when we use calculator or computer, the machine will convert and store the numbers in decimals and not in fractions. For example,

$\frac{36}{11}$ will be 3.2727

$\frac{1265}{99}$ will be 12.7778

This conversion gives birth to round-off errors.

7.5.3 Pitfalls of Gauss Elimination Method

Following are consequences associated with this method :

1. Division by zero.
2. Round-off errors.
3. ILL conditioned set of equation.

We have already discussed regarding *ill* conditioned set. Now, let us understand meaning of first two by an example.

Example 7.6 : *A company has three mass production units. One for manufacturing of bolts, one for manufacturing of nuts and one for manufacturing of washers. While transporting finished products, it is observed that a container 'A' contains 19883 washers and a nut. Container 'B' contains 2137 bolts, a washer and five nuts. Container 'C' contains 7307 nuts, 8 bolts and 5 washers. The mass contained in container A is 139.2 kg that in container B is 115.5 kg and that in container C is 139.3 kg. Determine mass of bolt, nut and washer individually.*

Solution : Let   mass of bolt be x,

               mass of nut be y,

and   mass of washer be z.

According to the description equation for

---

*   A decimal number can be expressed as fraction. For example, 0.271 can be expressed as $\frac{271}{1000}$.

    The fractions are of three types :

1. Proper fraction e.g. $\frac{3}{4}$.
2. Improper fraction e.g. $\frac{10}{4}$.
3. Mixed fraction e.g. $3\frac{5}{7}$.

Container 'A' is $\quad\quad\quad\quad\quad$ 19883z + y = 139.2

Container 'B' is $\quad\quad\quad\quad\quad$ 2137x + z + 5y = 115.5

Container 'C' is $\quad\quad\quad\quad\quad$ 7307y + 8x + 5z = 139.3

Let us arrange them in the form of matrices, therefore,

$$\begin{bmatrix} 0 & 1 & 19883 \\ 2137 & 5 & 1 \\ 8 & 7307 & 5 \end{bmatrix} \begin{bmatrix} x \\ y \\ z \end{bmatrix} = \begin{bmatrix} 139.2 \\ 115.5 \\ 139.3 \end{bmatrix}$$

Now, as per standard procedure, sequence 1 of row operations is,

$$R_1 - \left(\frac{2137}{0}\right) R_0, \quad R_2 - \left(\frac{8}{0}\right) R_0$$

Thus, we observe an undesired consequence of "Division by zero". To avoid such consequences we need to rearrange elements in matrix A, so that there will not be zero at diagonal position.

The diagonal elements are called as pivot elements because row transformations are based on these elements. For example, row transformations

$R_1 - a_{1,0}/a_{0,0} * R_0$, $R_2 - a_{2,0}/a_{0,0} * R_0$, ... are based on $a_{0,0}$ because every expression has a common element $a_{0,0}$ which is a diagonal element. So, as a conclusion, matrix A or set of equation should be arranged in such a way that any pivot element (diagonal element) will not be zero. Hence, we rearrange the equations as,

$$8x + 7307y + 5z = 139.3$$
$$0x + y + 19883z = 139.2$$
$$2137x + 5y + z = 115.5$$

The equations in the matrix form will be

$$\begin{bmatrix} 8 & 7307 & 5 \\ 0 & 1 & 19883 \\ 2137 & 5 & 1 \end{bmatrix} \begin{bmatrix} x \\ y \\ z \end{bmatrix} = \begin{bmatrix} 139.3 \\ 139.2 \\ 115.5 \end{bmatrix}$$

Now, as per standard procedure, the first sequence of row operation is, $R_1 - \left(\frac{0}{8}\right) R_0$, $R_2 - \left(\frac{2137}{8}\right) R_0$. Therefore,

$$\begin{bmatrix} 8 & 7307 & 5 \\ 0 & 1 & 19883 \\ 0 & -1951877.375 & -1334.625 \end{bmatrix} \begin{bmatrix} x \\ y \\ z \end{bmatrix} = \begin{bmatrix} 139.3 \\ 139.2 \\ -37095.013 \end{bmatrix}$$

The second sequence of row operations is, $R_2 - \left(\frac{-1951877.375}{1}\right) R_1$ that means $R_2 + 1951877.375\, R_1$ which will force us to handle a few elements of very large size as,

$$\begin{bmatrix} 8 & 7307 & 5 \\ 0 & 1 & 19883 \\ 0 & 0 & 38809176512.5 \end{bmatrix} \begin{bmatrix} x \\ y \\ z \end{bmatrix} = \begin{bmatrix} 139.3 \\ 139.2 \\ 271664235.6 \end{bmatrix}$$

And by back substitutions, answers are,

$$z = \frac{271664235.6}{38809176512.5} = 0.007$$
$$y = 139.2 - 19883 \times 0.007 = 0.019$$
$$z = \frac{139.3 - 7307 \times 0.019 - 5 \times 0.007}{8} = 0.054$$

Hence, mass of a bolt is 54 gm, that for a nut is 19 gm and that for a washer is 7 gm.

On the other hand, while rearranging the set of equations, if one arranges it as,

$$2137x + 5y + z = 115.5$$
$$8x + 7307y + 5z = 139.3$$
$$0x + y + 19883z = 139.2$$

Then the equations in the matrix form will be,

$$\begin{bmatrix} 2137 & 5 & 1 \\ 8 & 7307 & 5 \\ 0 & 1 & 19883 \end{bmatrix} \begin{bmatrix} x \\ y \\ z \end{bmatrix} - \begin{bmatrix} 115.5 \\ 139.3 \\ 139.2 \end{bmatrix}$$

By the first sequence of row operations i.e.

$$R_1 - \left(\frac{8}{2137}\right) R_0, \; R_2 - \left(\frac{0}{2137}\right) R_0$$

$$\begin{bmatrix} 2137 & 5 & 1 \\ 0 & 7306.981 & 4.996 \\ 0 & 1 & 19883 \end{bmatrix} \begin{bmatrix} x \\ y \\ z \end{bmatrix} = \begin{bmatrix} 115.5 \\ 138.868 \\ 139.2 \end{bmatrix}$$

By the second sequence of row operations i.e.

$$R_2 - \left(\frac{1}{7306.981}\right) R_1$$

$$\begin{bmatrix} 2137 & 5 & 1 \\ 0 & 7306.981 & 4.996 \\ 0 & 0 & 19882.999 \end{bmatrix} \begin{bmatrix} x \\ y \\ z \end{bmatrix} = \begin{bmatrix} 115.5 \\ 138.868 \\ 139.181 \end{bmatrix}$$

And by back substitutions, answers are,

$$z = \frac{139.181}{19882.999} = 0.007$$

$$y = \frac{138.868 - 4.996 \times 0.007}{7306.981} = 0.019$$

$$x = \frac{115.5 - 5 \times 0.019 - 0.007}{2137} = 0.054$$

Thus, we naturally arrive at the same answers. But the advantage is that we are not forced to handle abnormally large numbers in any calculations.

We got this advantage, because in each row, the element at diagonal place was largest.

In earlier case, due to presence of extremely large numbers, round-off error may get induced and propagated when we perform divisions with these large numbers in denominator.

7.5.4 Pivoting

Gauss elimination, hence must be supported with a process which will eliminate consequences of "Division by zero" and will reduce possibility of induction and propagation of "Round-off error". Pivoting is the process which helps in this regard.

Pivoting is a process that is carried out with matrix A. Each column is searched for the largest element* and then rows are interchanged to place the largest element in the pivot (diagonal) position. This is called partial pivoting. If, after completing search of largest element through columns, we conduct the similar activities for each row, the process is called complete pivoting. In Gauss elimination method, partial pivoting is beneficial. And it does not change the basic set of equations. On the other hand, complete pivoting will lead us to erroneous results as the coefficients are changed with respect to the variables. Hence, complete pivoting should never be carried out in Gauss elimination method.

7.5.5 Process of Partial Pivoting

- Scan through first column of matrix A for largest absolute value of element. Let the element be in the mth row, say.
- Interchange first and m^{th} rows, in both matrix A and matrix B.
- Scan through second column for largest absolute value of element, except first row. Let it be in k^{th} row.
- Interchange second and k^{th} row, in matrix A and matrix B. Repeat this procedure till you reach the last row.

---

* While searching for the largest element, it is important to take absolute value of each element. For example, if elements are 17, – 25, 3 then – 25 is the largest element and not 17.

Example 7.7 : Convert the following set of equations in the matrix form

$$-3a + 5b + 6c + 2d = 11$$
$$15a + 7b + 6c - 4d = 65$$
$$8a + 12b + 20c + 6d = 60$$
$$3a + 4b + 7c + 9d = 7$$

(a) Carry out partial pivoting and convert back to equations form.
(b) Carry out complete pivoting and convert back to equations form.

Solution : (a) Partial Pivoting :

$$\begin{bmatrix} -3 & 5 & 6 & 2 \\ 15 & 7 & 6 & -4 \\ 8 & 12 & 20 & 6 \\ 3 & 4 & 7 & 9 \end{bmatrix} \begin{bmatrix} a \\ b \\ c \\ d \end{bmatrix} = \begin{bmatrix} 11 \\ 65 \\ 60 \\ 7 \end{bmatrix}$$

In the first column, "15" is the largest element. Hence, interchange rows R_0 and R_1.

$$\begin{bmatrix} 15 & 7 & 6 & -4 \\ -3 & 5 & 6 & 2 \\ 8 & 12 & 20 & 6 \\ 3 & 4 & 7 & 9 \end{bmatrix} \begin{bmatrix} a \\ b \\ c \\ d \end{bmatrix} = \begin{bmatrix} 65 \\ 11 \\ 60 \\ 7 \end{bmatrix}$$

In the second column, "12" is the largest element. Hence, interchange rows R_1 and R_2.

$$\begin{bmatrix} 15 & 7 & 6 & -4 \\ 8 & 12 & 20 & 6 \\ -3 & 5 & 6 & 2 \\ 3 & 4 & 7 & 9 \end{bmatrix} \begin{bmatrix} a \\ b \\ c \\ d \end{bmatrix} = \begin{bmatrix} 65 \\ 60 \\ 11 \\ 7 \end{bmatrix}$$

In the third column, "7" is the largest element. (Not "20", because that row has been fixed already. So we are searching for largest element in the third column and rows R_2 and R_3 only). Therefore, interchange R_2 and R_3.

$$\begin{bmatrix} 15 & 7 & 6 & -4 \\ 8 & 12 & 20 & 6 \\ 3 & 4 & 7 & 9 \\ -3 & 5 & 6 & 2 \end{bmatrix} \begin{bmatrix} a \\ b \\ c \\ d \end{bmatrix} = \begin{bmatrix} 65 \\ 60 \\ 7 \\ 11 \end{bmatrix}$$

Thus partial pivoting is completed. Observe that we interchanged rows in matrix A and matrix B only and not in matrix X, still coefficients of a, b, c and d will not be changed. Converting back to equations form,

$$15a + 7b + 6c - 4d = 65$$
$$8a + 12b + 20c + 6d = 60$$
$$3a + 4b + 7c + 9d = 7$$
$$-3a + 5b + 6c + 2d = 11$$

Thus, we observe that individually equation is unchanged but the sequence of equations in the set is only changed.

(b) Complete Pivoting : Let us start from recent matrix form.

$$\begin{bmatrix} 15 & 7 & 6 & -4 \\ 8 & 12 & 20 & 6 \\ 3 & 4 & 7 & 9 \\ -3 & 5 & 6 & 2 \end{bmatrix} \begin{bmatrix} a \\ b \\ c \\ d \end{bmatrix} = \begin{bmatrix} 65 \\ 60 \\ 7 \\ 11 \end{bmatrix}$$

Now in first row "15" is the largest element and it is at pivoting position. So no interchange of columns at this stage. Now in second row "20" is the largest element so interchange second and third columns. The interchange is possible only in matrix A. Interchange in matrix B is not possible as it contains only one column.

$$\begin{bmatrix} 15 & 6 & 7 & -4 \\ 8 & 20 & 12 & 6 \\ 3 & 7 & 4 & 9 \\ -3 & 6 & 5 & 2 \end{bmatrix} \begin{bmatrix} a \\ b \\ c \\ d \end{bmatrix} = \begin{bmatrix} 65 \\ 60 \\ 7 \\ 11 \end{bmatrix}$$

In third row, "9" is the largest element. Hence, interchanging third and fourth columns. Thus,

$$\begin{bmatrix} 15 & 6 & -4 & 7 \\ 8 & 20 & 6 & 12 \\ 3 & 7 & 9 & 4 \\ -3 & 6 & 2 & 5 \end{bmatrix} \begin{bmatrix} a \\ b \\ c \\ d \end{bmatrix} = \begin{bmatrix} 65 \\ 60 \\ 7 \\ 11 \end{bmatrix}$$

It seems that the largest elements are more correctly placed at diagonal position in this matrix A.

Converting back to equation form,
$$15a + 6b - 4c + 7d = 65$$
$$8a + 20b + 6c + 12d = 60$$
$$3a + 7b + 9c + 4d = 7$$
$$-3a + 6b + 2c + 5d = 11$$

We observe that the equations are modified. Hence, solution after complete pivoting will never match with the solution of the given equations set.

Example 7.8 : At a stationary mart it was observed that a person purchased 7 pencils, 20 sharpners and 3 erasers. His bill was ₹ 111/-. A customer purchased 23 pencils and 7 erasers, but returned 11 sharpners which he had purchased earlier.
The shopkeeper agreed to return amount paid for those sharpners, so his bill was ₹ 161.50/-. Another customer purchased 10 pencils, 13 sharpners and 22 erasers. His bill was ₹ 190.50/-. What will be the amount of bill for a customer purchasing 15 pencils, 33 sharpners and 17 erasers ?

Solution : First we need to find rate of pencil, sharpner and eraser. Then determine amount of bill for fourth person.

Hence, writing the data for first three persons in equation form, assuming prices of pencil, sharpner and eraser to be x, y and z respectively, we get,

$$7x + 20y + 3z = 111$$
$$23x - 11y + 7z = 161.5$$
$$10x + 13y + 22z = 190.5$$

Convert these equations to matrix form.

$$\begin{bmatrix} 7 & 20 & 3 \\ 23 & -11 & 7 \\ 10 & 13 & 22 \end{bmatrix} \begin{bmatrix} x \\ y \\ z \end{bmatrix} = \begin{bmatrix} 111 \\ 161.5 \\ 190.5 \end{bmatrix}$$

For partial pivoting, search for the largest element in the first column. The largest element is "23". Hence, interchange R_0 and R_1.

$$\begin{bmatrix} 23 & -11 & 7 \\ 7 & 20 & 3 \\ 10 & 13 & 22 \end{bmatrix} \begin{bmatrix} x \\ y \\ z \end{bmatrix} = \begin{bmatrix} 161.5 \\ 111 \\ 190.5 \end{bmatrix}$$

In the second column the largest element is "23" and is already at diagonal. Hence, partial pivoting process is over. Now as per Gauss elimination standard method, perform row transformations, $R_1 - \left(\frac{7}{23}\right) R_0$, $R_2 - \left(\frac{10}{23}\right) R_0$.

$$\begin{bmatrix} 23 & -11 & 7 \\ 0 & 23.3478 & 0.8696 \\ 0 & 17.7826 & 18.9565 \end{bmatrix} \begin{bmatrix} x \\ y \\ z \end{bmatrix} = \begin{bmatrix} 161.5 \\ 61.8478 \\ 120.2826 \end{bmatrix}$$

Now row operations, $R_2 - \left(\frac{17.7826}{23.3478}\right) R_1$

$$\begin{bmatrix} 23 & -11 & 7 \\ 0 & 23.3478 & 0.8696 \\ 0 & 0 & 18.2942 \end{bmatrix} \begin{bmatrix} x \\ y \\ z \end{bmatrix} = \begin{bmatrix} 161.5 \\ 61.8478 \\ 73.1769 \end{bmatrix}$$

$$\therefore \quad z = \frac{73.1769}{18.2942} = 4$$

$$y = \frac{61.8478 - 4 \times 0.8696}{23.3478} = 2.5$$

$$x = \frac{161.5 + 11 \times 2.5 - 7 \times 4}{23} = 7$$

Thus, price of pencil is ₹ 7/-, for sharpner it is ₹ 2.50/- and an eraser costs ₹ 4/-. Therefore, amount of bill for customer who purchased 15 pencils, 33 sharpners and 17 erasers is

$$15 \times 7 + 33 \times 2.5 + 17 \times 4 = ₹\ 255.50/\text{-}$$

7.5.6 Pseudo Code for Gauss Elimination Method

- Get number for variables, n.
- Get all coefficients that means all elements of matrix A.
- Get all constant terms that means all elements of matrix B.
- Perform partial pivoting as,

```
for i = 0 to i = n – 2
{   max = a[i][i]
    row – num = i
    for j = i to j = n – 1
    {   if (a[j][i] > max)
        { row – num = j
          max = a[j][i]
        }
    }
}
for j = 0 to j = n – 1
{   temp = a[i][j]
    a[i][j] = a[row – num][j]
    a[row – num][j] = temp
}
temp = b[i]
b[i] = b[row – num]
```

b[row – num] = temp
  }
- Now perform row transformation as,
  for i = 0 to i = n – 2
  {   for j = i to j = n – 2
  {   mult[j] = a[j + 1][i]/a[i][i]}
  for j = i to j = n – 2
  {   for k = i to k = n – 1
  {a(j + 1)[k] = a[j+1][k] – mult[j]*a[i][k]}
  b[j + 1] = b[j + 1] – mult[j]*b[i]
  }
  }
- Step 5 calculates the required elements (upper triangle and diagonal) correctly but lower triangle is not equated to zero. Hence, make those elements zero as,
  for i = 1 to i = n – 1
  {   for j = 0 to j = i – 1
  {a[i][j] = 0}
  }
  Thus, matrix after elimination is formed.
- For back substitution, find the last unknown, as
  x[n – 1] = b[n – 1]/a[n – 1][n – 1]
- Rest of the unknowns are found as,
  for i = n – 1 to i = 0 decrement by 1
  {   sum = 0

  for j = i to j = n – 1
  { sum = sum + a[i – 1][j] * x[j]}
  x[i – 1] = (b[i – 1] – sum)/a[i – 1][i – 1]
  }
  Thus, all unknowns are found.
- End.

7.5.7 Flow Chart for Gauss Elimination Method

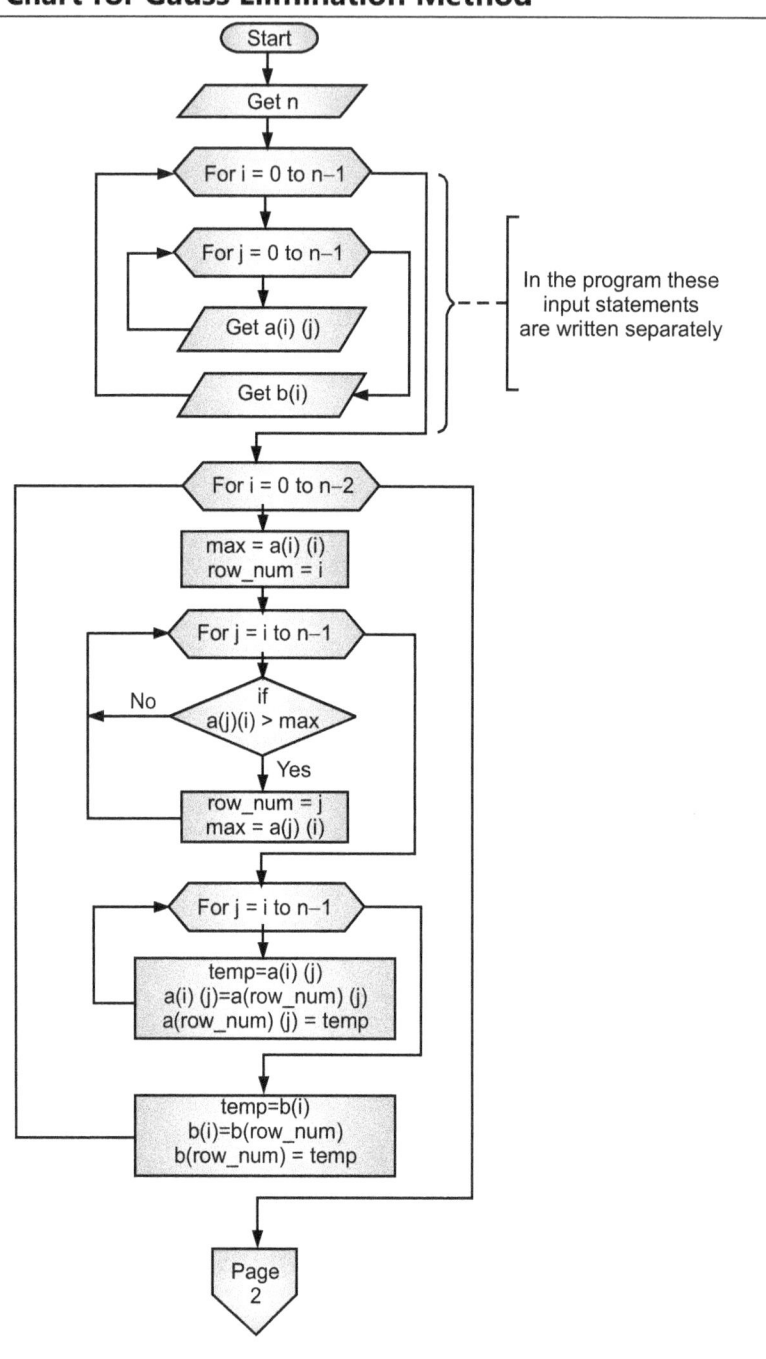

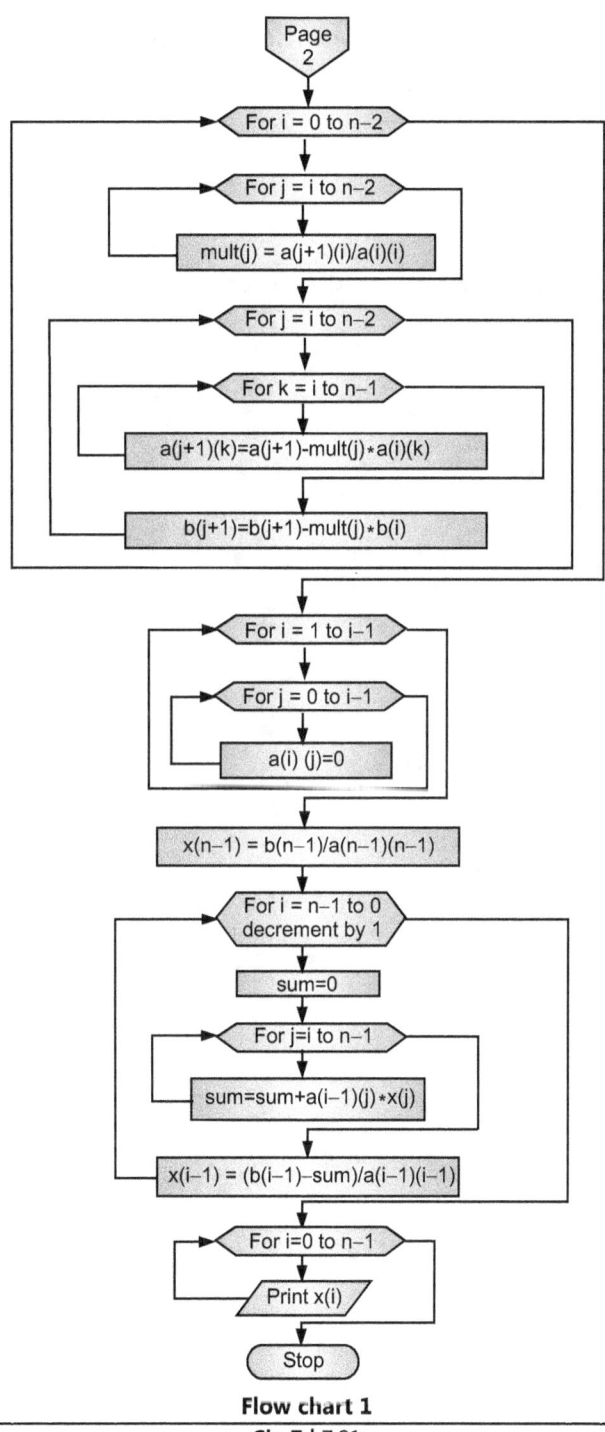

Flow chart 1

7.5.8 Matlab Code for Gauss Elimination Method

```
fprintf('\n******* GAUSS ELIMINITION METHOD **********');

%% MATRIX INPUT

n = input('\n Enter number of variables: ');
fprintf('\nEnter elements of Matrix A i.e. Coefficients matrix ...\n');

for i=1:n
    for j=1:n
            fprintf('\n A(%d,%d): ',i,j);
            a(i,j) = input('');
    end
    fprintf('\n B(%d): ',i);
    b(i) = input('');
end
b=b';

fprintf('[A][X]=[B]\twill look as ...\n\n');
for i=1:n
    for j=1:n
            fprintf('%f\t',a(i,j));
    end
    fprintf('x%d\t%f\n',i,b(i));
end

%% PARTIAL PIVOTING

fprintf('\nResult of Partial Pivoting ...\n\n');

for i=1:n-1
    max=a(i,i);
    row_num=i;
    for j=i:n
            if a(j,i)>max
```

```
                row_num=j;
                max=a(j,i);
            end
        end
        for j=1:n
            temp=a(i,j);
            a(i,j)=a(row_num,j);
            a(row_num,j)=temp;
        end
        temp=b(i);
        b(i)=b(row_num);
        b(row_num)=temp;
end

fprintf('\n[A][X]=[B]\twill look as ...\n\n');
for i=1:n
    for j=1:n
            fprintf('%f\t',a(i,j));
    end
    fprintf('x%d\t%f\n',i,b(i));
end

%% Gauss Elimination Method
%% Normalising Matrix
for i=1:n
    max=a(i,i);
    for j=1:n
        a(i,j)=a(i,j)/max;
    end
    b(i)=b(i)/max;
end

fprintf('\n[A][X]=[B]\twill look as ...\n\n');
for i=1:n
    for j=1:n
```

```
            fprintf('%f\t',a(i,j));
    end
    fprintf('x%d\t%f\n',i,b(i));
end

%% Upper Tringular Matrix
for k=1:n-1
    for i=k+1:n
            mult=a(i,k)/a(k,k);
            for j=1:n
            a(i,j)=a(i,j)-mult*a(k,j);
            end
            b(i)=b(i)-mult*b(k);
    end
end

fprintf('\n[A][X]=[B]\twill look as ...\n\n');
for i=1:n
    for j=1:n
            fprintf('%f\t',a(i,j));
    end
    fprintf('x%d\t%f\n',i,b(i));
end

%% Backward Substitution
for i=n:-1:1
    sum=0;
    for j=i:n
            if j>i
                sum=sum+a(i,j)*x(j);
            end
    end
    x(i)=(b(i)-sum)/a(i,i);
    fprintf('\n x(%d) = %f',i,x(i));
end
```

7.6 Gauss Jordan Method

Basics

The Gauss-Jordan Method is similar to the Gaussian Elimination.

- The method requires almost 50% more operations.
- The Gauss-Jordan method changes the matrix into the identity matrix.
- It doesn't require backward substitution like Gauss Elimination method.

Consider a set of simultaneous equations of size 'n' represented in matrix form as follows :

$$\begin{bmatrix} a_{11} & a_{12} & \cdots & a_{1n} \\ a_{21} & a_{22} & \cdots & a_{2n} \\ \cdots & \cdots & \cdots & \cdots \\ a_{n1} & a_{n2} & \cdots & a_{nn} \end{bmatrix} \begin{Bmatrix} x_1 \\ x_2 \\ \cdot \\ \cdot \\ x_n \end{Bmatrix} = \begin{Bmatrix} r_1 \\ r_2 \\ \cdot \\ \cdot \\ r_n \end{Bmatrix}$$

By performing row operations similar to Gauss Elimination method, reduced to upper triangular form.

Then in next step, by performing row operations, it further reduced to identity matrix as follows :

$$\begin{bmatrix} 1 & 0 & \cdots & 0 \\ 0 & 1 & \cdots & 0 \\ \cdots & \cdots & \cdots & \cdots \\ 0 & 0 & \cdots & 1 \end{bmatrix} \begin{Bmatrix} x_1 \\ x_2 \\ \cdot \\ \cdot \\ x_n \end{Bmatrix} = \begin{Bmatrix} r_1 \\ r_2 \\ \cdot \\ \cdot \\ r_n \end{Bmatrix}$$

Steps for Solving a System of Equations

Step 1: Elimination - use row operations to convert the matrix into an identity matrix.

Step 2: The new b vector is the solution to the x values.

Summary of Gauss Elimination and Gauss Jordon Method

- Gauss elimination is the most fundamental method for solving simultaneous linear algebraic equations.
- Gauss-Jordan is a variation of Gauss elimination.
- Both methods are used in engineering.

Consider simultaneous equations from previous illustration 7.7:

$$7x + 20y + 3z = 111$$
$$23x - 11y + 7z = 161.5$$
$$10x + 13y + 22z = 190.5$$

In matrix format, will appear as:

$$\begin{bmatrix} 7 & 20 & 3 \\ 23 & -11 & 7 \\ 10 & 13 & 22 \end{bmatrix} \begin{bmatrix} x \\ y \\ z \end{bmatrix} = \begin{bmatrix} 111 \\ 161.5 \\ 190.5 \end{bmatrix}$$

After reduction in upper triangular format, matrix will appear as follows:

$$\begin{bmatrix} 23 & -11 & 7 \\ 0 & 23.3478 & 0.8696 \\ 0 & 0 & 18.2942 \end{bmatrix} \begin{bmatrix} x \\ y \\ z \end{bmatrix} = \begin{bmatrix} 161.5 \\ 61.8478 \\ 73.1769 \end{bmatrix}$$

Now, dividing 2nd row by 23.3478 and 3rd row by 18.2942, we get,

$$\begin{bmatrix} 23 & -11 & 7 \\ 0 & 1 & 0.0372 \\ 0 & 0 & 1 \end{bmatrix} \begin{bmatrix} x \\ y \\ z \end{bmatrix} = \begin{bmatrix} 111 \\ 2.649 \\ 4 \end{bmatrix}$$

Then, $R_1 - 7R_3$ and $R_2 - 0.03272R_3$, we get,

$$\begin{bmatrix} 23 & -11 & 0 \\ 0 & 1 & 0 \\ 0 & 0 & 1 \end{bmatrix} \begin{bmatrix} x \\ y \\ z \end{bmatrix} = \begin{bmatrix} 83 \\ 2.5 \\ 4 \end{bmatrix}$$

Then, $R_1 - (-11)R_2$, we get,

$$\begin{bmatrix} 23 & 0 & 0 \\ 0 & 1 & 0 \\ 0 & 0 & 1 \end{bmatrix} \begin{bmatrix} x \\ y \\ z \end{bmatrix} = \begin{bmatrix} 161 \\ 2.5 \\ 4 \end{bmatrix}$$

Therefore, x = 7, y = 2.5 and z = 4.

7.7 LU Decomposition

Definition

- Let A be a square matrix that can be factored into the form A = LU, where 'L' is a lower triangular matrix and 'U' is an upper triangular matrix, this factoring is called an LU decomposition of A.
- Provides an efficient way to compute matrix inverse by separating the time consuming elimination of the Matrix [A] from manipulations of the right-hand side {B}.

- Gauss elimination, in which the forward elimination comprises the bulk of the computational effort, can be implemented as LU decomposition.

Note : Not every matrix has LU decomposition, and when it exists, it is not unique.

Steps for Problem Solving

- Let AX = B be a system of n equations in n variables, where A has LU decomposition
  A = LU
  $\Rightarrow$ LUX = B
  $\Rightarrow$ UX = Y (upper triangular) and LY = B (lower triangular)

LU Decomposition : Steps

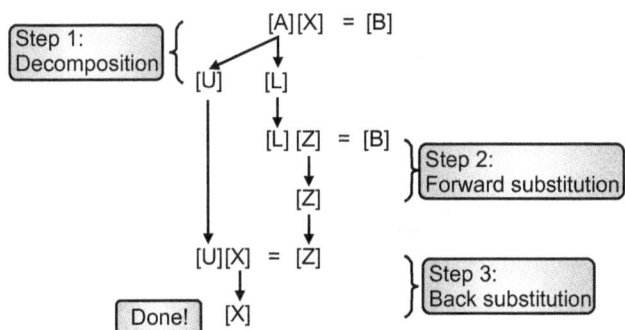

Fig. 7.2

A square matrix can be written as,

$$[A] = [L][U]$$

where, [L] is lower triangular matrix and
       [U] is upper triangular matrix.

In Gauss elimination method we convert [A] to [U] and find solution by backward substitution.

If we use [L] then we can find the same of solution by forward substitution.

e.g. Solve the following system of three equations using LU decomposition :

$x_1 - 3x_2 + 4x_3 = 12, -x_1 + 5x_2 - 3x_3 = -12, 4x_1 - 8x_2 + 23x_3 = 58$

$$\begin{bmatrix} 1 & -3 & 4 \\ -1 & 5 & -3 \\ 4 & -8 & 23 \end{bmatrix} \underset{\substack{R_2 + R_1 \\ R_3 - 4R_1}}{\approx} \begin{bmatrix} 1 & -3 & 4 \\ 0 & 2 & 1 \\ 0 & 4 & 7 \end{bmatrix} \underset{R_3 - 2R_2}{\approx} \begin{bmatrix} 1 & -3 & 4 \\ 0 & 2 & 1 \\ 0 & 0 & 5 \end{bmatrix}$$

These row operations lead to the following LU decomposition of A.

$$A = \begin{bmatrix} 1 & 0 & 0 \\ -1 & 1 & 0 \\ 4 & 2 & 1 \end{bmatrix} \begin{bmatrix} 1 & -3 & 4 \\ 0 & 2 & 1 \\ 0 & 0 & 5 \end{bmatrix}$$

- We again solve the given system LUX = B by solving the two sub systems LY = B and UX = Y

$$LY = B : \begin{bmatrix} 1 & 0 & 0 \\ -1 & 1 & 0 \\ 4 & 2 & 1 \end{bmatrix} \begin{bmatrix} y_1 \\ y_2 \\ y_3 \end{bmatrix} = \begin{bmatrix} 12 \\ -12 \\ 58 \end{bmatrix}$$

- This lower triangular system has solution $y_1 = 12$, $y_2 = 0$, $y_3 = 10$.

$$UX = Y : \begin{bmatrix} 1 & -3 & 4 \\ 0 & 2 & 1 \\ 0 & 0 & 5 \end{bmatrix} \begin{bmatrix} x_1 \\ x_2 \\ x_3 \end{bmatrix} = \begin{bmatrix} 12 \\ 0 \\ 10 \end{bmatrix}$$

- This upper triangular system has solution $x_1 = 1$, $x_2 = -1$, $x_3 = 2$.
- The solution to the given system is $x_1 = 1$, $x_2 = -1$, $x_3 = 2$.

7.8 Iterative Methods

As mentioned in the "Introduction" this is an iterative method. The difference in direct method and iterative method is that in iterative method the unknowns are given some initial guess values, then the method is iterated and new guess values are determined till the difference in guesses of two successive iterations is less than desired accuracy level. Partial pivoting advantage is applicable to this method also.

7.9 Jacobi's Method

Let there be 'n' unknowns as $x_0, x_1, \ldots x_{n-1}$.

Hence, 'n' simultaneous linear equations.

Conduct partial pivoting on the equations.

Then rewrite all the equations in such a way that first equation will have only x_0 on left side, second equation will have only x_0 on left side and so on, for all equations.

Basics
- The Jacobi's method and Gauss-Seidel Method allows the user to control round-off error.
- Elimination methods such as Gaussian Elimination and LU Decomposition are prone to prone to round-off error.
- Also, if the physics of the problem are understood, a close initial guess can be made, decreasing the number of iterations needed.

Basic Procedure

Consider set of algebraic equations :

$$\begin{bmatrix} a_{11} & a_{12} & \dots & a_{1n} \\ a_{21} & a_{22} & \dots & a_{2n} \\ \dots & \dots & \dots & \dots \\ a_{n1} & a_{n2} & \dots & a_{nn} \end{bmatrix} \begin{Bmatrix} x_1 \\ x_2 \\ \cdot \\ \cdot \\ \cdot \\ x_n \end{Bmatrix} = \begin{Bmatrix} r_1 \\ r_2 \\ \cdot \\ \cdot \\ \cdot \\ r_n \end{Bmatrix}$$

Step 1 : Algebraically solve each linear equation for xi, where 'i' is Row number.

$$x_i = \frac{r_i - \sum_{\substack{j=1 \\ j \neq i}}^{n} a_{ij} x_j}{a_{ii}}, i = 1, 2, \dots, n.$$

Step 2 : Assume an initial guess solution array

Step 3 : Solve for each x_i and repeat

Step 4 : Use absolute relative approximate error after each iteration to check if error is within a pre-specified tolerance.

Now, assume some values for unknowns $x_1, x_2 \dots x_{n-1}$ and evaluate x_0. Now evaluate x_1 using calculated value of x_0 and assumed values of $x_2, x_3, \dots x_{n-1}$. Keep on iterating the process till difference between two successive guesses of x_0 is greater than the expected accuracy level.

Let us solve the previous example of stationary mart billing to determine prices of pencil, sharpner and eraser.

Example 7.9 : *Determine prices of pencil, sharpner and eraser using the following data (from Example 7.8).*

Bill No.	Pencil (Qty.)	Sharpner (Qty.)	Eraser (Qty.)	Bill Amount (₹)
1	7	20	3	111
2	23	-11	7	161.5
3	10	13	22	190.5

Solution : After partial pivoting, equations will be,

$$23x - 11y + 7z = 161.5$$
$$7x + 20y + 3z = 111$$
$$10x + 13y + 22z = 190.5$$

Rewriting the equations,

$$x = \frac{161.5 + 11y - 7z}{23}$$

$$y = \frac{111 - 7x - 3z}{20}$$

$$z = \frac{190.5 - 10x - 13y}{22}$$

Assuming x = y = z = 0,

$$x = \frac{161.5 + 11*0 - 7*0}{23} = 7.022$$

$$y = \frac{111 - 7*0 - 3*0}{20} = 5.550$$

$$z = \frac{111 - 7*0 - 3*0}{20}$$

z = 8.659

Note : for calculation of x, y, z values for i^{th} iteration, values of previous iteration i.e. $(i-1)^{th}$ iteration are used. The iterative calculation results are as below,

Itn. No.	x	y	z
	0	0	0
1	7.022	5.550	8.659
2	7.041	1.794	2.188
3	7.214	2.758	4.399
4	7.002	2.365	3.751
5	7.011	2.537	4.079
6	6.994	2.484	3.973
7	7.001	2.506	4.012
8	6.999	2.498	3.996
9	7.000	2.501	4.002
10	7.000	2.500	3.999
11	**7.000**	**2.500**	**4.000**

7.10 GAUSS-SEIDEL METHOD

Gauss-Seidel method is similar to Jacobi's method in all respect. Only difference is it uses recent value of variables, making it faster than Jacobi's method.

Consider set following equations as per previous example :

After partial pivoting, equations will be,

23x – 11y + 7z = 161.5

$$7x + 20y + 3z = 111$$
$$10x + 13y + 22z = 190.5$$

Rewriting the equations,

$$x = \frac{161.5 + 11y - 7z}{23}$$

$$y = \frac{111 - 7x - 3z}{20}$$

$$z = \frac{190.5 - 10x - 13y}{22}$$

Assuming $y = z = 0$,

$$x = \frac{161.5}{23} = 7.02174$$

Now using this value of x and assumed value of z as zero,

$$y = \frac{111 - 7 \times 7.02174 - 0}{20} = 3.09239$$

Now using these values,

$$z = \frac{190.5 - 10 \times 7.02174 - 13 \times 3.09239}{22} = 3.64007$$

Going back to equation for x and using calculated values of y and z,

$$x = \frac{161.5 + 11 \times 3.09239 - 7 \times 3.64007}{23} = 7.39286$$

Again calculate y using

$$z = 3.64007 \text{ and } x = 7.39286$$

The iterative calculation results are as below,

Itn. No.	x	y	z
	0	0	0
1	7.02174	3.09239	3.64007
2	7.39286	2.41649	3.87077
3	6.99939	2.51960	3.98870
4	7.01281	2.49721	3.99582
5	6.99994	2.50065	3.99965
6	**7.000**	**2.500**	**4.000**

Note : Since most recent values of variables are used unlike Jacobi's method i.e. i^{th} and $(i-1)^{th}$ iteration for calculation of x, y, z values for i^{th} iteration are used, solution is faster.

7.10.2 Using MS-Excel for Gauss-Seidel Method

The voluminous work of iterative calculations may be easily completed in MS-Excel as solver for Gauss-Seidel method.

Let us solve Example 7.8 using MS-Excel :

1. Type zero in cells A1, A2, A3. These are initial guesses.
   (A1 – can be left blank).
2. Type formula for x as
   = (161.5 + 11 * A2 – 7 * A3)/23
   in cell B1
3. Type formula for y as
   = (111 – 7 * B1 – 3 * A3)/20
   in cell B2
4. Type formula for z as
   = (190.5 – 10 * B1 – 13 * B2)/22
   in cell B3
5. Now copy and paste cell B1 to B3 in multiple cells, say C1 to I1.

The worksheet will look as shown in Image 7.1.

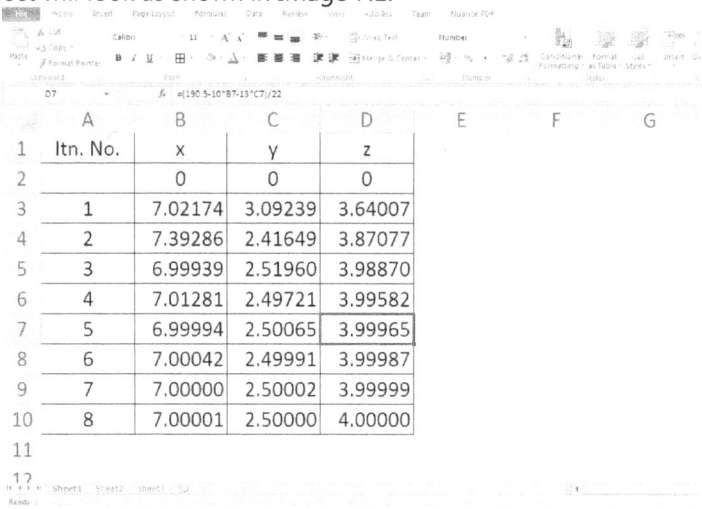

Image 7.1

The last cells I1, I2, I3 are representing the answers.

7.10.2 Using MS-Excel for Gauss-Seidel Method
Pseudo Code for Gauss-Seidel Method
1. Get number for variables, n.
2. Get all coefficients that means all elements of matrix A.
3. Get all constant terms that means all elements of matrix B.

4. Get initial guesses as,
   for i = 0 to i = n – 1
   {get x[i]}
5. Get accuracy level
6. Perform partial pivoting as,
   for i = 0 to i = n – 2
   { max = a[i][i]
   row_num = i
   for j = i to j = n – 1
   { if (a[j][i] > max)
      { row_num = j
        max = a[j][i]
      }
   }
   for j = 0 to j = n – 1
   { temp = a[i][j]
      a[i][j] = a[row_num][j]
      a[row_num][j] = temp
   }
   temp = b[i]
   b[i] = b[row_num]
   b[row – num] = temp
   }
7. Now calculate answers by iterative process as,
   do
   {   x_current = x[0]
   for i = 0 to i = n – 1
   { sum = 0
      for j = 0 to j = n – 1
      { if (i ≠ j)
        {sum = sum + a[i][j] * x[j]}
      }
      x[i] = (b[i] – sum)/a[i][j]
   }
   x_new = x[0]
   } while (fabs (x_new – x_current) > acc)
8. Answers are stored in x[i], so print them as,
   for i = 0 to i = n – 1
   {print x[i]}
9. End.

7.10.3 Flow Chart for Gauss-Seidel Method

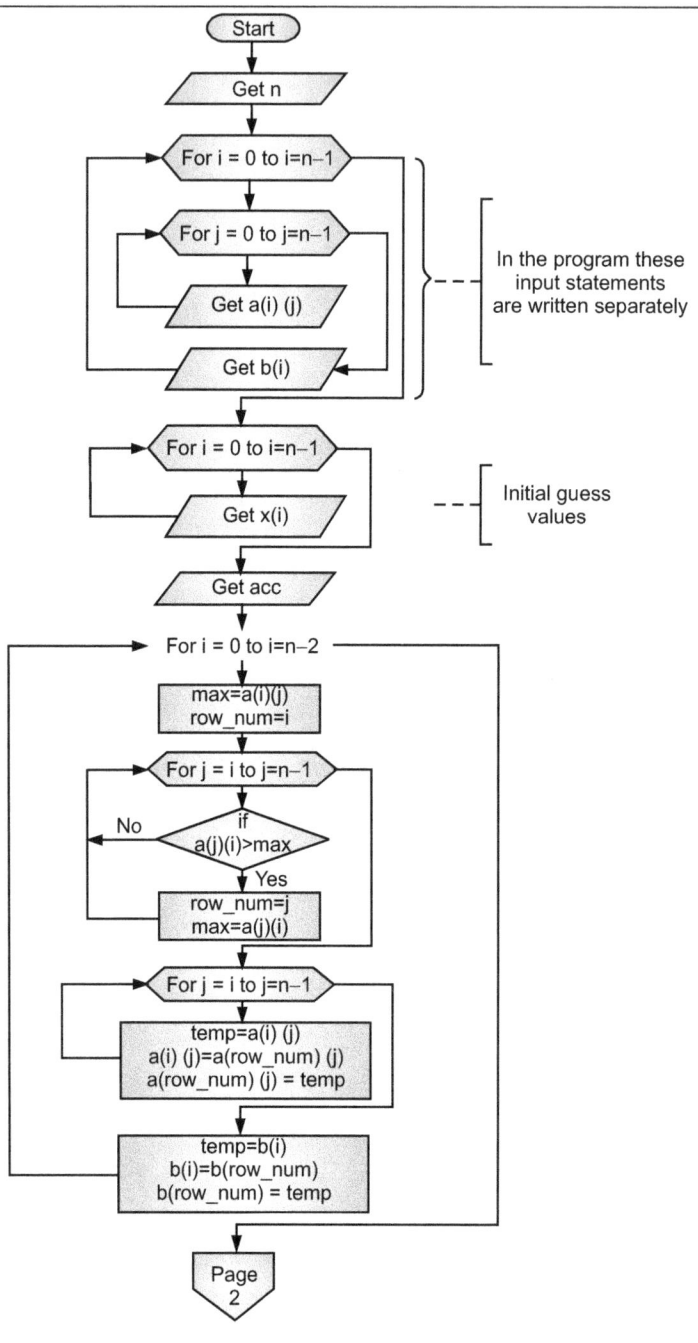

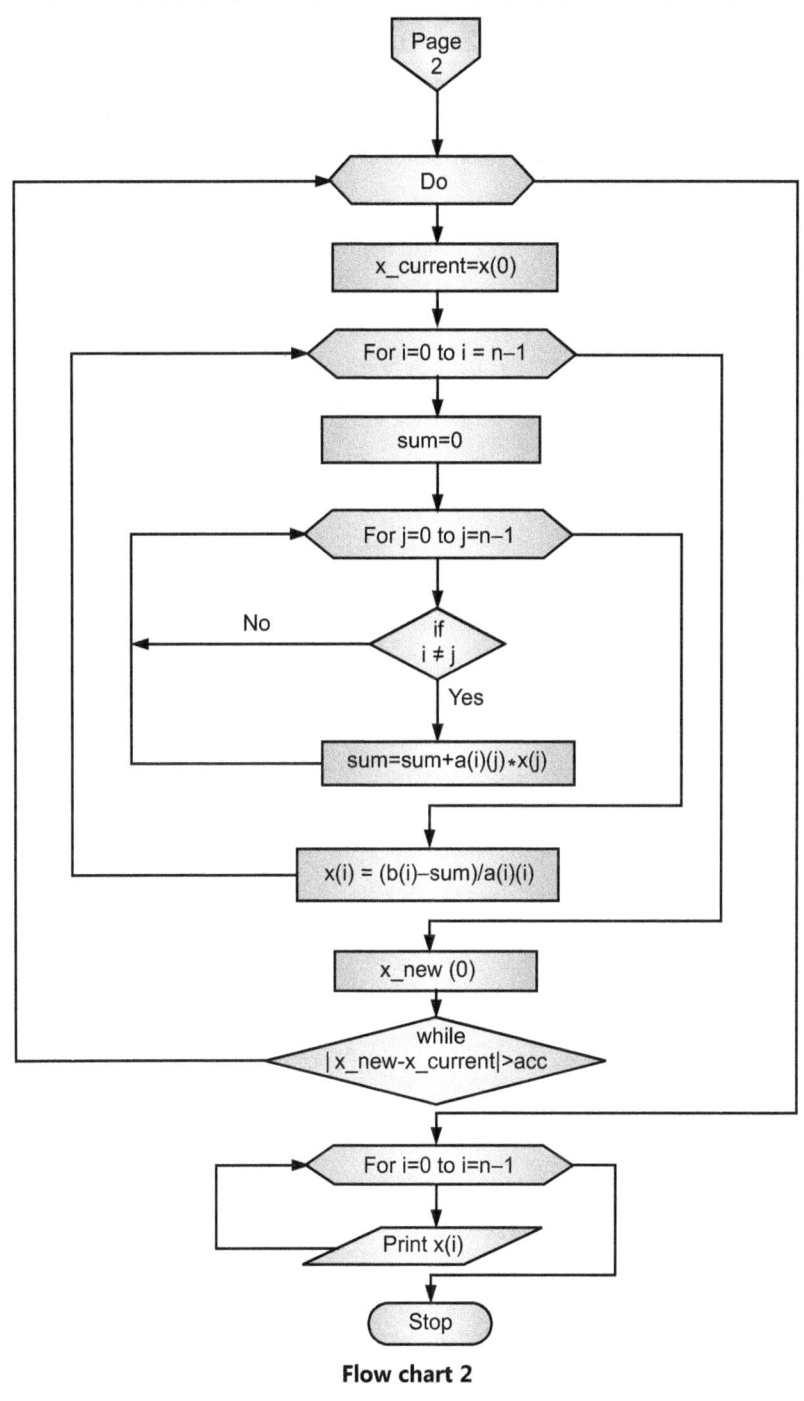

Flow chart 2

7.10.4 Matlab Code For Gauss-Seidal Method

```
fprintf('\n*****************************************************');
fprintf('\n*********** GAUSS SIEDEL METHOD ***************');
fprintf('\n*****************************************************');

%% MATRIX INPUT

n = input('\n Enter number of variables: ');
fprintf('\nEnter elements of Matrix A i.e. Coefficients matrix ...\n');

for i=1:n
    for j=1:n
            fprintf('\n A(%d,%d): ',i,j);
            a(i,j) = input('');
    end
end

fprintf('\nEnter elements of Matrix B i.e. Constant Terms matrix ...\n');
for i=1:n
    fprintf('\n B(%d): ',i);
    b(i) = input('');
    b=b';
end

fprintf('[A][X]=[B]\twill look as ...\n\n');
for i=1:n
    for j=1:n
            fprintf('%f\t',a(i,j));
    end
    fprintf('x%d\t%f\n',i,b(i));
end

%% PARTIAL PIVOTING

fprintf('\nResult of Partial Pivoting ...\n\n');
```

```
for i=1:n-1
    max=a(i,i);
    row_num=i;
    for j=i:n
            if a(j,i)>max
            row_num=j;
            max=a(j,i);
            end
    end
    for j=1:n
            temp=a(i,j);
            a(i,j)=a(row_num,j);
            a(row_num,j)=temp;
    end
    temp=b(i);
    b(i)=b(row_num);
    b(row_num)=temp;
end
fprintf('\n[A][X]=[B]\twill look as ...\n\n');
for i=1:n
    for j=1:n
            fprintf('%f\t',a(i,j));
    end
    fprintf('x%d\t%f\n',i,b(i));
end

%% Gauss Seidal Calculations
m = input('\n No. of Iterations [M] = ');
for i=1:n
    fprintf('\n Initial Guess Value of X(%d) = ',i);
    x(i) = input('');
end

for k=1:m
```

```
    for i=1:n
        sum=b(i);
        for j=1:n
        if i~=j                                    %% i is not equal to j
    sum=sum-a(i,j)*x(j);
        end
        x(i)=sum/a(i,i);
        end
        fprintf('\t x%d = %f',i,x(i));
end
    fprintf('\n');
end
```

7.11 Cholesky's Decomposition Method

From symmetric matrix, Lower triangular matrix (L) and upper triangular matrix (U) selected such that, U=LT, by decomposition as follows:

Step I - Perform decomposition :

$$\begin{bmatrix} l_{11} & 0 & 0 & 0 \\ l_{21} & l_{22} & 0 & 0 \\ l_{31} & l_{32} & l_{33} & 0 \\ l_{41} & l_{42} & l_{43} & l_{44} \end{bmatrix} \begin{bmatrix} u_{11} & u_{12} & u_{13} & u_{14} \\ 0 & u_{22} & u_{23} & u_{24} \\ 0 & 0 & u_{33} & u_{34} \\ 0 & 0 & 0 & u_{44} \end{bmatrix} = \begin{bmatrix} a_{11} & a_{12} & a_{13} & a_{14} \\ a_{21} & a_{22} & a_{23} & a_{24} \\ a_{31} & a_{32} & a_{33} & a_{34} \\ a_{41} & a_{42} & a_{43} & a_{44} \end{bmatrix}$$

where, Diagonal Elements are

$$u_{ii} = l_{ii} = \sqrt{a_{ij} - \sum_{k=1}^{i-1} l_{ik} u_{ki}} \quad , \quad i = 1, \ldots, n$$

and Non diagonal elements calculated by:

$$l_{ij} = \frac{a_{ij} - \sum_{k=1}^{j-1} l_{ik} u_{kj}}{u_{ii}} \quad j < i, \quad i = 2, \ldots, n$$

$$u_{ij} = \frac{a_{ij} - \sum_{k=1}^{i-1} l_{ik} u_{kj}}{l_{ii}} \quad i < j, \quad j = 2, \ldots, n$$

- Ax=b $\Rightarrow$ LLTx=b $\Rightarrow$ Ly=b $\Rightarrow$ LTx=y

7.12 GENERALIZED SOLUTION FOR LINEAR SIMULTANEOUS EQUATIONS USING MS-EXCEL

For given system of equations, we may follow below given steps to get the solution quickly using MS-Excel.

1. Fill in all coefficients, that means matrix A in row - column form.
2. Get inverse of matrix.
3. Fill in constant terms, that means matrix B in column form.
4. Perform matrix multiplication.
5. Due to multiplication $[A]^{-1}[B]$ we get solution as $[X]$.

Example 7.10 : Solve the following equations :

$$-3a + 5b + 6c + 2d = 11$$
$$15a + 7b + 6c - 4d = 65$$
$$8a + 12b + 20c + 6d = 60$$
$$3a + 4b + 7c + 9d = 7 \quad \text{using MS-Excel solver.}$$

Solution : Follow below given procedure :

1. Type all coefficients in row and column form as shown in Image 7.2.

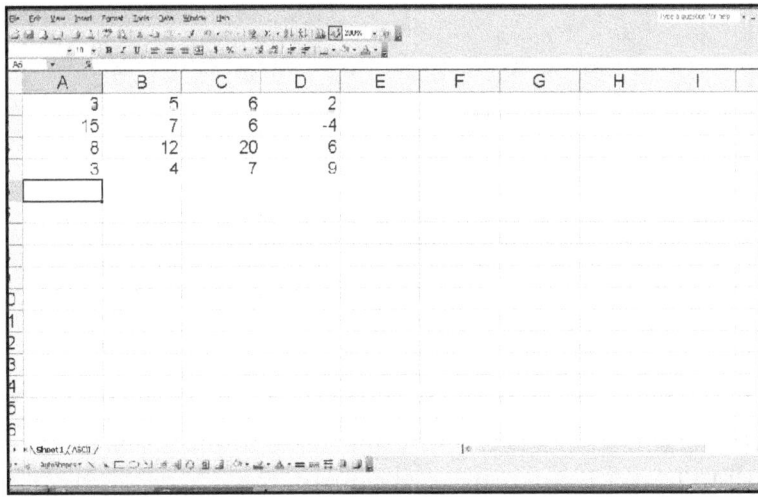

Image 7.2

2. Select cells A6 to D10 and type formula as = m inverse (A1 : D4). Do not simply press "Enter" key. Press Ctrl-Shift-Enter.
3. Inverse of matrix A is obtained as shown in Image 7.3.
4. Type matrix B, i.e. constant terms in cells F6 to F9.
5. Select cells H6 to H9 and type formula as = mmult (A6 : D9, F6 : F9).

Do not press only "Enter" key. Press Ctrl-Shift-Enter.

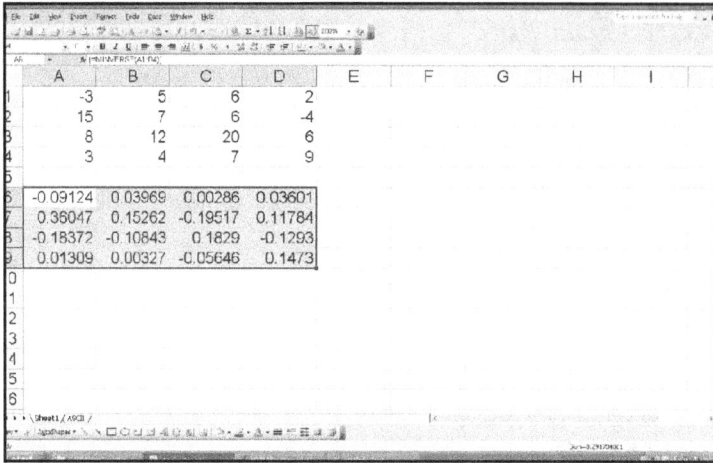

Image 7.3

The results are obtained as shown in Image 7.4. The values of a, b, c and d are displayed in cells H6, H7, H8 and H9 respectively.

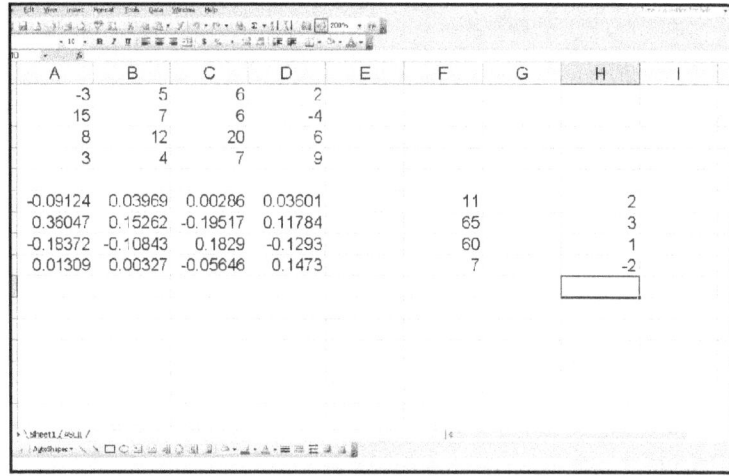

Image 7.4

Thus, solution is,

a = 2, b = 3, c = 1, d = –2

7.13 MATLAB SOLVERS FOR LINEAR SIMULTANEOUS EQUATIONS

In MATLAB, matrix can be input by following method:

A = [7 20 3; 23 -11 7; 10 13 22]

Where 'space' will distinguish between two numbers in a row and 'semicolon' will work as row terminator.

e.g.
>> A = [7 20 3; 23 – 11 7; 10 13 22]
A =
   7   10   3
   23 –11   7
   10   13   22
>> B = [111; 161.5;190.5]
B =
   111.0000
   161.5000
   190.5000
>> B = [111 161.5 190.5]
B =
   111.000   161.5000   190.5000

Linear simultaneous problems can be solved by using MATLAB as follows:

1. by using **linsolve** function
>> linsolve (A, B)
ans =
   7.0000
   2.5000
   4.0000

2. by using **rref** function
>> rref ([A B])
ans =
   1.0000   0   0   7.000
      0   1.0000   0   2.5000
      0   0   1.0000   4.0000

3. by using **Matrix inverse method**
>> x = inv (A) * B
X =
   7.0000
   2.5000
   4.0000
>> X = A\B
X =
   7.0000
   2.5000
   4.0000

SOLVED EXAMPLES

Example 7.11 : Solve the following equations :
$$-3a + 5b + 6c + 2d = 11$$
$$15a + 7b + 6c - 4d = 65$$
$$8a + 12b + 20c + 6d = 60$$
$$3a + 4b + 7c + 9d = 7$$
using MatLab.

Solution : Follow the procedure given below :

```
>> a = [–3 5 6 2; 15 7 6 –4; 8 12 20 6; 3 4 7 9];
>> b = [11; 65; 60; 7];
>> c = inv (a) * b
   c =
      2.0000
      3.0000
      1.0000
     –2.0000
>>
```

Thus solution is quickly obtained in MatLab.

Example 7.12 : Solve the following equations using (i) Gauss elimination method, (ii) Gauss-Jordan Method.
$$3x + 6y + z = 16$$
$$2x + 4y + 3z = 13$$
$$x + 3y + 2z = 9$$

Solution :

The matrix form for equations is

$$\begin{bmatrix} 3 & 6 & 1 \\ 2 & 4 & 3 \\ 1 & 3 & 2 \end{bmatrix} \begin{bmatrix} x \\ y \\ z \end{bmatrix} = \begin{bmatrix} 16 \\ 13 \\ 9 \end{bmatrix}$$

After partial pivoting the matrices remain unchanged.

(i) Gauss Elimination Method :

Performing row transformations as

$$R_1 - \left(\frac{2}{3}\right) R_0 \text{ and } R_2 - \left(\frac{1}{3}\right) R_0$$

$$\begin{bmatrix} 3 & 6 & 1 \\ 0 & 0 & 2.3333 \\ 0 & 1 & 1.6667 \end{bmatrix} \begin{bmatrix} x \\ y \\ z \end{bmatrix} = \begin{bmatrix} 16 \\ 2.333 \\ 3.6667 \end{bmatrix}$$

According to rules of standardization of Gauss Elimination, we must perform 2 sequences of row transformations. But due to $a_{11} = 0$ second sequence of row transformation is not possible, which will lead to erroneous results.

Hence, changing order of equations we rewrite matrices as,

$$\begin{bmatrix} 1 & 3 & 2 \\ 2 & 4 & 3 \\ 3 & 6 & 1 \end{bmatrix} \begin{bmatrix} x \\ y \\ z \end{bmatrix} = \begin{bmatrix} 9 \\ 13 \\ 16 \end{bmatrix}$$

Partial pivoting will rearrange the equations as earlier.

Hence, performing row transformations without partial pivoting as,

$$R_1 - 2R_0 \text{ and } R_2 - 3R_0$$

$$\begin{bmatrix} 1 & 3 & 2 \\ 0 & -2 & -1 \\ 0 & -3 & -5 \end{bmatrix} \begin{bmatrix} x \\ y \\ z \end{bmatrix} = \begin{bmatrix} 9 \\ -5 \\ -11 \end{bmatrix}$$

Now $R_2 - \left(\dfrac{3}{2}\right) R_1$

$$\begin{bmatrix} 1 & 3 & 2 \\ 0 & -2 & -1 \\ 0 & 0 & -3.5 \end{bmatrix} \begin{bmatrix} x \\ y \\ z \end{bmatrix} = \begin{bmatrix} 9 \\ -5 \\ -3.5 \end{bmatrix} \quad \ldots \ldots \text{[A]}$$

$\therefore \quad z = 1$

and by backward substitutions,

$$-2y - z = -5$$

$\therefore \quad y = 2$

and $\quad x + 3y + 2z = 9$

$\therefore \quad x = 1$

Thus, solution is **x = 1, y = 2, z = 1.**

(ii) Gauss Jordan Method :

Refer Equation [A], we have

$$\begin{bmatrix} 1 & 3 & 2 \\ 0 & -2 & -1 \\ 0 & 0 & -3.5 \end{bmatrix} \begin{bmatrix} x \\ y \\ z \end{bmatrix} = \begin{bmatrix} 9 \\ -5 \\ -3.5 \end{bmatrix} \quad \text{........................ [A]}$$

or

$$\begin{bmatrix} 1 & 3 & 2 \\ 0 & 2 & 1 \\ 0 & 0 & 1 \end{bmatrix} \begin{bmatrix} x \\ y \\ z \end{bmatrix} = \begin{bmatrix} 9 \\ 5 \\ 1 \end{bmatrix}$$

Now $R_1 - 2*R_3$ and $R_2 - R_3$, we get

$$\begin{bmatrix} 1 & 3 & 0 \\ 0 & 2 & 0 \\ 0 & 0 & 1 \end{bmatrix} \begin{bmatrix} x \\ y \\ z \end{bmatrix} = \begin{bmatrix} 7 \\ 4 \\ 1 \end{bmatrix} \Rightarrow \begin{bmatrix} 1 & 3 & 0 \\ 0 & 1 & 0 \\ 0 & 0 & 1 \end{bmatrix} \begin{bmatrix} x \\ y \\ z \end{bmatrix} = \begin{bmatrix} 7 \\ 2 \\ 1 \end{bmatrix}$$

Now $R_1 - 3*R_2$, we get

$$\begin{bmatrix} 1 & 0 & 0 \\ 0 & 1 & 0 \\ 0 & 0 & 1 \end{bmatrix} \begin{bmatrix} x \\ y \\ z \end{bmatrix} = \begin{bmatrix} 1 \\ 2 \\ 1 \end{bmatrix}$$

Thus, solution is **x = 1, y = 2, z = 1.**

Example 7.13 : *Solve following equations for five iterations using*
(i) Jacobi's Method and (ii) Gauss-Seidel method,

$$4x_1 + 2x_3 = 4$$
$$5x_2 + 2x_3 = 3$$
$$5x_1 + 4x_2 + 10x_3 = 2$$

Solution : Rewriting the equations,

$$x_1 = \frac{4 - 2x_3}{4} = \frac{2 - x_3}{2}$$

$$x_2 = \frac{3 - 2x_3}{5}$$

$$x_3 = \frac{2 - 5x_1 - 4x_2}{10}$$

(i) Jacobi's Method :

With initial guesses as $x_2 = x_3 = 0$

Iteration 1: $x_1 = \dfrac{2-0}{2} = 1$

$x_2 = \dfrac{3-2\times 0}{5} = 0.6$

$x_3 = (2-5\times 0-4\times 0)/10 = 0.20$

Iteration 2: $x_1 = (2-0.2)/2 = 0.90$

$x_2 = (3-2\times 0.2)/5 = 0.520$

$x_3 = (2-5\times 1-4\times 0.6)/10 = -0.540$

Note: Please refer table for further calculations:
Answer after 5th iteration, $x_1 = $ **1.3807**, $x_2 = $ **0.9046** and $x_3 = $ **-0.7278** ... Ans.
Answer after 20th iteration, $x_1 = $ **1.4574**, $x_2 = $ **0.9660** and $x_3 = $ **-0.9151** ... Ans.

(ii) Gauss-Seidel Method :
with initial guesses as $x_2 = x_3 = 0$

Iteration 1: $x_1 = \dfrac{2-0}{2} = 1$

$x_2 = \dfrac{3-2\times 0}{5} = 0.6$

$x_3 = \dfrac{2-5\times 1-4\times 0.6}{10} = -0.54$

Iteration 2: $x_1 = \dfrac{2-(-0.54)}{2} = 1.27$

$x_2 = \dfrac{3-2\times(-0.54)}{5} = 0.816$

$x_3 = \dfrac{2-5\times 1.27-4\times 0.816}{10}$

$= -0.7614$

Iteration 3: $x_1 = \dfrac{2-(-0.7614)}{2} = 1.3807$

$x_2 = \dfrac{3-2\times(-0.7614)}{5} = 0.90456$

$x_3 = \dfrac{2-5\times 1.3807-4\times 0.90456}{10} = -0.8522$

Iteration 4: $x_1 = \dfrac{2-(-0.8522)}{2} = 1.4261$

$$x_2 = \frac{3 - 2 \times (-0.8522)}{5} = 0.94088$$

$$x_3 = \frac{2 - 5 \times 1.4261 - 4 \times 0.94088}{10} = -0.8894$$

Iteration 5 :

$$x_1 = \frac{2 - (-0.8894)}{2} = 1.4447$$

$$x_2 = \frac{3 - 2 \times (-0.8894)}{5} = 0.95576$$

$$x_3 = \frac{2 - 5 \times 1.4447 - 4 \times 0.95576}{10} = -0.9047$$

Thus, solution at the end of fifth iteration is, **$x_1 = 1.4447$, $x_2 = 0.95576$, $x_3 = -0.9047$** ... Ans.
Answer after 10th iteration, $x_1 = $ **1.4575**, $x_2 = $ **0.9660** and $x_3 = $ **-0.9151** ... Ans.

Itn. No.	Jacobi's Method			Gauss-Seidel Method		
	x_1	x_2	x_3	x_1	x_2	x_3
	0	0	0	0	0	0
1	1.0000	0.6000	0.2000	1.0000	0.6000	-0.5400
2	0.9000	0.5200	-0.5400	1.2700	0.8160	-0.7614
3	1.2700	0.8160	-0.4580	1.3807	0.9046	-0.8522
4	1.2290	0.7832	-0.7614	1.4261	0.9409	-0.8894
5	**1.3807**	**0.9046**	**-0.7278**	**1.4447**	**0.9558**	**-0.9047**
6	1.3639	0.8911	-0.8522	1.4523	0.9619	-0.9109
7	1.4261	0.9409	-0.8384	1.4555	0.9644	-0.9135
8	1.4192	0.9354	-0.8894	1.4567	0.9654	-0.9145
9	1.4447	0.9558	-0.8837	1.4573	0.9658	-0.9150
10	1.4419	0.9535	-0.9047	**1.4575**	**0.9660**	**-0.9151**
11	1.4523	0.9619	-0.9023			
12	1.4512	0.9609	-0.9109			
13	1.4555	0.9644	-0.9100			
14	1.4550	0.9640	-0.9135			
15	1.4567	0.9654	-0.9131			
16	1.4565	0.9652	-0.9145			
17	1.4573	0.9658	-0.9144			
18	1.4572	0.9657	-0.9150			
19	1.4575	0.9660	-0.9149			
20	**1.4574**	**0.9660**	**-0.9151**			

Example 7.14 : Determine solution of following set of linear simultaneous equations using appropriate method.

$$3x_1 + 2x_2 = 1$$
$$x_1 + 5x_2 + 4x_3 = 4$$
$$-3x_2 + 2x_3 + x_4 = 10$$
$$4x_3 + 7x_4 = 29$$

Solution : Writing the equations in the matrix form, we get,

$$\begin{bmatrix} 3 & 2 & 0 & 0 \\ 1 & 5 & 4 & 0 \\ 0 & -3 & 2 & 1 \\ 0 & 0 & 4 & 7 \end{bmatrix} \begin{bmatrix} x_1 \\ x_2 \\ x_3 \\ x_4 \end{bmatrix} = \begin{bmatrix} 1 \\ 4 \\ 10 \\ 29 \end{bmatrix}$$

The coefficient matrix that means matrix A is tridiagonal matrix. Hence, we will use Thomas algorithm to get the solution.

Accordingly,

Step 1 : Decomposition of matrix A.

$$l_1 = \frac{l_1}{d_0} = \frac{1}{3} = -0.3333$$

$$d_1 = d_1 - l_1 \cdot u_0 = 5 - 0.3333 \times 2 = 4.3333$$

$$l_2 = \frac{l_2}{d_1} = \frac{-3}{4.3333} = -0.6923$$

$$d_2 = d_2 - l_2 \cdot u_1 = 2 - (-0.6923) \times 4 = 4.7692$$

$$l_3 = \frac{l_3}{d_2} = \frac{4}{4.7692} = 0.8387$$

$$d_3 = d_3 - l_3 \cdot u_2 = 7 - 0.8387 \times 1 = 6.1613$$

Step 2 : Forward substitution, i.e. transformations on matrix B,

$$b_1 = b_1 - l_1 \cdot b_0 = 4 - 0.3333 \times 1 = 3.6667$$
$$b_2 = b_2 - l_2 \cdot b_1 = 10 - (-0.6923) \times 3.6667 = 12.5385$$
$$b_3 = b_3 - l_3 \cdot b_2 = 29 - 0.8387 \times 12.5385 = 18.484$$

Step 3 : Back substitutions

$$x_3 = \frac{b_3}{d_3} = \frac{18.484}{6.1613} = 3.00001623$$

$$x_2 = \frac{(b_2 - u_2 \cdot x_3)}{d_2} = \frac{(12.5385 - 1 \times 3.00001623)}{4.7692}$$

$$= 2.000017565$$

$$x_1 = \frac{(b_1 - u_1 \cdot x_2)}{d_1}$$

$$= \frac{(3.6667 - 4 \times 2.000017565)}{4.3333}$$

$$= -1.000016214$$

$$x_0 = \frac{(b_0 - u_0 \cdot x_1)}{d_0}$$

$$= \frac{(1 - 2 \times (-1.000016214))}{3}$$

$$= 1.000010809$$

Thus solution is,

$$x_0 = 1, \quad x_1 = -1, \quad x_2 = 2, \quad x_3 = 3$$

According to variable names given in the problem statement, the solution is,

$$x_1 = 1, \quad x_2 = -1, \quad x_3 = 2, \quad x_4 = 3 \quad \quad \ldots \text{Ans.}$$

Example 7.15 : *Solve following set of equations by Gauss elimination method :*

$$10p - 7q + 3r + 5s = 6$$
$$-6p + 8q - r - 4s = 5$$
$$3p + q + 4r + 11s = 2$$
$$5p - 9q - 2r + 4s = 7$$

Solution : In matrix form, the equations are written as,

$$\begin{bmatrix} 10 & -7 & 3 & 5 \\ -6 & 8 & -1 & -4 \\ 3 & 1 & 4 & 11 \\ 5 & -9 & -2 & 4 \end{bmatrix} \begin{bmatrix} p \\ q \\ r \\ s \end{bmatrix} = \begin{bmatrix} 6 \\ 5 \\ 2 \\ 7 \end{bmatrix}$$

Partial pivoting keeps the matrices unchanged.

Performing row transformations as,

$$R_1 - \left(\frac{-6}{10}\right) R_0, \quad R_2 - \left(\frac{3}{10}\right) R_0 \text{ and } R_3 - \left(\frac{5}{10}\right) R_0$$

$$\begin{bmatrix} 10 & -7 & 3 & 5 \\ 0 & 3.8 & 0.8 & -1 \\ 0 & 3.1 & 3.1 & 9.5 \\ 0 & -5.5 & -3.5 & 1.5 \end{bmatrix} \begin{bmatrix} p \\ q \\ r \\ s \end{bmatrix} = \begin{bmatrix} 6 \\ 8.6 \\ 0.2 \\ 4 \end{bmatrix}$$

Now $R_2 - \left(\frac{3.1}{3.8}\right) R_1$ and $R_3 - \left(\frac{-5.5}{3.8}\right) R_1$

$$\begin{bmatrix} 10 & -7 & 3 & 5 \\ 0 & 3.8 & 0.8 & -1 \\ 0 & 0 & 2.4474 & 10.3158 \\ 0 & 0 & -2.3421 & 0.0526 \end{bmatrix} \begin{bmatrix} p \\ q \\ r \\ s \end{bmatrix} = \begin{bmatrix} 6 \\ 8.6 \\ -6.8158 \\ 16.4474 \end{bmatrix}$$

Next, $R_3 - \left(\dfrac{-2.3421}{2.4474}\right) R_2$

$$\begin{bmatrix} 10 & -7 & 3 & 5 \\ 0 & 3.8 & 0.8 & -1 \\ 0 & 0 & 2.4474 & 10.3158 \\ 0 & 0 & 0 & 9.9249 \end{bmatrix} \begin{bmatrix} p \\ q \\ r \\ s \end{bmatrix} = \begin{bmatrix} 6 \\ 8.6 \\ -6.8158 \\ 9.9249 \end{bmatrix}$$

From the last row,

$$s = \dfrac{9.9249}{9.9249} = 1$$

By backward substitution, from row R_2,

$2.4474\, r + 10.3158\, s = -6.8158$

$\therefore \quad r = -6.99992 \doteq -7$

From row R_1,

$3.8q + 0.8r + s = 8.6$

$\therefore \quad q = \dfrac{8.6 - 0.8 \times (-7) + 1}{3.8} = 4$

From row R_0,

$10p - 7q + 3r + 5s = 6$

$\therefore \quad p = \dfrac{6 + 7 \times 4 - 3 \times (-7) - 5}{10} = 5$

Thus solution is,

p = 5, q = 4, r = -7, s = 1 ...Ans.

PROBLEMS FOR PRACTICE

1. Solve using Gauss-Seidel method.

   $83x + 11y - 4z = 95$

   $7x + 52y + 13z = 104$

   $3x + 8y + 29z = 71$

   Ans.: $x = 1.058$, $y = 1.37$, $z = 1.96$

2. Perform partial pivoting with following matrix.

$$\begin{bmatrix} -7 & 3 & 20 & 7 & 19 & 13 \\ 17 & -4 & 8 & 3 & 0 & 32 \\ 19 & 25 & 26 & -12 & 8 & 7 \\ 33 & 19 & 17 & 22 & -25 & 18 \\ 3 & 0 & 21 & 19 & -10 & -20 \\ 32 & 27 & 35 & -46 & 18 & 36 \end{bmatrix}$$

Ans. : $\begin{bmatrix} 33 & 19 & 17 & 22 & -25 & 18 \\ 32 & 27 & 35 & -46 & 18 & 36 \\ 19 & 25 & 26 & -12 & 8 & 7 \\ 3 & 0 & 21 & 19 & -10 & -20 \\ -7 & 3 & 20 & 7 & 19 & 13 \\ 17 & -4 & 8 & 3 & 0 & 32 \end{bmatrix}$

3. Solve using Gauss elimination method.

$$x_2 + 2x_3 = 5$$
$$x_1 + 2x_2 + 4x_3 = 11$$
$$-3x_1 + x_2 - 5x_3 = -12$$

Ans. : $x_1 = 1$, $x_2 = 1$, $x_3 = 2$

5. Solve following system of equations using Gauss elimination method.

$$10x_1 + x_2 + x_3 = 12$$
$$2x_1 + 11x_2 + 2x_3 = 15$$
$$3x_1 + 4x_2 + 9x_3 = 16$$

Ans. : $x_1 = x_2 = x_3 = 1$

7. Solve following set of equations to the accuracy of 0.01 using Gauss-Seidel method.

$$3.15x - 1.96y + 3.85z = 12.95$$
$$2.13x + 5.12y - 2.89z = -8.61$$
$$5.92x + 3.05y + 2.15z = 6.88$$

Ans. : $x = 1.7$, $y = -1.8$, $z = 1.05$

9. An engineer has listed some equations as below :

$$3a + 4b - f = 37$$
$$2b - 6d + 4e - 7f = 59$$
$$3d - 2e + 11f = 103$$
$$a - b + 7d = 36$$

$$5b + 7e - 4f = 24$$

Comment on sufficiency of the equations.

10. State whether following set of equations is ill conditioned or well conditioned.
$$5p + 7.5q - 2r = 33.5$$
$$5.1p - 12q + 5r = -14.8$$
$$3p - 12q + 5.1r = -18.3$$

Ans. : It is well conditioned. All coefficients in any two equations are not close to each other hence it is not ill conditioned.

11. Solve following system of linear equations by appropriate direct method.

$$\begin{bmatrix} 0 & 7 & 9 & 5 & 0 \\ 1 & 2 & 3 & 0 & 0 \\ 0 & 0 & 0 & 2 & 8 \\ -3 & 4 & 0 & 0 & 0 \\ 0 & 0 & 3 & 4 & 2 \end{bmatrix} \begin{bmatrix} a \\ b \\ c \\ d \\ e \end{bmatrix} = \begin{bmatrix} 4 \\ 3 \\ 46 \\ -17 \\ 16 \end{bmatrix}$$

(**Hint :** Rearrange rows in [A] and [B] so that [A] will become a tridiagonal matrix, then use Thomas algorithm, which is an appropriate method for solution.)

Ans. : $a = 7$, $b = 1$, $c = -2$, $d = 3$, $e = 5$

REVIEW QUESTIONS

1. Solve the following equations using Gauss-Elimination method.
   $$3x + 6y + z = 16$$
   $$2x + 4y + 3z = 13$$
   $$x + 3y + 2z = 9$$

2. Using Gauss Seidal iteration method solve following simultaneous equations (five iterations only)
   $$4x_1 + 2x_3 = 4$$
   $$5x_2 + 2x_3 = 3$$
   $$5x_1 + 4x_2 + 10x_3 = 2$$

3. Explain partial pivoting and full pivoting.
4. Write flow chart for back substitution.
6. Draw a flow chart for Gauss Seidal method with relaxation.
7. Using Gauss-Seidal Method solve the following set of simulations equations.
   $$x_1 + 20x_2 + 9x_3 = -23$$
   $$2x_1 - 7x_2 - 20x_3 = -57$$
   $$20x_1 + 2x_2 + 6x_3 = 28$$
   Show four iterations in the tabular form.

8. Draw a flow chart for Gauss-Elimination method.
9. Using Gauss Seidal method, solve the following set of simultaneous equations up to 03 decimal places.
   x + 2y + z = 0; 3x + y – z = 0; x – y + 4x = 3
11. Using Gauss Elimination Method, solve the following set of simultaneous equations.
    2x + 4y – 6z = –4; x + 5y + 3z = 10; x + 3y + 22 = 5
13. Solve the following set of simultaneous equations using Gauss Elimination method
    $10x_1 + x_2 + x_3 = 12$; $2x_1 + 11x_2 + 2x_3 = 15$; $3x_1 + 4x_2 + 9x_3 = 16$
15. Solve the following set of simultaneous equations using Gauss Seidal method.
    $9x_1 + 2x_2 + 4x_3 = 20$
    $x_1 + 10x_2 + 4x_3 = 6$
    $2x_1 – 4x_2 + 10x_3 = –15$
17. Use Gauss Elimination method to find v_1, v_2 and v_3
    $2v_1 – v_2 + 3v_3 = 5$; $–4v_1 – 3v_2 – 2v_3 = 8$; $3v_1 + v_2 – v_3 = 4$
18. Write a step by step procedure for Gauss Elimination method, develop a flow chart for Gauss-Elimination method.
19. Explain following statement with graphical representation "Gauss Seidal method and successive approximation method are same and in both method intersections of lines is taken as a solution."
20. Apply Gauss-Elimination method to solve the equations as follows :
    x + 3y + 3z = 16; x + 4y + 3z = 18; x + 3y + 4z = 19
21. Explain step by step procedure for Gauss Seidal method to compute solution of simultaneous equation and draw a flowchart.
22. What is meant by Partial Pivoting in Gauss Elimination to solve simultaneous equations ? And explain its importance in convergence of solution.
23. Using Gauss Seidel iterative method to solve the following system of simultaneous equations 9x + 4y + z = –17, x – 2y – 6z = 14, x + 6y = 4 perform four iterations.
24. Draw flowchart of Thomas algorithm.
25. Find the numerical solution of the system of equations x – y + 4z = 16, 3x + 2y + z = 18 and x + 4y – 2z = 12 correct up to 3 decimal places, using Gauss elimination method with partial pivoting.
26. Draw a flowchart for Gauss-Seidal method with partial pivoting.
27. Solve the following equation by Gauss-Seidal method,
    5x + 2y + z = 12, x + 4y + 2z = 15, x + 2y + 5z = 20
28. Solve the following equation by Gauss Elimination method
    2x + y + z = 10, 3x + 2y + 3z = 18, x + 4y + 9z = 16
29. Explain partial complete pivoting with suitable example.

Unit - V

Chapter 8
FINITE ELEMENT ANALYSIS

8.1 INTRODUCTION

Finite Element Method (FEM) is a numerical method for solving a differential or integral equation. This method is useful to obtain solution for problems with complex shapes, boundary conditions and loads. It can be applied to a number of physical problems, where the governing differential equations are available. The method essentially consists of assuming the piecewise continuous function for the solution and obtaining the parameters of the functions in a manner that reduces the error in the solution. The solutions obtained are approximate in nature.

Due to its diversity and flexibility as an analysis tool, it is receiving much attention in engineering. Some of the popular packages are NASTRAN, ANSYS, NISA, etc. Using these packages one can analyze several complex structures. The finite element analysis originated as a method of stress analysis in the design of aircrafts. It started as an extension of matrix method of structural analysis.

Today this method is used not only for the analysis in solid mechanics, but even in the analysis of fluid flow, heat transfer, electric and magnetic fields and many others. Mechanical engineers use this method extensively for the analysis of plates, components, assemblies of various machine components. Both static and dynamic problems can be handled by finite element analysis. This method is used extensively used for the analysis and design of ships, aircrafts, space crafts, electric motors and heat engines.

8.1.1 Advantages of the Finite Element Method (FEM)

- Can readily handle complex geometry :
- Can handle complex analysis types :
  - Vibration
  - Transients
  - Nonlinear
  - Heat transfer
  - Fluids
- Can handle complex loading :
  - Node-based loading (point loads).
  - Element-based loading (pressure, thermal, inertial forces).
  - Time or frequency dependent loading.

- Can handle complex restraints :
  - Indeterminate structures can be analyzed.
- Can handle bodies comprised of nonhomogeneous materials :
  - Every element in the model could be assigned a different set of material properties.
- Can handle bodies comprised of non-isotropic materials :
  - Orthotropic
  - Anisotropic
- Special material effects are handled :
  - Temperature dependent properties.
  - Plasticity
  - Creep
  - Swelling
- Special geometric effects can be modeled :
  - Large displacements.
  - Large rotations.
  - Contact (gap) condition.

8.1.2 Disadvantages of the Finite Element Method (FEM)

A specific numerical result is obtained for a specific problem. A general closed-form solution, which would permit one to examine system response to changes in various parameters, is not produced.

8.2 FINITE ELEMENT ANALYSIS

In engineering problems there are some basic unknowns. If they are found, the behaviour of the entire structure can be predicted. The basic unknowns or the Field variables which are encountered in the engineering problems are displacements in solid mechanics, velocities in fluid mechanics, electric and magnetic potentials in electrical engineering and temperatures in heat flow problems.

In a continuum, these unknowns are infinite. The finite element procedure reduces such unknowns to a finite number by dividing the solution region into small parts called elements and by expressing the unknown field variables in terms of assumed approximating functions (Interpolating functions/Shape functions) within each element.

The approximating functions are defined in terms of field variables of specified points called nodes or nodal points. Thus in the finite element analysis the unknowns are the field variables of the nodal points. Once these are found the field variables at any point can be found by using interpolation functions. After selecting elements and nodal unknowns next step in finite element analysis is to assemble element properties for each element. For example, in solid mechanics, we have to find the force-displacement i.e. stiffness characteristics of each individual element. Mathematically this relationship is of the form

$$[k]_e\{\delta\}_e = \{F\}_e$$

Where, $[k]_e$ is element stiffness matrix, $\{\delta\}_e$ is nodal displacement vector of the element and $\{F\}_e$ is nodal force vector. The element of stiffness matrix kij represent the force in coordinate direction 'i' due to a unit displacement in coordinate direction 'j'. Four methods are available for formulating these element properties viz. direct approach, variational approach, weighted residual approach and energy balance approach. Any one of these methods can be used for assembling element properties.

In solid mechanics variational approach is commonly employed to assemble stiffness matrix and nodal force vector (consistent loads). Element properties are used to assemble global properties/structure properties to get system equations [k] {δ} = {F}. Then the boundary conditions are imposed. The solution of these simultaneous equations gives the nodal unknowns. Using these nodal values additional calculations are made to get the required values e.g. stresses, strains, moments, etc. in solid mechanics problems.

8.3 TERMINOLOGY

Discretization : Model body by dividing it into an equivalent system of many smaller bodies or units (finite elements) interconnected at points common to two or more elements (nodes or nodal points) and/or boundary lines and/or surfaces.

Nodes : A node is a coordinate location in space where the degrees of freedom (DOFs) are defined. The DOFs for this point represent the possible movement of this point due to the loading of the structure.

The DOFs also represent which forces and moments are transferred from one element to the next. The results of a finite element analysis, (deflections and stresses), are usually given at the nodes. In the real world, a point can move in 6 different directions, translation in X, Y, and Z, and rotation about X, Y, and Z. In FEA, a node may be limited in the calculated motions for a variety of reasons.

For example, there is no need to calculate the out of plane translation on a 2-D element; it would not be a 2-D element if its nodes were allowed to move out of the plane. The DOF for the generic element types are given in Table 8.1.

Table 8.1 : Degrees of Freedom for Element Types

Element Type	Translation			Rotation		
	X	Y	Z	X	Y	Z
Truss, spring, gap	Yes	Yes	Yes			
Beam	Yes	Yes	Yes	Yes	Yes	Yes
2-D		Yes	Yes			
Membrane	Yes	Yes	Yes			
Plate, shell	Yes	Yes	Yes	Yes*	Yes*	
Brick, tetrahedral	Yes	Yes	Yes			

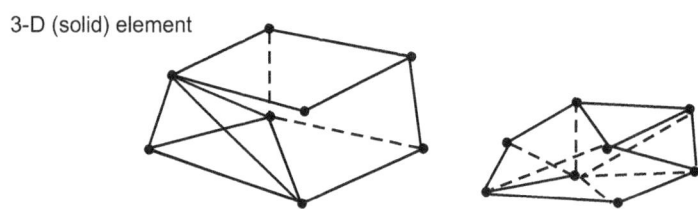

1-D (line) element

(Spring, truss, beam, pipe, etc)

2-D (plane) element

(Membrane, plate, shell, etc)

3-D (solid) element

(3-D fields-temperature, dispalcement, stress, flow velocity)

Fig. 8.1

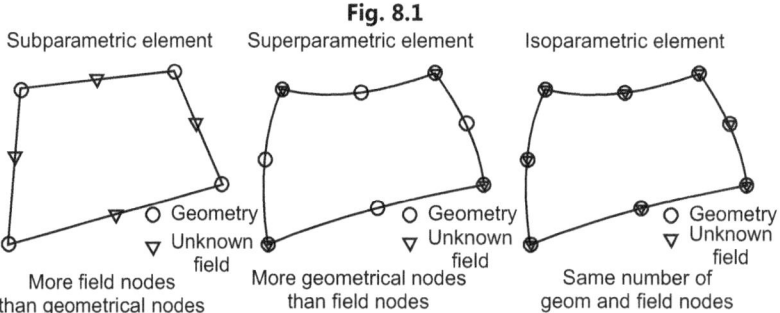

Subparametric element — More field nodes than geometrical nodes

Superparametric element — More geometrical nodes than field nodes

Isoparametric element — Same number of geom and field nodes

○ Geometry
▽ Unknown field

Fig. 8.2

Elements : An element is the basic building block of finite element analysis. There are several basic types of elements. Which type of element for finite elements analysis that is used depends on the type of object that is to be modeled for finite element analysis and the type of analysis that is going to be performed. An element is a mathematical relation that defines how the degrees of freedom of a node relate to the next. These elements can be lines (trusses or beams), areas (2-D or 3-D plates and membranes) or solids (bricks or tetrahedral). It also relates how the deflections create stresses.

Based on the shapes elements can be classified as :
(1) One dimensional elements.
(2) Two dimensional elements.
(3) Axi-symmetric elements and
(4) Three dimensional elements.

8.3.1 Types of Finite Elements

The boundary conditions are the specified values of the field variables (or related variables such as derivatives) on the boundaries of the field.

Interpolation Functions : The values of the field variable computed at the nodes are used to approximate the values at non-nodal points (that is, in the element interior) by interpolation of the nodal values. For the three-node triangle example, the field variable is described by the approximate relation :

$\varphi(x, y) = N_1(x, y) \varphi_1 + N_2(x, y) \varphi_2 + N_3(x, y) \varphi_3$

Where φ_1, φ_2, and φ_3 are the values of the field variable at the nodes, and N_1, N_2 and N_3 are the interpolation functions, also known as shape functions or blending functions.

8.4 INTERPOLATION FUNCTIONS FOR GENERAL ELEMENT FORMULATION

In finite element analysis, solution accuracy is judged in terms of convergence as the element "mesh" is refined. There are two major methods of mesh refinement :

- In the first, known as h-refinement, mesh refinement refers to the process of increasing the number of elements used to model a given domain. Consequently, reducing individual element size.
- In the second method, p-refinement, element size is unchanged but the order of the polynomials used as interpolation functions is increased.
- The objective of mesh refinement in either method is to obtain sequential solutions that exhibit asymptotic convergence to values representing the exact solution.

Stiffness Matrix

The primary characteristics of a finite element are embodied in the element stiffness matrix. For a structural finite element, the stiffness matrix contains the geometric and material behaviour information that indicates the resistance of the element to deformation when subjected to loading. Such deformation may include axial, bending, shear, and torsional effects. For finite elements used in non-structural analyses, such as fluid flow and heat transfer, the term stiffness matrix is also used, since the matrix represents the resistance of the element to change when subjected to external influences.

8.5 STEPS IN FINITE ELEMENT ANALYSIS

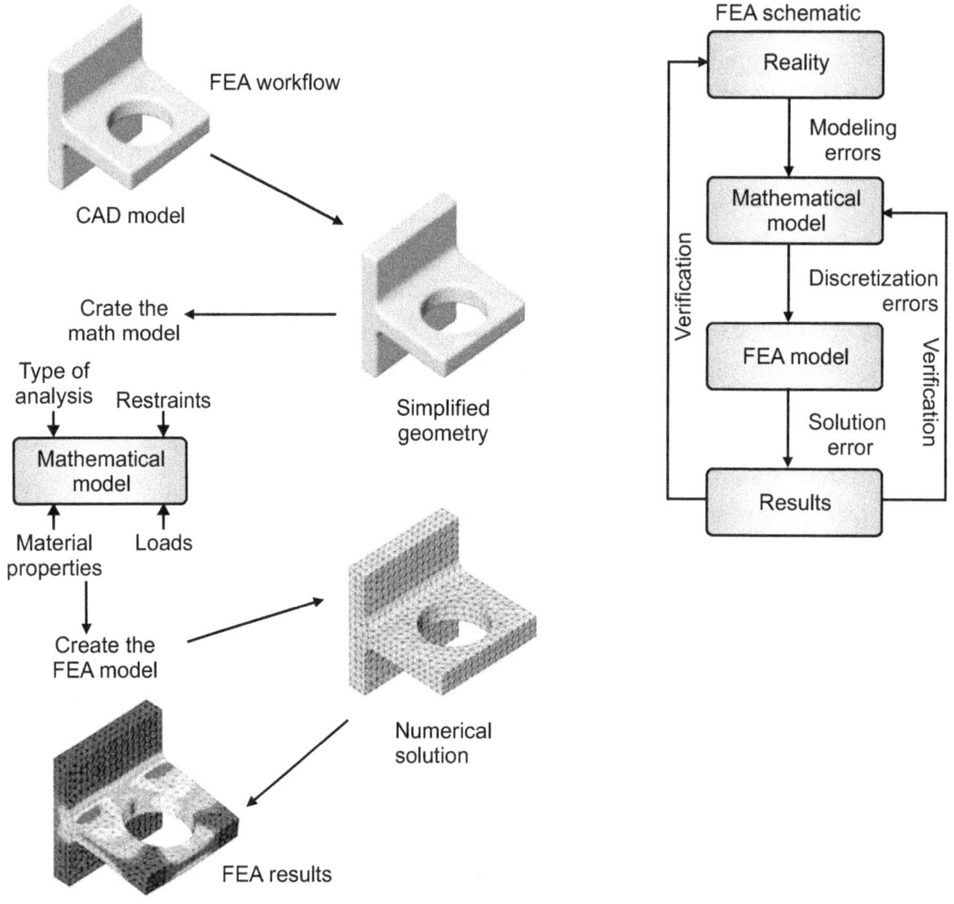

Fig. 8.3

The various steps involved in the finite element analysis as shown in Fig 8.3 are :

(1) Pre-Processing :
- Select suitable field variables and the elements viz. material information, element type, etc.
- Meshing or Discretize the continua.

- Select interpolation functions.
- Find the element properties.
- Assemble element properties to get global properties.
- Apply loads and boundary conditions.

(2) Solution :
- Solve the system equations to get the nodal unknowns.
- Make the additional calculations to get the required values by back substitution to compute additional, derived variables viz. reaction force, element stress, heat flow, etc.

(3) Post Processing :
- Plot Results.
- Print Reports.

8.6 General Approach

The steps involved in finite element analysis are clarified by taking the stress analysis of a tension strip with fillets (Refer Fig. 8.4). In this problem stress concentration is to be studies in the fillet zone. Since the problem is having symmetry about both x and y axes, only one quarter of the tension strip may be considered as shown in Fig. 8.5. About the symmetric axes, transverse displacements of all nodes are to be made zero. The various steps involved in the finite element analysis of this problem are discussed below:

Step 1 : Four noded isoparametric element (refer Fig 8.6) is selected for the analysis. The four noded isoparametric element can take quadrilateral shape also as required for elements 12, 15, 18, etc. As there is no bending of strip, only displacement continuity is to be ensured but not the slope continuity. Hence displacements of nodes in x and y directions are taken as basic unknowns in the problem.

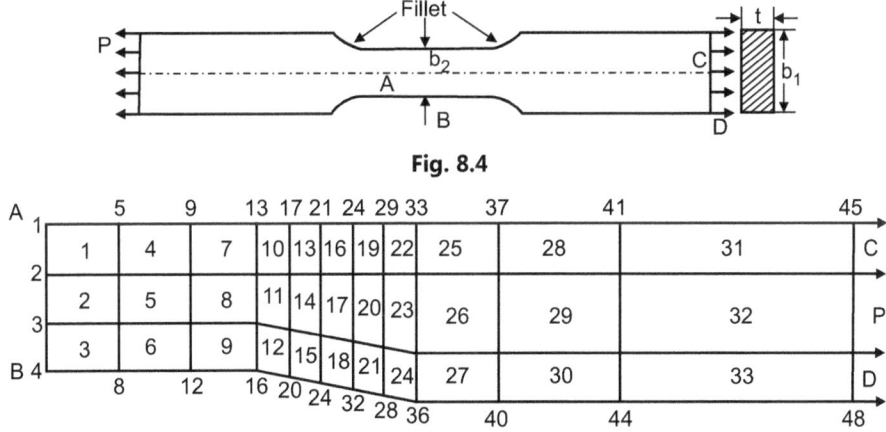

Fig. 8.4

Fig. 8.5 : Discretisation of quarter of tension flat

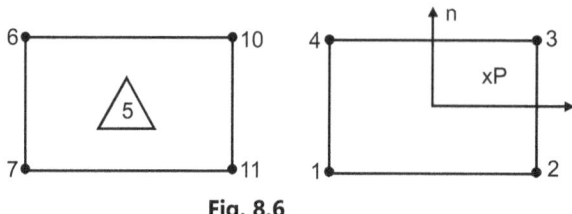

Fig. 8.6

Step 2 : The portion to be analysed is to be discretised. Fig. 8.4 shows discretized portion. For this 33 elements have been used. There are 48 nodes. At each node unknowns are x and y components of displacements. Hence in this problem total unknowns (displacements) to be determined are 48 × 2 = 96.

Step 3 : The displacement of any point inside the element is approximated by suitable functions in terms of the nodal displacements of the element. For the typical element (Fig. 8.4 b), displacements at P are

$$u = \Sigma N_i u_i = N_1 u_1 + N_2 u_2 + N_3 u_3 + N_4 u_4$$

and

$$v = \Sigma N_i v_i = N_1 v_1 + N_2 v_2 + N_3 v_3 + N_4 v_4 \quad ...(8.1)$$

The approximating functions N_i are called shape functions or interpolation functions. Usually they are derived using polynomials.

Step 4 : Now the stiffness characters and consistant loads are to be found for each element. There are four nodes and at each node degree of freedom is 2. Hence degree of freedom in each element is 4 × 2 = 8. The relationship between the nodal displacements and nodal forces is called element stiffness characteristics. It is of the form $[k]_e \{\delta\}_e = \{F\}_e$, as explained earlier.

For the element under consideration, k_e is 8 × 8 matrix and δ_e and F_e are vectors of 8 values. In solid mechanics element stiffness matrix is assembled using variational approach i.e. by minimizing potential energy.

If the load is acting in the body of element or on the surface of element, its equivalent at nodal points are to be found using variational approach, so that right hand side of the above expression is assembled. This process is called finding consistant loads.

Step 5 : The structure is having 48 × 2 = 96 displacement and load vector components to be determined. Hence global stiffness equation is of the form

$$[k] \quad \{\delta\} = \{F\}$$
$$96 \times 96 \quad 96 \times 1 \quad 96 \times 1$$

Each element stiffness matrix is to be placed in the global stiffness matrix appropriately. This process is called assembling global stiffness matrix. In this problem force vector F is zero at all nodes except at nodes 45, 46, 47 and 48 in x direction. For the given loading nodal equivalent forces are found and the force vector F is assembled.

Step 6 : In this problem, due to symmetry transverse displacements along AB and BC are zero. The system equation [k] {δ} = {F} is modified to see that the solution for {δ} comes out with the above values. This modification of system equation is called imposing the boundary conditions.

Step 7 : The above 96 simultaneous equations are solved using the standard numerical procedures like Gauss elimination or Choleski's decomposition techniques to get the 96 nodal displacements.

Step 8 : Now the interest of the analyst is to study the stresses at various points. In solid mechanics the relationship between the displacements and stresses are well established. The stresses at various points of interest may be found by using shape functions and the nodal displacements and then stresses calculated. The stress concentrations may be studies by comparing the values obtained at various points in the fillet zone with the values at uniform zone, far away from the fillet (which is equal to $P/b^2 t$).

8.7 FEM 1-D Elements

I-D elements are broadly classified on the load applied on them as spar or truss element for axial load, torsion element for torque load and beam element for bending in one or two planes through neutral axis/plane. Stiffness matrix of each of these elements can be derived based on the well known relations in strength of materials.

Truss Element

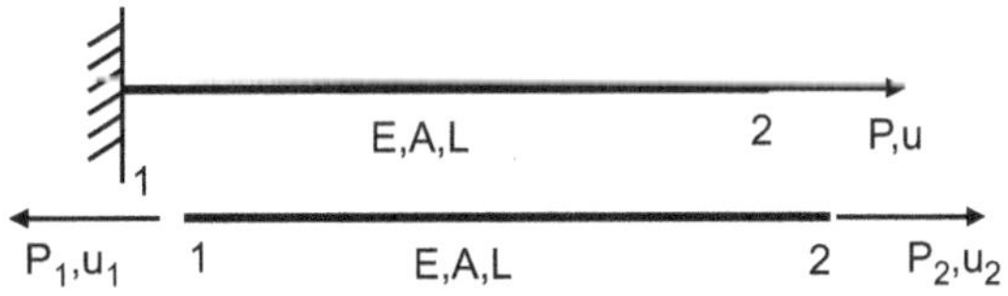

Fig. 8.7

$$\sigma = P/A = E\varepsilon = Eu/L$$

or
$$P = (AE/L)u - Ku \qquad \ldots(8.2)$$

The familiar relation for axial load carrying element fixed at one end and load applied at the free end with displacement 'u' at the free end 2.

In general, if loads P_1 and P_2 are applied at the two ends of an element resulting in displacements u_1 and u_2 at these two ends, stress is proportional to $(u_2 - u_1)$.

Then,
$$-P_1 = P_2 = \left(\frac{AE}{L}\right)(u_2 - u_1) \qquad \ldots(8.3)$$

In matrix notation,
$$\begin{Bmatrix} P_1 \\ P_2 \end{Bmatrix} = [K] \begin{Bmatrix} u_1 \\ u_2 \end{Bmatrix}$$

Where,
$$[K] = \left(\frac{AE}{L}\right) \begin{bmatrix} 1 & -1 \\ -1 & 1 \end{bmatrix} \qquad \ldots(8.4)$$

Review Questions

1. State advantages of Finite Element Method. (FEM).
2. State disadvantages of Finite Element Method. (FEM).
3. Explain the Finite Element Analysis.
4. What are the terminology of Finite Element Methods (FEM) ?
5. What are the types of Finite Elements ?
6. Explain the Interpolation Functions for General Elements.
7. Write a short note on steps in Finite Element Analysis.
8. Explain the general approach of finite element.
9. Describe the 1-D elements of Finite Element Method (FEM).

Chapter 9
FINITE DIFFERENCE METHODS

9.1 Introduction

As discussed in previous chapter, various differential equations can be solved by using methods like Euler's method, Runge Kutta method, where only initial conditions are known. But some practical problems like deflection of beam loaded with uniformly distributed load and supported at two ends, deflection is zero. These type of problems require a solution of differential equation in a given area subjected to the various conditions on the boundary of region. Practical applications like deflection of beam, falling of object due to gravity, etc. where equation is exact differential equation.

Let us consider the problem $\dfrac{d^2y}{dx^2} + f(x) \cdot \dfrac{dy}{dx} + g(x) \cdot y(x) = r(x)$

i.e. $y''_{(x)} + f(x) \cdot y'_{(x)} + g(x) \cdot y(x) = r(x)$

with boundary conditions $y(x_0) = a$ and $y(x_n) = b$.

These type of problems can be solved by :
1. Finite Difference Method,
2. The Shooting Method,
3. The Collocation Method.

Out of these three methods, finite difference method is much popular and discussed in following section.

9.2 Finite Difference Method

In this method, derivatives appearing in the differential equation and the boundary conditions are replaced by their finite difference approximations and the resulting linear system of equations are solved by standard procedures. The roots are the values of the required solution at the pivotal points.

The finite difference approximations to the various derivatives are derived as under :

If $y(x)$ and its derivatives are single valued continuous functions of x, then by Taylor's Expansion, we have

$$y_{(x+h)} = y_{(x)} + h \cdot y'_{(x)} + \dfrac{h^2}{2!} y''_{(x)} + \dfrac{h^3}{3!} y'''_{(x)} + \ldots \quad \ldots (9.1)$$

and

$$y_{(x-h)} = y_{(x)} - h \cdot y'_{(x)} + \dfrac{h^2}{2!} y''_{(x)} - \dfrac{h^3}{3!} y'''_{(x)} + \ldots \quad \ldots (9.2)$$

From equation (9.1), we get

$$y'_{(x)} = \frac{1}{h}[y_{(x+h)} - y(x)] - \frac{h}{2!}y''_{(x)} - \frac{h^3}{3!}y''''_{(x)} + \ldots$$

$$\therefore \quad y'_{(x)} = \frac{1}{h}[y_{(x+h)} - y_{(x)}] + O(h)$$

Which is **Forward Difference Approximation** of $y'_{(x)}$ with an error of the order h.

Similarly, equation (9.2) gives,

$$y'_{(x)} = \frac{1}{h}[y_{(x)} - y_{(x-h)}] + O(h)$$

Which is **Backward Difference Approximation** of error order h.

Subtracting equation (9.2) from (9.1), we get

$$y'_{(x)} = \frac{1}{2h}[y_{(x+h)} - y_{(x-h)}] + O(h^2)$$

Which is the **Central Difference Approximation** of $y'_{(x)}$ with an error of the order h^2.

Clearly central difference approximation is better than forward and backward difference approximation to $y'_{(x)}$ and hence should be preferred.

Adding equations (9.1) and (9.2), we get

$$y''_{(x)} = \frac{1}{h^2}[y_{(x+h)} - 2y_{(x)} + y_{(x-h)}] + O(h)^2$$

which is central difference approximation of $y''_{(x)}$ with error of order h^2.

Note : The accuracy of this method depends upon step size or sub-interval (h) and also on the order of approximation.

As we reduce h, accuracy improves but number of equations to be solved increases.

Generalized Equations are :

1. **Forward difference method** $\Rightarrow y'_i = \frac{1}{h}[y_{i+1} - y_i]$

2. **Backward difference method** $\Rightarrow y'_i = \frac{1}{h}[y_i - y_{i-1}]$

3. **Central difference method** $\Rightarrow y''_i = \frac{1}{h^2}[y_{i+1} - 2y_i + y_{i-1}]$

9.3 Difference between FEM and FDM -

The finite difference method (FDM) is an alternative way of approximating solutions of PDEs. The differences between FEM and FDM are :

Sr. No.	Finite Element Method	Finite Difference Method
1.	FEM make piecewise approximation i.e. it ensures the continuity at node points as well as along the sides of the element.	FDM makes pointwise approximation to the governing equations i.e. it ensures continuity only at the node points. Continuity along the sides of grid lines are not ensured.
2.	FEM can give the values at any point. However the values obtained at points other than nodes are by using suitable interpolation formulae.	FDM do not give the values at any point except at node points. It do not give any approximating function to evaluate the basic values (deflections, in case of solid mechanics) using the nodal values.
3.	FEM can consider the sloping boundaries exactly. If curved elements are used, even the curved boundaries can be handled exactly.	FDM makes stair type approximation to sloping and curved boundaries.
4.	FEM needs fewer nodes to get good results.	FDM needs larger number of nodes to get good results.
5.	The most attractive feature of the FEM is its ability to handle complicated geometries (and boundaries) with relative ease.	While FDM in its basic form is restricted to handle rectangular shapes and simple alterations.
6.	Arbitrary geometry can be modeled.	Approximations based on rectangular discretization.
7.	Boundary conditions is more systematic.	Treatment of boundary conditions needs extra care.
8.	Making higher order approximation is tedious	Making higher order approximation is easy.
9.	FEM is an indirect method - works on a weak form.	FDM is a direct method replaces differential equations by a difference.
10.	The quality of a FEM approximation is often higher than in the corresponding FDM approach, but this is extremely problem dependent and several examples to the contrary can be provided.	The quality of a FDM approximation is often lesser than in the corresponding FEM approach.

11.	Very difficult to implement.	The most attractive feature of finite differences is that it can be very easy to implement.
12.	Generally, FEM is the method of choice in all types of analysis in structural mechanics (i.e. solving for deformation and stresses in solid bodies or dynamics of structures).	Computational Fluid Dynamics (CFD) tends to use FDM or other methods like finite volume method (FVM).

SOLVED EXAMPLES

Example 9.1 : Solve the equation $\frac{d^2y}{dx^2} = x + y$ with boundary conditions $y_{(0)} = y_{(1)} = 0$, consider $h = 0.25$.

Solution : Given data : $x_0 = 0$, $y_0 = 1$

$$h = 0.25$$

$$\therefore \quad n = \frac{x_n - x_0}{h} = \frac{1-0}{0.25}$$

$$\therefore \quad n = 4$$

$$\therefore \quad x_1 = x_0 + h = 0 + 0.25$$

$$\therefore \quad x_1 = 0.25$$

$$\therefore \quad x_2 = x_1 + h$$

$$\therefore \quad x_2 = 0.25 + 0.25$$

$$\therefore \quad x_2 = 0.50$$

Similarly, $x_3 = 0.75$ and $x_4 = 1$
we have, $x_4 = 1.0$, $y_4 = 1.0$

By using generalized formula for Central Difference Method,

$$\frac{1}{h^2}[y_{i+1} - 2y_i + y_{i-1}] = y_i'' \text{ where } i = 1, 2, 3$$

$$\therefore \quad \frac{1}{(0.25)^2}[y_{i+1} - 2y_i + y_{i-1}] = x_i + y_i$$

$$\therefore \quad 16[y_{i+1} - 2y_i + y_{i-1}] = x_i + y_i$$

$$\therefore \quad 16y_{i+1} - 33y_i + y_{i+1} = x_i \quad \ldots \text{(I)}$$

By using equation (I) and substituting values $y_0 = y_4 = 0$ and $x_1 = 0.25$, $x_2 = 0.5$, and $x_3 = 0.75$

$i = 1 \Rightarrow$ $16y_2 - 33y_1 + y_0 = x_1$ $\Rightarrow$ $16y_2 - 33y_1 + 0 = 0.25$

$i = 2 \Rightarrow$ $16y_3 - 33y_2 + y_1 = x_2$ $\Rightarrow$ $16y_3 - 33y_2 + y_1 = 0.50$

$i = 3 \Rightarrow$ $16y_4 - 33y_3 + y_2 = x_3$ $\Rightarrow$ $-33y_3 + y_2 = 0.75$

Therefore,

$$-33y_1 + 16y_2 = 0.25$$

$$y_1 - 33y_2 + 16y_3 = 0.50$$
$$y_2 - 33y_3 = 0.75$$

Solving these equations simultaneously, we get
$$y_1 = -0.03488$$
$$y_2 = -0.05632$$
$$y_3 = -0.05003 \quad \text{... Ans.}$$

Example 9.2 : Solve the equation $\dfrac{d^2y}{dx^2} - \dfrac{14}{x}\dfrac{dy}{dx} + x^3 \cdot y = 2x^3$, for $y\left(\dfrac{1}{3}\right)$ and $y\left(\dfrac{2}{3}\right)$. Boundary conditions are $y(0) = 2$, $y(1) = 0$.

Solution : Given data : $x_0 = 0$, $y_0 = 2$, $h = \dfrac{1}{3}$

$\therefore \quad \dfrac{d^2y}{dx^2} - \dfrac{14}{x}\dfrac{dy}{dx} + x^3 y = 2x^3$

$\therefore \quad \dfrac{1}{h^2}[y_{i+1} - 2y_i + y_{i-1}] - \dfrac{14}{x}\left[\dfrac{1}{2h}(y_{i+1} - y_{i-1})\right] + x_i^3 \cdot y_i = 2x_i^3$

Putting $h = \dfrac{1}{3}$, we get

$$\left[1 + \dfrac{7}{3x_i}\right] y_{i-1} - \left[2 - \dfrac{1}{9}x_i^3\right] y_i + \left[1 - \dfrac{7}{3x_i}\right] y_{i+1} = \dfrac{2}{9} 2x_i^3$$

Putting $i = 1, 2$ and $x_1 = \dfrac{1}{3}$ and $x_2 = \dfrac{2}{3}$, we get

$$8y_0 - \dfrac{485}{243} y_1 - 6y_2 = \dfrac{2}{243} \quad \text{... (I)}$$

$$\dfrac{9}{2} y_1 - \dfrac{478}{243} y_2 - \dfrac{5}{2} y_3 = \dfrac{18}{243} \quad \text{... (II)}$$

Using $y_0 = y_{(0)} = 2$, $y_3 = y_{(1)} = 0$ in equations (I) and (II), we get

$$485 y_1 + 145 y_2 = 3886 \quad \text{... (III)}$$
$$218 y_1 - 956 y_2 = 36 \quad \text{... (IV)}$$

Solving equations (III) and (IV) simultaneously, we get

$$y_1 = y\left(\dfrac{1}{3}\right) = 1.0315$$

$$y_2 = y\left(\dfrac{2}{3}\right) = 2.3222 \quad \text{... Ans.}$$

Example 9.3 : Solve the equation $\dfrac{d^2y}{dx^2} - x \cdot y = 0$. Boundary conditions are $x_i = 0, \dfrac{1}{3}, \dfrac{2}{3}, 1$ and $y(1) = 1$, $y(0) + y'_{(0)} = 1.0$.

Solution : Given data :

$$\frac{d^2y}{dx^2} - xy = 0 \quad \text{i.e.} \quad y'' = xy$$

By Finite Difference Equivalent, we have

$$\frac{1}{h^2}[y_{i+1} - 2y_i + y_{i-1}] = x_i y_i$$

i.e. $\quad y_{i+1} - 2y_i + y_{i-1} = 9 \cdot x_i y_i$

∴ $\quad y_{i-1} - (2 - 9x_i) y_i + y_{i+1} = 0$ ... (I)

We have, $\quad y'_i = \dfrac{y_{i+1} - y_{i-1}}{2h}$ ... (II)

Substituting $i = 0$ in equation (II), we get

$$y'_0 = \frac{y_1 - y_{-1}}{2h}$$ ... (III)

By using Boundary Condition, we have

$$y_0 + y'_0 = 1$$

∴ $\quad y_0 + \dfrac{y_1 - y_{-1}}{2h} = 1$

$$h = \frac{1}{3}$$

∴ $\quad 2y_0 + 3(y_1 - y_{-1}) = 2$

∴ $\quad 2y_0 + 3y_1 - 3y_{-1} = 2$

∴ $\quad y_{-1} = \dfrac{2y_0 + 3y_1 - 2}{3}$ ... (IV)

In Equation (I), substituting $x_0 = 0$, $i = 0, 1, 2$, we have

$$y_{-1} - 2y_0 + y_1 = 0$$

$$y_0 - \frac{55}{27} y_1 + y_2 = 0$$

$$y_1 - \frac{56}{27} y_2 + y_3 = 0$$

Second Boundary Condition, $y_3 = 1$ and using value of y_{-1} from equation (IV), we get

$\quad -2y_0 + 3y_1 = 0 \quad \Rightarrow \quad -2y_0 + 3y_1 = 0$

$\quad y_0 - \dfrac{57}{27} y_1 + y_2 = 0 \quad \Rightarrow \quad y_0 - 2.0740\, y_1 + y_2 = 0$

$\quad y_1 - \dfrac{56}{27} y_2 = -1 \quad \Rightarrow \quad y_1 - 2.074\, y_2 = -1$

Solving these equations simultaneously, we get

$$y_0 = y_{(0)} = -0.9880$$

$$y_1 = y\left(\frac{1}{3}\right) = -0.3253$$

$$y_2 = y\left(\frac{2}{3}\right) = 0.3253 \qquad \text{... Ans.}$$

Example 9.4 : Solve the boundary value problem for $x = 0.5$

$$\frac{d^2y}{dx^2} + y + 1 = 0$$

Boundary conditions are $y_{(0)} = y_{(1)} = 0$

Solution : Given data : $x_0 = 0$, $y_0 = 0$, $x_n = 1$

Consider $h = 0.25$

$$\therefore \quad n = \frac{x_n - x_0}{h} = \frac{1-0}{0.25} = 4$$

$\therefore \quad x_1 = x_0 + h = 0.25$

$\quad\quad x_2 = x_1 + h = 0.50$

$\quad\quad x_3 = x_2 + h = 0.75$

$\quad\quad x_4 = x_3 + h = 1.0 = x_n \Rightarrow y_4 = 0$ Boundary Condition

We have

$$\frac{d^2y}{dx^2} + y + 1 = 0$$

$$\therefore \quad \frac{1}{h^2}[y_{i+1} - 2y_i + y_{i-1}] + y_i + 1 = 0$$

$$h = 0.25 = \frac{1}{4} \Rightarrow h^2 = \frac{1}{16}$$

Multiplying equation by 16, we get

$\therefore \quad y_{i+1} - 2y_i + y_{i-1} + 16y_i + 16 = 0$

$\therefore \quad y_{i-1} + 14y_i + y_{i+1} + 16 = 0$

Putting $y_0 = y_4 = 0$ – Boundary Conditions

$\therefore \quad\quad 14y_1 + y_2 = -16$

$\quad\quad\quad y_1 + 14y_2 + y_3 = -16$

$\quad\quad\quad y_2 + 14y_3 = -16$

Solving these equations simultaneously by Gauss Elimination Method, we get

$$y_2 = y_{(0.50)} = -0.989691 \qquad \text{... Ans.}$$

Example 9.5 : Solve the boundary value problem :

$xy'' + y = 0, y(1) = 1, y(2) = 2$

Solution : Given data : $x_0 = 1, y_0 = 1, x_n = 2, y_n = 2$

We have

$$x \cdot y'' + y = 0$$

By using difference formula, we get

$$x \times \frac{1}{h^2} [y_{i+1} - 2y_i + y_{i-1}] + \frac{1}{2h} [y_{i+1} - y_{i-1}] = 0 \qquad \ldots (I)$$

Take h = 0.25

$$\therefore \quad n = \frac{x_n - x_0}{h} = \frac{2-1}{0.25} = 4$$

$$\therefore \quad x_0 = 1$$

$$x_1 = x_0 + h$$

$$\therefore \quad x_1 = 0.25, x_2 = 0.50, x_3 = 0.75, x_4 = 1.0$$

We have, $\quad y_0 = 1.0, y_4 = 2.0 \quad$ Boundary Conditions

Substituting h = 0.25 = $\frac{1}{4}$ in equation (I), we get

$$x_i \times \frac{1}{16} [y_{i+1} - 2y_i + y_{i-1}] + \frac{1}{8} [y_{i+1} - y_{i-1}] = 0$$

Multiplying equation by 16,

$$x_i [y_{i+1} - 2y_i + y_{i-1}] + 2 [y_{i+1} - y_{i-1}] = 0$$

$\therefore \quad x_i y_{i+1} - 2x_i y_i + x_i \cdot y_{i-1} + 2y_{i+1} - 2y_{i-1} = 0$

$\therefore \quad (x_i + 2) y_{i+1} - 2x_i \cdot y_i + (x_i - 2) y_{i-1} = 0$

$\therefore \quad (x_i - 2) y_{i-1} - 2x_i y_i + (x_i + 2) y_{i+1} = 0$

$\quad (x_i - 2) \cdot y_{i-1} - 2x_i y_i + (x_i + 2) y_{i+1} = 0$

Substituting i = 1, 2, 3 and $x_1 = 0.25, x_2 = 0.5$ and $x_3 = 0.75$, we get

$(x_1 - 2) \cdot y_0 - 2x_1 \cdot y_1 + (x_1 + 2) \cdot y_2 = 0 \Rightarrow -1.75 y_0 - 0.5 y_1 + 2.25 y_2 = 0$

$(x_2 - 2) \cdot y_1 - 2x_2 \cdot y_2 + (x_2 + 2) \cdot y_3 = 0 \Rightarrow -1.50 y_1 - y_2 + 2.50 y_3 = 0$

$(x_3 - 2) \cdot y_1 - 2x_3 \cdot y_3 + (x_3 + 2) \cdot y_4 = 0 \Rightarrow -1.25 y_2 - 1.5 y_3 + 2.75 y_4 = 0$

Boundary Conditions $\Rightarrow y_0 = 1$ and $y_4 = 2$

$\therefore \qquad -1.75 - 0.5 y_1 + 2.25 y_2 = 0$

$\Rightarrow \qquad -0.5 y_1 + 2.25 y_2 = 1.75$

$\qquad -1.5 y_1 - y_2 + 2.5 y_3 = 0$

$\therefore \qquad -1.25 y_2 - 1.5 y_3 + 5.5 = 0$

$\Rightarrow \qquad -1.25 y_2 - 1.5 y_3 = -5.50$

Solving these equations simultaneously by Gauss Elimination Method, we get

$$y_1 = y_{(0.25)} = -3.50$$
$$y_2 = y_{(0.50)} = 1.35$$
$$y_3 = y_{(0.75)} = 1.56 \quad \text{... Ans.}$$

Example 9.6 : *Solve the boundary value problem* $\frac{d^2y}{dx^2} - 64y + 10 = 0$ *with* $y(0) = y(1) = 0$. *Using finite difference method, calculate* $y(0.5)$, *taking step size* $h = 0.025$.

Solution : Given data : Boundary Conditions $x_0 = 0$, $y_0 = 0$

$$x_n = 1, \; y_n = 0$$
$$h = 0.25$$

$\therefore \qquad n = \dfrac{x_n - x_0}{h}$

$$= \dfrac{1 - 0}{0.25}$$

$\therefore \qquad n = 4$
$\therefore \qquad x_0 = 0$
$\therefore \qquad x_1 = 0 + 0.25 = 0.25$
$\therefore \qquad x_2 = 0.25 + 0.25 = 0.50$
$\therefore \qquad x_3 = 0.50 + 0.25 = 0.75$
$\therefore \qquad x_4 = 0.75 + 0.25 = 1.0 = x_n$ and $y_4 = 0$

Differential Equation $\Rightarrow \quad \dfrac{d^2y}{dx^2} = 64y + 10 = 0$

By Finite Difference Equivalent for $\dfrac{d^2y}{dx^2}$, we have

$$\dfrac{1}{h^2}[y_{i+1} - 2y_i + y_{i-1}] - 64\,y_i + 10 = 0$$

Since $h = 0.25 = \dfrac{1}{4}$, we have

$$[y_{i+1} - 2y_i + y_{i-1}] - 64\,y_i + 10 = 0$$

$\therefore \qquad 16\,[y_{i+1} - 2y_i + y_{i-1}] - 64\,y_i + 10 = 0$
$\therefore \qquad 16\,y_{i+1} - 32\,y_i + 16\,y_{i-1} - 64\,y_i + 10 = 0$
$\therefore \qquad 16\,y_{i+1} - 96\,y_i + 16\,y_{i-1} + 10 = 0$

$$y_{i+1} - 6\,y_i + y_{i-1} = -\dfrac{10}{16}$$

$$y_{i+1} - 6\,y_i + y_{i-1} = -\dfrac{5}{8} \qquad \text{... (I)}$$

By using i = 1, 2, 3 in equation (I), we get

$$y_2 - 6y_1 + y_0 = -\frac{5}{8}$$

$$y_3 - 6y_2 + y_1 = -\frac{5}{8}$$

$$y_4 - 6y_3 + y_2 = -\frac{5}{8}$$

Since $y_0 = 0$ and $y_4 = 0$, we have

$$y_2 - 6y_1 = -\frac{5}{8} \Rightarrow -6y_1 + y_2 = -\frac{5}{8} \quad ...(II)$$

$$y_3 - 6y_2 + y_1 = -\frac{5}{8} \Rightarrow y_1 - 6y_2 + y_3 = -\frac{5}{8} \quad ...(III)$$

$$-6y_3 + y_2 = -\frac{5}{8} \Rightarrow y_2 - 6y_3 = -\frac{5}{8} \quad ...(IV)$$

By solving equations (II), (III) and (IV) simultaneously, we get

$$\begin{bmatrix} -6 & 1 & 0 \\ 1 & -6 & 1 \\ 0 & 1 & -6 \end{bmatrix} \begin{bmatrix} y_1 \\ y_2 \\ y_3 \end{bmatrix} = \begin{bmatrix} -\frac{5}{8} \\ -\frac{5}{8} \\ -\frac{5}{8} \end{bmatrix}$$

$$y_1 = 0.1287 = y(0.25)$$
$$y_2 = 0.1471 = y(0.50)$$
$$y_3 = 0.1287 = y(0.75) \qquad \text{... Ans.}$$

Example 9.7 : The deflection of a strut with one end built in (x = 0) and other subjected to end thrust P, satisfies the equation

$$\frac{d^2y}{dx^2} + 4y = 0.1\,(40 - x)$$

subjected to boundary conditions $\quad y(0) = 0,\ y(40) = 0$

Considering h = 10, find out y(10), y(20), y(30)

Solution : Given data : h = 10, $x_0 = 0$, $x_1 = 10$, $x_2 = 20$, $x_3 = 30$, $x_4 = 40$

$$\frac{d^2y}{dx^2} + 4y = 4 - 0.1\,x$$

By using Finite Difference Equivalent for $\frac{d^2y}{dx^2}$, we have

$$\frac{1}{h^2}[y_{i+1} - 2y_i + y_{i-1}] + 4y_i = 4 - 0.1 x_i$$

Since h = 10

∴ $$\frac{1}{100}[y_{i+1} - 2y_i + y_{i-1}] + 4y_i = 4 - 0.1 x_i$$

∴ $y_{i+1} - 2y_i + y_{i-1} + 400 y_i = 400 - 10 x_i$

∴ $y_{i+1} + 399 y_i + y_{i-1} = 400 - 10 x_i$ ... (I)

Substituting i = 1, 2, 3, we get

$y_2 + 399 y_1 + y_0 = 400 - 10 x_1 = 400 - 10 \times 10$

∴ $y_0 + 399 y_1 + y_2 = 300$ ... (II)

$y_3 + 399 y_2 + y_1 = 400 - 10 x_2 = 400 - 10 \times 20$

∴ $y_1 + 399 y_2 + y_3 = 200$ ... (III)

$y_4 + 399 y_3 + y_2 = 400 - 10 x_3 = 400 - 10 \times 30$

∴ $y_2 + 399 y_3 + y_4 = 100$ ... (IV)

$y_0 + 399 y_1 + y_2 = 300$

$y_1 + 399 y_2 + y_3 = 200$

$y_2 + 399 y_3 + y_4 = 100$

Since $y_0 = 0$ and $y_4 = 0$

∴ $399 y_1 + y_2 = 300$

$y_1 + 399 y_2 + y_3 = 200$

$y_2 + 399 y_3 = 100$

By solving above equations, we get

$$\begin{bmatrix} 399 & 1 & 0 \\ 1 & 399 & 1 \\ 0 & 1 & 399 \end{bmatrix} \begin{bmatrix} y_1 \\ y_2 \\ y_3 \end{bmatrix} = \begin{bmatrix} 100 \\ 200 \\ 300 \end{bmatrix}$$

∴ $y_1 = 0.2494 = y(100)$

∴ $y_2 = 0.4987 = y(200)$

∴ $y_3 = 0.7506 = y(100)$

Example 9.8 : A cantilever beam of length 'l' and weighing 'w' kg per meter is subjected to horizontal compressive force 'P' at free end.

The governing differential equation is given by $\frac{d^2 y}{dx^2} + 0.001 y = (-2 \times 10^{-6}) x^2$.

Initial boundary condition is given by,

y(0) = 0 and y(1000) = 1 mm, find out y(250), y(500) and y(750).

Solution : Given data :

$$\frac{d^2y}{dx^2} + 0.001\, y = -0.02\, x^2$$

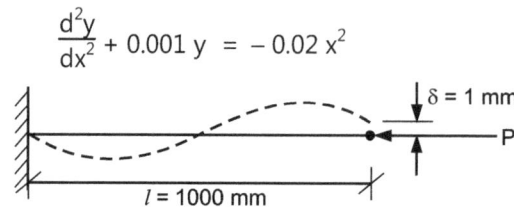

Fig. 9.1

$x_0 = 0$, $y_0 = 0$, $x_1 = 250$, $x_2 = 500$, $x_3 = 750$, $x_4 = 1000$, $y_4 = 1$ mm.

By Definite Difference Equivalent of $\frac{d^2y}{dx^2}$, we have

$$\frac{1}{h^2}[y_{i+1} - 2y_i + y_{i-1}] + 0.001\, y_i = (-2 \times 10^{-6}) \cdot x_i^2$$

Since $h = 250$, multiply by 62500, we get

$$\frac{63500}{(250)^2}[y_{i+1} - 2y_i + y_{i-1}] + 62500 \times 0.001\, y_i = 62500 \times (-2 \times 10^{-6})\, x_i^2$$

$$y_{i+1} - 2y_i + y_{i+1} + 62.5\, y_i = -0.1250\, x_i^2$$

∴ $\qquad y_{i-1} + 60.5\, y_i + y_{i+1} = -0.1250\, x_i^2$

For $i = 1$, we get

$$y_0 + 60.5\, y_i + y_2 = -0.1250 \times (250)^2$$

∴ $\qquad y_0 + 60.5\, y_1 + y_2 = 7812.5$

∴ $\qquad 60.5\, y_1 + y_2 = 7812.5$

∴ $\qquad y_0 = 0$ ... (I)

For $i = 2$,

$$y_1 + 60.5\, y_2 + y_3 = -0.1250 \times (500)^2$$

∴ $\qquad y_1 + 60.5\, y_2 + y_3 = -31250$ ... (II)

For $i = 3$

$$y_2 + 60.5\, y_3 + y_4 = -0.1250 \times (750)^2$$

∴ $\qquad y_2 + 60.5\, y_3 + y_4 = -70313$

∵ $\qquad y_4 = 0, \Rightarrow y_2 + 60.5\, y_3 = -70313$ ... (III)

Solving (I), (II), (III) simultaneously we get

$$y_1 = 0.1374 = y(250)$$
$$y_2 = -0.4997 = y(500)$$
$$y_3 = -1.1539 = y(750) \qquad \text{... Ans.}$$

Example 9.9 : It has found experimentally that acceleration of a spring loaded with weight 'w' at time 't' is given by

$$\frac{d^2y}{dt^2} = -0.1 \times \frac{196}{3} \cos \frac{14}{\sqrt{3}} t$$

Given conditions :

$$y(0) = 15 \text{ cm}$$
$$y(2) = 5 \text{ cm}$$

Find displacement at t = 1 sec.

Solution : Given data : h = 1 sec.

t = 0, y_0 = 15 cm

t = 2, y_2 = 5 cm

By Law,

$$\frac{d^2y}{dt^2} = -0.1 \times \frac{196}{3} \cos \frac{14}{\sqrt{3}} t$$

$$\frac{1}{h^2}[y_{i-1} - 2y_i + y_{i+1}] + 0.1 \times \frac{196}{3} \cos \frac{14}{\sqrt{3}} \cos \frac{14}{\sqrt{3}} t_i = 0$$

∴ For i = 1, we have

$$y_0 - 2y_i + y_2 + 0.1 \times \frac{196}{3} \cos \left(\frac{14}{\sqrt{3}} \times t_1\right) = 0$$

∴ $15 - 2y_1 + 5 + 0.1 \times \frac{196}{3} \cos \left(\frac{14}{\sqrt{3}} \times 1\right) = 0$

∴ $20 + 0.1 \times \frac{196}{3} \times (-0.2269) = 2y_1$

∴ $y_1 = \frac{1}{2}(20 - 1.4826)$

∴ **y_1 = 9.2587 = y(1)** ... Ans.

Example 9.10 : A non-insulated metallic bar of 1 m long is held in a air which is at temperature of 20°C.

One end of the bar is maintained at 100°C while the other is at 40°C. The temperature distribution along the length at steady state may be assumed as :

$$\frac{d^2T}{dx^2} + h(T_a - T) = 0$$

where T is the temperature in degree Celcius, x is the distance from hot end, T_a is atmospheric temperature in °C and h = 0.01.

Calculate the rod temperature at 250 mm, 500 mm and 750 mm from the hot end.

Solution : Given data :

$$\frac{d^2T}{dx^2} + h(T_a - T) = 0 \quad \ldots (I)$$

$$\therefore \quad \frac{d^2T}{dx^2} = -h \cdot (T_a - T)$$

$$\therefore \quad \frac{d^2T}{dx^2} = -0.01(20 - T) \quad \text{where } h = 0.01 \text{ and } T_a = 20°C$$

$$\therefore \quad \frac{d^2T}{dx^2} = 0.01\,T - 0.20$$

Boundary Conditions are given as follows :
At $x = x_0 = 0$ mm, $T = T_0 = 100°C$
At $x = x_n = 1000$ mm, $T_{(n)} = 40°C$

By using Finite Difference Equation for equation (I), we get

$$\frac{d^2T}{dx^2} - 0.01\,T = -0.20$$

$$\frac{T_{i+1} - 2T_i + T_{i-1}}{h^2} - 0.01\,T_i = -0.20$$

where $h = 250$ mm or 0.25 m

$$\therefore \quad T_{i+1} - 2T_i + T_{i-1} - 0.01\,T_i \times h^2 = -0.20\,h^2$$

$$\therefore \quad T_{i+1} - (2 + 0.01 \times h^2)T_i + T_{i-1} = -0.2\,h^2$$

For $i = 1, 2, 3$, we have

$$T_2 - 2T_1 + T_0 = -0.2 \times (0.25)^2$$

$$\Rightarrow \quad T_0 - 2T_1 + T_2 = -0.00125$$

$$T_1 - 2T_2 + T_3 = -0.00125$$

$$T_2 - 2T_3 + T_4 = -0.00125$$

But $T_0 = 100°C$, $T_4 = 40°C$

$$\therefore \quad -2T_1 + T_2 = -0.00125 - 100 = -100.00125$$

$$T_1 - 2T_2 + T_3 = -0.00125$$

$$T_2 - 2T_3 = -0.00125 - 40 = -40.00125$$

We have

$$\begin{bmatrix} -2 & 1 & 0 \\ 1 & -2 & 1 \\ 0 & 1 & -2 \end{bmatrix} \begin{bmatrix} T_1 \\ T_2 \\ T_3 \end{bmatrix} = \begin{bmatrix} -10.00125 \\ -0.00125 \\ -40.00125 \end{bmatrix}$$

$\therefore$ Temperature distribution in rod is

$$T_0 = T_{(0)} = 100°C \text{ (Given)}$$

$T_1 = T_{(250)} = 84.93°C$

$T_2 = T_{(500)} = 70.0025°C$

$T_3 = T_{(750)} = 55.009°C$

$T_4 = T_{(1000)} = 40°C$ (Given) ... Ans.

9.4 Introduction to Partial Differential Equations

As per discussion in previous chapter, differential equation involving two or more than two independent variables is known as Partial Differential Equation.

Example, $\dfrac{\partial^2 u}{\partial x^2} + \dfrac{\partial^2 u}{\partial y^2} = f(x, y)$

where u is dependent variable, and x and y are independent variables.

Partial Differential Equation has wide spread applications in science and engineering field.

General form of Partial Differential Equation is given by

$$A \cdot \dfrac{\partial^2 u}{\partial x^2} + B \cdot \dfrac{\partial^2 u}{\partial x \cdot \partial y} + C \dfrac{\partial^2 u}{\partial y^2} + D = 0$$

where, A, B, C are functions of x and y, and D is a function of x, y, u, $\dfrac{\partial u}{\partial x}$ and $\dfrac{\partial u}{\partial y}$.

Depending upon the values of A, B and C, Partial Differential Equations are classified as :

$B^2 - 4AC = 0$ — Parabolic equation

$B^2 - 4AC < 0$ — Elliptical equation

$B^2 - 4AC > 0$ — Hyperbolic equation

9.5 Finite Difference Approximation to Partial Derivatives

Consider a rectangular region in x, y plane. This rectangular region is divided into a mesh of size h in x direction and k in y direction.

The points of intersection of dividing lines are called as mesh points, nodes or grid points.

As per discussion in previous section, the finite difference approximations for partial derivatives in x-direction are

$$u_x = \dfrac{\partial u}{\partial x} = \dfrac{u(x+h, y) - u(x, y)}{h} + O(h)$$

$$= \dfrac{u(x, y) - u(x-h, y)}{h} + O(h)$$

$$= \dfrac{u(x+h, y) - u(x-h, y)}{2h} + O(h)^2$$

and $u_{xx} = \dfrac{\partial^2 u}{\partial x^2} = \dfrac{u(x-h, y) - 2u(x, y) + u(x+h, y)}{h^2} + O(h^2)$

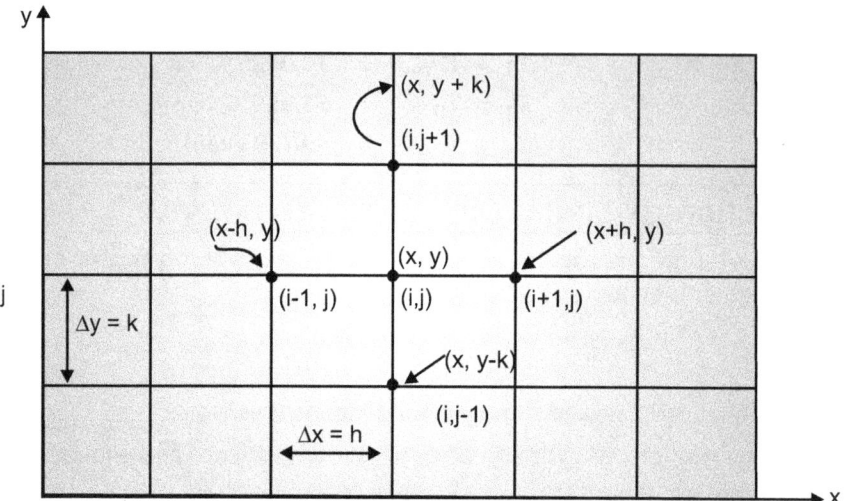

Fig. 9.2

Writing these approximations $u(x,y)$ as $u_{i,j}$ and neglecting error terms, we get

$$u_x = \frac{u_{i+1,j} - u_{i,j}}{h} \quad \ldots (9.3)$$

$$= \frac{u_{i,j} - u_{i-1,j}}{h} \quad \ldots (9.4)$$

$$= \frac{u_{i+1,j} - u_{i-1,j}}{2h} \quad \ldots (9.5)$$

and $$u_{xx} = \frac{u_{i-1,j} - 2u_{i,j} + u_{i+1,j}}{h^2} \quad \ldots (9.6)$$

Similarly, approximations for partial derivatives w.r.t. y, we get

$$u_y = \frac{u_{i,j+1} - u_{i,j}}{k} \quad \ldots (9.7)$$

$$= \frac{u_{i,j} - u_{i,j-1}}{k} \quad \ldots (9.8)$$

$$= \frac{u_{i,j+1} - u_{i,j-1}}{2k} \quad \ldots (9.9)$$

and $$u_{yy} = \frac{u_{i,j-1} - 2u_{i,j} + u_{i,j+1}}{k^2} \quad \ldots (9.10)$$

Replacing the derivatives in any partial differential equation by their corresponding difference approximation given in equations (9.3) to (9.10), we obtain finite-difference analogues of the given equation.

9.6 ELLIPTICAL EQUATIONS

Consider Partial Differential Equation :

$$A \cdot \frac{\partial^2 u}{\partial x^2} + B \cdot \frac{\partial^2 u}{\partial x \partial y} + C \cdot \frac{\partial^2 u}{\partial y^2} + D = 0$$

If $B^2 - 4AC < 0$, then equation is called as Elliptic Equation.

e.g.
$$\frac{\partial^2 u}{\partial x^2} + \frac{\partial^2 u}{\partial y^2} = 0$$

– Laplace Equation (steady-state flow and potential problems)

$$\frac{\partial^2 u}{\partial x^2} + \frac{\partial^2 u}{\partial y^2} = f(x, y)$$

– Poisson's Equation (fluid mechanics, torsion, magnetism problems)

9.6.1 Laplace Equation

Consider rectangle for which u(x, y) is known at the boundary as shown in Fig. 9.3. Let divide this region in square mesh having size h in x-direction and k in y-direction.

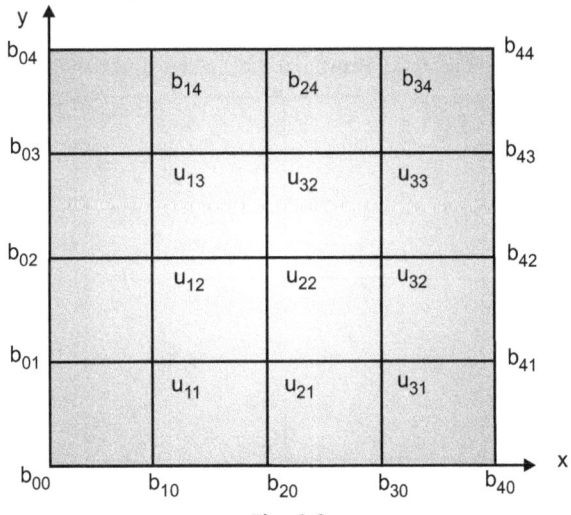

Fig. 9.3

Laplace equation is given by

$$\frac{\partial^2 u}{\partial x^2} + \frac{\partial^2 u}{\partial y^2} = 0 \quad \text{i.e.} \quad u_{xx} + u_{yy} = 0 \quad \ldots (9.11)$$

Replacing the derivatives with difference approximations, we have

$$\frac{1}{h^2}[u_{i-1,j} - 2u_{i,j} + u_{i+1,j}] + \frac{1}{k^2}[u_{i,j-1} - 2u_{i,j} + u_{i,j+1}] = 0 \quad \ldots (9.12)$$

When h = k = 1 (unit) then by simplifying equation (II), we get

$$u_{i,j} = \frac{1}{4}[u_{i-1,j} + u_{i+1,j} + u_{i,j-1} + u_{i,j+1}] \qquad \ldots (9.13)$$

As per equation (9.13), value of u of interior point is average of values of its neighbouring points as shown in Fig. 9.4. Formula (9.13) is known as Standard 5 Point Formula.

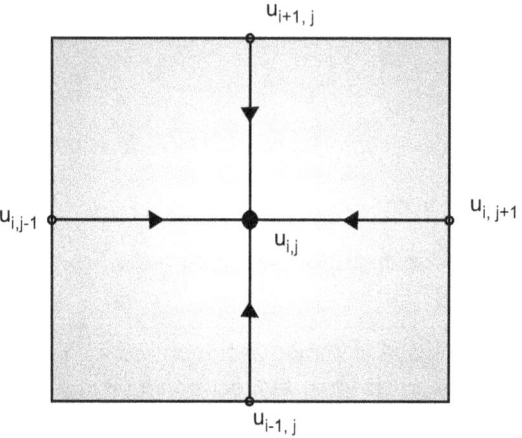

Fig. 9.4 : Standard 5 point formula

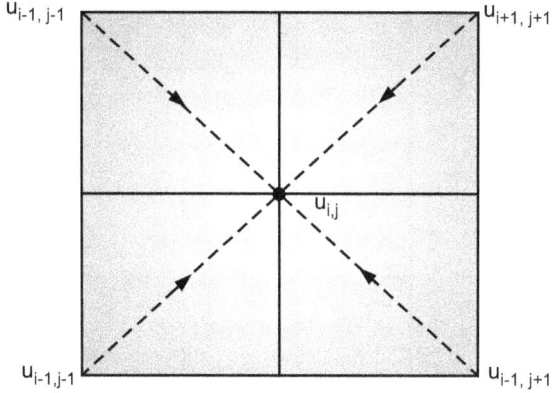

Fig. 9.5 : Diagonal 5 point formula

In case, values of neighboring points are not available, then value of $u_{i,j}$ is calculated as average of its neighboring diagonal points as shown in Fig. 9.5. It is called as diagonal 5-point formula.

$$u_{i,j} = \frac{1}{4}[u_{i-1,j+1} + u_{i+1,j-1} + u_{i-1,j-1} + u_{i+1,j+1}] \qquad \ldots (9.14)$$

Note : Diagonal 5-point formula is less accurate than standard 5-point formula, but it can be used to get initial guess value only, if alternate is not possible.

SOLVED EXAMPLES

Example 9.11 : Solve $\dfrac{\partial^2 u}{\partial x^2} + \dfrac{\partial^2 u}{\partial y^2} = 0$, correct upto 3 decimal places for boundary values as shown in Fig. 9.6.

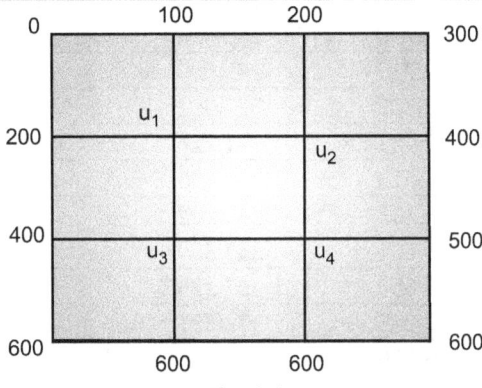

Fig. 9.6

Solution : To get initial values of u_1, u_2, u_3 and u_4, we assume $u_4 = 0$ and by using standard formulae, we get

$$u_1^{(0)} = \frac{1}{4}[0 + u_4 + 200 + 400] \qquad \text{... by diagonal formula}$$

$$u_1^{(0)} = \frac{1}{4}[0 + 0 + 200 + 400] = 150$$

$$u_2^{(0)} = \frac{1}{4}[u_1 + 400 + 200 + u_4] \qquad \text{... standard 5-point formula}$$

$$= \frac{1}{4}[150 + 400 + 200 + 0]$$

$$\therefore \quad u_2 = 187.50$$

$$u_3^{(0)} = \frac{1}{4}[400 + u_4 + u_1 + 600] \qquad \text{... standard 5-point formula}$$

$$\therefore \quad u_3^{(0)} = 287.50$$

Now, by using Standard 5-Point Formula, we have

$$u_1^{(i)} = \frac{1}{4}\left[100 + 200 + u_2^{(i-1)} + u_3^{(i-1)}\right]$$

$$u_2^{(i)} = \frac{1}{4}\left[u_1^{(i)} + 400 + 200 + u_4^{(i-1)}\right]$$

$$u_3^{(i)} = \frac{1}{4}\left[u_1^{(i)} + 400 + 600 + u_4^{(i-1)}\right]$$

$$u_4^{(i)} = \frac{1}{4}\left[u_3^{(i)} + 500 + 600 + u_2^{(i)}\right]$$

By using above four equations and by iterations, we get

Iteration No. (i)	u_1	u_2	u_3	u_4
0	150.000	187.500	287.500	0.000
1	193.750	198.438	298.438	399.219
2	199.219	299.609	399.609	449.805
3	249.805	324.902	424.902	462.451
4	262.451	331.226	431.226	465.613
5	265.613	332.806	432.806	466.403
6	266.403	333.202	433.202	466.601
7	266.601	333.300	433.300	466.650
8	266.650	333.325	433.325	466.663
9	266.663	333.331	433.331	466.666
10	266.666	333.333	433.333	466.666

∴ Required solution is

u_1 = 266.666
u_2 = 333.333
u_3 = 433.333
u_4 = 466.666

Example 9.12 : Solve Laplace equation $u_{xx} + u_{yy} = 0$ for following square mesh with boundary conditions.

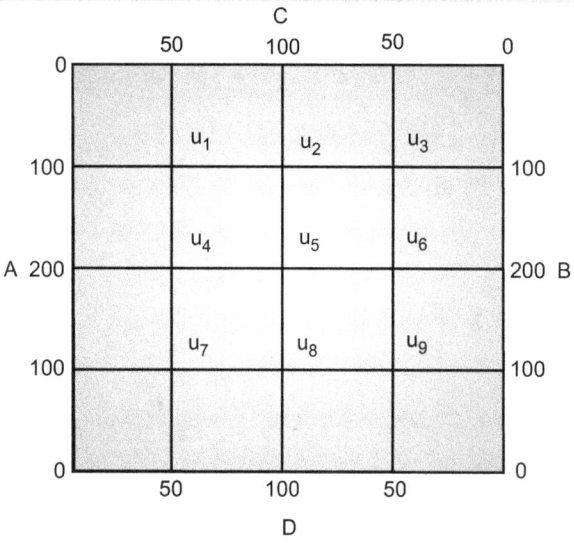

Fig. 9.7

Solution : Since mesh is symmetrical about AB and CD.

∴ $\quad u_1 = u_7 = u_9 = u_3$

Therefore it is sufficient to find u_1, u_2, u_4 and u_5 to get complete solution.

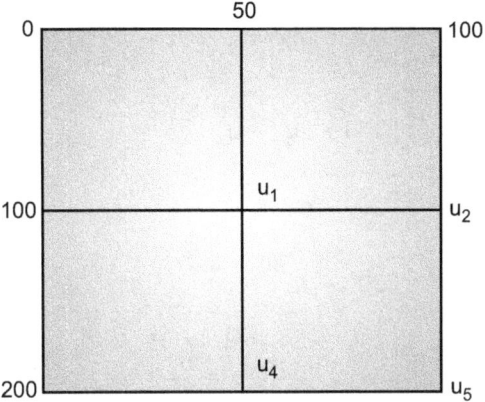

Fig. 9.8

We have,

$$u_5 = \frac{1}{4}[100 + 100 + 200 + 200] \quad \text{... Standard 5-point formula}$$

$$u_5^{(0)} = 150$$

$$u_1 = \frac{1}{4}[0 + 200 + 100 + u_5]$$

$$u_1 = \frac{1}{4}[0 + 200 + 100 + 150] \quad \text{... Diagonal 5-point formula}$$

∴ $\quad u_1^{(0)} = 112.5$

$$u_2 = \frac{1}{4}[u_1 + 100 + u_3 + u_5] \quad \text{... } u_1 = u_3 = 112.5$$

$$u_2 = \frac{1}{4}[112.5 + 100 + 112.5 + 150] \quad \text{... Standard 5-point formula}$$

∴ $\quad u_2^{(0)} = 118.75$

$$u_4 = \frac{1}{4}[u_1 + u_5 + u_7 + 200] \quad \text{... } u_1 = u_7 = 112.5$$

$$u_4 = \frac{1}{4}[112.5 + 150 + 112.5 + 200] \text{ ... Standard 5-point formula}$$

∴ $\quad u_4^{(0)} = 143.75$

Now, by using values of $u_1^{(0)}, u_2^{(0)}, u_4^{(0)}$ and $u_5^{(0)}$ and standard 5-point formula, we get

$$u_1^{(i)} = \frac{1}{4}\left[50 + u_2^{(i-1)} + u_4^{(i-1)} + 100\right] \quad \ldots \text{(I)}$$

$$u_2^{(i)} = \frac{1}{4}\left[100 + u_3^{(i-1)} + u_5^{(i-1)} + u_1^{i}\right]$$

∴ $$u_2^{(i)} = \frac{1}{4}\left[100 + 2u_1^{(i)} + u_5^{(i-1)}\right] \quad \because u_1 = u_3 \quad \ldots \text{(II)}$$

$$u_4^{(i)} = \frac{1}{4}\left[200 + u_1^{(i)} + u_5^{(i-1)} + u_7^{(i)}\right] \quad \ldots u_1 = u_7$$

∴ $$u_4^{(i)} = \frac{1}{4}\left[200 + 2u_1^{(i)} + u_5^{(i-1)}\right] \quad \ldots \text{(III)}$$

$$u_5^{(i)} = \frac{1}{4}\left[u_4^{(i)} + u_2^{(i)} + u_6^{(i)} + u_8^{(i)}\right] \quad \ldots u_2 = u_8 \text{ and } u_4 = u_6$$

∴ $$u_5^{(i)} = \frac{1}{4}\left[2u_4^{(i)} + 2u_2^{(i)}\right] \quad \ldots \text{(IV)}$$

By using equations (I), (II), (III) and (IV) upto 15th iterations, we get

$u_1 = u_3 = u_7 = u_9 = 93.751$

$u_4 = u_6 = 125.001$

$u_2 = u_8 = 100.001$

$u_5 = 112.501$

Iteration No. (i)	u_1	u_2	u_3	u_4
0	112.500	118.750	143.750	150.00
1	103.125	114.063	139.063	126.563
2	100.781	107.031	132.031	119.531
3	97.266	103.516	128.516	116.016
4	95.508	101.758	126.758	114.258
5	94.629	100.879	125.879	113.379
6	94.189	100.439	125.439	112.939
7	93.970	100.220	125.220	112.720
8	93.860	100.110	125.110	112.610
9	93.805	100.055	125.055	112.555
10	93.777	100.027	125.027	112.527
11	93.764	100.014	125.014	112.514

12	93.757	100.007	125.007	112.507
13	93.753	100.003	125.003	112.503
14	93.752	100.002	125.002	112.502
15	93.751	100.001	125.001	112.501

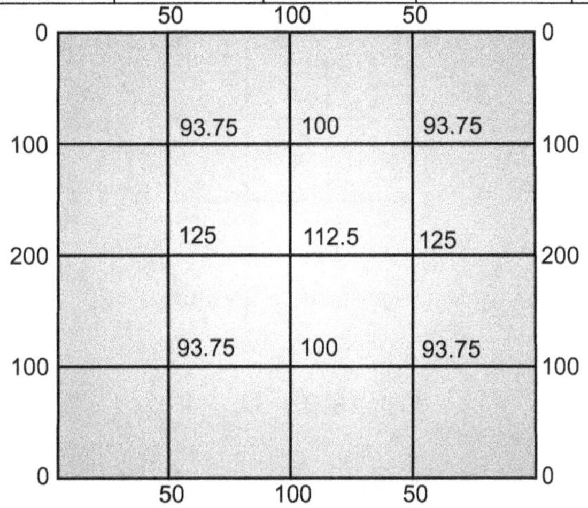

Fig. 9.9

Example 9.13 : A steel plate of 150 mm × 150 mm has its four sides held at 100, 80, 50 and 0°C as shown in Fig. 9.10. Estimate the steady-state temperature distribution at interior points assuming grid size of 50 mm.

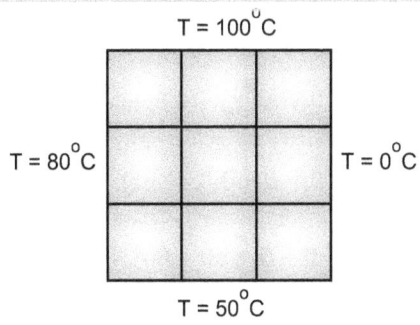

Fig. 9.10

Solution : By using standard 5-point formula, we get

$$u_1 = \frac{1}{4}(100 + u_2 + u_3 + 80)$$

$$u_2 = \frac{1}{4}(100 + 0 + u_4 + u_1)$$

$$u_3 = \frac{1}{4}(u_1 + u_4 + 50 + 80)$$

$$u_4 = \frac{1}{4}(u_2 + 0 + 50 + u_3)$$

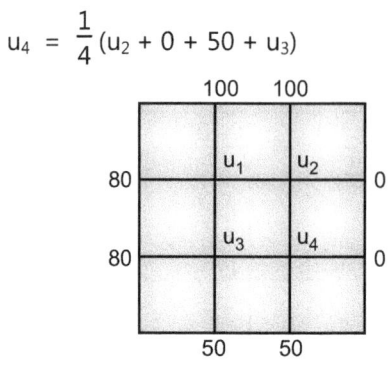

Fig. 9.11

To get initial values of u_1, u_2, u_3 and u_4 assume u_2, u_3 and $u_4 = 0$.

Iteration (1) :

$$u_1^{(1)} = \frac{1}{4}(100 + 0 + 0 + 80) = 45$$

$$u_2^{(1)} = \frac{1}{4}(100 + 0 + 0 + 45) = 36.25$$

$$u_3^{(1)} = \frac{1}{4}(45 + 0 + 50 + 80) = 43.75$$

$$u_4^{(1)} = \frac{1}{4}(36.25 + 0 + 50 + 43.75) = 32.50$$

Iteration (2) :

$$u_1^{(2)} = \frac{1}{4}(100 + 36.25 + 43.75 + 80) = 65.0$$

$$u_2^{(2)} = \frac{1}{4}(100 + 0 + 32.5 + 65) = 49.375$$

$$u_3^{(2)} = \frac{1}{4}(65.0 + 0 + 50 + 80) = 56.875$$

$$u_4^{(2)} = \frac{1}{4}(49.375 + 0 + 50 + 56.875) = 39.063$$

Iteration (3) :

$$u_1^{(3)} = 71.563$$

$$u_2^{(3)} = 52.656$$

$$u_3^{(3)} = 60.156$$

$$u_4^{(3)} = 40.703$$

Iteration (4) :

$$u_1^{(4)} = 73.203$$
$$u_2^{(4)} = 53.477$$
$$u_3^{(4)} = 60.977$$
$$u_4^{(4)} = 41.113$$

Iteration (5) :

$$u_1^{(5)} = 71.613$$
$$u_2^{(5)} = 53.682$$
$$u_3^{(5)} = 61.182$$
$$u_4^{(5)} = 41.216$$

After 10th iteration, we get

$$u_1^{(10)} = 73.750$$
$$u_2^{(10)} = 53.750$$
$$u_3^{(10)} = 61.250$$
$$u_4^{(10)} = 41.250$$

9.6.2 Algorithm-Laplace Method

1. Input size of square plate.
2. h=1.
3. Calculate n.
4. Assign all elements of matrix u = 0.
5. Input boundary conditions, number of iterations and accuracy.
6. for k =1 to itn, inc. itn by 1.
7. maxerr = 0.
8. for i =2 to n-1, inc. i by 1.
9. for j =2 to n-1, inc. j by 1.
10. Calculate t and err.
11. if err > acc, then err = maxerr.
12. u(i,j) = t.
13. End j.
14. End i.
15. Print results.
16. End k.

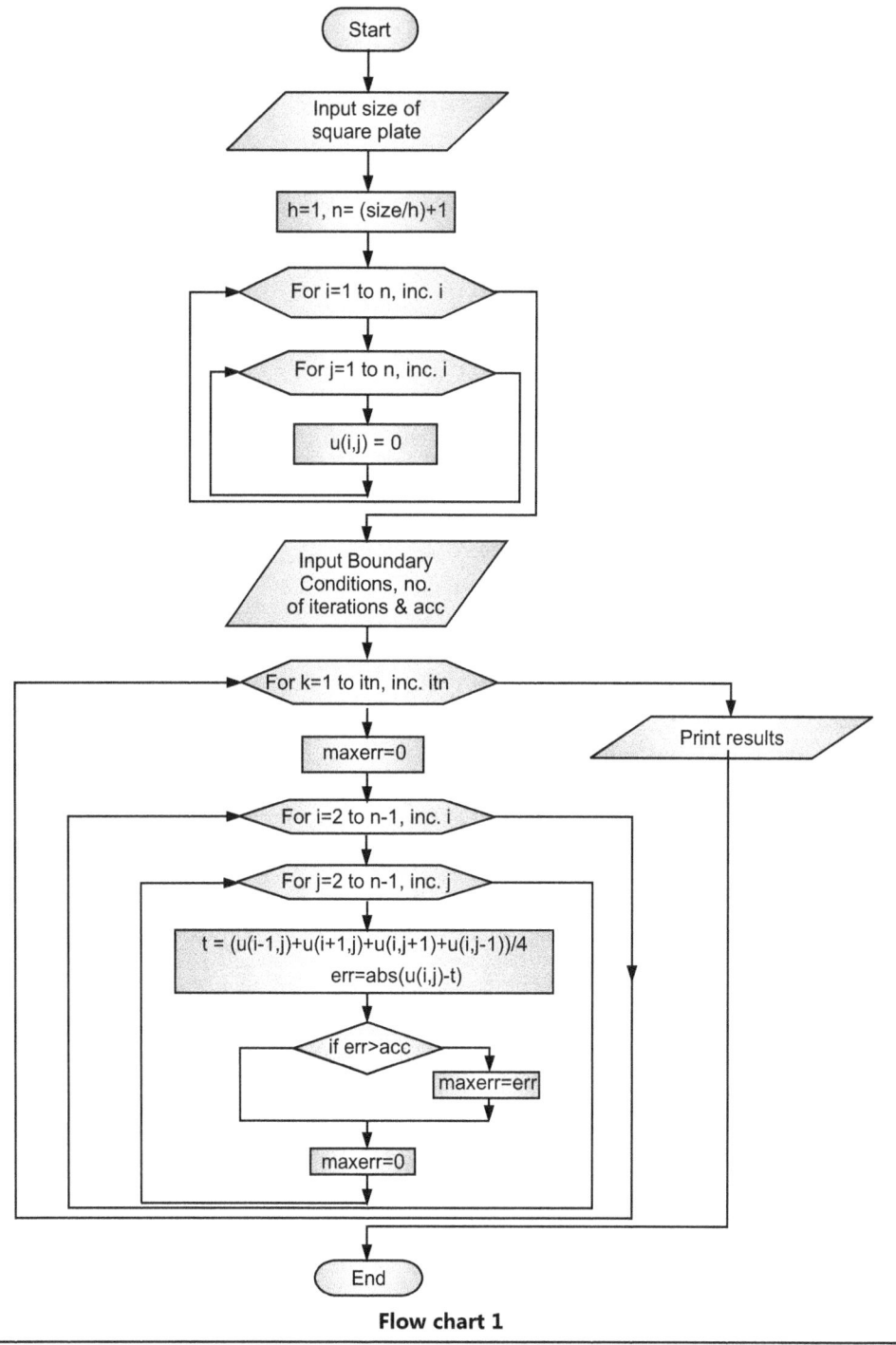

Flow chart 1

9.6.3 Elliptical Equation : Laplace Equation Using C Language

```
clc;
close all;
clear all;

% Numerical Solution of Partial Differential Equations by Laplace Method

disp(sprintf(['\n    Uxx + Uyy = 0']))

size = input('\n Enter Size of Square Plate : ');
h = 1;
n = (size/h)+1;
fprintf('\n No. of Grid Points>>> %g X %g',n,n);

for i = 1:n
   for j = 1:n
      u(i,j) = 0;
   end
end

fprintf('\n Boundary Condition along X axis >>> Upper Side :');
fprintf('\n Values from Left to Right>>> ');
for i = 1:n
   u(1,i) = input('\n Enter u = ');
end

fprintf('\n Boundary Condition along X axis >>> Lower Side :');
fprintf('\n Values from Left to Right>>> ');
for i = 1:n
   u(n,i) = input('\n Enter u = ');
end
fprintf('\n Boundary Condition along Y axis >>> Left Side :');
fprintf('\n Values from Top to Bottom: Excluding first>>> ');
for i = 2:n-1
   u(i,1) = input('\n Enter u = ');
```

```
end
fprintf('\n Boundary Condition along Y axis >>> Right Side : ');
fprintf('\n Values from Top to Bottom: Excluding first>>> ');
for i = 2:n-1
    u(i,n) = input('\n Enter u = ');
end

itn = input('\n Enter no. of Iterations : ');
acc=input('\n Enter Accuracy for Solution : ');

for k = 1:itn
    maxerr = 0;
    for i = 2:n-1
        for j = 2: n-1
            t = (u(i-1,j)+u(i+1,j)+u(i,j+1)+u(i,j-1))/4;
            err=abs(u(i,j)-t);
            if err>acc
                maxerr=err;
            end
            u(i,j)=t;
        end
    end

    fprintf('\n Iteration No. %g \n',k);
    for i = 1:n
        for j = 1:n
            fprintf('\t %.2f',u(i,j));
        end
        fprintf('\n');
    end
end
```

Output :

% Numerical solution of partial differential equations by Laplace method

Uxx + Uyy = 0

Enter Size of Square Plate : 3

No. of Grid Points>>> 4 X 4
Boundary Condition along X axis >>> Upper Side :
Values from Left to Right
Enter u = 0
Enter u = 40
Enter u = 80
Enter u = 120
Boundary Condition along X axis >>> Lower Side :
Values from Left to Right
Enter u = 80
Enter u = 110
Enter u = 160
Enter u = 210

Boundary Condition along Y axis >>> Left Side :
Values from Top to Bottom: Excluding first
Enter u = 20
Enter u = 40

Boundary Condition along Y axis >>> Right Side :
Values from Top to Bottom: Excluding first
Enter u = 110
Enter u = 180
Enter no. of Iterations : 2
Enter Accuracy for Solution : 0.01
Iteration No. 1

0.00	40.00	80.00	120.00
20.00	15.00	51.25	110.00
40.00	41.25	108.13	180.00
80.00	110.00	160.00	210.00

Iteration No. 2

0.00	40.00	80.00	120.00
20.00	38.13	84.06	110.00
40.00	74.06	124.53	180.00
80.00	110.00	160.00	210.00

9.6.4 Poisson's Equation (Elliptical Equation)

Poisson's Equation is given by

$$\frac{\partial^2 u}{\partial x^2} + \frac{\partial^2 u}{\partial y^2} = f(x, y)$$

By replacing the derivatives with difference approximations, we have

$$\frac{1}{h^2}[u_{i-1,j} - 2u_{i,j} + u_{i+1,j}] + \frac{1}{k^2}[u_{i,j-1} - 2u_{i,j} + u_{i,j+1}] = f(x_i, y_i)$$

If $h = k$, multiplying whole equation by h^2, we get

$$u_{i-1,j} - 2u_{i,j} + u_{i+1,j} + u_{i,j-1} - 2u_{i,j} + u_{i,j+1} = h^2 \cdot f(x_i, y_i)$$

$$u_{i-1,j} + u_{i+1,j} + u_{i,j-1} + u_{i,j+1} - 4 \cdot u_{i,j} = h^2 \cdot f(x_i, y_i) \quad \ldots (I)$$

By applying equation (I) at each interior mesh point, we arrive at linear equations in the nodal values of $u_{i,j}$. These set of equations can be solved by Gauss-Seidal Method.

Note : Use suitable method to solve linear simultaneous equations to get values of $u_1, u_2 \ldots u_n$.

Example 9.14 : Solve the equation $\frac{\partial^2 u}{\partial x^2} = -10(x^2 + y^2 + 10)$ over the square of sides $x = y = 0$ to $x = y = 3$ with $u = 0$ on boundary and mesh size $= 1$.

Solution : Given data : $h = k = 1$.

∴ Standard 5-point formula for Poisson's Equation is

$$u_{i-1,j} + u_{i+1,j} + u_{i,j-1} + u_{i,j+1} - 4u_{i,j} = h^2[-10(x_i^2 + y_i^2 + 10)]$$

For u_1, $i = 2$ and $j = 1$, $x = 1$, $y = 2$

∴ $u_3 + 0 + 0 + u_2 - 4u_1 = (1)^2 \times [-10(1 + 4 + 10)]$

∴ $u_3 + u_2 - 4u_1 = -150$

∴ $4u_1 - u_2 - u_3 = 150$

∴ $u_1^{(0)} = \frac{1}{4}[u_2 + u_3 + 150]$ ... (I)

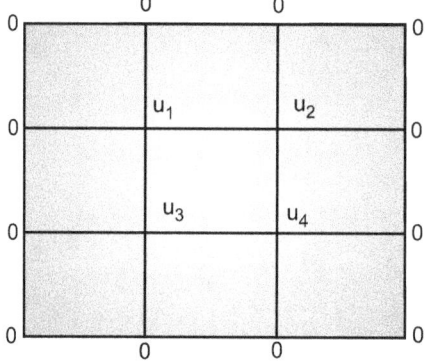

Fig. 9.12

For u_2, $i = 2$, $j = 2$, $x = 2$, $y = 2$

$$u_1 + 0 + 0 + u_4 - 4u_2 = -10[2^2 + 2^2 + 10]$$

$$\therefore u_2^{(0)} = \frac{1}{4}[u_1 + u_4 + 180] \quad \ldots \text{(II)}$$

For u_3, $i = 1$, $j = 1$ i.e. $x = 1$, $y = 1$

$$\therefore 0 + u_1 + u_4 + 0 - 4u_3 = -10[1^2 + 1^2 + 10]$$

$$\therefore u_3^{(0)} = \frac{1}{4}[u_1 + u_4 + 120] \quad \ldots \text{(III)}$$

For u_4, $i = 1$, $j = 2$, $x = 2$, $y = 1$

$$\therefore u_3 + u_2 + 0 + 0 - 4u_4 = -10[2^2 + 1^2 + 10]$$

$$\therefore u_4^{(0)} = \frac{1}{4}[u_2 + u_3 + 150] \quad \ldots \text{(IV)}$$

By using equations (I), (II), (III), (IV) and using Gauss-Seidal method, assume u_2, u_3 and $u_4 = 0$, then

Iteration No (i)	u_1	u_2	u_3	u_4
0		0	0	0
1	37.5	54.375	39.375	60.9375
2	60.9375	75.4688	60.4688	71.4844
3	71.1844	80.7422	65.7422	74.1211
4	74.1211	82.0605	67.0605	74.7803
5	74.7803	82.3901	67.3901	74.9451
6	74.9451	82.4725	67.4725	74.9863
7	74.9863	82.4931	67.4931	74.9966
8	74.9966	82.4983	67.4983	74.9991
9	74.9991	82.4996	67.4996	74.9998
10	74.9998	82.4999	67.4999	74.9999
11	74.9999	82.5000	67.5000	75.0000
12	75.0000	82.5000	67.5000	75.0000

$$\therefore u_1 = 75$$
$$u_2 = 82.5$$
$$u_3 = 67.5$$
$$u_4 = 75 \quad \ldots \textbf{Ans.}$$

Example 9.15 : Solve the Poisson's equation $\nabla^2 u = 2x^2y^2$ over the square domain $0 \leq x \leq 3$ and $0 \leq y \leq 3$ with $u = 0$ on the boundary and $h = 1$.

Solution : The domain is divided into square of one unit size as illustrated in Fig. 9.13.

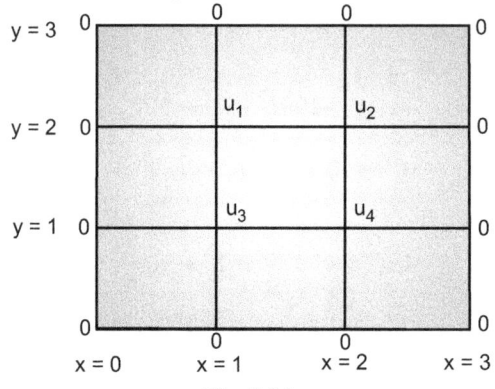

Fig. 9.13

By using 5-point formula for Poisson's Equation, we have

$$u_{i-1,j} + u_{i+1,j} + u_{i,j-1} + u_{i,j+1} - 4u_{ij} = h^2 f(x_i, y_i)$$

For u_1 : When $i = 2, j = 1$ and $x = 1, y = 2$

$\therefore \quad u_3 + 0 + 0 + u_2 - 4u_1 = 2 \times 1^2 \times 2^2$

$\therefore \quad -4u_1 + u_2 + u_3 = 8$ ... (I)

For u_2 : When $i = 2, j = 2$ and $x = 2, y = 2$

$\therefore \quad u_4 + 0 + u_1 + 0 - 4u_2 = 2 \times 2^2 \times 2^2$

$\Rightarrow u_1 - 4u_2 + u_4 = 32$ ... (II)

For u_3 : When $i = 1, j = 1$ and $x = 1, y = 1$

$\therefore \quad 0 + u_1 + 0 + u_4 - 4u_3 = 2 \times 1^2 \times 1^2$

$\Rightarrow u_1 - 4u_3 + u_4 = 2$ ... (III)

For u_4 : When $i = 1, j = 2$ and $x = 2, y = 1$

$\therefore \quad 0 + u_2 + u_3 + 0 - 4u_4 = 2 \times 2^2 \times 1^2$

$\Rightarrow u_2 + u_3 - 4u_4 = 8$ ... (IV)

Rewriting these equations, we get

$-4u_1 + u_2 + u_3 + 0.u_4 = 8$

$u_1 - 4u_2 + 0u_3 + u_4 = 32$

$u_1 + 0u_2 - 4u_3 + u_4 = 2$

$0.u_1 + u_2 + u_3 - 4u_4 = 8$

By using Gauss Elimination Method, we get

$u_1 = -5.5$

$u_2 = -10.75$

$u_3 = -3.25$

$u_4 = -5.5$ ... **Ans.**

9.6.5 Elliptical Equation : Poisson's Equation

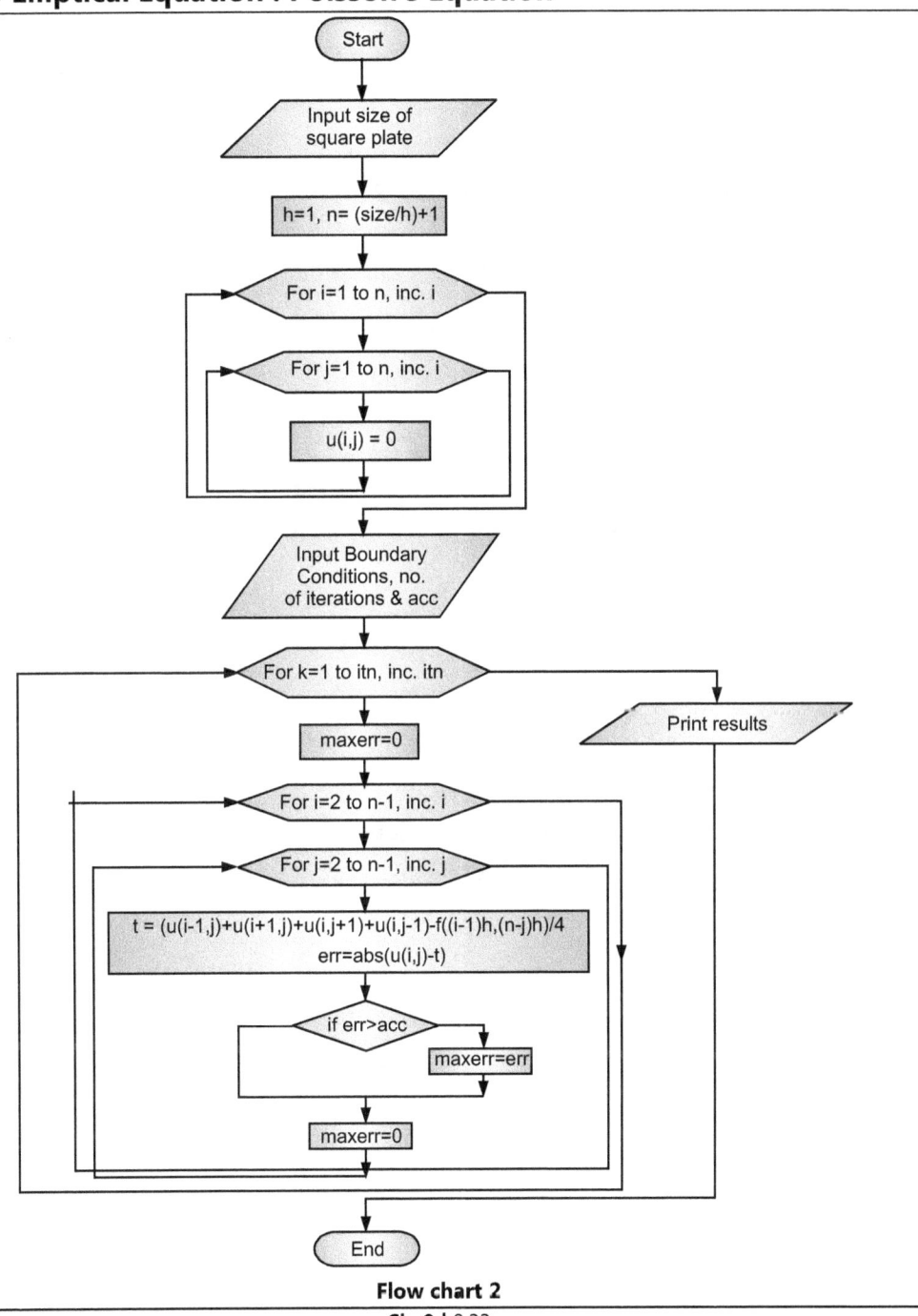

Flow chart 2

9.6.6 Matlab Code

```
clc;
close all;
clear all;

% Numerical Solution of Partial Differential Equations by Poisson Method

fstr = input('\n Input function String on RHS of equation >>>','s');   %% Function definition
f=inline(fstr);
disp(sprintf(['\n    Uxx + Uyy = f(x,y) =' fstr]))

size = input('\n Enter Size of Square Plate : ');
h = input('\n Enter Step Size (h) of Square Plate : ');
n = (size/h)+1;
fprintf('\n No. of Grid Points>>> %g X %g',n,n) ;

for i = 1:n
   for j = 1:n
      u(i,j) = 0;
   end
end

fprintf('\n Boundary Condition along X axis >>> Upper Side :') ;
fprintf('\n Values from Left to Right>>> ');
for i = 1:n
   u(1,i) = input('\n Enter u = ');
end

fprintf('\n Boundary Condition along X axis >>> Lower Side :');
fprintf('\n Values from Left to Right>>> ');
for i = 1:n
   u(n,i) = input('\n Enter u = ');
end

fprintf('\n Boundary Condition along Y axis >>> Left Side :');
```

```
fprintf('\n Values from Top to Bottom: Excluding first>>> ');
for i = 2:n-1
   u(i,1) = input('\n Enter u = ');
end

fprintf('\n Boundary Condition along Y axis >>> Right Side : ');
fprintf('\n Values from Top to Bottom: Excluding first>>> ');
for i = 2:n-1
   u(i,n) = input('\n Enter u = ');
end

itn = input('\n Enter no. of Iterations : ') ;
acc=input('\n Enter Accuracy for Solution : ') ;

for k = 1:itn
   maxerr = 0;
   for i = 2:n-1
      for j = 2: n-1
            t=(u(i-1,j)+u(i+1,j)+u(i,j+1)+u(i,j-1)-f(h*(i-1),h*(n-j)))/4;
            err=abs(u(i,j)-t),
            if err>acc
         maxerr=err;
      end
         u(i,j)=t;
      end
   end

   fprintf('\n Iteration No. %g \n',k);
   for j = 1:n
      for i = 1:n
         fprintf('\t %.2f',u(i,j));
      end
      fprintf('\n');
   end
end
```

Output :

% Numerical Solution of Partial Differential Equations by Poisson Method

Uxx + Uyy = f(x,y) =-4*(x+y)

Enter Size of Square Plate : 3

Enter Step Size (h) of Square Plate : 1

No. of Grid Points>>> 4 X 4

Boundary Condition along X axis >>> Upper Side :

Values from Left to Right

Enter u = 0

Enter u = 0

Enter u = 0

Enter u = 0

Boundary Condition along X axis >>> Lower Side :

Values from Left to Right) Enter u = 0

Enter u = 0

Enter u = 0

Enter u = 0

Boundary Condition along Y axis >>> Left Side :

Values from Top to Bottom : Excluding first

Enter u = 0

Enter u = 0

Boundary Condition along Y axis >>> Right Side :

Values from Top to Bottom : Excluding first

Enter u = 0

Enter u = 0

Enter no. of Iterations : 5

Enter Accuracy for Solution : 0.01

Iteration No. 1

0.00	0.00	0.00	0.00
0.00	3.00	4.75	0.00
0.00	2.75	4.88	0.00
0.00	0.00	0.00	0.00

Iteration No. 2

0.00	0.00	0.00	0.00
0.00	4.88	6.44	0.00

| 0.00 | 4.44 | 5.72 | 0.00 |
| 0.00 | 0.00 | 0.00 | 0.00 |

Iteration No. 3

0.00	0.00	0.00	0.00
0.00	5.72	6.86	0.00
0.00	4.86	5.93	0.00
0.00	0.00	0.00	0.00

Iteration No. 4

0.00	0.00	0.00	0.00
0.00	5.93	6.96	0.00
0.00	4.96	5.98	0.00
0.00	0.00	0.00	0.00

Iteration No. 5

0.00	0.00	0.00	0.00
0.00	5.98	6.99	0.00
0.00	4.99	6.00	0.00
0.00	0.00	0.00	0.00

Example 9.16 : Given that $2\frac{\partial u}{\partial t} = \frac{\partial^2 u}{\partial x^2}$; $u(0, t) = 0$; $\frac{\partial u}{\partial x}(5, t) = 0$ and $u(x, 0) = 100$, find values of u upto 5 seconds. Take h = 1.

Solution : Given data : $2\frac{\partial u}{\partial t} = \frac{\partial^2 u}{\partial x^2}$ i.e. $\frac{\partial u}{\partial t} = \frac{1}{2} \cdot \frac{\partial^2 u}{\partial x^2}$

We have general form of parabolic equation

$$\frac{\partial u}{\partial t} = \alpha^2 \cdot \frac{\partial^2 u}{\partial x^2}$$

∴ $\alpha^2 = \frac{1}{2}$

$h = 1$

We have, $\lambda = \frac{k \cdot \alpha^2}{h^2}$

Consider $\lambda = \frac{1}{2}$

∴ $\frac{1}{2} = \frac{k \cdot \alpha^2}{h^2}$

$$\therefore \quad k = \frac{h^2}{2\alpha^2} = \frac{1^2}{2 \times \frac{1}{2}}$$

$$\therefore \quad k = 1$$

By using Schmidt's Explicit Formula with $\lambda = \frac{1}{2}$, we have

$$u_{i,j+1} = \frac{1}{2}[u_{i-1,j} + u_{i+1,j}] \qquad \ldots (I)$$

By using Boundary Conditions :

$u(0, t) = 0$ i.e. value of u = 0 at x = 0 for all values of t

$u(x, 0) = 100$ i.e. value of u = 100 at all x when t = 0

Also, $\left(\dfrac{\partial u}{\partial x}\right)_{5, t} = 0$

i.e. $\left(\dfrac{\partial u}{\partial x}\right)_{(x_5, t_j)} = 0$

$$\therefore \quad \left[\frac{u_{i+1,j} - u_{i-1,j}}{2h}\right]_{i=5} = 0$$

$$\therefore \quad \frac{u_{6,j} - u_{4,j}}{2h} = 0$$

$$\therefore \quad u_{6,j} = u_{4,j}$$

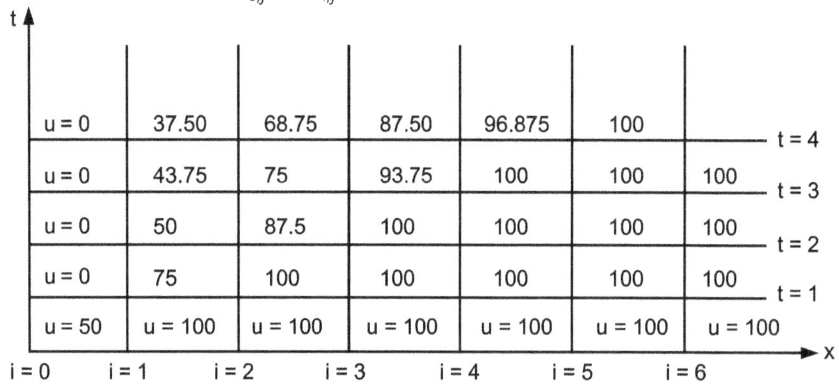

u = 0	37.50	68.75	87.50	96.875	100		t = 4
u = 0	43.75	75	93.75	100	100	100	t = 3
u = 0	50	87.5	100	100	100	100	t = 2
u = 0	75	100	100	100	100	100	t = 1
u = 50	u = 100	u = 100	u = 100	u = 100	u = 100	u = 100	
i = 0	i = 1	i = 2	i = 3	i = 4	i = 5	i = 6	

Fig. 9.14

We have, $u(0, 0) = 0$ by boundary condition $u(0, t) = 0$

and $u(0, 0) = 100$ by boundary condition $u(x, 0) = 100$

u is discontinuous at (0, 0).

$$\therefore \quad u(0, 0) = \frac{1}{2}(0 + 100) = 50 - \text{Aug. of both conditions.}$$

Values of interior points can be calculated by using formula (I) values of $u_{i,j}$ as per following table.

j ↓ \ i →	0	1	2	3	4	5	6
0	50	100	100	100	100	100	100
1	0	75	100	100	100	100	100
2	0	50	87.5	100	100	100	100
3	0	43.75	75	93.75	100	100	100
4	0	37.50	68.75	87.50	96.875	100	96.875
5	0	34.375	62.50	82.8125	93.75	96.875	93.75

Example 9.17 : Solve $\dfrac{\partial^2 u}{\partial x^2} - \dfrac{\partial u}{\partial t} = 0$ subjected to $u(0, t) = u(5, t) = 0$ and $u(x, 0) = x^2 (25 - x^2)$. Find values upto 3 sec. Take $h = 1$.

Solution :

$$\dfrac{\partial^2 u}{\partial x^2} = \dfrac{\partial u}{\partial t}$$

∴ $\alpha^2 = 1$

For $\lambda = \dfrac{k \cdot \alpha^2}{h^2} = \dfrac{1}{2}$

∴ $k = \dfrac{h^2}{2\alpha^2} = \dfrac{1}{2}$

∴ for t = 3 sec, j = 0, 1, 2, 3, 4, 5, 6

By using Schmidt's Method, we have

$$u_{i, j+1} = \dfrac{1}{2} [u_{i-1, j} + u_{i+1, j}] \quad \ldots \text{(I)}$$

By Boundary Conditions,

$u(0, t) = u(5, t) = 0$

i.e. $u = 0$ for all t values at $x = 0$

Also, $u(x, 0) = x^2(25 - x^2)$

When $x = 0,\ u(0, 0) = 0$
 $x = 1,\ u(1, 0) = 24$
 $x = 2,\ u(2, 0) = 2^2 (25 - 2^2) = 84$
 $x = 3,\ u(3, 0) = 3^2 (25 - 3^2) = 144$
 $x = 4,\ u(4, 0) = 4^2 (25 - 4^2) = 144$
 $x = 5,\ u(5, 0) = 5^2 (25 - 5^2) = 0$

Therefore in x-t table by using formula (I), we get

i → j ↓	0	1	2	3	4	5
0	0	24	84	144	144	0
1	0	42	84	114	72	0
2	0	42	78	78	57	0
3	0	39	60	67.5	39	0
4	0	30	53.25	49.5	33.75	0
5	0	26.625	39.75	43.5	24.75	0
6	0	19.875	35.0625	32.25	21.75	0

Example 9.18: Calculate the finite difference solution of the equation $\frac{\partial u}{\partial t} = \frac{\partial^2 u}{\partial x^2}$ ($0 \leq x \leq 1$) subjected to the conditions

$u = \sin \pi x$ when $t = 0$ for $0 \leq x \leq 1$
$u = 0$ at $x = 0$ and $x = 1$ for $t > 0$

taking $h = 0.1$ and $k = 0.001$ for all locations at $t = 0.002$ by using Schmidt's method.

Solution: Given data: $\frac{\partial u}{\partial t} = \frac{\partial^2 u}{\partial x^2}$, $h = 0.1$, $k = 0.001$

∴ $\alpha^2 = 1$

∴ $\lambda = \frac{k \cdot \alpha^2}{h^2} = \frac{0.001 \times 1}{0.1} = 0.01$

Also, $u = \sin \pi x$

$x = 0.1$ $u = 0.3090$
$x = 0.2$ $u = 0.5877$
$x = 0.3$ $u = 0.8090$
$x = 0.4$ $u = 0.9510$
$x = 0.5$ $u = 1.000$
$x = 0.6$ $u = 0.9510$
$x = 0.7$ $u = 0.8090$
$x = 0.8$ $u = 0.5877$
$x = 0.9$ $u = 0.3090$
$x = 1$ $u = 0$

By Schmidt's Explicit Method,

$$u_{i, j+1} = \lambda \cdot u_{i-1, j} + (1 - 2\lambda) u_{i,j} + \lambda \cdot u_{i+1, j}$$

where, $\lambda = 0.1$

$\therefore \quad u_{i,j+1} = 0.1\, u_{i-1,j} + 0.8\, u_{i,j} + 0.1\, u_{i+1,j}$

for i = 1, 2,...10 and j = 1, we have

$$u_{1,1} = 0.1\, u_{0,1} + 0.8\, u_{1,1} + 0.1\, u_{2,1}$$
$$= 0.1\,[u_{0,1} + 8u_{11} + u_{2,1}]$$
$$= 0.1 \times [0 + 8 \times 0.3091373 + 0.5879898] = 0.3061088$$
$$u_{2,1} = 0.1[u_{1,1} + 8u_{2,1} + u_{3,1}]$$
$$= 0.1\,[0.3091373 + 8 \times 0.5879898 + 0.8092399]$$
$$= 0.5822296$$

By using same procedure, values of $u_{3,1} \ldots u_{9,1}$ and $u_{1,2}$ to $u_{9,2}$ are calculated as tabulated below :

X =	0	0.1	0.2	0.3	0.4	0.5	0.6	0.7	0.8	0.9	1
i→ j↓	0	1	2	3	4	5	6	7	8	9	10
0	0	0.3091373	0.5879898	0.8092399	0.9512127	0.9999998	0.9512127	0.8092399	0.5879898	0.3091373	0
1	0	0.3061088	0.5822296	0.8013122	0.9418941	0.9902424	0.9418941	0.8013122	0.5822296	0.3061088	0
2	0	0.3031100	0.5765258	0.7934621	0.936708	0.9805727	0.9326708	0.7934621	0.5765258	0.3031100	0

Problems for Practice

1. The transverse displacement 'u' of a point at a distance 'x' from one end and at any time 't' of the vibrating string satisfies the equation, $\dfrac{\partial^2 u}{\partial t^2} = 4\dfrac{\partial^2 u}{\partial x^2}$ with boundary conditions u = 0 at x = 4, t > 0 and initial conditions u = x(4 − x) and $\dfrac{\partial u}{\partial t} = 0$, $0 \le x \le 4$.

   Solve this equation numerically for one half period of vibration, taking h = 1 and k = 0.5.

   $$\text{Ans.} \begin{bmatrix} & \lambda = 1 & u_1 & u_2 & u_3 \\ t = 0 & & 3 & 4 & 3 \\ t = 0.5 & & 2 & 3 & 2 \\ t = 1 & & 0 & 0 & 0 \\ t = 1.5 & & -2 & -3 & -2 \end{bmatrix}$$

2. A steel plate of 150 mm × 150 mm has its four sides held at 100, 80, 50 and 0°C as shown in Fig. 9.15.
   Estimate the steady-state temperature distribution at interior points assuming grid size of 50 mm.

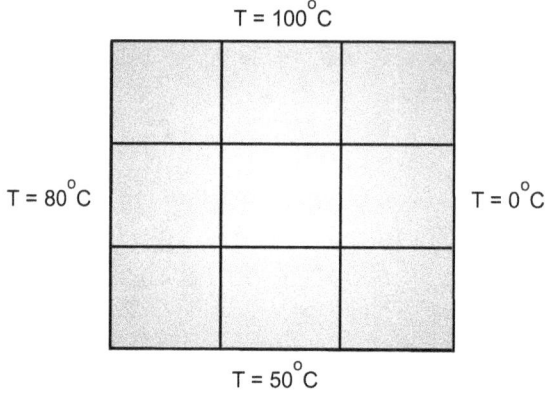

Fig. 9.15

3. The steady-state two dimensional heat flow in the metal plate is given by,
$$\frac{\partial^2 T}{\partial x^2} + \frac{\partial^2 T}{\partial y^2} = 0.$$

Given the boundary conditions as shown in Fig. 9.16. Find the temperatures T_1, T_2, T_3 and T_4.

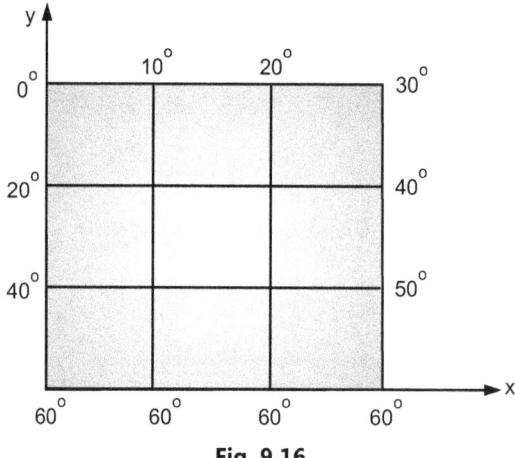

Fig. 9.16

Ans. After 3rd Iteration :
$$\begin{bmatrix} u_1 = 24.61 \\ u_2 = 32.30 \\ u_3 = 42.30 \\ u_4 = 46.15 \end{bmatrix}$$

4. Solve Laplace equation for given grid and boundary conditions and find temperatures T_1, T_2, T_3 and T_4.

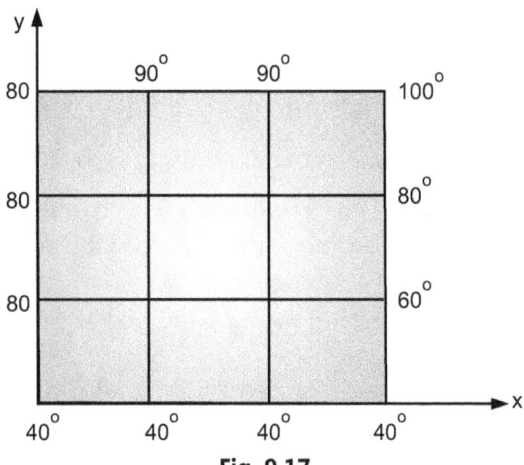

Fig. 9.17

$$\text{Ans. After 3}^{rd}\text{ Iteration : }\begin{bmatrix} u_1 = 74.92 \\ u_2 = 75.59 \\ u_3 = 63.09 \\ u_4 = 59.67 \end{bmatrix}$$

Review Questions

1. A body of mass of 5 kg is attached to a spring with stiffness of 12. The differential equation governing the displacement of the body (a) and time (t) is given by $\frac{d^2x}{dt^2} + 5\frac{dx}{dt} - 12x = 0$. Find the displacement (x) at time t = 2, given that x(0) = 4 and y(0) = –5. Use Runge Kutta Second order method.

2. Solve the boundary value problem $\frac{d^2y}{dx^2} - 64y + 10 = 0$. Initial conditions, y(0) = 1, y(1) = 1, take step size, h = 1/3 compute y(1/3) and y(2/3).

3. Second order differential equation is $x^2 \frac{d^2y}{dx^2}(x-2)\frac{dy}{dx} - 3y = 10x$. subject to consideration y(0) = 0, y(0.3) = 10, h = 0.1.
   Solve by Finite difference method.

4. Solve $y_{tt} = y_{xx}$ upto t = 0.2 with a spacing of 0.1 subject to y(0, t) = 0, y(1, t) = 0, $y_1(x, 0) - 0$ and y(x – 0) = 10 + x(1 – x).

5. Solve $\frac{\partial u}{\partial t} = \frac{\partial^2 u}{\partial x^2}$, for the following condition using Crank-Nicolson method.
   At x = 0 and x = 3, u = 0 for all values of t

At t = 0, u = x^2 for 0 < x < 3

Take increment in x as 1 and increment in t as 0.1. Find all values of u for t = 0 to t = 0.3.

6. Solve $\frac{\partial u}{\partial t} = \frac{\partial u}{\partial x^2}$ for the following conditions using explicit finite difference scheme at t = 0, u = sin πx (0 < x < 1) at x = 0 and x = 1, u = 0 for all values of t. Taking increment in t as 0.002 and increment in x as 0.2 tabulate values of u for t = 0 to 0.006 and x = 0 to 1.

7. Solve Laplace equation (2D heat flow) w.r.t. the grid as shown in Fig. 9.18. Compute temperatures T_1, T_2, T_3 and T_4.

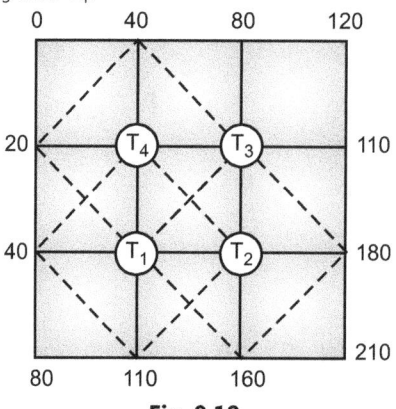

Fig. 9.18

8. Evaluate the pivotal values of the equation $u_{tt} = 16$ taking Δx ≡ 1 upto t = 1.25. The boundary conditions are u(0, t) = u(5, t) = 0, u_t(x, 0) = 0 and u(x, 0) = x^2(5 − x).

9. Given the value of u(x, y) on the boundary of the square in Fig. 9.19. Evaluate the function u(x, y) satisfying the Laplace equation $\nabla^2 u = 0$ at the pivotal points of Fig. 9.19.

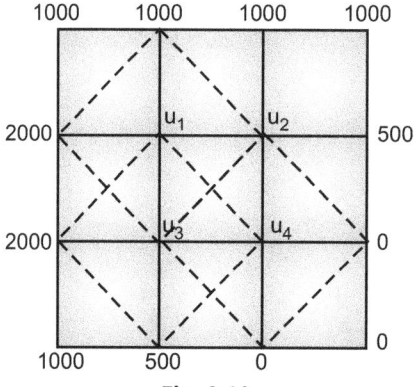

Fig. 9.19

10. Solve the Laplace equation $\frac{\partial^2 T}{\partial x^2} + \frac{\partial^2 T}{\partial y^2} = 0$ with respect to the grid and boundary conditions as shown in Fig. 9.20 Calculate temperatures T_1, T_2, T_3 and T_4. If required assume suitable accuracy.

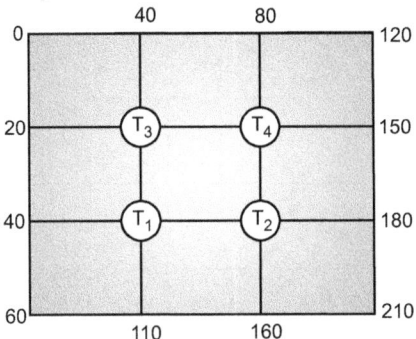

Fig. 9.20

11. Solve $\frac{\partial u}{\partial t} = \frac{\partial^2 u}{\partial x^2}$ for the following conditions using explicit finite difference scheme

    at $t = 0$, $u = \sin \pi x$, at $x = 0$ and $x = 1$, $u = 0$ for all values of t. Taking increment in t as 0.002 and increment in x as 0.2, tabulate values of u for $t = 0$ to 0.006 and $x = 0$ to 1.

12. Draw flow chart for the above problem.

13. Initial temperature within an insulated cylindrical metal rod of 4 cm length is given by, $T = 50(4 - x)$, $0 < x < 4$, where x is distance from one end in cm.

    Both the ends are maintained at 0°C.

    Find the temperature as a function of x and t ($0 \le t \le 1.5$) if the heat flow is governed by $\frac{\partial T}{\partial t} = 2\frac{\partial^2 T}{\partial x^2}$, $\Delta x = 1$ and $\Delta t = 0.25$.

14. Draw a flow-chart for solution of wave equation.

15. Draw a Flowchart for solution of Poisson's equation.

16. Draw a Flowchart for solution of wave equation.

17. Solve $\delta^2 u/\delta t^2 = 4 \cdot \delta^2 u/\delta x^2$ with boundary conditions $u(0, t) = u(4, t) = 0$ and initial condition $u_t(x, 0) = 0$ and $u(x, 0) = x(4 - x)$ taking $h = 1$, $k = \frac{1}{2}$.

18. Draw a flowchart for solving Elliptical equation.

19. Solve the equation $\nabla^4 u = -10(x^2 + y^2 + 10)$ over the square with sides $x = 0$, $y = 0$ and $x = 3$, $y = 3$ with $u = 0$ on the boundary and the mesh length $= 1$.

20. Solve the equation, $\dfrac{d^2u}{dx^2} + 2\dfrac{d^2u}{dy^2} = \dfrac{1}{x \cdot y}$ corresponding to grid shown in following Fig. 9.21.

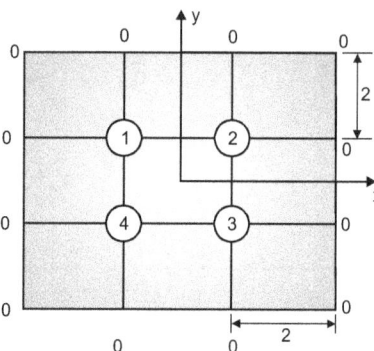

Fig. 9.21

21. Draw a flowchart for solving Laplace's equation.

22. Consider a plate 2.4m × 3.0m that is subjected to the boundary conditions shown below. Find the temperature at the interior at the nodes using a square grid with a length of 0.6 m by using the direct method.

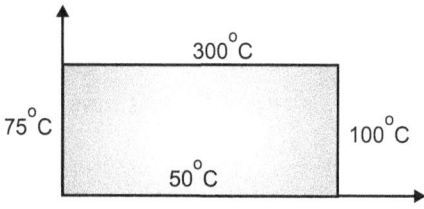

Fig. 9.22

23. What is difference between implicit method and explicit method for better convergence and stability which is best suitable.

24. Consider a steel rod that is subjected to a temperature of 100° C on the left end and 25° C on the right end .If the rod is of length 0.5 m, use the implicit method to find the temperature distribution in the rod from t=0 and t=9seconds.

    Use $\Delta x = 0.01$m and $\Delta t = 3$ sec.

25. Draw a flow chart for Crank Nicholas method for solution of parabolic partial differential equation.

26. Given the values of u (x, y) on the boundary of the square is as follows, evaluate the function u (x, y) satisfying the Laplace equation $\nabla^2 u = 0$.

    Boundary conditions,

    Top = 1000;

    Bottom = 500;

    Left = 2000;

    Right = 500 with 3 × 3 grid points.

27. Explain Liberman's method to solve Partial Differential Equation. Write down step by step procedure.

28. Write down step by step procedure for solution of PDE of Laplace Equation and develop a flow chart to write a program.

29. Solve the equation $\nabla^2 = -10 (x^2 + y^2 + 10)$ over the square with sides x = 0 = y, x = 3 = y with u = 0 on the boundary and mesh length = 1.

30. Solve using Crank-Nicolson's method, solve $\frac{\partial u}{\partial t} = \frac{1}{16} \frac{\partial^2 u}{\partial x^2}$, 0 < x < 1, t > 0 given that

    u (x, 0) = 0, u (0, t) = 0, u = (1, t) = 50 t.

    Compute u for two steps in t direction taking h = ¼ and λ = 1.

31. Draw a flow chart for solution of wave equation.

32. Draw flow chart to solve Parabolic Equation by Explicit method.

33. Solve the Parabolic equation $\frac{\partial u}{\partial t} = \frac{\partial^2 u}{\partial x^2}$ subject to condition u (x, 0) = sin πx, 0 ≤ x ≤ 1,

    u (0, t) = u (1, t) = 0 using Crank-Nicolson method, do two iterations taking h = 1/3, k = 1/36.

34. Draw flow chart to solve Laplace Equation for given no. of iterations.

    (1) Derive the difference equation corresponding to :

    (a) Laplace equation

    (b) Poisson's equation

    (c) Hyperbolic equation

    (d) Parabolic equation

    (2) What is the difference between implicit and explicit equations ?

    (3) Draw flow chart for :

(a) Laplace equation
   (b) Poisson's equation
   (c) Hyperbolic equation
   (d) Parabolic equation
35. State practical applications of
   (a) Laplace equation
   (b) Poisson's equation
   (c) Hyperbolic equation
   (d) Parabolic equation

www.ingramcontent.com/pod-product-compliance
Lightning Source LLC
Chambersburg PA
CBHW080540230426
43663CB00015B/2653